PROGRESS THROUGH REGRESSION

The Cobb-Douglas regression, a statistical technique developed to estimate what economists called a 'production function', was introduced in the late 1920s. For several years, only economist Paul Douglas and a few collaborators used the technique, while vigorously defending it against numerous critics. By the 1950s, however, several economists beyond Douglas's circle were using the technique, and by the 1970s, Douglas's regression, and more sophisticated procedures inspired by it, had become standard parts of the empirical economist's toolkit. This volume is the story of the Cobb-Douglas regression from its introduction to its acceptance as general-purpose research tool. The story intersects with the histories of several important empirical research programs in twentieth century economics, and vividly portrays the challenges of empirical economic research during that era. Fundamentally, this work represents a case study of how a controversial, innovative research tool comes to be widely accepted by a community of scholars.

JEFF E. BIDDLE is a Professor of Economics at Michigan State University.

HISTORICAL PERSPECTIVES ON MODERN ECONOMICS

Series Editor: Professor Harro Maas, *Walras-Pareto Centre for the History of Economic and Political Thought, University of Lausanne*

This series contains original works that challenge and enlighten historians of economics. For the profession as a whole, it promotes better understanding of the origin and content of modern economics.

Other books in the series:

Erwin Dekker, *The Viennese Students of Civilization* (2016)

Steven G. Medema, Anthony M. C. Waterman (eds.), *Paul Samuelson on the History of Economic Analysis: Selected Essays* (2014)

Floris Heukelom, *Behavioral Economics: A History* (2014)

Roger E. Backhouse, Mauro Boianovsky, *Transforming Modern Macroeconomics: Exploring Disequilibrium Microfoundations, 1956–2003* (2013)

Susan Howson, *Lionel Robbins* (2012)

Robert Van Horn, Philip Mirowski, Thomas A. Stapleford (eds.), *Building Chicago Economics: New Perspectives on the History of America's Most Powerful Economics Program* (2012)

Arie Arnon, *Monetary Theory and Policy from Hume and Smith to Wicksell: Money, Credit, and the Economy* (2011)

Malcolm Rutherford, *The Institutionalist Movement in American Economics, 1918–1947: Science and Social Control* (2011)

Samuel Hollander, *Friedrich Engels and Marxian Political Economy* (2011)

Robert Leonard, *Von Neumann, Morgenstern, and the Creation of Game Theory: From Chess to Social Science, 1900–1960* (2010)

Simon J. Cook, *The Intellectual Foundations of Alfred Marshall's Economic Science: A Rounded Globe of Knowledge* (2009)

Samuel Hollander, *The Economics of Karl Marx: Analysis and Applications* (2008)

Donald Moggridge, *Harry Johnson: A Life in Economics* (2008)

Filippo Cesarano, *Monetary Theory and Bretton Woods: The Construction of an International Monetary Order* (2006)

Timothy Davis, *Ricardo's Macroeconomics: Money, Trade Cycles, and Growth* (2005)

Progress through Regression

The Life Story of the Empirical Cobb–Douglas Production Function

JEFF E. BIDDLE
Michigan State University

CAMBRIDGE
UNIVERSITY PRESS

CAMBRIDGE
UNIVERSITY PRESS

University Printing House, Cambridge CB2 8BS, United Kingdom

One Liberty Plaza, 20th Floor, New York, NY 10006, USA

477 Williamstown Road, Port Melbourne, VIC 3207, Australia

314–321, 3rd Floor, Plot 3, Splendor Forum, Jasola District Centre, New Delhi – 110025, India

79 Anson Road, #06–04/06, Singapore 079906

Cambridge University Press is part of the University of Cambridge.

It furthers the University's mission by disseminating knowledge in the pursuit of education, learning, and research at the highest international levels of excellence.

www.cambridge.org
Information on this title: www.cambridge.org/9781108492263
DOI: 10.1017/9781108679312

First published 2021

A catalogue record for this publication is available from the British Library.

ISBN 978-1-108-49226-3 Hardback

For Kay, Jeb, John, and Stevie

Contents

Contents

Figures

Acknowledgments

This book has its origin in an invitation I received from Marcel Boumans to participate in the 2011 *History of Political Economy* conference, Histories on Econometrics. My contribution to that conference became the kernel of Chapter 5 of this book, and the research I did for that paper led me to believe that a more comprehensive history of the Cobb–Douglas regression was worth writing. Following up on that belief has been a rewarding project, in the course of which I have learned a lot more about the history of economics than is found in these pages. I would like to thank Marcel for the invitation that reawakened my dormant interest in the history of empirical economic research in the twentieth century, and for the comments he has given on various parts of the manuscript that I have sent him through the years. Discussions with other fellow historians of economics have also helped make this a better book; I would like to mention Ross Emmett, Mary Morgan, Tom Stapleford, and the series editor, Harro Maas, in particular.

I also owe thanks to the Department of Economics at Michigan State University for providing a hospitable environment in which to do this sort of research. Although this book is not really what my colleagues think of as economics, the department has never failed to support my historical research and was generous enough to fund two trips to archives related to this book.

I spent the spring semester of 2014 as a senior research fellow at the Center for the History of Political Economy at Duke University, and I am grateful to Bruce Caldwell and the faculty and staff of the center for their support and collegiality during that time. The center is a wonderful place for a historian of economics to work, and not surprisingly, I made significant progress on the book during my time there.

Some of the material in this book draws from research I previously published elsewhere. Portions of Chapter 1 are based on Biddle (2011) and Biddle (2012), and Chapter 5 draws on Biddle (2011). I thank the American Economic Association and Duke University Press for permission to reproduce and paraphrase passages from those articles.

I would finally like to take this opportunity to acknowledge my tremendous debt, as a historian of economics, to Craufurd Goodwin and Warren Samuels. Craufurd Goodwin's teaching helped me to see the history of economics as a fascinating research field full of interesting questions. While I was still a graduate student, he convinced me that I could contribute to the field, and that I would enjoy doing so. Throughout my career Craufurd was generous with his comments on my work and never failed to provide valuable support and encouragement. Warren Samuels was my colleague at Michigan State University beginning in 1985. Warren was the ideal mentor during the early years of my career, and I continued to benefit from our friendship until his death in 2011. Through word and example, he showed me how to be a better historian and a better scholar. And it is still not unusual these days for me to pause and think about how much I would enjoy – and learn from – having Warren to talk to about some intriguing question or difficult matter to which my research has drawn my attention.

Introduction

At the 1927 meetings of the American Economic Association, Paul Douglas presented a paper entitled "A Theory of Production," which he had coauthored with Charles Cobb. The paper proposed the now familiar Cobb–Douglas function as a general mathematical representation of the relationship between the amounts of capital and labor employed in the US manufacturing sector and the quantity of output produced by that sector. The paper's innovation, however, was not the function itself, as this functional form had been previously proposed by Knut Wicksell and others, but the use of the function as the basis of a statistical procedure for estimating the parameters of this relationship.[1] It is this procedure, a linear regression of the log of a measure of the output of some production activity on the logs of measures of inputs used in the activity, that I call in this book "the Cobb–Douglas regression." In a broader sense, the paper's innovation was the idea motivating and underlying the particular linear regression used by Cobb and Douglas: that a stable, quantifiable relationship between the inputs to and outputs of production processes existed and could be discovered through regression analysis, and that knowledge of this relationship would help to answer important questions of economic theory and policy.

Paul Douglas's innovation of 1927 was a very successful one. The production function regression, in which a measure of output is regressed on measures of inputs, has become a general-purpose empirical tool in economics. Production function regressions are today seen as a means of answering a wide range of questions in a number of fields of economics. They are estimated with cross section, time series, and panel data sets,

[1] Lloyd (2001) discusses previous theoretical uses of the Cobb–Douglas production function to describe the relationship between inputs and outputs.

using variables measured at the level of the individual production process, the firm, the industry, and the national economy. Douglas's idea that such regressions yield meaningful and useful information is widely accepted, and even the original Cobb–Douglas form of the regression continues to be used by economists. This book tells the story of the introduction and diffusion of the Cobb–Douglas regression.

I have two purposes in writing this book. The first is to provide a detailed and accurate historical case study of the introduction and diffusion of an important empirical research technique in economics. Though a history of a single empirical technique may seem very narrow in focus, the life story of the Cobb–Douglas regression has the potential to shed light on several aspects of the history of twentieth-century economics. First, it provides a valuable new perspective on the development of empirical research in economics in the twentieth century, much as did Mary Morgan's (1990) case studies of the estimation of supply and demand curves and of empirical business cycle research in her *History of Econometrics.* Also, it will become clear that the history of the Cobb–Douglas regression intersects with the histories of several research areas and policy debates in economics. I have focused in particular on the role of the Cobb–Douglas regression in the field of agricultural economics and in the history of empirical research into economic growth. However, Douglas's idea that the parameters of something called a production function could be estimated using regression analysis has come to be central to other areas of economics as well, including, since the 1970s, research and policy advice related to education, and, since the 1990s, the empirical analysis of oligopoly behavior and its implications for antitrust law.

As a historical case study, the book focuses on the period from the mid-1920s, when Douglas was doing the preliminary statistical work that led to the 1927 paper, to the late 1960s, when Douglas's idea had come to be widely accepted by economists, and the Constant Elasticity of Substitution (CES) production function was emerging as the first popular alternative to the Cobb–Douglas function for use in empirical production function research. The main source material for this history is the published economic literature. I review and analyze the articles, books, reviews, comments and rejoinders in which the regression was used, praised, criticized, or defended. The decision to focus on published economic literature is warranted, I would argue, because economists in their roles as researchers were the initial and crucial gatekeepers determining whether the Cobb–Douglas regression would indeed come to be a widely used research tool. The diffusion of the technique could only occur if and when a significant number of economists decided that it produced trustworthy information relevant to questions they believed to be important. Economists' decisions to accept or reject the Cobb–Douglas regression and the results it produced were made largely on the basis of technical considerations related to the specialized disciplinary knowledge of their field, and the published literature is the central source for one who wishes to understand these considerations.

My perspective on this material is in the main that of a historian of econometrics, or more accurately, a historian of the use of statistical evidence by economists. The economists in my narrative who sought to estimate production functions faced a variety of challenges, which in many cases were specific forms of generic challenges that hindered empirical research in economics in the mid-twentieth century. The procedure required measures of inputs and outputs, measures that often had to be constructed from imperfect and incomplete statistical data. Throughout the period I examine, linear regression was the statistical method used to estimate production functions, but the decision to use linear regression necessitated a number of subsidiary decisions, such as the form to be taken by the estimating equation. Theory gave, at best, uncertain guidance to the economist making these decisions; this, combined with the quality of the available data, ensured that any decision made was vulnerable to criticism. Further, the interpretation of the results of the regression required an assessment of problems arising from inaccuracies in the construction of input and output measures, or failures in the statistical assumptions required for linear regression to produce reliable estimates. I give particular attention to describing these challenges, the strategies used by researchers to deal with them, and the roles played by statistical and economic theory in both the development and the criticism of those strategies.

Although Paul Douglas is the most important person in the story of the Cobb–Douglas regression, readers will find that this book is not, even in part, a biography of Douglas. Douglas's 1971 autobiography, *In the Fullness of Time*, reveals him to be a fascinating individual – intelligent, energetic, ambitious, and a complex man who had a highly successful career as an academic economist, culminating in his election as president of the American Economic Association, and in politics, including three terms as a US senator. A good biography of Douglas would be most welcome, but this book is about the life of his most enduring creation, not the life of the creator. I only refer to biographical material on Douglas when I believe it provides insights into the choices he made in his production function research.

Douglas's 1927 paper with Cobb (published in 1928) marked the beginning of a twenty-year research program in which Douglas, working with various collaborators, estimated the Cobb–Douglas regression using a variety of data sets. Part I of the book describes that research and reactions to it by various groups of critics, both friendly and unfriendly. The research program can be divided into two phases: the first, which included Douglas's 1934 book, *The Theory of Wages*, in which he estimated the regression with annual time-series data from the manufacturing sector as a whole, and the second, from about 1937 to 1947, in which he used a cross-section version of the regression with input and output data aggregated to the level of individual industries.

The original time-series regression of the 1928 Cobb–Douglas paper arose out of Douglas's prior research interests and represented cutting-edge work in empirical economics. Between 1928 and the publication of *The Theory of Wages*, Douglas came to understand and represent his work with the regression as a contribution to a larger effort by sophisticated empirical economists to build a body of empirical knowledge on the "valuable theoretical scaffolding" of "the neoclassical school" (Douglas 1934, xii), or, as he sometimes put it, to make economics "a more progressive science."

From *The Theory of Wages* onward, one finds two consistent and strongly argued claims in Douglas's production studies: The Cobb–Douglas regression could produce results that were economically meaningful and important, and their meaning was closely related to the marginal productivity theory of distribution. In the cross-section studies of the late 1930s and early 1940s, however, Douglas and his coauthors took shifting and sometimes inconsistent positions on a number of subsidiary questions related to these themes. These included questions of inference and statistical procedure, such as "Under what circumstances does a least squares regression based on the Cobb–Douglas production function produce meaningful information?" or "How does one judge whether a particular application of the Cobb–Douglas regression to a data set has produced useful estimates of economically important quantities and relationships?" as well as questions related to the theoretical and practical significance of the results, such as "Could the results be used to test the marginal productivity theory? To detect the presence or absence of competitive conditions in some part of the economy? To provide quantitative measures of key theoretical relationships identified by the marginal productivity theory?"

There are several reasons for this ambiguity. One is that after 1935, Douglas worked with coauthors and allowed them to write their own defenses and interpretations of the Cobb–Douglas regression procedure into jointly authored publications. Another is that numerous innovative statistical practices were being introduced into the economic literature during the period, and Douglas wanted to keep his research program at the cutting edge of empirical economics – indeed, this was one reason for his eagerness to work with coauthors. A third reason was the existence in the profession of more than one conceptualization of the marginal productivity theory. And it could simply be said that Douglas was in the process of learning about the technique he had introduced to the profession in 1927, developing, with the help of his coauthors and critics, a firmer grasp on its potential and its limitations.

Douglas began his first successful campaign for the US Senate in 1948, effectively ending his research career. However, applications of Douglas's regression multiplied over the following two decades – a 1963 survey article in a leading economics journal cited more than thirty published books and articles in which estimated Cobb–Douglas regressions could be found (Walters 1963a). Criticisms of the procedure also continued to appear, some making new points and some essentially reiterating points made by earlier critics.

Part II of the book is concerned with the diffusion of the Cobb–Douglas regression, and begins with a chapter that discusses three important moments in the story of the Cobb–Douglas regression after 1947. The first is the appearance in Lawrence Klein's (1953) econometrics textbook of an econometric model that included a Cobb–Douglas production function. The second is E. H. Phelps Brown's 1957 article criticizing Douglas's applications of the regression. The third is the introduction of the CES production function in 1961 by Kenneth Arrow, Hollis Chenery, Bagicha Minhas, and Robert Solow.

However, the bulk of my discussion of the postwar (and post-Douglas) spread of Douglas's regression takes the form of two case studies: (i) the adoption of the Cobb–Douglas regression by agricultural economists and (ii) the story of how the Cobb–Douglas regression came to be used as a tool for the measurement and explanation of economic growth and technical change. In both cases, I begin by describing the preexisting situation in the area of research into which the regression was introduced. Each had its own set of motivating questions, theoretical framework(s), cache of relevant data, and associated empirical challenges. In both cases, a small group of researchers introduced the Cobb–Douglas regression as a means of answering one or more of the important questions in the field. As these innovators described how the regression could be applied to the questions they cared about, some of the existing claims and counterclaims about what Douglas's versions of the regression could or could not accomplish, and under what circumstances, became irrelevant, while the new applications led to new challenges to, and new modifications of, Douglas's regression procedure. In each of the two fields, the regression, and Douglas's broader idea about the fruitfulness of using regression analysis to estimate input-output relationships, gained a foothold, creating yet another genus of the Cobb–Douglas regression (with associated species) that sidestepped at least some of the criticisms leveled at Douglas's original studies. In the process, each field also became home to a new constituency with a vested interest in defending the value and legitimacy of its version of the regression.

My second purpose in writing this book is to explore possible answers to two questions raised by the story of the Cobb–Douglas regression: First, what explains the success of the Cobb–Douglas regression, that is, what factors contributed to its gradual transformation from an innovative and controversial statistical procedure to a widely accepted general-purpose tool in empirical economics? As a historical matter, the acceptance of the Cobb–Douglas regression was the crucial first step in the process by which economists would embrace and more fully implement Douglas's innovative idea of using regression analysis to estimate production relations. Further, the factors that contributed to economists' acceptance of the Cobb–Douglas regression shaped in important ways the more general strategies and techniques that economists would eventually develop in pursuing the many research questions embodied in Douglas's idea. So, explaining the success of the Cobb–Douglas regression goes a long way towards explaining the success of the regression approach to estimating production relations.

The second and related question is whether the analysis of factors that contributed to the success of the Cobb–Douglas regression offers more general insights into the factors that determine the success or failure of innovative research techniques in the social and perhaps natural sciences. In posing this second question, I have in mind a variety of types of innovative research tools, techniques, or procedures: new statistical techniques, like the Cobb–Douglas regression, but also new experimental methods, new modeling strategies, new conceptual frameworks, and so on. I regard an innovation as having become "successful" when it comes to be used by a large number of researchers, and a significant number of researchers who do not actually use the technique believe that it can contribute to the advance of knowledge, and regard as credible the knowledge it has produced. This broad consensus on the value of the tool should persist for a while – decades, not years – and would be evidenced by a steady and substantial stream of peer reviewed or otherwise professionally approved published research in which the tool is used.[2] Few economists would dispute that the production function regression was, and remains, a success in this sense.[3]

I reflect on the first question, that is, what factors led to the success of the Cobb–Douglas regression, at various points in the book. Some of these reflections are brief and quite speculative, but there are four potential reasons for the success of Douglas's regression that I elaborate in more detail in a final chapter. A first reason is the decision by Douglas to link his procedure, and his interpretation of the estimates it produced, to fundamental concepts of the neoclassical approach to economics, which was destined to grow in influence over the course of the twentieth century. A second is what I call the adaptability of the Cobb–Douglas regression. As I have mentioned, one could discern from Douglas's papers several "versions" of the Cobb–Douglas regression. There were the two "actual" versions (the time series and the industry-level cross section), but Douglas endorsed the idea that other versions should be developed as well (firm level, or time series within a single industry, or cross section with aggregate data from different states or countries, or any of the above with alternative functional form assumptions). As the Cobb–Douglas regression came to be adopted by other researchers in other fields of economics, for purposes other than those originally envisioned by Douglas, even more versions

[2] Using this standard of success, it is not hard to also find examples of unsuccessful attempts to introduce innovative research tools. Three cases of innovative empirical tools/approaches introduced into twentieth-century economics research that were not successful by my definition would be the measures of business cycle behavior developed by Arthur Burns and Wesley Mitchell (1946, discussed in Morgan [1990]); Ragnar Frisch's confluence analysis (Hendry and Morgan 1989); and "periodogram analysis" (Cargill 1974).

[3] Some citation-based evidence of this success can be offered as well. A 2003 article proposing an improved approach to production function estimation, "Estimating Production Functions Using Inputs to Control for Unobservables" (Levinsohn and Petrin 2003) has been cited over 1,000 times. A subsequent related article, "On Estimating Firm-Level Production Functions Using Proxy Variables to Control for Unobservables" (Wooldridge 2009) has been cited 160 times. An empirical article demonstrating a "production function approach" to measuring the effect of health on economic growth (Bloom, Canning, and Sevilla 2003) has been cited over 250 times. By way of comparison, the median article published in one of the five most prestigious journals in economics in 2007 had received 50 cites by 2015 (Hamermesh 2018).

were born. I believe that the fact that many versions and interpretations of Douglas's regression existed, both actual and potential, contributed to the growth in its use by economists. Criticisms that were devastating to one version of the regression were often irrelevant to others. Rejection of the results that the Douglas group was actually publishing did not constitute rejection of the broader idea represented by Douglas's program: One could still believe that if one used the right type of data, rather than the type that Douglas had used, a regression of the log of output on logged measures of inputs could yield useful information, although perhaps not the information that Douglas claimed it would yield.

Another explanation of the success of Douglas's innovation involves a discussion of Douglas's rhetoric of persuasion. It will become clear that Douglas was, at times, the model of the objective scientist: open and frank about the limitations of his method, about the weaknesses of his data, about the potential biases in the results he had produced, and about the wide gap between the conditions his regression procedure assumed and the conditions under which the data he used were actually generated. But at other times, he adopted the tone and rhetoric of an advocate. When responding to critics, their weaker criticisms were identified and rebutted but strong ones ignored or twisted into a form more easy to dismiss. When Douglas summarized his past work, he often stressed or exaggerated positive results and glossed over or ignored negative ones. Even particular results that he identified as problematic when originally published would sometimes be represented in subsequent accounts as part of the body of evidence that supported the legitimacy of the procedure.

More important, perhaps, than Douglas's ability to persuade was his audience's willingness to be persuaded. Simply put, economists really wanted to believe in Douglas's idea, if not his regression. Douglas's production function research faced harsh, detailed, and technically competent criticisms from the very beginning, some of which called into question not just Douglas's particular applications of his regression but also the general feasibility of estimating neoclassical production functions. At the same time, early articles that use or endorse the future potential of Douglas's regression seem to show an *eagerness to believe*. My argument is not that there was simply some critical mass of economists who were so carried away by the potential of the Douglas's method that they were willing to ignore criticisms or accept deficient defenses of the method. Instead, I think it is important that many economists were sufficiently excited by the potential of the method that, rather than abandoning it in the face of warranted criticism, they were willing to continue to teach it and use it while working towards improvements in data and statistical methodology that would rescue it.

To put this argument in a more concrete form, I focus on two economists, Earl Heady and Zvi Griliches, who responded to the new research tool in a similar way. (Heady's work with the regression is described in detail in Chapter 5, and Griliches's in Chapter 6). Both men became early and frequent users of the technique, in research that displayed a solid understanding of how it worked as a research tool as well as the various problems associated with its application. More importantly, they communicated, by words and example, the attitude that despite its weaknesses, the technique was potentially very valuable, that the best way to realize that potential was to continue using the technique while working to address the weaknesses, and that even while this process of improvement was going on, the technique was still able to contribute to knowledge. I propose that the efforts of these men, or more precisely, the manner in which they advocated for the new technique, was an important factor in its eventual success.

PART I

PAUL DOUGLAS AND HIS REGRESSION, 1927–1948

1

The Origins of Douglas's Production Function Research Program and His Initial Time Series Studies

Paul H. Douglas received his Ph.D. in economics from Columbia University in 1920. He had begun his graduate education at Columbia University in 1913, spent a year at Harvard University taking theory courses, and taken his first college teaching post in 1915. In 1920 he accepted a position at the University of Chicago, where he would remain on the faculty until 1948.[1]

Douglas was a prolific researcher, and began in the late teens to produce a steady stream of articles and books on topics related to labor legislation and working-class living standards. In 1921 he entered an ongoing debate on the trend in real wages in the United States since 1890 (Douglas and Lamberson 1921), and in 1924 started work on *Real Wages in the United States, 1890–1926*, a comprehensive statistical exploration of recent trends in wages, prices, employment, and unemployment rates (Douglas 1930). While assembling this statistical evidence, he was also developing a theoretical framework through which to interpret it. In 1926 he submitted a "Treatise on the Theory of Wages" to a competition sponsored by Hart, Schaffner, and Marx, and was awarded the $5,000 first prize. The prize-winning manuscript, which included "a more or less original explanation of general wages drawn in terms of relative elasticities of supply" and "the theory of occupational and geographical differences in wage rates" was too long to be published, and Douglas agreed to distill it into a book (Douglas 1934, xi). Seven years passed before this book appeared under the title *The Theory of Wages*. It was substantially altered from its 1926 form, and at its core was the Cobb–Douglas regression.

[1] Douglas's (1971) autobiography is the richest source of details on his life.

Douglas recounted the origin story of the Cobb–Douglas regression in several places, including this version in his autobiography:

> One spring day in 1927, while lecturing at Amherst, I charted on a logarithmic scale three variables I had laboriously compiled for American manufacturing for the years 1899 to 1922: an index of total fixed capital corrected for the change in the cost of capital goods (C), an index of the total number of wage earners employed in manufacturing (L), and an index of physical production (P). I noticed that the index of production lay between those for capital and labor and that it was from one third to one quarter of the relative distance between the lower index of labor and the higher index of capital. After consulting with my friend Charles W. Cobb, the mathematician, we decided to try to find on the basis of these observations the relative contributions which each of the two factors of production, labor and capital, had upon production itself. We chose the Euler formula of a simple homogeneous function of the first degree, which that remarkable Englishman Philip Wicksteed had developed some years before ($P = bL^kC^{1-k}$). We found the values of k and 1-k by the method of least squares to be .75 and .25, and that b was merely 1.01
>
> (Douglas 1971, 46–47).[2]

The results of this investigation were presented at the American Economic Association (AEA) meetings in 1927, and published in article form the next year as "A Theory of Production" (Cobb and Douglas 1928). They would be republished in *The Theory of Wages*, embedded in a discussion of the marginal productivity theory and a defense of that theory as a framework for the inductive study of production and distribution. In this chapter I review in detail the contents of these two publications, as well as the reactions of Douglas's fellow economists to them. I also describe the final study in the "time series" phase of Douglas's research with the regression, in which he applied the technique to data from the Australian state of Victoria. Prior to doing so, however, I discuss some of the theoretical concepts and research questions that motivated Douglas to pursue a program of research revolving around the estimation of the Cobb–Douglas regression, and also influenced how other economists responded to his work. Also, because many of the debates over the usefulness of the Cobb–Douglas regression as a research tool involved discussions of its properties as a statistical procedure, I review the state of empirical research

[2] See also Douglas (1948, 6) and Douglas (1976, 904). Samuelson (1976, 926) discusses Douglas's apparent confusion between the work of Wicksteed and Wicksell on the relationship between linear homogenous production functions and the marginal productivity theory.

methodology in economics during the initial years of Douglas's work with the regression.

PRODUCTION AND DISTRIBUTION THEORY IN THE 1920S

Both Douglas's decisions about how and why to pursue the research program that began with "A Theory of Production" and the reactions of other economists to his work with the Cobb–Douglas regression reflected certain theoretical and conceptual frameworks important to economic researchers working in the early twentieth century, some of which had their roots in the "classical economics" of the nineteenth century. Central to classical economics was a desire to discover the "laws of production," or the determinants of the amount of "wealth" that a society would produce, and the "laws of distribution," or the determinants of how that wealth was divided among society's members.[3] In seeking laws of production, the classical economists began with a conceptualization of production in which wealth was created by combining "labor," or human effort; "land," or the free gifts of nature; and "capital," which meant previously existing wealth that was used up in the process of creating new wealth. The conceptualization could be applied at the level of a single farm or factory, an industry, or society as a whole. It was understood that land, labor, and capital were aggregated categories of heterogeneous elements, but for analytical purposes they were often treated as three distinct and homogenous requisites to the production of wealth, and termed the "agents" or "factors" of production.

This conceptualization created questions of interest for the classical economists regarding the relationship between the quantities of the three factors employed in a production process and the amount of wealth produced. One question concerned the impact on the quantity of wealth produced of increasing all the factors of production by the same proportion. If, for example, the amounts of land, labor, and capital used in production were all doubled, would the amount of wealth produced also double, fall short of doubling, or more than double? By the early twentieth century, these three possibilities were commonly labeled "constant returns

[3] For example, John Stuart Mill, in the introduction to his summary of classical economic doctrines (Mill 1987 [1848]) explained that "writers on Political Economy profess . . . to investigate the nature of Wealth, and the laws of its production and distribution." Early classical writer J. B. Say (1855) [1803] defined political economy as the science that deals with "the production, distribution, and consumption of wealth."

to scale," "decreasing returns to scale," and "increasing returns to scale" in production.

A second question concerned the impact of increasing the quantity of one factor of production while leaving the quantities of the other factors unchanged. The classical economists assumed that the "law of diminishing returns" provided the answer to this question: successive, equal-sized increases of any factor of production, holding constant the amounts of the other two factors employed, would lead to successively smaller increases in wealth. This "law," when applied to the production of wealth by society as a whole, became a fundamental assumption underlying some of the most important propositions of classical economic theory.

The classical economists' discussion of the distribution of wealth ran in terms of three social classes, landlords, laborers, and capitalists, each consisting of the owners of one of the factors of production. The share of society's wealth claimed by each of these classes depended on the price of the factor of production they owned – the rent of land, the wage rate for labor, and the rate of profit on the money that producers spent on capital. There were competing theories about how these factor prices were determined, and how they were likely to change over time with the growth of population and of the quantity of society's wealth set aside as capital for future production, but assumptions about returns to scale and diminishing returns – that is, the assumed laws of production – played key roles in those theories.

During the 1870s, several economists made similar and strikingly innovative contributions to economic theory. The work of these economists and their immediate followers has been called "the marginal revolution" in economics, and it led to the creation of a new approach to and body of economic theory that came to be known as "neoclassical economics."[4] Neoclassical economics would eventually become the dominant paradigm in economics in the United States and Western Europe, but this process had hardly begun at the time Cobb and Douglas introduced the Cobb–Douglas regression. The decades of the 1920s, 1930s, and 1940s have been well described as the period of "interwar pluralism" in economics, during which the literature of the subject included arguments for and

[4] Whether the theoretical innovations introduced during this period really constituted a scientific revolution in any well-defined sense, and the extent of continuity between neoclassical economics and the classical economics it eventually supplanted, remain unsettled questions among historians of economics but are not particularly relevant to this book. The contributions in Black, Coats, and Goodwin (1973) provide a good introduction to these questions.

examples of a variety of distinct approaches to economic analysis, each characterized by different ideas about the scope and method of economics, including the role of statistical data in economic research, and about the assumptions that should form the starting point for economic theory (Morgan and Rutherford 1998). Further, a single economist might employ theories and concepts drawn from more than one of these approaches, Paul Douglas himself being one example.

Certain aspects of the emerging neoclassical school are particularly relevant to the story of the Cobb–Douglas regression. A first was the belief of many neoclassical economists that the first language of economic theory should be mathematics; that is, to as great an extent as possible, the assumptions of an economic theory should be expressed in mathematical form, and the propositions of the theory derived from those assumptions through mathematical analysis. This idea, to which almost no classical economist would have subscribed, was pushed by only some of the marginalist pioneers, and during the interwar period, both the degree of enthusiasm for it and the extent to which it was put into practice, while increasing, still varied considerably across enthusiasts for the neoclassical approach.[5]

Second, central to the contributions of the marginalist pioneers and the subsequent neoclassical school of economics was a new theory of distribution, one that was tightly linked to a theory of production, and that proposed a single principle, "marginal productivity," to explain the price received by sellers of any specific factor of production, for example, a tool, a building, an acre of grazing land, an hour of labor of an accountant, or an of hour unskilled labor. The theory sought to describe the determination of the prices of factors of production in settings in which producers sought to maximize profits, and all factors of production and outputs of production were traded in perfectly competitive markets.[6] It did so by characterizing an equilibrium in such markets, a balance of economic forces that rested ultimately on the preferences of the people participating in the markets and the technologies available for creating goods and services from factors of production, an equilibrium that would change in predictable ways should preferences or technological knowledge change.

The basics of this "marginal productivity theory of distribution" can be presented efficiently using mathematical notation, an approach that was

[5] Mirowski (1991) and Backhouse (1998) discuss and document the growing use of mathematics in economics during the twentieth century.

[6] The creation of the most useful definition of the abstract concept of "perfect competition" in markets was itself a part of the neoclassical research program.

becoming common by the interwar period. Consider first a twice differentiable mathematical function describing the relationship between some quantity of good or service produced (y), and the quantities of the m factors of production ($x_1, x_2 \ldots x_m$) used to create the good or service:

$$y = f(x_1, x_2 \ldots x_m) \tag{1.1}$$

By the mid-twentieth century, it was becoming standard for neoclassical economists to refer to a function such as Eq. (1.1) as a "production function." Also, the x's were increasingly being referred to a "inputs," and y the "output" of the production function, although the language of "factors of production" was still commonly used.

Choices could be made about the characteristics of this function to embody the common types of assumptions that had been employed by the classical economists in theorizing about production. The derivative of the function with respect to some x_j, that is, $\partial y/\partial x_j$, was termed the "marginal productivity" of input x_j, and was trivially assumed to be positive for all inputs. If the second derivative of the function with respect to an input was negative, then that input was said to be characterized by diminishing marginal productivity, or to use the older phrasing, subject to the law of diminishing returns. A common assumption in the basic form of the theory was that all inputs were subject to the law of diminishing returns. Assumptions about the form of the function also determined the nature of the "returns to scale" in production (decreasing, constant, or increasing), which might be different for different levels of output.[7]

Letting r_j represent the price, or rental rate, of a unit of input x_j, the marginal productivity theory held that in equilibrium, for every factor of production,

$$r_j = p\frac{\partial y}{\partial x_j} \tag{1.2}$$

where p was the price per unit of y. The quantity on the right was termed the "value marginal product" of x_j, that is, the increase in the producer's revenue obtained by increasing the amount of input x_j by one unit, although sometimes in describing this central implication of the theory, the word "value" was left implicit. Also, if the input x_j was used in the

[7] If, as a matter of mathematical analysis, a simultaneous and equal percentage increase in all of the x's led to a larger/smaller/equal percentage increase in y, then the production function was characterized by increasing/decreasing/constant returns to scale.

production of many goods and services (as was, for example, unskilled labor), the value marginal product of x_j in the production of any of those goods and services would be equal to r_j. Put another way, there would be only one price for the input x_j no matter how it was used. The condition (1.2) characterizing the prices of factors of production also explained incomes – the income of an individual would be the sum received from selling the factors of production he owned. So, for example, the total income of an unskilled laborer who had no input to sell except labor would be the hourly wage rate (the value of his marginal product in any type of production activity) times the number of hours worked.

Again, Eq. (1.2) describes the equilibrium state of an economic environment in which markets are perfectly competitive and the preferences of individuals, technological knowledge, and the supplies of non-manufactured inputs (in particular, labor inputs) are held constant. Neoclassical economists understood this to be an abstraction, not a description of reality in any part of the economy. They believed, however, that circumstances and processes in the real economy were often close enough to those captured by the abstract theory for the theory to provide compelling explanations for observed differences or changes in the prices of factors of production, and thus the incomes of the owners of those factors.

Douglas saw the Cobb–Douglas regression as a means of determining the characteristics of actual production functions using statistical data. Given the close relationship between the characteristics of the production function and the distribution of income posited by the marginal productivity theory, it is obvious how valuable such a procedure could be to the neoclassical research program.[8] For example, knowledge of the rate at which the productivity of unskilled labor diminished (the second derivative of a function like Eq. (1.2) with respect to unskilled labor) would provide quantitative answers to questions about how wages would be affected by changes in the quantity of unskilled labor due to migration, population growth, or education. And Douglas would, beginning in the 1930s, argue that his procedure could provide a statistical test of the marginal productivity theory itself, via a comparison of actual wage levels

[8] As will be discussed in Chapter 2, in the mid-1930s, Douglas began to use data sources that led him to adopt a version of the production function in which the left and side variable was the monetary "value added" of the production process – the market value of the output (py) minus the costs of all non-labor inputs to production that were not classified by the data collectors as "capital" (e.g., raw materials).

to the statistically determined value of marginal product of labor in production.

During the interwar and early postwar decades, there was a certain flexibility in the way that the neoclassical production function concept was used, in the sense that a production function might be assumed to describe the relationship between inputs employed and output created in the production of one particular good, or by a single firm, or by an industry (several firms producing the same output), or in the economy as a whole. In the latter case, the analysis ran in terms of concepts similar to those employed by the classical economists – land, labor, and capital as factors of production, and an aggregated, homogenized total output concept. This last type of production function came to be known as an aggregate production function, as did the production function used by Douglas, which portrayed the relationship between inputs employed by and output produced by the US manufacturing sector taken as a whole.

This flexibility reflects another important aspect of neoclassical economics at this time: Several distinct variants of the marginal productivity theory existed, two of which are particularly important to understanding Douglas's own arguments about what his empirical technique could accomplish, and the reaction of other economists to Douglas's research with the technique. The first variant had its roots in the version of the theory proposed by American economist John Bates Clark. His was a theory of how the wealth produced by society as a whole ended up being divided between the owners of two factors of production, labor and capital, with land being considered by Clark to be a form of capital. The marginal productivity of a homogenous "social" labor input in the production of wealth determined the single wage rate in the economy, while the marginal productivity of a social fund of capital determined the rate of interest. Clark's version of the theory, then, was compatible with an aggregate production function defined at the level of the economy as a whole.

A second variant of the marginal productivity theory can be called the "Walrasian" variant, as it was built on the theoretical contributions of the early French marginalist Leon Walras. Like the other marginalist pioneers, Walras was particularly interested in understanding how the prices of goods and productive factors were determined in a competitive market economy. He insisted, however, that an adequate theoretical account of the process of price determination must embody the interrelatedness of all markets in such an economy, in the sense that the price of any one of the myriad of unique goods or productive factors in an economy would depend on the conditions affecting the supply of and demand for every other good and productive factor – that potentially, the price of ice cream could be affected by a change in the demand for, or the technology for producing, hammers. This, coupled with a belief that economic theory should be expressed in mathematical form, led him to represent the equilibrium of input and output prices in a competitive market economy as the solution to a system of simultaneous equations.[9]

Economists who built on Walras's contributions still arrived at the conclusion expressed in Eq. (1.2), that the price of any input to production would be equal to its value marginal productivity, but in their models they assumed (as did Walras) that each good in the economy had a distinct production function. Aggregation – grouping goods together into categories for the purposes of analysis –was something the Walrasian neoclassicists worked hard to avoid, as it obscured some of the intermarket relationships that they considered a crucial feature of price determination. In describing factors of production, a term like "capital" might be used but only as a category label for a heterogeneous collection of "capital goods," or goods used in the process of production, like the various types of buildings, tools, and machines. Using a homogenous "capital" concept for analytical purposes could be misleading. Similarly, although there might be a mathematical relationship between the quantity of a somehow aggregated collection of goods and services, and the quantities of somehow aggregated collections of capital goods and labor types used in their production, these relationships would necessarily be complicated and difficult to disentangle amalgams of the production relationships that really mattered for the determination of prices and the distribution of income – those characterizing the production functions of distinct individual goods. As shall become more clear, many economists who embraced the Walrasian variant of the marginal productivity theory were critical of Douglas's use of the phrase "production function" to describe the relationships he estimated using the Cobb–Douglas regression.

EMPIRICAL ECONOMICS IN THE 1920s

At the time that Cobb and Douglas's "A Theory of Production" appeared, there was something of a revolution underway in empirical economic research. Prior to World War I, as today, economists used statistical data

9 Stigler (1941) is an excellent technical analysis of the differences between the versions of marginal productivity theory developed by the early marginalists and inherited by the neoclassical writers of the mid-twentieth century.

to discern and represent what was really going on in the economy, to buttress claims about the causes and effects of economic phenomena and policies, to defend or test the assumptions and conclusions of theory, and so on. But with the exception of the work of a few pioneers such as Wesley Mitchell, Warren Persons, and Irving Fisher, most economists who used statistical data simply presented raw numbers or percentage shares in tables or in the text of their books and articles, making no use of derived statistical measures such as means, standard deviations, or index numbers. This began to change, and change rather quickly, during the 1920s, and by the end of that decade, the well-trained empirical economist understood basic statistical theory and applied it in constructing index numbers, tabulating frequency distributions, and calculating summary statistics.[10]

Douglas's own development as an economic statistician paralleled these changes in what represented good statistical practice for economists. For example, in his early work on immigrant skill levels and labor turnover, he reported numbers and percentages in tables and text (Douglas 1918, 1919). In his research during the 1920s on trends in real wages and working conditions, however, Douglas showed his ability to construct and critique index numbers, and to calculate means and measures of average deviation to illustrate relevant points (Douglas 1921, 1930). It seems likely that Douglas taught himself the statistical skills necessary to keep up with the advancing field during the 1920s, as his account of his graduate education makes only the briefest reference to a class in statistics, while offering several hints that he needed to work on his own to make up for general deficiencies in his graduate training.[11]

Douglas's work on real wages also exemplifies an important strand of the 1920s literature in empirical economics. Often the chief task of an author was simply to provide, through statistics, as accurate a portrayal as possible of some aspect of economic activity, such as recent movements of the retail price level or the pattern of international trade flows. Because

[10] Biddle (1999) documents this transition, while Ayres (1927) provides a contemporary account.

[11] At one point he comments on how the student at Columbia University had little interaction with the faculty, and was "largely thrown on his own resources." He also recounts taking a class from Frank Taussig at Harvard University, who seemed to take pleasure in illustrating the shortcomings of Douglas's Columbia training. Douglas recalled that in response, "I left each session soaked with perspiration, and hurried back to my room to change my clothes and start studying for the next day. I kept at the texts until midnight and rose early each morning to begin again" (Douglas 1971, 28, 33–34). In Douglas (1939) he mentions taking a class given by pioneering econometrician H. L. Moore, but getting little out of it.

government programs for collecting economic statistics were still in their infancy, one of the more valued skills of a good empirical economist was the ability to construct a credible and comprehensive quantitative account of some economic phenomenon of interest from the fragmentary statistical evidence available on that phenomenon. Among other things, this required the researcher to locate the relevant data sources, to extrapolate from time periods or sectors for which data were relatively complete to time periods or sectors in which they were more scarce, and to defend or assess the likely accuracy of the results using logic, implicit theorizing, and various consistency checks across data from different sources. For example, the US Census of Manufactures might provide comprehensive statistics on manufacturing output at five-year intervals, while a trade organization might provide annual data on output for a particular industry. An author might then use information from two censuses on the ratio of the latter industry's output to total manufacturing output to produce annual estimates of total manufacturing output for intercensal years. Data from a few state-level censuses from these years might then be used as a check on the results. This type of work required detailed reporting and explanation of the various steps used to build up estimates, and also a fair amount of persuasion, as the author tried to convince readers not only that the steps taken to produce the estimates were the most reasonable ones under the circumstances but also that the resulting statistical picture, with all its shortcomings, was still accurate enough to be useful.

As noted, this type of statistical work and argumentation was an essential feature of Douglas's work on real wages, but it was also an important part of his work with the Cobb–Douglas regression, especially in the early years. And while critics of this aspect of Douglas's work sometimes faulted the strong claims he made for the accuracy of his results, they seldom criticized the thoroughness of his search for data sources or his decisions about how to build estimates from the limited data resources available to him.

Douglas's initial research employing the Cobb–Douglas regression also had two features in common with work at the frontier of empirical economics in the late 1920s and early 1930s. One was the use of least squares regression and correlation analysis. The second was the explicit attempt to estimate, using statistical data, functional or causal relationships implied by economic theory. During the 1920s and early 1930s, there was a growing literature in which regression techniques were used in an attempt to estimate the real-world counterparts of the supply and demand curves of theory. As Morgan (1990) has shown, this work played an important role in shaping the approach to combining statistical methods and economic theory that become the standard econometric practice in the later decades of the twentieth century. Still, it should be remembered that at the time it first appeared, this research program, which I shall call the neoclassical-econometric program, was rather speculative and esoteric. Douglas, however, saw it as the wave of the future, and in *The Theory of Wages* explicitly linked his own work to it:

> It has long seemed to me that the inductive, statistical, and quasi-mathematical method must be used if we are ever to make economics a truly fruitful and progressive science. The neoclassical school has constructed a valuable theoretical scaffolding according to which the value of commodities and the rates of return to land, labor, and capital are fixed at the intersection of the various supply and the demand curves. This is a beginning but only a beginning. For in order to make the analysis precise, to forecast, and to detect interactions in economic society it is necessary to determine the slopes of the demand and supply curves …. An excellent beginning has been made in this direction by such scholars as Henry L. Moore, Schultz, Ezekiel, Bean, Working, and Marschak …. (T)he skill of these pioneers and their followers is growing and they are using ever more powerful techniques with a resultant narrowing of the margin of error and uncertainty. This line of attack has, therefore, more than justified itself in dealing with the problem of prices and the values of commodities ….
>
> There is a need for a similar approach to the problems of distribution. We need to know whether the assumed curves of diminishing incremental productivity are merely imaginative myths or whether they are real, and if the latter, what their slopes are. We need to know more about the supply functions of the factors and whether the actual processes of distribution furnish any degree of corroboration to the inductive tendencies discovered. This book is an attempt to do just that (Douglas 1934, xii).

So, when the Cobb–Douglas regression made its debut, it represented a bold attempt by an established empirical economist to join up-to-date statistical methods with a still-controversial theoretical framework. During the 1930s, new and more technically sophisticated statistical methods were being introduced into the empirical economics literature, and acceptance of the neoclassical framework by economists was increasing. The debate over Douglas's production function research would reflect both these trends.

THE DEBUT OF THE COBB–DOUGLAS REGRESSION: "A THEORY OF PRODUCTION"

As noted above, the results of estimating a Cobb–Douglas regression first appeared in 1928 in the article "A Theory of Production" (Cobb and

Douglas 1928). And while Douglas's 1934 book *The Theory of Wages* would make very clear the connection he saw between the estimation of the Cobb–Douglas regression and the project of testing and giving quantitative content to the marginal productivity theory of distribution, this connection was at most implicit in the 1928 article. The article opened with a statement of goals. Given that "refined" measures of the volume of manufacturing output for recent years now existed, Douglas argued, it seemed worthwhile to attempt to measure the relative amounts of labor and capital used to produce that output. If these amounts could be even approximately ascertained, a number of interesting tasks could be undertaken. They included determining the extent to which increases in output were due to increases in the quantities of labor and capital vs. improvements in technique; measuring the marginal physical product of labor and capital; discovering whether the "theories of decreasing imputed productivity" were historically valid, and if so, attaching quantitative approximations to these "assumed tendencies"; and finally, with estimates of imputed physical product in hand and measures of real wages available, determining "whether or not the processes of distribution are modeled at all closely upon those of the production of value." This vague assertion of a possible relationship between production and distribution was clarified a bit at the end of the paper, when Douglas argued that he had revealed a decided tendency for distribution to follow the laws of imputed productivity while noting that this alone allowed no ethical or policy conclusions to be drawn (Cobb and Douglas 1928, 139–40, 163–64).

Douglas next described and defended his measures of capital and labor. Capital presented the greatest challenge. On the way to presenting an index of the amount of capital employed in US manufacturing from 1899–1922, Douglas catalogued a daunting array of problems with the existing data on capital along with his solutions to these problems, solutions that he frankly critiqued but also defended as adequate to the task at hand. For example, Douglas believed that the "capital" he should be measuring was fixed capital (buildings, tools, equipment, and machinery), but not "working capital," which included raw materials, goods in process, and inventories. While every Census of Manufactures reported the total value of capital employed, only some of them segregated out the value of buildings, machinery, and equipment.[12] Douglas described how he used the share

[12] The Census of Manufactures, conducted every ten years from 1879 to 1899, every five years from 1899 to 1919, and again in 1921, endeavored to compile statistics on capital, employment, and output for every manufacturing establishment in the United States.

of total capital represented by fixed capital in the census years for which it was reported to estimate a trend in this proportion, and then used this estimated trend to assign a value to fixed capital for census years in which it was not separately reported. Douglas defended his procedure by pointing out that the value it produced for 1922 (fixed capital representing 46.5 percent of total capital) was close the value reported for Missouri in that state's 1923 census.

A tougher problem was created by the fact that, according to an expert Douglas queried at the Census Bureau, dollar values of capital reported to the census probably represented original cost rather than current value, requiring Douglas to (i) estimate what proportion of a given year's fixed capital stock had been added in each of a number of preceding years and (ii) reduce each year's estimated increment to the value of the fixed capital stock to a constant dollar value, using a capital-price index of some sort. Without getting into the details of how Douglas handled this problem, suffice it to say that it required him to construct price and quantity indexes for two categories of capital goods using partial data on the production and prices of various basic commodities (e.g., pig iron and coke) along with an index of money wages, liberally applying proportionality assumptions throughout the process.[13]

These brief descriptions of Douglas's methods of producing his capital series actually underrepresent their complexity and the number of heroic assumptions upon which they rested, and indicate the large number of potential points of contention presented to any critic of Douglas's work. It should not be forgotten, however, that these were the sort of things that empirically oriented economists of the time did, and felt they had to do, in order to build up the statistical pictures of economic activity that they believed were required for economic science to move forward.

Estimating the aggregate quantity of labor used in manufacturing was more straightforward, at least in census years, in which manufacturing

[13] It is often the case that economic quantities are reported in monetary form, for example, dollars' worth of goods produced, or dollars' worth of inputs used. A change between two time periods in the dollar value of a quantity of goods reflects both the change in the price per unit of the good and the change in the number of units of the good. If economists are interested in knowing the change in the number of units of the good represented by the change in measured monetary quantity, they must somehow adjust the monetary measure for the change in prices, or "deflate" the monetary measure. Beginning in the late 1800s, the "price index number" was the statistical tool used for this procedure. The best way to construct a price index number for various purposes, and the relative strengths and weaknesses of various actual price indexes used in empirical research, were (and remain) a subject of research and controversy in economics.

establishments reported the average number of "wage earners" employed throughout the year. Employment numbers for intercensal years were filled in with the help of annual employment counts from New Jersey, Massachusetts, and Pennsylvania along with reasonable rules for dealing with the differences in employment growth between census years in these states vs. the nation as a whole. Douglas commented that the measure would have been better if it had included clerical workers, and better still if it had been based on man-hours rather than number of men. As a measure of the output of the manufacturing sector, Douglas borrowed "E. E. Day's well known index of the physical volume of production for the years 1899–1922" (Cobb and Douglas 1928, 149–50; Day and Persons 1920), noting later in the paper that this involved the assumption that the level of manufacturing output moved proportionately with the level of total output. Douglas presented his three series for capital, labor and product (C, L and P) as index numbers taking the value of 100 in 1899.[14]

The first of two sections written by Cobb (the paper's initial footnote identified which sections were written by each author) presented the paper's promised "theory of production": aggregate manufacturing output was a linear homogenous function of aggregate labor and aggregate capital; the general form of the function was $P = bL^{k}C^{1-k}$; and the specific form of the function was $P = 1.01L^{.75}C^{.25}$. Beyond mentioning that the values chosen for b and k were the "best . . . in the sense of the Theory of Least Squares," no details of the estimation procedure were reported (152).[15]

Using P' to represent the value of the production index predicted by the regression and P the actual value, Cobb portrayed the goodness of fit of the regression in a number of ways: tabulating and plotting the percentage deviation of P from P' in each year, calculating the mean absolute (percentage) deviation (4.2 percent), noting that P was closer to P' than to its own three-year moving average, reporting the correlation coefficients between P and P' (.97), and between the deviations of P and P' from their respective moving averages (.93).

Cobb's second section discussed and derived mathematical properties of the fitted function, including its implied functions for the productivities of total capital and total labor, the marginal productivities of capital and

[14] Judged by the standards of the time, Douglas's construction of these series alone would have been enough to make the paper an important contribution to empirical economics. His index of physical capital appears to have been the first such time series constructed by an economist.

[15] The value of k was the slope coefficient obtained by a linear regression of log(P/C) on log (L/C).

labor, and the elasticities of product with respect to capital and labor. Then, using the actual values of P, L, and C along with formulas for marginal productivity, he plotted the values of marginal productivity of capital and labor implied by the data along the theoretical curves of marginal productivity implied by the estimated regression.

It remained for Douglas to make the case that "the equation $P = 1.01L^{3/4}C^{1/4}$ describes in a fairly accurate manner the actual processes of production in manufacturing during this period." He reviewed the evidence of goodness of fit, both the "close consilience between P and P'" and the clustering of data-based measures of marginal productivity along the theoretically derived marginal productivity functions. He raised the possibility that the good fits were due to spurious correlation between trending series, noting that "it has some times been charged that . . . equally good results would be secured by comparing the relative movements of hogs in Wisconsin, cattle in Wisconsin, with the physical product in manufacturing," but dismissed this charge by arguing that there was an a priori theoretical connection between capital, labor and output that did not exist for pigs, cattle, and output, and by reminding readers of the high correlation between the deviations of P and P' from their three-year moving averages. Employing a tactic that he would use throughout his 20-year defense of his production research, Douglas then explained that even observations for which P' was a poor approximation for P strengthened the case for the estimated equation. If one looked at years with large differences between predicted and actual output, those in which P was below P' were recession years, and those in which P was above P' were years of prosperity. Since the capital index measured existing capital rather than capital utilized, and the labor index was men rather than man-hours, one would expect this pattern: in a recession, when plants were idled and overtime eliminated, the capital and labor indexes overstated the amount of the inputs actually employed, and so the equation produced a predicted output that was too high. Likewise, prosperities were periods of full capital utilization and long, intense hours for workers, leading the indexes to understate true input use (Cobb and Douglas 1928, 160–61).

Douglas's final argument in defense of the validity of his "theory of production" was to show that "the process of distribution approximate(s) the apparent laws of production." Doing so required additional constructive data work. Combining Cobb's formulas for marginal product with his own basic data series for L, C, and P allowed Douglas to create an index of physical productivity of labor. He converted this to a value-product series by using the wholesale price indexes published by the Bureau of Labor

Statistics (BLS) to construct an annual series of the price of manufactured goods relative to all goods. The resulting index of value product per worker was then compared to an index of real wages in manufacturing that Douglas had recently created (Douglas 1926). Douglas reported that the wage and value-product series had a correlation of .69. Douglas also cited a number that ended up having a large impact on readers of the Cobb–Douglas paper: the National Bureau of Economic Research (NBER) had estimated that over the 1909–19 period, wages and salaries represented 74 percent of the total value added in manufacturing, a number stunningly close to the .75 estimate for k produced by the production regression.

The law of production had not been "solved," Douglas concluded, but an approximation had been made and a line of attack on the problem indicated. Much more work remained to be done. The series for labor, capital, and output could all be refined. Other formulas, including one that allowed k to vary over time, could be tested. Other sets of data could be analyzed, eventually allowing comparisons between manufacturing and other sectors and international comparisons as well. Natural resources could be included as a productive factor in future work. Interestingly, Cobb had also included an assessment of where the research stood and where it should go in one of his sections, and it was somewhat more tentative than Douglas's: "It is the purpose of this paper, then, not to state results, but to illustrate a method of attack. In choosing a definite Norm for Production as a first approximation, it is not at all certain that we have arrived at the best possible. The advantage of choosing a norm at all seems to be that it involves us in logical consequences that can be compared to the facts as we get the facts." (Cobb and Douglas 1928, 156).

REACTIONS TO "A THEORY OF PRODUCTION"

Douglas made bold claims in "A Theory of Production": Using generally available data and accessible statistical techniques, he had shown that the actual relationship between the amount of capital and labor used in manufacturing and the quantity of manufacturing output could be closely approximated by a simple function, one that embodied and allowed quantification of the hypothesis of diminishing marginal productivity of labor and capital. He had demonstrated a relationship between the characteristics of this "law of production" and the distribution of income between labor and capital, a relationship posited by a well-known but still-contested theory of distribution. It is thus not surprising that the paper attracted the attention of a number of economists.

Sumner Slichter was assigned to discuss the paper at the AEA meetings, and his comments were decidedly negative. He harshly criticized Douglas's capital index, citing the known unreliability of census capital figures and of the price data that Douglas had used to deflate capital values. He showed how small biases caused by inaccurate price indexes in early years of the series could cumulate, and noted that the capital series was altered considerably if different years were chosen as base years for deflating. These problems "rob[bed] Prof. Cobb's computations of the significance they would otherwise possess" (Slichter 1928, 168).

Slichter's complaints went beyond issues of data quality, however, as he believed the entire project to be wrong-headed. Despite the fact that the marginal productivity theory was not explicitly mentioned in the paper, Slichter thought he could see a hidden agenda, and he did not approve: "Professors Cobb and Douglas conclude that it has been statistically demonstrated that the relationship between the agents of production on one hand and the volume of output on the other meets the requirements of the marginal productivity hypothesis." Slichter disputed this specific claim, and argued more generally that marginal productivity theory had little to offer as a framework for thinking about distribution. "The description of the relationship between productive agents and physical output sheds little light upon what happens in the market place where distribution of income actually takes place." (Slichter 1928, 168) Marginal productivity theory required instantaneous and complete adjustment of factor prices to changes in output prices and vice versa, something that clearly was not the case, since "every one knows" that factors like land and capital are obtained on long-term contracts and that wages are sticky. Entrepreneurs could not know the marginal contribution of each agent, and, for that matter, entrepreneurship had not even been included as a factor in the Cobb–Douglas analysis. Nor was there any element of the equation that accounted for possible technological change. Slichter closed with a final indictment of the research:

> "There is probably no more important single cause for our meagre knowledge of the distributive process than the fact that the subject has been so largely studied within the narrow limits imposed by the assumptions of static economics .... Quantitative economics, by helping to provide the raw materials for a realistic theory, can be of great use in liberating the study of distribution from the tyranny of economic statics. But it can be of little assistance if statisticians and mathematical economists are too completely preoccupied with verifying the propositions of static doctrine."
>
> (Slichter 1928, 170)

Douglas recalled in later years that his initial work with the Cobb–Douglas production function was, in general, poorly received by the profession (Douglas 1979, 905; 1971, 614; Samuelson 1979, 924). This is not quite true: while almost all economists who commented on or reviewed "A Theory of Production" or *The Theory of Wages* did find fault with various details of Douglas's method, most of them expressed considerable enthusiasm for the "method of attack" represented by the research, and some offered constructive suggestions for pushing the research program forward.

A good example of a "friendly critic" of this sort is J. M. Clark, whose article "Inductive Evidence on Marginal Utility" appeared within a few months of "A Theory of Production" and was devoted solely to discussing issues raised by the Cobb–Douglas paper (Clark 1928). His criticisms were numerous, but most were constructive, aimed at improving the Cobb–Douglas analysis of marginal productivity rather than discrediting it. Like Slichter, he questioned the accuracy of Douglas's capital and labor series, but took it for granted that "they will be improved and refined as the authors continue their researches," offering several suggestions for how this might be done (Clark 1928, 451). He suggested an approach for estimating the return to fixed capital using only the (more reliable) data on total capital, and even estimated his own augmented version of the Cobb–Douglas regression. Clark believed that the Cobb–Douglas equation offered a good account of the "normal" or long-run relationship between labor, capital, and output, but did a poor job of representing the impact of cyclical fluctuations in labor and capital utilization, which were governed by a "different law." He proposed altering the function so that the normal relationship between capital and labor could be adjusted by a factor representing cyclical swings, and suggested $P = L^k C^{1-k}(L/L_n)^m$, where L_n represented the "normal" level of employment, meaning that which the capital stock was designed to accommodate.[16] Clark defined L_n as a seven-year centered moving average of Douglas's L. He fixed k at 2/3, as Cobb had found this to fit the prewar years better than k=.75, and Clark believed the war years too abnormal to include in the analysis. A sort of grid search procedure was used to set .63 as the value for m. For the years Clark

[16] This formula allows the marginal increases in labor input to have a magnified impact on output if they are allowing idled capital to be put back into use. Clark admitted that it would not capture the phenomenon of a diminishing marginal return to labor as plant capacity was pressed and exceeded during booms, but argued that this was a relatively unimportant case during the period covered.

included, 1902–16, his formula produced a lower sum of squared errors than the Cobb–Douglas formula, because it did a better job of matching the amplitude of the cyclical fluctuations in P.

Clark was troubled by the fact that the Cobb–Douglas regression left no room for improvements in technology to affect productivity. Accurate measurement of marginal products required that the impact of technological progress be isolated or eliminated, but experience suggested that such progress was the main cause of the growth of output observed in the data. Clark argued that either some means of adjusting the capital and labor series to remove the impact of technological development should be developed, or else the growth in output attributed by the regression to growth in capital should be partly attributed to "progress." His tentative suggestion as to how such data adjustments or attributions might be made only served to indicate how difficult this problem was. But it could be solved, Clark believed, if not with data based on historical aggregates, then with comparative studies of "simultaneous" data from different industries. Clark concluded that the Cobb–Douglas study was "a bold and significant piece of pioneer work in a hitherto neglected field," which he clearly hoped would be followed up by others (Clark 1928, 467).

Another prominent early critic who believed that the Cobb–Douglas approach should be "modified, not abandoned" was Douglas's colleague from University of Chicago Henry Schultz (Schultz 1929). Schultz's main criticism was that Cobb and Douglas's statistical procedure, which employed time series data but made no adjustment for secular changes, could not result in a verification of a static theory like the marginal productivity theory.[17] Referring to his own approach to estimating neoclassical supply and demand curves, Schultz described the strategy of adjusting the data to remove long-term trends, then correlating deviations from those trends in order to isolate relationships that were closer in principle to the concepts of static theory. Long-term relationships between variables, such as those estimated by Cobb and Douglas, were likely to be interesting for their own sake, but by adopting alternative methods, perhaps including some of those employed in empirical studies of demand, one could also potentially identify short-run marginal productivity curves and the factors that shifted them.

[17] As Morgan (1990, section 5.2) explains, possible approaches to testing a static theory with time series data were much discussed in the literature on estimating supply and demand relationships, to which Schultz was a major contributor.

The second published estimates of Cobb–Douglas regressions appeared in 1930 in a short article by Cobb, in which he used time series data from the annual Massachusetts Census of Manufacturing to estimate the regression. Cobb reported that he had encountered difficulties in attempting to estimate the Cobb–Douglas regression, and had sought the advice of Ragner Frisch. As a result, Cobb made two changes in the estimation method: he estimated the coefficients of capital and labor separately, thus relaxing the assumption that the production function was linear homogenous, and he estimated the function using "diagonal mean regression." Diagonal mean regression had been proposed by Frisch in part as a solution to what Morgan (1990, 138) called the "regression choice problem": in using regression to estimate the relationship between several economic variables, which variable should be chosen as the dependent variable?[18] Frisch began with an assumption that there was a deterministic relationship between the variables, and that the only reason the actual data did not reveal this exact relationship was because variables were measured with error. For example, if two variables were related by the linear equation $X_1 = a + bX_2$, and both variables were measured with error, the true value of b would be bounded by the regression estimate of b obtained using X_1 as the dependent variable and the estimate obtained using X_2 as the dependent variable. Where within these bounds the true b fell depended on the relative variances of the measurement errors in X_1 and X_2. Frisch's diagonal mean regression amounted to estimating the true b as the geometric mean of the two bounds. It was a concession to the fact that the variances of the errors were typically unknown, and also an unsuccessful attempt to produce regression estimates that were invariant to changes in the scale of measurement of the variables.

It is easy to imagine why Cobb felt that the diagonal mean regression estimator was "particularly well adapted" to his project (Cobb 1930, 705), as it was clear that all three of his variables were measured with error, while there was no solid information concerning which were more error-ridden. Cobb gave no economic reason for wanting to relax the restriction that the coefficients summed to one. In any case, following Frisch's suggestions created difficulties for Cobb rather than solving them. Estimating the regression for six different industries and for manufacturing as a whole

[18] At the time, this was often referred to as choosing the direction of minimization. Classical regression minimizes the distance of the data points from the regression surface in the direction parallel to the axis of the variable chosen as "dependent."

in three different time periods, Cobb got coefficient estimates that were all over the map, including negative values and values greater than one. The sum of the coefficients in these regressions ranged from .94 to 5.17. When he applied the same method to the US data from the Cobb–Douglas paper, the coefficient for labor was 1.63 and for capital .48. Beyond a few unconvincing attempts to make economic sense of some of the more bizarre results, Cobb had little to say about what had happened, and this paper marked the end of his work with the Cobb–Douglas regression.

Cobb's article should be classed as a criticism of Douglas's research program because it raised very serious questions about the credibility of marginal productivity estimates produced by estimating the Cobb–Douglas function. Douglas's reaction to it was rather curious – he ignored it completely, even in subsequent works in which he discussed his own estimates derived from the same Massachusetts data,[19] and even though Douglas would wrangle with other critics for several years over how the regression choice problem should be treated in the case of production function estimation.[20]

The reasons for the differing reactions of Cobb and Douglas to Cobb's discouraging results – with Cobb moving on to other areas of research and Douglas deciding that further work with the regression was a potential path to establishing his scientific respectability (Douglas 1967) are largely a matter of speculation, but I would argue that one reason is the difference in the two men's academic training and orientation. Douglas's undergraduate and graduate training was in economics, during which he read the classical works in the field and used several of the standard economics textbooks of the time. Cobb was trained as a mathematician, serving on the faculty of mathematics at Amherst and having received a Ph.D. in mathematics from the University in Michigan in 1912 (Collier 2016).[21] In his reminiscences about the writing of "A Theory of Production," Douglas would refer to

[19] He did mention it in Douglas (1976), but cited a result that did not appear in Cobb's paper, and made no reference to the negative results that Cobb did report.

[20] Also, as discussed in Chapter 2, while Douglas did adopt the practice of estimating the coefficients of capital and labor separately, on repeated occasions he attributed this change in approach to a suggestion of David Durand (1937), not to Cobb.

[21] Cobb's dissertation was in part concerned with the decidedly mathematical topic, "the asymptotic development for a certain integral function of zero order" (Cobb 1913). His later publications in economic journals were concerned almost exclusively with matters of applied statistical theory.

Cobb as a friend and a mathematician. I suspect that the Cobb–Douglas collaboration was not the result of a shared interest in the economic questions underlying Douglas's research at the time, but one of convenience – Douglas had an essentially economic question, in that he wanted to characterize the relationship between capital, labor, and output that he saw in his time series data with a simple mathematical function, and sought help from a mathematician that he had befriended during his short time in Amherst. And Cobb had a quick answer for Douglas (Douglas 1934).

But the two men thought about the regression they had fit to the economic data in two different ways. Cobb saw it as a mathematical-statistical object, with results to be interpreted with the aid of statistical theory. When thinking about the changes in the coefficient estimates associated with changing the choice of what variable was "dependent" in the regression, Cobb was drawn to Frisch's approach to the problem, which involved considering the relative error variances of the three statistical variables involved, and/or altering the objective function to be minimized. Douglas, however, thought about the regression as an economic object, so that economic theory had a role to play in specifying the regression and interpreting the results. He has already indicated this in "A Theory of Production," when he responded to the criticism that "equally good results would be secured by comparing the relative movements of hogs in Wisconsin, cattle in Wisconsin, with the physical product in manufacturing" by commenting that "there is a logical and economic connection between labor, capital, and product which is not present in the attempted *reductio ad absurdum*" (Cobb and Douglas 1928, 160). In Douglas's view, the choice of dependent variable in the Cobb–Douglas regression was obvious because economic theory and common sense clearly indicated the causation ran from the quantity of the inputs to the quantity of the output, and he would later make this point forcefully when the sensitivity of the regression results to the choice of dependent variable became an important issue on the debate over the value of Douglas's technique.

BRINGING THE MARGINAL PRODUCTIVITY THEORY TO THE FOREFRONT: *THE THEORY OF WAGES*

Though clearly stung by some of the criticisms of "A Theory of Production," Douglas pushed ahead with his new method, making the

Cobb–Douglas regression the centerpiece of his *The Theory of Wages*.[22] The first section of the book was devoted to a history of production and distribution theory and an explication of the marginal productivity theory, focusing mainly on J. B. Clark's version of that theory. Several pages were devoted to explaining the meaning of the assumption of constant returns to scale and its relationship to linear homogenous functions, Euler's theorem and the question of whether paying all factors their marginal contributions would exhaust the product. He defended this assumption, which was of course embodied in the original Cobb–Douglas regression, by variously labeling it a "common sense" assumption, the "most probable" relationship between inputs and outputs, and a good first approximation to the true relationship. He also cited the arguments of A. A. Cournot and Knut Wicksell that increasing returns would lead to widespread monopoly and decreasing returns to an economy of one-man firms, neither of which obtained in the real world.

Perhaps with an eye to critics like Slichter, Douglas included a chapter on the assumptions of the marginal productivity theory, both explicit and implicit, with long discussions of the extent to which each was valid for the United States. After arranging the key assumptions on a scale ranging from "largely valid but not wholly so" to "partially true but on the whole not true" he commented that

> many, who have seen the degree of variance between real life and the assumptions of the productivity school, have in their impatience declared that because of this defective basis, the conclusions which have been drawn from the productivity theory are not worthy of credence and hence should be disregarded. But an attitude such as this ignores the fact that the assumptions do represent real tendencies which in the aggregate are more powerful than those of a conflicting nature
>
> (Douglas 1934, 94–95).

Such critics, Douglas argued, seemed ignorant of the fact that the method of deduction and abstraction used to build the marginal productivity theory was also the method that had achieved great success in the natural sciences.

22 Douglas 1967, 17; 1971, 47. Over half of *The Theory of Wages* was devoted to Douglas's attempts to estimate the elasticities of supply of the major productive factors, particularly labor. This second part of the book received less attention from the profession than did the part concerning the "theory of production," and I limit my attention here to that first part of the book.

Another type of unfriendly critic was exemplified by Douglas's colleague Frank Knight, who argued that the key concepts of (neoclassical) economic theory were essentially static and abstract, while historical data was dynamic, reflecting the action of forces that were assumed away in static theory. Thus, statistical methods could never quantify theoretical concepts.[23] Douglas dismissed such arguments rather undiplomatically in *The Theory of Wages*:

> The high priests of "pure" theory are never tired of pointing out that they are dealing with only static conditions – as of one moment in time for one community. When statistical series dealing with time sequences or even relative distributions in space are brought forward, the armchair theorists brush these aside on the ground that they may include shiftings of the curves or different curves. These series are then dismissed as being merely historical or empirical ....
>
> Now it is true that one of the aims of statistical economics ... should be to approximate as far as possible the static concepts and give concrete meaning and definite value to them. But if this cannot be completely carried out ... [s]hould we abandon all efforts at the inductive determination of economic theory and remain in the ivory tower of "pure" theory[?] If this is what is done, we may as well abandon all hope of further developing the science of economics and content ourselves with merely the elaboration of hypothetical assumptions which will be of little aid in solving problems since we will not know the values. Or shall we try to make economics a progressive science?
>
> (Douglas 1934, 107)

The inductive portion of Douglas's book began with a slightly revised version of "A Theory of Production." In his discussion of the data, he now addressed those who had questioned his capital series on the basis of the Census Bureau's own misgivings about its capital statistics. These "doubting Thomases," Douglas noted, had overlooked the fact that he had taken specific steps to address the concerns of the bureau's statisticians. He also cited a new study estimating the capital of American corporations in the 1920s and showed that its results could be made fairly consistent with his own, although this required considerable work. He created an alternative version of his labor series that accounted for changes

23 Letter from F. Knight to Douglas, October 12, 1932, Frank Knight papers, Box 58, Folder 16. Special Collections Research Center, University of Chicago Library. Knight was generally hostile to empirical work in economics (Reder 1982). Later in life, Douglas would attribute this criticism to "neoclassicists ... irate at our attempt to quantify the theory which they had contemplated in the abstract as unquantified." (Douglas 1967, 17) Although I could find no extended published articulation of this particular criticism, Douglas's sense that it represented a widespread opinion may have been due to the fact that Knight's opinions carried considerable weight with a number of younger University of Chicago faculty members at the time. See Douglas (1976, 905).

in salaried and clerical employment as well as that of wage earners, and that also reflected changes in man-hours rather than employment, but these adjustments made little difference to the results.

In rewriting Cobb's section of the 1928 paper, Douglas referred to the estimation method as "modified least squares," without offering elaboration, though later he listed the normal equations that were solved in constructing the estimates. He also expanded his response to the argument that his results might be due to spurious correlation, and added a reference to a study by two of his students in which the regression was estimated using the trend ratios of his three series, producing .84 as an estimate of k.[24]

The Theory of Wages also reported results from estimating the Cobb–Douglas regression using other data sets. In one chapter, Douglas thanked Cobb for allowing him to publish the results of Cobb's analysis of the data from Massachusetts. But the results published were not those Cobb had published in 1930. Only the aggregate data for all industries were used. There was no mention of Cobb's experiment with diagonal mean regression, nor his relaxation of the linear homogeneity assumption. Instead, "values for b and k were chosen so that the squares of the deviations of the computed P' from P would approach a minimum" (161). This led to an estimated k of .743 when data covering 1890–1926 were used, almost identical, Douglas noted, to the estimate obtained from US data. However, Douglas admitted, this estimate changed considerably if the years after 1920 were excluded from the sample. The deviations of P from P' in both absolute and percentage terms were tabulated and averaged, and by this measure the fit for Massachusetts was not as good as the fit for the United States. Also, the pattern in which the predicted P' exceeded actual P in recessions but fell short of it in prosperities, a pattern that Douglas believed enhanced his claim to have estimated the true normal relationship between inputs and output in manufacturing, was not present in the Massachusetts case, and Douglas had no ready explanation for this.

[24] The trend ratios of a series divided the original series value by the value predicted by fitting a linear trend to the series. Using trend ratios alleviated concerns with spurious correlation, and was a method favored by Henry Schultz in his work estimating demand elasticities. Douglas's comments in a memorial tribute to Schultz would suggest that Douglas regularly sought Schultz's advice on statistical matters (Douglas 1939), but Douglas expressed ambivalence about this particular procedure, opining that to remove the shared trend from the series was to throw the baby out with the bath water.

University of Chicago graduate student Aaron Director had estimated the Cobb–Douglas regression using annual manufacturing data from New South Wales from the years 1900 to 1921, and Douglas devoted a chapter to describing Director's data and reviewing his results. For New South Wales, k was .65, and the average annual deviation of P' from P smaller than for the United States.

With these results in hand, Douglas returned to the question of the relationship between the estimated laws of production and the processes of distribution. He reminded readers of the striking correspondence between his estimated coefficient of labor for the United States and the NBER's estimate of labor's average share of manufacturing output, and then moved to comparisons of the movements over time of value product per worker and real wages. Now, however, he conducted this analysis for each of nine manufacturing sectors and for coal mining. To do so, he drew on government data sources, the estimated indexes of various sorts he had compiled for *Real Wages in the United States*, and some series specifically created for this analysis. When the real wage indexes were plotted on a graph along with the average productivity indexes on an industry-by-industry basis, Douglas was confronted with a welter of conflicting evidence: productivity indexes soaring above wage indexes in some industries, productivity and wages fluctuating in opposite directions in others, and in a few industries, such as coal, close co-movements of the two series. Working to make sense of these graphs that agreed with neither each other nor the strict marginal productivity theory, Douglas cited various industry-specific factors such as data problems, wartime dislocations of production, and monopoly power. He took the position that the marginal productivity theory implied only long-run or "normal" relationships between movements in productivity and wages, and was less likely to hold for cyclical fluctuations, and noted that the consilience between productivity and wage movements would have been closer had he graphed moving averages. All things considered, he was willing to assert that he had found a "striking agreement" between movements of real wages and "social marginal productivity" up until 1922, and that "the failure of this correspondence to continue . . . may have been responsible in part for the cumulative breakdown which began in 1929" (Douglas 1934, 183–192, 488).

Simple correlation coefficients between the industry-level wage and productivity measures provided friendlier evidence for Douglas. They ranged from .3 to .8, with most above .6. In keeping with the idea that the marginal productivity theory described long-term rather than short-term relationships, correlations increased when five-year moving averages were used, and decreased (but remained positive) when deviations from the trend were used. Douglas was willing to invoke theory to provide some meaning to these positive correlations, concluding that "since the movements of average value productivity are beyond doubt the causative factors, this relationship furnishes further statistical corroboration that the principles of imputed marginal productivity do appreciably determine what the movements of real wages will be" (Douglas 1934, 198).[25]

The New South Wales' data provided another challenge for Douglas. Director had estimated a coefficient of .65 for labor in New South Wales' manufacturing, but when Douglas calculated, on an annual basis, the share of value added in manufacturing formed by wages and salaries, the average value was 56 percent. However, Douglas was willing to submit that these two numbers were "not greatly at variance" (Douglas 1934, 198). The year-to-year movements in real wages and value product were only weakly correlated, but Douglas reminded readers that the expected relationship between wages and productivity was a long-run relationship, and might not show up when annual movements were correlated, especially in a place like New South Wales, where the basic wage rate was set by state agencies. To reveal the "normal" relationship between wages and productivity, Douglas graphed and correlated the five-year moving averages of the two series. He reported a correlation of .97 with a probable error of .011, which could "only cause one to believe that there is a remarkably close relationship between changes in the 'normal' amount of value which is imputed to each worker and changes in the 'normal' movement of real wages" (Douglas 1934, 202). Examination of the graph showing the five-year moving averages, however, could only cause one to wonder how a correlation of .97 could be found between the two series, and indeed this figure is erroneous. The actual correlation between these two series is .41.[26]

[25] This assertion came at the end of a section devoted specifically to the discussion of coal-industry statistics, which had probably provided the strongest support for Douglas's case. Although it may seem to imply a relationship involving time lags, Douglas never introduced lagged relationships into his statistical analyses.

[26] I have confirmed the correlation reported by Douglas for the annual values of the two series, and the reported coefficients of the production function estimated by Director. As Douglas noted in the introduction to the book, "Many millions of computations have been made, and it is possible that there still may be some undetected errors." (Douglas 1934, xvii). Still, one wonders how Douglas could have failed to notice the discrepancy between the high correlation coefficient and the lack of visual evidence of a strong relationship between the two variables. It suggests an incomplete understanding of what actually lay behind a calculated correlation coefficient, or perhaps excessive haste in summarizing such a large quantity of statistical results.

Douglas had much to say about the implications of the results he had presented and how they might be built upon. He cautioned readers strongly that the "close correspondence" between the estimated marginal productivity of labor and the wages of workers did not "furnish an ethical justification for the present economic order," and that the equation of production "need not be the same for all periods and economies." Differences in the exponent of labor might arise because of different capital/labor ratios, or differences in the mix of industries making up the manufacturing sector, given that different industries might have different values for k (Douglas 1934, 202–3). He reviewed many of Clark's (1928) comments on the original Cobb and Douglas paper, including the proposed modifications to the Cobb–Douglas regression, and noted that while Clark's formula led to a better fit in the prewar years, it did worse than the original in the postwar years. Still, Douglas allowed, an augmented version of the original Cobb–Douglas formula that allowed the coefficients to vary over time might be in order, and he reviewed a suggestion along these lines that he had received in private correspondence from Sidney Wilcox (Douglas 1934, 216, 224–25).

The suggestion that the value of k might vary over time was linked by Douglas to the observation that the original Cobb–Douglas function implied that labor's share in distribution would be at least approximately constant over time. He pointed out that studies by Arthur Bowley and Josiah Stamp of income data in the United Kingdom seemed to indicate such a constancy of labor's share in distribution for that country, but that German data showed large fluctuations in labor's share. Douglas believed that the data from the United States were still insufficient to allow a firm conclusion to be drawn concerning the behavior of labor's share over time. However, looking at distribution data from five countries and various time periods, he found it striking that labor's average share of national income seemed limited to a narrow range between 60 and 71 percent, which, he believed, pointed to some broadly similar influences at work in all the countries. And, taking the logic of the Cobb–Douglas function one step further, he made the pregnant suggestion that if one were willing to assume that processes of distribution followed those of production, data on the shares of national income going to labor and capital would allow one to estimate the elasticities of the marginal productivity curves of those factors (Douglas 1934, 221–24, 490–91).

In both 1928 and 1934, Douglas had listed as an important end to be sought in his production research the determination of the extent to which increases in output over time had been due to technological progress.

However, he admitted, it was a "disconcerting feature" of his analysis based on the Cobb–Douglas regression that it "seems to eliminate 'progress' or dynamic improvements in the quality of capital, labor, and the industrial arts from the industrial history of the periods studied" (Douglas 1934, 209). As noted, this misgiving had been raised in print by Clark (1928), but also according to Samuelson (1979), by Joseph Schumpeter.[27]

Douglas's first response to this potential problem with his procedure was to point out how it actually represented a move forward in attempts to understand economic progress. In the past, he noted, some had viewed the increase of total production as a measure of progress, but this was clearly wrong, as it ignored the fact that rising output accompanied by rising population could mean that labor productivity and average consumption were both declining. Output per worker, the measure of progress most commonly used by modern economists, was also flawed in that it could increase solely because of increases in the quantity of capital per worker with no change in "technical efficiency." The Cobb–Douglas procedure corrected this flaw by explicitly taking into account the quantity of capital as well as the quantity of labor.

However, in each set of data to which the procedure was actually applied, the whole of the increase in total production over the sample period was accounted for, with a seemingly high level of accuracy, by mere quantitative increases in labor and capital. In the face of the obvious revolution in manufacturing technique in these periods, such a conclusion was "incredible"; it was a paradox demanding a reconciliation between "the reality of qualitative progress and the validity of the formula" (Douglas 1934, 210–11).

Douglas admitted that he had no such reconciliation to offer, only some suggestions on this "tangled question." He proposed that when the equation was estimated for a particular time period, one might suspect the existence of technical progress in shorter periods within or adjacent to that period during which the growth of output exceeded what one would predict using the estimated equation, or which led to different estimated coefficients for the equation than those produced by the entire period. Douglas pointed to the period 1921–26 as one that showed progress by this

[27] It is easy to accept Samuelson's report that Schumpeter was "shocked" by Douglas's apparent assumption of no technological progress over the 1890–1922 period. Even so, Schumpeter should be classed as a friendly critic of Douglas's production function research, as he described *The Theory of Wages* as "one of the boldest ventures in econometrics ever undertaken," and the research in general as "an impressive series of econometric studies" (Schumpeter (1954), 942, 1042).

metric. Douglas also suggested that the some of the progress in US manufacturing from 1899 to 1922 was "concealed in and made possible" the reduction in the average work week and the falling ratio of production to non-production workers. Further, Douglas argued, there was reason to believe that the quality of the average worker had been increasing along with the quality of capital, and he quoted at length J. M. Clark's (1928) argument that part of the estimated productivity of capital was due to the improved quality of capital. Douglas did not, however, develop the statistical implications of possible improvements in the quality of labor and capital for his method of estimating the marginal productivity of these two factors, beyond saying that if the qualitative improvement of workers balanced the qualitative improvement of capital, progress could have affected the size of the total product without being reflected in his marginal productivity estimates.

Douglas reported having had useful conversations on the topic of technical progress with William Ogburn and S. C. Gilfillan, two colleagues with demonstrated expertise on the subject.[28] Douglas was particularly interested in Gilfillan's classification of the 120 inventions of the last generation "with the most important social effects" into the categories of labor saving, land saving, capital saving, and developments of consumer goods (Douglas 1934, 214; Gilfillan 1932). Douglas noted the ratio of capital- and land-saving inventions to labor-saving inventions (1 to 1.5), and related Gilfillan's opinion, conveyed in an unpublished communication to Douglas, that while labor-saving inventions tend to raise the capital/labor ratio, and capital-saving inventions to lower it, the second effect is offset somewhat by the necessary investment in new types of capital and the reduced need for labor to operate the reduced quantity of capital. In reading these passages, one senses that Douglas believed that these observations were very relevant to the question of how technical change affected the meaning of the estimates produced by his regression, but also understood that he was not yet seeing all the necessary connections.

[28] Ogburn, a prominent sociologist, was on the University of Chicago faculty and was known for his work on the social impact of technological change. Sociologist S. Colum Gilfillan also wrote copiously on the topic of inventions, spent much of his career in the Chicago area, and was in the early 1930s working for the President's Research Committee on Social Trends. This committee, established by President Hoover in service to the same general vision that motivated the *Recent Economic Changes* project, produced a volume entitled *Recent Social Trends in the United States* (1933), with a chapter coauthored by Ogburn and Gilfillan and entitled "The Influence of Invention and Discovery."

Another communication received by Douglas bearing on the relationship between his regression and technical change came from Morris Copeland, in which Copeland reported the results of fitting a straight-line trend to the logarithm of Douglas's output per worker series. The resulting regression predicted actual output just as well as the Cobb–Douglas regression, leading Copeland to conclude that the hypothesis that all the growth in labor productivity was due to technical change was as firmly supported by Douglas's data as the hypothesis that it was all due to a growing quantity of capital. This finding clearly troubled Douglas,[29] as it would others who later encountered it in *The Theory of Wages*, and Douglas closed his discussion of "Progress and the Equation of Production" by admitting that "the whole question needs to be gone into more thoroughly" (Douglas 1934, 215).

RESPONSES TO *THE THEORY OF WAGES*

The Theory of Wages was widely discussed in the social science literature, both in standard reviews and in longer articles. The reviews were generally favorable in tone: Douglas had performed "an invaluable service" (Bigge 1934); the book was "brilliantly incisive and appallingly exhaustive," and would "endure as an outstanding pioneer accomplishment in the synthesis of abstract and realistic materials" (Dickenson 1934). Rowe (1934) also called Douglas a "true pioneer," with his equation of production representing the book's most original and interesting contribution to knowledge. Such reviews were not without criticisms. Berman (1934), who called the book "one of the most important works of a theoretical nature ever published in this country," still expressed concern about the quality of the data. Bigge thought Douglas's causality claims were too strong, and several reviewers expressed misgivings about the problems raised for Douglas's equation by technological progress. Some were impressed by the goodness of fit of the estimated equation of production, others by the correspondence between coefficient estimates and distributive shares. An outlier was Don Lescohier (1935), a student of J. R. Commons from Wisconsin. He was not impressed by the good fit produced by Douglas's production equation, arguing that the analytical method was designed specifically to produce a good fit, and he remained "unconvinced of the

[29] He spoke of Copeland's "weighty criticisms of the theory and the significance of our results that should be recognized" (Douglas 1934, p. 215).

quantitative conclusions" drawn concerning marginal productivities, as the procedure was based on so many untrue assumptions.

Lescohier's doubts about the significance of Douglas's results, like those of Slichter (1928), were in part a result of Lescohier's rejection of the marginal productivity theory of distribution. Another important set of reactions to *The Theory of Wages*, however, came from mathematical economists who embraced marginal productivity theory, and who were trying to make sense of the relationship between Douglas's regression equation and the equations of their theoretical systems. In the November 1934 issue of the *Quarterly Journal of Economics*, Wassily Leontief took up the question of whether or under what conditions the regressions estimated by Douglas could be squared with "the marginal productivity theory of interest as it appears to emerge from the writings of Jevons, Bohm-Bawerk, Wicksell, and their successors."[30] Leontief's main criticism was that the Cobb–Douglas production function did not allow for the time-consuming nature of production, nor for the fact that that the length of the period of production (or the rate of turnover of capital) was likely a choice variable for the entrepreneur. Starting with a production function that did have these characteristics, Leontief developed a mathematical model of the profit-maximizing firm and used it to evaluate Douglas's methods and results. Leontief was a friendly critic, however. He was not rejecting Douglas's idea, only Douglas's function, and offering his own modified production function as a better basis for the statistical investigation of the laws of distribution (156). Leontief concluded that whatever flaws subsequent investigators might find in Douglas's work, "it is not to be spoken of without admiration. It will remain a most outstanding contribution to economic literature" (Leontief 1934, 156, 161).

Jacob Marschak (1935) also expressed support for Douglas' project. Pure theory was valuable, he noted, but could only go so far. It could indicate the likely signs of relationships between economic variables, but not the magnitudes. Douglas was boldly attempting to find, using statistical data, the shape of the production function of economic theory. Marschak saw

[30] This particular line of theorizing was based on Bohm-Bawerk's idea that the productivity of labor was increasing in the length of time between the expenditure of labor and the appearance of the final product (the period of production) and that the period of production increased if and only if the amount of capital used in production was increased. Thus, capital had a marginal productivity. Although Leontief referred to this as the "current" and the "predominating" theory of interest, many who embraced the marginal productivity theory at this time (e.g., Frank Knight and Irving Fisher) rejected it root and branch.

problems in Douglas's execution, however. Like Leontief, Marschak embraced the Bohm-Bawerk/Wicksell view of capital and interest, and thus he asserted that Douglas's use of a single measure of aggregate capital was theoretically suspect under the assumption that units of capital consumed at different points in the production process had different marginal productivities. Marschak's larger concern was statistical. Like Schultz's (1929) comments on the Cobb–Douglas paper, Marschak's statistical critique grew out of contemporary debates over the estimation of supply and demand functions. Citing Elmer J. Working's (1927) article on statistical identification of supply and demand relationships, Marschak explained that Douglas's curve-fitting procedure implicitly assumed that observed variations in output were not due to changes in the production function to be estimated, but occurred because the amounts of capital and labor employed were changing for other reasons. Marschak noted that this was not a condemnation of Douglas's method, but a warning that those who used it should take care in thinking about the issue of which relationships in their data were shifting and which were stable.

David Durand provided the most detailed scrutiny of the relationship between the estimated production relationships in Douglas's *The Theory of Wages* and the concepts of marginal productivity theory, which, in Durand's case, meant the version of that theory associated with French economist Leon Walras. Durand's (1937) article, "Some Thoughts on Marginal Productivity Theory, with Special Reference to Professor Douglas' Analysis," began with a mathematical description of equilibrium on the production side of a Walrasian economy with fixed output prices. Durand assumed that each firm had a distinct production function in which output could be a very general (but differentiable) function of inputs, described how profit maximization led to a situation in which factors received payments equal to their marginal productivity, explained how entry and exit drove firms to the point of their production function characterized by constant returns to scale and minimum cost, and counted equations and unknowns to establish the existence of equilibrium values for all factor prices. Having laid out this "clear and precise statement of the marginal productivity theory," Durand proceeded to explain why there was absolutely no relationship between the concepts and elements of this theory and the quantities estimated by Douglas. According to Durand, marginal productivity theory "can be applied only to individual firms. It is a great mistake to attempt to extend the theory to industrial society in general, to the so-called social organism" (Durand 1937, 745). There was no way to aggregate the different outputs of individual firms to a single total output. Aggregation problems arose in dealing with productive factors as well, as the theory required that they be very specifically defined, rather than being grouped as land, labor, and capital. The theory was static, assuming that factor supplies were constant, and that marginal increments of factors supplied to one firm were bid away from another, while the marginal increments of a factor to society were newly created.

Turning specifically to Douglas's statistical analysis, Durand objected to the assumed linear homogeneity of the Cobb–Douglas function. Theoretical production functions could not be linear homogeneous throughout their range, as was the Cobb–Douglas function, or there would be no single minimum cost point and no determinate equilibrium. Nor did anything in the theory justify the idea of an industry-level production function with constant returns to scale – such a conclusion would have to be established empirically. Also, Douglas placed undue emphasis on the good fit of his regression. A good fit showed only that the function was statistically accurate, not that it was theoretically accurate, nor that it revealed causal relationships. Other functional forms fit the data just as well. These good fits were all a consequence of the fact that the three series Douglas worked with were highly collinear. Durand's review of Douglas's attempts to deal with trends in the data and cyclical fluctuations served to illustrate further the uncertainty about what the estimates of the Cobb–Douglas regression actually represented.

Then, however, Durand took an unexpected turn, and placed himself firmly in the camp of Douglas's friendly critics. "All that has been said thus far," he wrote, "might be construed as a decrial of quantitative studies of production. This is not the case. Statistical studies of all sorts are desirable, and Professor Douglas's is no exception." Douglas simply should have chosen a function that was "a little more general." Durand proposed two adjustments to the Cobb–Douglas equation: first, the assumption of constant returns to scale should be relaxed, and the coefficients of labor and capital estimated separately. Second, the formula should be adjusted to allow those coefficients of labor and capital to change over time. Durand implemented the first suggestion himself with Douglas's data, and found very little change in the results. He also made some calculations to show that Douglas's data suggested a value of k that changed over time, thus supporting the need for his second adjustment. Pushing Douglas's program forward, Durand concluded, would be difficult but desirable (Durand 1937, 755).

Douglas, in all his subsequent production function studies, would estimate the coefficients of capital and labor separately, attributing this idea to Durand,[31] and would offer Durand's concern with a changing k value as one reason for his switch from using time series to cross-section data in those studies. It is worth mentioning, however, one thing Durand did not do in his article. Having argued at length that there was no relationship between the quantities estimated by Douglas and the concepts and relationships of marginal productivity theory, Durand offered few hints regarding what he thought one did or should hope to obtain from "quantitative studies of production" in the Douglas mode. Although his arguments in support of his proposed adjustments to the Cobb–Douglas formula seemed to indicate a belief that the relationship between inputs and output in an economy with growth and technological change could be characterized by a stable function (Durand 1937, 754–55), the matter of the theoretical significance of the estimated parameters of such a function was left undiscussed.

In *The Theory of Wages*, Douglas usually referred to the regression equation he was estimating as a law of production or a theory of production, and only rarely as a production function. It was in the articles by Leontief, Durand, and Marschak, as well as the very critical article by Mendershausen discussed in Chapter 2, that the label "production function" was first consistently applied to the relationship that Douglas was seeking to estimate, although Douglas quickly adopted the phrase himself. This labeling of the Douglas regression, while arguably contributing to its eventual widespread acceptance, also altered the nature of the discussion surrounding its validity and significance.

In the mid-1930s, the phrase "production function" was rare in the economics literature, used almost exclusively by those engaged in the program of mathematical formalization of some version of the neoclassical model and/or the statistical estimation of the components of those models. As mentioned earlier, in 1934 Douglas presented his production studies as part of the neoclassical-econometric research program, a complement to efforts to estimate the supply and demand curves of neoclassical theory. In referring to Douglas's regression as a production function, leading young econometricians such as Leontief, Marschak, and Oskar Lange (1939) were affirming this conception of Douglas's. In doing so, they linked the Cobb–Douglas equation more closely to a research program that was on the ascendency, identifying the equation as a starting point or possible

[31] See, for example, Douglas (1948, 8) or Douglas (1976, 904). This attribution is somewhat puzzling, given that Cobb (1930) had estimated Cobb–Douglas regressions of this form.

building block for the mathematical and econometric systems that constituted the research output of the program.

However, while the neoclassically oriented econometricians of the late 1930s and early 1940s were embracing Douglas's program as complementary to their own, they were also redefining the objectives of the program, and developing criteria for evaluating Douglas's methods and results that Douglas himself would not have accepted. This is partly because these pioneering econometricians were operating with versions of neoclassical value and distribution theory different from the one that had motivated Douglas as he developed his empirical research strategy in the late twenties and early 1930s. They thought about marginal productivity theory within the context of Walrasian general equilibrium theory, in which the production function was a characteristic of a firm, or Marshallian theory, in which it was the characteristic of an industry. As a result, when they contemplated the output of estimating a production function using time series data aggregated over several industries, or cross-section data at the industry level, certain questions naturally seemed crucial: Did the estimated coefficients say anything useful about the true parameters of the underlying industry or firm production functions? Were they averages of those parameters in some sense? If so, in what sense? I would argue, however, that because of the way Douglas was trained, these questions were never crucial for him, nor were they even at the forefront of his mind as he began his research. As he notes in his autobiography, he was taught theory at Columbia University by John Bates Clark, and received "a thorough drilling in (the marginal productivity) principle, which served me well a decade later when I started my own inductive work in the theory" (Douglas 1971, 29). But Clark's formal analysis of factor-price determination, unlike that of Walras or Alfred Marshall, ran in terms of aggregates: the basic wage rate and the interest rate depended on the marginal products of "social" capital and "social" labor (Stigler 1941, 307). A student of Clark would have had no trouble thinking of an aggregate production function as a primal entity to be estimated, and its parameters as significant theoretical quantities.

During the years that Douglas was defending his production function studies, when critics questioned whether there was any relationship between his estimates and theoretical parameters of production functions of firms or industries, Douglas was not dismissive, but neither was he particularly bothered. The production functions of single firms should be estimated if and when firm-level data became available, but currently they were "nonoperational" concepts for the purposes of inductive studies.

Production functions estimated with cross-industry data or aggregate time series data were "different type(s)" of production functions from each other and from those of Walrasian theory, but interesting in their own right (Bronfenbrenner and Douglas, 1939, 779, 780–82; Douglas 1948, 9, 22–23).

This attitude also grew out of a methodological difference between Douglas and many critics, both friendly and unfriendly, who raised the issue of the relationship between Douglas's estimates and the production functions of individual firms. In *The Theory of Wages*, Douglas had commented:

> It will be noticed that I have treated the marginal productivity and supply curves for labor and capital in society as a whole and not for particular industries and plants. This has been done in part because as Willard Gibbs once remarked 'the whole is simpler than its parts' and because it seemed to me to be the more significant problem . . . the forces at work in society as a whole need to be analyzed. For surely general results are more significant than are those for particular branches of industry and in turn are conditioning forces upon these subgroups.
>
> (Douglas 1934, xv)

When Durand provided the first extended treatment of the question of whether Douglas's regression yielded estimates of the production functions of (Walrasian) neoclassical theory and answered in the negative, he went on to implicitly endorse Douglas's methodological position concerning the existence and significance of an aggregate production function. Discussion of the issue of whether the parameters of a Cobb–Douglas (or any) production function estimated with cross-industry or aggregate time series data could be rigorously related to the parameters of the firm-level production functions of theory, and, if not, what theoretical or practical significance they held, would continue. It would be taken over, however, by members of the neoclassical econometric research program who were more fully committed to methodological individualism, in a form something like that articulated by Haavelmo (1944) and defended by Tjalling Koopmans in his well-known "Measurement without Theory" debate with Vining (Koopmans 1947; Vining and Koopmans 1949). From this standpoint, parameters that described the preferences and constraints of individual actors, including parameters of firm-level production functions, were the holy grail of econometrics, and statistical methods and results were to be judged largely on the basis of what they revealed about these parameters.[32]

[32] Reder (1982, 3) commented that "While Douglas was anxious to give theoretical interpretation to his statistical calculations, he was not fully aware of, or greatly concerned with, the analytical problems that such interpretation involved. Attempts to interpret the

DOUGLAS'S FINAL TIME SERIES STUDY: HANDSAKER AND DOUGLAS (1937–1938)

Following the publication of *The Theory of Wages*, Douglas continued to work on production studies from 1935 until fall of 1942, when he enlisted in the Marine Corps. These were also years during which a small group of econometricians was introducing new ways of thinking about empirical work in economics that involved novel and explicit applications of the mathematical theory of probability in the design, discussion, and evaluation of statistical methods and results. Although their work had little impact on the practice of empirical research in the profession as a whole prior to 1950 (Biddle 1999), these econometricians were disproportionately represented among those who cited Douglas's production studies, and in the neoclassical econometric research program in which Douglas was now a participant. Thus, the econometricians were an important group for Douglas to persuade, and after 1935 his presentations, discussions, and defenses of his own statistical methods and results were increasingly conducted within their conceptual frameworks using their analytical tools.

A small move in this direction can be seen in Douglas's first study following the publication of *The Theory of Wages*, which appeared as a two-part article in the *Quarterly Journal of Economics* coauthored with University of Chicago graduate student Majorie Handsaker. This study, the last one in which Douglas estimated the regression with time series data, was the first in which a standard error for the k estimate was reported. Douglas had in previous work reported either the standard errors or probable errors of the correlation coefficients he presented, but had said next to nothing about the meaning or significance of these measures.[33]

properties of estimated production functions have inspired major developments in econometric technique, but Douglas took little part in the technical development that stemmed from his research."

[33] The probable error of an estimate is equal to .67 times the standard error; the sample estimate will be within one probable error of the population parameter 50 percent of the time. The relationship between the standard error and the probable error was explained in the standard textbooks of the time, such as Mills (1924). Douglas did occasionally mention the ratio between the coefficient and its error measure; perhaps this reflects the influence of Bowley's (1901) statistics text, in which it was argued that one could infer causation from a correlation that was over six times the size of its probable error (Morgan 1990, 137). Handsaker and Douglas also reported the standard errors of correlation coefficients, sometimes incorrectly referring to them as probable errors. At a few points, they remarked on the high ratio of the correlation coefficients to their standard errors but made no explicit claim about causality on that basis.

This use of a standard error along with an estimated regression coefficient to place a bound on the true value of some parameter is based on the assumption, usually implicit, that one's data represent a random sample from a larger population. This way of thinking about data has now become a fundamental feature of applied econometrics but was not at all common in the 1930s (Biddle 2017). Indeed, Frederick Mills, in his widely read statistics textbook, warned readers that the standard formulas derived from probability theory for calculating the likely errors of estimates should be used with great care, because the assumption that one's data were a random sample from some population of interest would seldom be met (Mills 1924, chapter 16). Be that as it may, Handsaker and Douglas did not articulate any formal, sample/population framework for thinking about their time series sample or their estimates, but simply asserted the probability theory–based bounds on the estimate of k without further explanation.[34] The introduction and use of the standard error of k may have been Handsaker's idea. For reasons discussed more fully below, I believe that after 1935 Douglas sought coauthors who could, among other things, bring cutting edge statistical knowledge to the project, helping Douglas to understand the implications of his results, to explain them to the econometricians in his audience and, more importantly, to rebut the criticisms of those econometricians.

In most other respects, the Douglas/Handsaker article, which estimated the Cobb–Douglas regression using data from the Australian state of Victoria, looked much like the previous Cobb–Douglas regression studies. The article began with a review of those studies, with emphasis on the goodness of fit of the Cobb–Douglas equation and the close correspondence between labor's share in distribution and the coefficient of labor in the production function. Analysis of data from another economy, the authors argued, would help to establish whether the Cobb–Douglas function was adequate to represent "real facts of economic life," or whether this seemingly positive evidence had been merely "accidental" (Handsaker and Douglas 1937, 4).

A brief review of differences between the manufacturing sector in Victoria and in the United States was followed by a discussion of how data from Victoria's Census of Manufactures had been used to construct the time series for product, labor, and capital. The task was made easier by the

[34] This exemplifies Haavelmo's (1944, iii) complaint that empirical economists often used the tools of statistical inference without adopting any explicit probabilistic framework, even though the tools had no meaning without such a framework.

fact that the Victorian census data were annual, so that no interpolation was required, but it did require an index of total manufacturing output to be built up from data on a subset of manufacturing industries,[35] and it still involved creating price indexes for capital in order to convert annual additions to the value of buildings, plant, and machinery into estimates of annual increases in the stock of physical capital. The tone of the discussion was that the data were adequate for the task, but no reader could complain that potential weaknesses in the data had been hidden.

Using the three constructed series, the least squares value of k in the function $P' = bL^kC^{1-k}$ was .79. For the first time, Douglas provided a derivation of the formula used to estimate k, making it clear that it resulted from a linear regression involving logs of the series values. The estimated regression was then put through the familiar paces. P' was compared to P on a year-by-year basis both graphically and in tables, and in both absolute and percentage terms. This, readers were told, represented a "stringent test" of the equation of production. The average absolute deviation was slightly smaller than that found for the US data, and the correlation coefficient between P and P' was .97. It was argued that most of the large deviations could be explained by business-cycle factors, as was the case in the US data, or by the disruption of labor supply and the reallocation of capital caused by the war, although it was admitted that a few large deviations escaped easy rationalization. The authors concluded that all in all, actual production in Victoria was "fairly closely approximated" by the estimated function.

Next came the test of marginal productivity theory via the comparison of the k estimate to labor's share of the value of output.[36] The results were somewhat unsatisfactory, as the average annual share of the net value of product paid in wages was about 61 percent, which was deemed to be an "appreciable" deviation from the 71 percent one would have expected from the regression results, and far larger than the deviation found for the United States. It was not mentioned that the deviation between labor's share and the labor coefficient in Director's study of the neighboring state of New South Wales was almost equally large, though Douglas had

35 The index was based mostly on data for physical quantities produced, but there were some monetary series included as well, which Douglas deflated with specially constructed price indexes.

36 The computation of the latter ratio using the Australian data was nontrivial, as numerous deductions had to be made from the total sales value of output to get the value added in manufacture, many of which, such as depreciation allowances and insurance costs, had to be estimated.

pronounced the two New South Wales quantities to be "not greatly at variance."

Handsaker and Douglas offered an array of possible explanations for the deviation they had found. The first argument was based on the standard error of the k estimate, which, as discussed earlier, had been reported along with the coefficient estimate. In an argument that would certainly have been quite novel to most readers of the *Quarterly Journal*, Handsaker and Douglas explained that since the standard error of the coefficient estimate was .065, the true value of the coefficient for Victoria could be as low as .71 minus .065, which would bring it much closer to the average value of labor's share. They did not report the formula used to calculate the standard error, nor did they cite a source, and they did not explain why one standard error was used to construct their lower bound rather than some other multiple.[37]

Handsaker and Douglas next argued that there were good reasons for believing that their estimate of the growth of the capital stock overestimated the true growth, which would cause the regression procedure to overestimate the labor coefficient. Two additional possible reasons for the deviation between the k estimate and labor's share of value added were based on economic theory. The equality of wage and marginal product was a theoretical prediction for economies with competitive labor markets, the authors noted, but wages in Victoria were set by government fiat. Australian data showed that government-set wages had lagged far behind price increases during periods of inflation. During those same periods, labor's share was below its average for the entire period. Further, if one looked only at a period of stable prices, labor's share averaged 65 percent, close to the lower bound for k calculated by subtracting one standard error from the estimate.

The newly developed theory of imperfect competition provided a final possible explanation for the relatively low value of labor's share. Citing Edward Chamberlain (1933) and Joan Robinson (1933), Handsaker and Douglas explained that when a firm was large enough relative to its industry that its output level influenced product price, marginal revenue would deviate from average revenue (i.e., price), and the firm would produce the

[37] Later in the paper, Douglas and Handsaker would again use the standard error estimate in this way to argue for the consistency of k estimates across all four data sets examined so far, claiming that the standard error of .065 would "possibly bring the value of k up to above the Massachusetts and United States values and also down to the New South Wales value" (Handsaker and Douglas 1938, 244).

level of output at which marginal cost equaled marginal revenue. They continued:

> This vitally affects the theory of distribution. For whereas, under perfect competition, labor would receive marginal physical product valued at the constant average price, it receives, under imperfect competition, marginal physical product multiplied by the marginal revenue of the last unit. As consumers, however, laborers will pay the higher price per unit for the articles so that in terms of real wages the payment will be marginal physical product multiplied by the ratio of marginal revenue to average revenue, or $\frac{\partial P}{\partial L} \cdot \frac{MR}{AR}$.
>
> There will, therefore, be an exploitation of the factors of production, as Mrs. Robinson states, and labor will receive less than it would under a condition of "pure" or "perfect" competition. In addition, as Mrs. Robinson has pointed out, monopsony, or monopolistic buying of the factors of production, may introduce a further divergence between the actual processes of distribution and those which we might expect under perfect competition
>
> (Handsaker and Douglas 1938, 229).

Robinson's (1933) book had actually analyzed several models in which imperfect competition of one form or another would lead to monopolistic or monopsonistic exploitation of labor. In the passage quoted above, Handsaker and Douglas referred to a chapter in Robinson's book dealing with "the monopolistic exploitation of labor," in which Robinson analyzed models of a single industry, assuming that changes in employment in that industry would have no significant effect on other industries or the general level of prices. However, Handsaker and Douglas's reference to the impact on real wages of the higher prices brought about by imperfect competition, along with the equation they presented to describe labor's marginal physical product under imperfect competition, suggest that they were actually thinking in terms of another model of monopolistic exploitation that Robinson presented in her chapter on "A World of Monopolies" (Robinson 1933, 307–12). That model involved an economy in which different competitive industries produced different commodities that were imperfect substitutes for one another, with factors of production supplied perfectly elastically to the industries, though fixed in total supply. Robinson analyzed the consequences for that economy of placing output decisions for each industry into the hands of a different monopolist, with the owners of the existing firms being converted into salaried managers and nothing else changing. Assuming no collusion between the monopolists, she described the "monopolistic exploitation" that would characterize the resulting equilibrium, giving a verbal specification for the equilibrium wage that matched Handsaker and Douglas's formula (Robinson 1933, 311).

I think it likely that Handsaker and Douglas were raising the possibility that the manufacturing sector of Victoria approximated Robinson's "world of monopolies," with "a considerable degree of collusive and non-competitive fixing of prices behind the tariff wall" (Handsaker and Douglas 1938, 231). The manufacturing sector was a large enough segment of the total economy that the impact of monopoly prices on real wages was non-negligible. And if the Victorian manufacturing sector approximated Robinson's "world of monopolies," labor's share of value added in manufacturing, averaged over all the industries, would be below an accurate measure of the true k. In any case, Handsaker and Douglas did not ultimately place too much stock in imperfect competition as an explanation of the deviation of labor's share from k in Victorian manufacturing. After citing statistics bearing on the level of industry concentration in Australian manufacturing, they pointed out that although US manufacturing seemed to be no less concentrated than Victorian manufacturing, labor's share in the United States equaled the estimated value of k for the United States. Also, they had nothing more to say about the possibility of monopsonistic exploitation beyond the sentence in the passage quoted earlier. However, the nature of monopolistic and monopsonistic exploitation, and the possibilities for detecting it statistically with a Cobb–Douglas regression, would soon become a controversial issue for Douglas's research program.

As in Douglas's earlier studies, the legitimacy of the Cobb–Douglas function was also tested by looking at correlations between the year to year movements of real wages and the estimated marginal physical productivity of labor (which, given the Cobb–Douglas function, would be proportional to movements in average product per laborer). After explaining the complicated process used to construct indexes of real earnings, Handsaker and Douglas reported correlation coefficients above .8 between various measures of the two variables, including four-year moving averages.

The Handsaker and Douglas paper is the only one of Douglas's production studies that presents empirical evidence on the relationship between the return to capital and the productivity of capital. The authors noted that the marginal productivity of capital implied by the Cobb–Douglas function, as proxied by P/C, had declined by 30 percent over the sample period, while the return to capital, as proxied by the return on Australian government bonds, had risen by 43 percent. Although the authors admitted that this evidence would seem to "completely disprove" the productivity theory underlying their study, they provided two possible grounds for rejecting the Australian interest rate as a measure of the return to capital. First, appealing to Irving Fisher, they argued that Australian interest rates would include a premium for expected inflation, and that the middle of the sample period had been a period of rapid inflation. Second, appealing to J. M. Keynes, they speculated that interest rates might have been pushed upward by a secular increase in liquidity preference, although they admitted that they could identify no obvious cause for such a secular shift (Handsaker and Douglas 1938, 249–51).

Douglas and Handsaker also responded to some of Douglas's friendly critics. Durand's (1937) arguments against imposing the constant returns to scale assumption when estimating an aggregate production function were pronounced "just"; relaxing the assumption led to an estimate of .84 for k, and .23 for the coefficient of capital, which Douglas now labeled j. While this version of the regression, which will henceforth be referred to as the unrestricted Cobb–Douglas regression, fit the data "slightly better" than the original or restricted Cobb–Douglas equation, Douglas seemed to want to cast doubt on its validity, as he pointed out the fact that the least squares value of b dropped from 1 to .715 "raise[d] a very decided question as to the practical meaning of the results."[38]

A footnote mentioned Schultz's (1929) proposal that a linear trend be added to the regression, but this suggestion was not taken up. Leontief's suggestion that working capital be included as a separate term in the production function could not be implemented, as Handsaker and Douglas had no measure of working capital, but J. M. Clark's (1928) analysis of how the inclusion of working capital would influence the coefficient estimates was reviewed (24, 245–46). Douglas and Handsaker also tested Clark's method of adjusting the Cobb–Douglas equation to capture cyclical fluctuations in capital utilization; the fit of the augmented equation was "slightly" better than that of the original. The authors concluded the article by reminding readers that they did not claim to have found "the precise production exponents" or "the exact slopes of the marginal productivity curves of the two major factors," only an approximation to conditions in Victorian manufacturing. Readers were reminded, however, that there was a "striking" degree of agreement between the

[38] Douglas seemed troubled by the fact that in calculating P', "the set of values obtained by using L and C with their stated exponents had to be deflated by 28.5%," and implied that a b value other than one meant that the sum of k and j no longer represented the percentage increase in output to be obtained from a 1 percent increase in both inputs. This is not the case, however. Whatever the value of b, the coefficient of each input will still represent the elasticity of output with respect to changes in that input.

Victorian results and those for the United States, Massachusetts, and New South Wales (Handsaker and Douglas 1938, 250).

Although the Handsaker and Douglas study was the last in which Douglas would estimate the Cobb–Douglas regression using original time series data, it presages two characteristics of Douglas's work with the cross-section version of the Cobb–Douglas regression over the next five years. The first has already been mentioned, that is, the effort to stay up to date in terms of the statistical tools and methods used to present and interpreting the statistical results. The second is Douglas's consistent emphasis on the economic nature of the economic/statistical tool that he had developed. Handsaker and Douglas attempted to make sense of their results using not only the statistical theoretical concept of the standard error, but also novel economic theoretical models and concepts taken from Joan Robinson and J. M. Keynes. In subsequent studies Douglas would continue to rely on arguments from both statistical and economic theory, both when rebutting the attacks of his critics and when making the positive case that his statistical results were revealing valid information about fundamental economic relationships.

2

The Douglas–Mendershausen Debate and the Cross-Section Studies

Some time in 1937 or 1938, Paul Douglas and his assistants developed an approach to estimating the Cobb–Douglas regression using cross-section data, in which all observations came from a single economy in a single year, and each observation described an industry or a group of related industries. This began what I have called the second phase of Douglas's research with the Cobb–Douglas regression, which ended with Douglas's enlistment in the Marine Corps in 1942. In the cross-section studies, the unrestricted Cobb–Douglas equation $P = bL^kC^j$ became the standard specification for the analysis, allowing for statistical tests of the constant returns to scale assumption, although results based on the restricted version were usually reported as well.

In the early cross-section studies, Douglas and his coauthors offered a number of reasons for believing that the information on production relations provided by estimating the Cobb–Douglas regression with cross-section, industry-level data represented an important complement to, if not advance upon, what had been learned from the Douglas's time series studies. As it happens, the cross-section studies also proved an important source of material for Douglas to use during a contentious debate with Horst Mendershausen, an econometrically sophisticated critic who raised serious doubts about the central claim of the Douglas production research program – that Douglas's applications of the Cobb–Douglas regression procedure were estimating "production functions," that is, revealing a stable relationship between the inputs to and outputs of a productive process.

This chapter begins by describing in detail Mendershausen's initial criticism of Douglas's original time series results. I then describe the several cross-section studies that Douglas produced with the help of various coauthors. Looking at these studies as a group, one sees not only

Douglas's definitive response to Mendershausen's criticisms but also the emergence of new and sometimes conflicting claims about what could be learned from the estimates produced by a Cobb–Douglas regression.

THE FIRST MAJOR ECONOMETRIC CRITIQUE: MENDERSHAUSEN AND CONFLUENCE ANALYSIS

In 1938 there appeared in *Econometrica* an article "On the Significance of Professor Douglas's Production Function." It was written by Horst Mendershausen, an econometrician trained by Ragner Frisch, and a decidedly unfriendly critic of Douglas's production studies. Douglas would later comment that Mendershausen and Frisch "believed sincerely that the analysis should be abandoned and, in the words of Mendershausen, all past work should be torn up and consigned to the wastepaper basket."[1] Mendershausen's stated purpose in the *Econometrica* article was to show that the function estimated by Cobb and Douglas in their 1928 paper "does not give a reliable description of a real production function" (Mendershausen 1938, 143). Mendershausen was not specific about what a "real" production function was, but implicit in his article seems to be an acceptance of the idea that a stable relationship between measures of inputs and outputs aggregated over a number of manufacturing industries does represent a real production function, and that the goal of estimating such a relationship was a legitimate one. The thrust of his article is that Douglas had failed to achieve this goal.

Mendershausen first found fault with Douglas's capital series, dubbing it "highly estimative," and referring to Slichter's (1928) critical remarks on that score. He argued that production function estimation should be based on measures of capital and labor actually used, whereas Douglas's capital series, by his own admission, best represented available capital, including capital that might be idle due to slack demand. Mendershausen also attacked Douglas's assumptions that neither technological progress nor improvements in efficiency of labor had occurred over the sample period. These assumptions were "manifestly in contradiction to all economists know about industrial development during this period," (Mendershausen 1938, 145) and in reality, the changing input ratios and output levels

[1] Douglas's comment is in Douglas (1975). I have been unable to find the remark about the wastepaper basket in Mendershausen's published writings pertaining to Douglas's work, which actually included comments to the effect that Douglas's estimates measured something of interest, just not what Douglas believed they measured.

observed in Douglas's data might be due to movements from one production function to another.

Mendershausen next questioned Douglas's decision to assume that the production function was characterized by constant returns to scale. He explained to readers that while the Cobb–Douglas equation was a theoretical relationship between three variables, Douglas's decision to estimate only k, and to restrict the coefficient of capital to equal 1–k, made the estimated Cobb–Douglas regression a statistical relationship between only two variables, P/C and L/C. Mendershausen believed that the question of returns to scale should be settled by the data, not imposed upon it, and explained that it was possible to do so in principle by estimating the coefficients of labor and capital separately (estimating the unrestricted regression), and seeing whether the resulting k estimate was close to Douglas's estimate. Mendershausen found, as had Durand (1937), that Douglas's data passed this test. However, he cautioned readers that it would be "rash" to take this as support for Douglas's assumption of constant returns to scale, because Douglas's three series were a "nearly perfectly *multicollinear set*."[2] This, it turns out, was to be the central theme of Mendershausen's criticism of Douglas's work: multicollinearity in Douglas's data made it impossible for Douglas to estimate a real production function using the statistical approach he had adopted.

As discussed in Chapter 1, in the late 1920s and early 1930s Mendershausen's mentor, Ragner Frisch, had been exploring the problem of estimating a deterministic linear relationship between economic variables when all those variables were potentially measured with error. By 1934, this research had blossomed into Frisch's "Confluence Analysis," which Hendry and Morgan (1989, 35) called "the first general statistical method especially designed for econometric research." The starting point for confluence analysis remained the problem of estimating a deterministic relationship that was assumed to exist between several economic variables, each of which was measured with error, but to this Frisch had added the complicating assumption that more than one exact linear relationship between the true variables might hold simultaneously.[3] As Hendry and Morgan pointed out, the econometric problems that arise in this assumed

[2] The emphasis is in the original. A search of JSTOR indicates that this is the first time the word "multicollinear" had appeared in a major English language statistics or economic journal; multicollinearity had appeared once earlier in the year in an article by Jan Tinbergen.

[3] The measurement errors were assumed to be "classical," that is, uncorrelated with each other and with the true values of variables.

stochastic environment included several that have since come to be labeled and analyzed separately. For example, in the confluence-analysis framework, ordinary least squares estimation of a linear relationship could lead to inconsistent coefficient estimates both because all variables were measured with error (the "errors in the variables" problem) and because more than one deterministic relationship linked the variables (simultaneous equations bias). The simultaneous existence of many linear relationships between variables could also lead to what came to be called the identification problem, and/or to an excess sensitivity of the estimated coefficients to small changes in sample composition, which eventually came to be called the multicollinearity problem. Confluence analysis involved the application of a single novel statistical method, bunch-map analysis, to help econometricians deal with all these difficulties as they attempted to discover and quantify economically interesting relationships in their data.

Bunch maps were diagrams that allowed the analyst to look at two general questions: first, how did the estimated regression relationship between any two variables in the data change when a different direction of minimization was used (that is to say, when a different variable was used as the dependent variable)? Given Frisch's assumptions, this provided information about the nature of measurement error in the data. Second, how did the regression coefficient between any two variables change when additional variables were included in the regression equation? This, Frisch believed, would help the analyst decide which multivariate relationships could or should be estimated. So, with Douglas's data, for example, one could see how the simple regression coefficient between P and L changed when L rather than P was used as the dependent variable, how the regression coefficient between P and L changed when C was also included in the regression, and how the estimate of k (the regression coefficient between P and L, holding constant C) changed when the three possible choices about the direction of minimization were made.[4]

It is worth mentioning two additional characteristics of confluence analysis that distinguished it from other approaches to econometrics that were emerging in the late 1930s and early 1940s, approaches upon which

[4] Each bunch-map diagram plotted how the regression coefficient between a pair of variables changed with different choices about the direction of minimization, holding constant the list of other variables included in the regression, and the diagrams were presented in sets, since there were many possible variable pairs and many possible choices about what variables to include in the regression. Mendershausen referred to a set of diagrams as a bunch map, but I follow later usage by referring to each diagram in the set as a bunch map.

Douglas would draw in countering Mendershausen's criticisms. First, Frisch shared with many of the econometricians of the 1920s and 1930s the belief that statistical methods based in probability theory were not appropriate for the analysis of most economic data. As a result, probability theory entered confluence analysis only through the distributional assumptions imposed on the measurement errors, and it did not involve any formal inference procedures based on probability theory. However, as Morgan (1990, section 8.2) describes, some econometricians in the early 1930s were beginning to make use of probability-based conceptual frameworks, or at least to employ formal inferential tools based in probability theory such as significance tests, with Douglas and Handsaker's construction of a lower bound for k being one example. Secondly, confluence analysis, at least as conceived by Frisch and practiced by Mendershausen, entailed a certain diffidence towards economic theory as a guide to identifying, prior to estimation, the relationships likely to exist and the specific forms they were likely to take in the data. Instead, confluence analysis was seen as a way of exploring the data to discover the relationships that actually did exist, both those suggested by theory and others.

Mendershausen's application of confluence analysis to Douglas's data began with the statement that Douglas's problem of the "nearly perfectly collinear set" was "very well exhibited" by a set of bunch maps. Although Mendershausen's paper marked the first appearance of bunch maps in an English-language economics journal, he offered no further explanation of how they had been constructed, what they represented, or how they should be interpreted. He did, however, present some other, more transparent, evidence. He pointed out that the pairwise correlations between Douglas's three series were all above .9. He showed that when estimating the unrestricted version of the regression, one obtained very different estimates of k, ranging from -1.06 to 2.23, depending on which direction of minimization was used. And one could not choose between these three regressions based on fit, as all three fit the data equally well. According to Mendershausen, all of this was due to the fact that there was more than one determinate relationship among the three variables.

He then presented the following set of graphs to illustrate the problem with Douglas's data and results:

The graphs represent two perspectives on the three-dimensional space formed by the positive portions of the log P, log C, and log L axes. The observations in Douglas's data are presented as the heads of pins of various heights stuck into the log L-by-log C plane, which serves as the "floor" of the space. Mendershausen made two points using these graphs. First, in

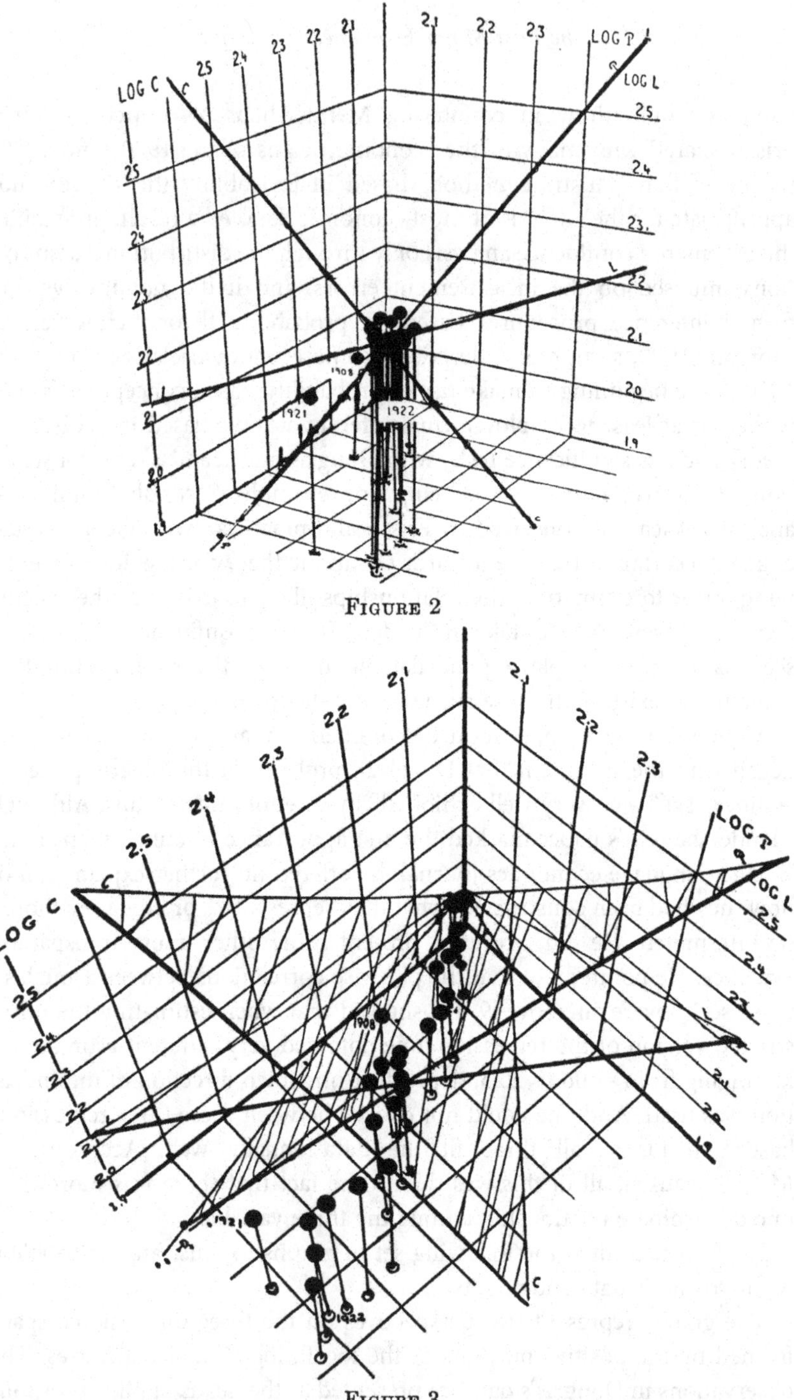

Figure 2.1 Mendershausen's illustrations of multicollinearity in Douglas's data

order for Douglas's regression to produce a good estimate of the separate effects on product of changes in labor and changes in capital, it was required that the pinheads in this three-dimensional space seem (approximately) to be points on a tilted plane suspended above the floor. Douglas's data did not meet this requirement. Instead, in the frontal view (Mendershausen's Figure 2) the pinheads seemed to be bunched around a point, and cannot provide stable support to a plane, while in the view from above (Mendershausen's Figure 3) most of the pinheads seemed to be grouped around a tilting line that runs through the space so that several planes of very different orientations could be said to pass closely by all the points. The three planes sketched into Mendershausen's Figure 3 were the three planes implied by estimating Douglas's equation with the three different directions of minimization – a pictorial representation of the widely differing estimates for k that resulted from choosing the three different directions of minimization.

A second point of Mendershausen's was that when most of the pinheads seemed to run along a line, the estimation procedure, in determining the orientation of the best approximate plane, would give special attention to the few pinheads that were distant from the point or line. In Douglas's data these were the points for 1908, 1921, and 1922. However, by Douglas's own admission, 1908 and 1921 were years of depression, for which Douglas's capital series (measuring capital available) was a particularly poor approximation of capital actually utilized, the theoretically desired variable. Douglas's estimate of the value of k was being determined largely by pieces of data known to be unreliable.

Mendershausen demonstrated this in another way by removing the observations for 1908, 1921, and 1922 and then redrawing the bunch maps and reestimating the unrestricted version of the regression. Again, no explanation accompanied the bunch maps beyond the remark that "the bunch map of the three-set shows still stronger 'explosion,'" (Mendershausen 1938, 150) a statement that could only have mystified all but a very few readers. They could see, however, that the k estimate was very sensitive to the removal of a few observations.

According to Mendershausen, all of this indicated Douglas's US data could not be used to ascertain any sort of production law or production function between three variables. As for the production function estimates based on data from other economies reported in *The Theory of Wages*, Mendershausen was willing to assert that, based on a "superficial examination of the data used," they were "very probably" subject to the same criticisms (Mendershausen 1938, 152).

Mendershausen closed by asking if Douglas's estimate of k represented any "real phenomenon." He concluded that it did. With some mathematical manipulation, he showed that if log L, log C, and log P all had approximately linear time trends, the k estimate produced by the original Cobb–Douglas regression would equal the ratio of the percentage growth rate of labor to the percentage growth rate of capital. A k of less than one meant that economic growth in manufacturing had been relatively capital intensive. He then fit trend lines to the logged versions of Douglas's labor and capital series and showed that indeed, the ratio of the trends was .75, thus corroborating his interpretation of Douglas's k.[5]

It is my belief that the potential impact of Mendershausen's critique of Douglas's methods and results was considerably reduced by Mendershausen's rhetorical style. At a time when only a minority of economists had more than a basic knowledge of statistical measures, he was discussing relatively subtle statistical points and applying novel tools of analysis, and doing so using an arcane vocabulary, probably comprehensible to few, if any, outside Frisch's circle of students. He did not speak of variables but "variates." Douglas's data was a "three-set." Douglas's k could be regarded as an "empirically found coefficient" when estimated with a two-set, but not when estimated with a three-set. When Mendershausen critiqued Douglas's assumption that the coefficients of labor and capital summed to one, he eschewed the "returns to scale" terminology familiar to most economists, instead giving readers a footnote formula for something called a "passus coefficient," which was meant to clarify statements like "This procedure stands and falls with the presence or absence of an assumed *pari passu* law in the reality reflected by the material" (Mendershausen 1938, 146).[6] The unexplained bunch maps have already been mentioned.

But Mendershausen's article did include several bits of evidence that I think a large proportion of *Econometrica's* readership would have recognized as problematic for Douglas's estimates. The discussion of the regression-choice problem had by now been going on for over a decade, and many readers would have known well that there was a problem when

[5] This calculation actually had no bearing on the correctness of Douglas's interpretation of his own estimates, as this result also follows if log L and log C have linear trends and production is characterized by the original Cobb–Douglas equation.

[6] "Pari passu" was Frischian for "constant returns to scale," while Mendershausen's reference to an "ultra passum law" meant increasing returns to scale. JSTOR searches indicate that this way of speaking of the returns to scale of a production function never become part of the vocabulary of English-speaking economists.

different choices of direction of minimization led to very different coefficient estimates. Testing the sensitivity of regression coefficient estimates to changes in sample composition was also a standard method of measuring the reliability of those estimates prior to the full-scale adoption of standard error measures based in probability theory. And those who spent enough time looking at Mendershausen's renditions of Douglas's data in three-dimensional space would have seen that those pinheads did not provide a solid basis for estimating a plane. In any case, whatever its impact on the profession, Douglas took Mendershausen's criticisms very seriously, particularly the ones related to the econometric problem of multicollinearity, and they spurred him to introduce a number of changes in both his approach to estimating the Cobb–Douglas regression and his methods of defending the results.

A NEW DIRECTION: THE SHIFT TO CROSS-SECTION DATA AND THE RESPONSE TO MENDERSHAUSEN

The cross-section approach to estimating the Cobb–Douglas regression, which was introduced in a paper that Douglas coauthored with graduate student Martin Bronfenbrenner[7] (Brofenbrenner and Douglas 1939), made use of data from various nations' censuses of manufacturing, each of which presented information for one particular year for each of a nation's manufacturing industries, allowing the creation of a data set in which each observation described an industry or group of related industries. The labor variable in these studies was the number of employees in an industry. The capital variable was most often the value of "total capital," a variable expressed in monetary terms that included not only the values of buildings, tools, equipment, and machinery (fixed capital) but also working capital and goods in process, and sometimes the value of land. The product variable was the value added by the industry, which was a monetary value, as opposed to the indexes of physical output used to measure product in the time series studies. Unlike the capital and labor variables, which were directly reported in the census data used for the cross-section studies, this value-added figure had to be calculated using other census variables (such as total value of output and total costs of raw materials, energy, and so on)

[7] Martin Bronfenbrenner (1914–97) received his Ph.D. in economics from the University of Chicago in 1939 and became a very prolific researcher, serving on the faculties of several leading universities (Blaug 1999).

and estimates made by Douglas and his coauthors of items like taxes, insurance, and depreciation.

Overall, however, the amount of estimation involved in preparing the cross-section data for regression analysis was trivial compared to what had been required for the time series studies, and this, as Douglas realized, answered a persistent criticism of those studies – that the data upon which they were based were not trustworthy. Using the cross-section industry data eliminated the need to invoke questionable proportionality assumptions to interpolate between census years, or to estimate the vintage of various increments to the capital stock, or to construct price indexes to deflate the increments of capital value assigned to different years, just to mention a few of the procedures that had concerned Slichter and others.

The cross-section approach addressed other common criticisms of the earlier studies as well. The frequently expressed objection that the good fit of the Cobb–Douglas regression did not capture a causal relationship, but only the extent to which all three series were strongly correlated with time, could not be applied to the cross-section results. As each cross-section study was based upon data from a single year, the need to either deal with or assume away technological progress was eliminated, as was any problem caused by changes over time in the value of k.[8] The complaint that Douglas's capital variable measured available capital rather than capital actually used was blunted if the year chosen for the cross-section study was a year of prosperity.

Perhaps just as importantly, there were numerous data sets in existence, from a variety of economies and time periods, to which the new cross-section approach could be applied (Douglas 1976, 905). This allowed Douglas to pursue more effectively the strategy of establishing the credibility and usefulness of his methodology by piling up plausible-looking results from a variety of time periods and economies. It was a fairly robust strategy: to the extent that results of estimating the Cobb–Douglas regression with data from different times or places differed (provided that they were still somewhat reasonable), the method could be advertised as one that helped to reveal important differences between economies and to shed light on their causes. To the extent that the method produced similar results for different times and places, it could be argued that the estimation of the production function was revealing something fundamental about

[8] Douglas and coauthors described the ways in which the cross-section approach dealt with criticisms of the time series studies in a number of places, including Bronfenbrenner and Douglas (1939, 762, 777–81), and Gunn and Douglas (1940, 401–03).

capitalist economies. One can find Douglas arguing along both lines in the cross-section studies, but by his 1947 AEA presidential address the similarity of results from different times and places had become one of Douglas's key selling points for his program.

While each cross-section study was intended to advance Douglas's program by providing yet another example of a fruitful application of the Cobb–Douglas regression, they also provided a platform for defending the program from critics. As noted above, the switch to the cross-section approach had in a stroke rendered irrelevant a number of objections to the earlier studies, but Douglas still felt a need to undermine Mendershausen's arguments concerning multicollinearity and the sensitivity of results to the direction of minimization. These were econometrically sophisticated arguments, and in the first two cross-section studies, Bronfenbrenner and Douglas (1939) and Gunn and Douglas (1940), econometrically sophisticated rebuttals were presented. Each of these papers, however, had a distinct approach to dealing with Mendershausen's concerns, suggesting that these rebuttals were largely the work of Douglas's coauthors, and that by this time Douglas had decided that the best way to keep his research program up to date econometrically was to enlist the aid of young, recently trained economists.

THE DEBUT OF THE CROSS-SECTION METHOD: BRONFENBRENNER AND DOUGLAS (1939)

Like the last time series study with Handsaker, Douglas's first cross-section study with Bronfenbrenner began with a brief review of the research program: "The Cobb–Douglas function was applied in 1927–1928 to the statistical verification of the marginal productivity theory of distribution," readers were told, and they were reminded of the good fits achieved in past applications as well as the close alignment between the estimate of k and labor's share in total product predicted by marginal productivity theory. But these studies had not been without critics, the authors admitted. Because they were based on time series of labor, capital, and product, all of which had upward trends, many had suggested that the results demonstrated "the effects of time, not productivity." Then Bronfenbrenner and Douglas made a striking announcement: using cross-section data from the United States, data that were not subject to time trends, they had produced estimates of k within one percentage point of the estimate produced in the US time series study, making it "apparent that the results of neither temporal or cross-section studies can be due to the operation of the time factor alone" (Bronfenbrenner and Douglas 1939, 761–62).

Bronfenbrenner and Douglas's data came from the 1909 Census of Manufactures, conducted in a year of moderate prosperity. The authors divided the data into 90 industry categories, and labor, capital, and product (that is, value added) variables were created for each category. The census reported values of total capital in each industry (including land and working capital), leading Bronfenbrenner and Douglas to construct an alternative fixed capital variable as well, using industry-level estimates from the 1904 census of the percentage of total capital represented by buildings, machinery, tools, and equipment. As noted above, creating the product variable from census data required additional estimation, with the construction of industry-level depreciation allowances being the authors' toughest task.

The cross-section industry data, in theory at least, allowed Douglas and Bronfenbrenner to develop some interesting new tests and extensions of the methodology. Subsamples for industry groupings such as "food and beverages" or "highly capitalistic industries" were created, to look for systematic differences in k and to identify samples where increasing returns might be expected to prevail. A monopolistic subsample and a "sweated trades" subsample were defined to test the possibility of the Cobb–Douglas function "proving too much," that is, if k in these subsamples equaled labor's share, there would be "grounds for suspicion" (Bronfenbrenner and Douglas 1939, 765–66).

Bronfenbrenner pushed the Douglas research program further towards a formalistic econometrics based on classical sampling theory. For the first time in a Douglas production study, readers were provided with a complete set of formulas for all the coefficient estimates to be calculated and their standard errors. Formal statistical tests of significance were outlined both for the constant returns to scale hypothesis and the equality of k to labor's share: "The critical comparison is that of j+k with unity. If a significant difference ($>3s_{j+k}$) exists, we may have evidence of production under increasing or decreasing cost conditions." And "the Cobb–Douglas function was developed as a statistical test of the theory of marginal productivity. If this theory were applicable, and competition approximately pure, the share of labor in total product would equal $(L\partial P/\partial L)/P$, or k in the Cobb–Douglas function. In the case the observed share of labor, which we call w, were significantly different from k (different by more than $3s_k$, w not being considered subject to measurable sampling error), we should have evidence of the invalidity of one or both of our assumptions"

(Bronfenbrenner and Douglas 1939, 767–68).[9] Readers were cautioned, however, that given various limitations of the data, the evidence of these tests could not be considered conclusive.

One of these limitations would be a source of confusion and apparent inconsistency throughout Douglas's subsequent cross-section studies. It was a result of the change in the P variable from an index of physical output to a measure of value added by industry, which could fluctuate both with the physical output of an industry and the price of its product. Because of this change, the authors explained, "Our figures do not distinguish value of marginal product from value of marginal physical product. Accordingly they provide no method for detecting 'monopolistic' as distinguished from 'monopsonistic' exploitation." Thus, while a finding that k did not equal labor's share could still be taken as evidence of the inaccuracy of the Cobb–Douglas function and/or a lack of competition, a finding that k was equal to labor's share was consistent with perfect or imperfect competition in product markets, and could only be taken as evidence of competition in factor markets. In light of this, readers might have wondered about the authors' rationale for the previously described strategy of examining a subsample of monopolistic industries for evidence of exploitation.

About a quarter of the article's text was devoted to "the problem of stability," that is, Mendershausen's main critique of Douglas's work. Bronfenbrenner gave a succinct account of the issues using a verbal description of Mendershausen's pinhead graphs: when the data points were on or close to a plane in three-dimensional space, the estimates of the Cobb–Douglas regression parameters would be invariant to the choice of direction of minimization.[10] But if the independent variables were highly correlated, the points would seem to lie along a "pencil" in space, and the choice of minimization direction would have a large effect on the estimated coefficients. Unless one direction of minimization could be justified in some way, any set of estimates produced from such data should be considered statistically unstable.

The Bronfenbrenner–Douglas response to this problem was two pronged: first, admit that multicollinearity was a problem, but one that could be detected by tests and that did not plague all cross-section samples;

9 s_{j+k} stood for the standard error of the sum of the j and k coefficients, and s_k the standard error of the k coefficient.

10 I attribute the details of the rebuttal of Mendershausen to Bronfenbrenner, for reasons already given.

second, develop a priori arguments based in economic and statistical theory as to why Douglas's approach of using P as the dependent variable in the regression (minimizing in the P direction) was appropriate. With respect to the first, three "stability conditions" were defined, and readers were told that results from samples that did not satisfy these conditions would be "disregarded."[11] Two of the stability conditions were "'rules of thumb' unjustified as yet by the mathematical theory of sampling" relating to the level of intercorrelation between variables. The third required that all estimated coefficients be statistically significant, that is, more than three times their standard errors. Although the full sample satisfied these conditions, most subsamples did not (Bronfenbrener and Douglas 1939, 769–70). In the article's conclusion, the situation was summarized thusly:

> The instability problem, of course, is real, and should not be overlooked. It makes our function appear as one of the exotic hot-house plants of economic statistics. It will not grow, this function, wherever planted. If the soil be too rocky, or temperature too low, or the terra firma subject to the unstabilizing influence of earthquakes, no amount of statistical cultivation can remedy the deficiencies. The plant will then be a nonviable monstrosity, perishing in embryo. But given rare and optimal conditions, the plant will grow to maturity and fruition, with a percentage of viable results as great as can be anticipated in other branches of experimental botanizing (782).[12]

To defend the choice of P as the dependent variable, Bronfenbrenner offered readers an alternative to Mendershausen's approach to choosing the direction of minimization:

> The logical meaning of minimizing in any particular direction is the assumption that all deviations from the fitted function are due to random errors in measurement of the dependent variable *or are residual deviations due to random operation of various causes not included in the formula* .... Since the economic analysis underlying the relationship P= f(L,C) implies causation of P by L and C, these residual deviations are of necessity confined to the P values. These deviations are caused by the actual effect upon product (P) of various causes other than quantities of labor (L) and capital (C), which may operate in practice, and it is assumed that these effects have a random distribution about the 'pure' effects upon P of L and C alone. Since the movement of causation is from L and C to P, and not vice versa, we would expect that such random deviations or residuals would be present in the

11 Actually, results from both stable and unstable samples were reported and discussed, although results from stable samples were marked in tables and privileged in discussion.

12 These words were probably Bronfenbrenner's, given that the stability tests did not appear in subsequent Douglas production studies, and that colorful language and metaphor characterized Bronfenbrenner's style throughout his subsequent career.

observed P quantities, and hence would justify minimizing in this direction, although if all the deviations were caused by measurement error this would not be justifiable

(Bronfenbrenner and Douglas 1939, 771–72, emphasis added).

The key feature of Bronfenbrenner's approach that allowed him to reach different conclusions from those of Mendershausen was his willingness to make analytical use of assumptions about causality. In the confluence-analysis framework, it was assumed that a number of exact linear relationships might hold between economic variables, but no analytical distinction was made between relationships that were causal and those that were not, and thus there was no role to play for assumptions about direction of causality. Bronfenbrenner began with the assumption, based in economic theory, that at least one of the relationships between the variables (the production function) was a causal relationship, and that the direction of causality was known. This allowed him to introduce the idea that when the caused variable (in this case, P) was used as the dependent variable, the failure of the estimated version of the relationship to fit perfectly was due not only to measurement error in the variables, as in the confluence-analysis framework, but also to unmeasured factors that had a causal influence on the dependent variable. From the point of view of statistical theory, the unobserved factors that causally influenced P, even after accounting for the influence of C and L, had the same impact on estimation as did measurement error in P – they biased the coefficient estimates if P was used as an independent variable, but not if P was used as the dependent variable. Prior treatments of the problem of choosing the direction of minimization (including Frisch's) had led to a widely held belief that the variable with the most measurement error should serve as the dependent variable. Bronfenbrenner was arguing that when estimating a causal relationship, the influence of unobserved factors on the caused variable should be considered along with the measurement error in that variable when deciding the direction of minimization.[13]

[13] From the point of view of econometrics as it would develop in later decades, Bronfenbrenner's analysis was correct, given his assumptions. He had assumed away what came to be known as simultaneous equations bias by ruling out any causal effect of P on C or L, and with P as the dependent variable, correlations, causal or otherwise, between C and L would not bias the coefficient estimates and thus not lead the coefficient estimates to be sensitive to the chosen direction of minimization. Another important assumption that the unobserved factors that causally influenced P did not also causally influence L or C through some avenue other than their influence on P (no omitted

Bronfenbrenner also pointed out another important omission from Mendershausen's analysis. In thinking about the relative amounts of measurement error in the variables, it was only important to consider random, as opposed to systematic, errors of measurement. For example, there was a general tendency across industries to overestimate the value of capital, but this was a systematic measurement error. It might lead the average error in the measurement of capital to be greater than the average value of measurement error in the other two variables, but what mattered was the variance of the measurement error in capital, which arose only from random measurement error, and thus might be smaller than the variance of the measurement errors of the other two variables.

Following this econometric discussion, estimation results were presented for the full sample and for seven subsamples, using both the fixed and the total capital measure, for the unrestricted function and then for the restricted. It was the full sample of 90 industries, using the total capital measure, that yielded the noteworthy k=.74 estimate. Once again readers were reminded that the US time series estimate for k had been .75, an occurrence that "would certainly seem to be more than accidental and to corroborate in large degree the results of previous studies" (773). Something not highlighted was that the near equality of k and labor's average share that was such an important selling point for the US time series study did not characterize the 1909 cross-section results, for which labor's share was .67. Instead, the authors commented that when the total capital measure was used, the results "checked closely" with observed distributive shares.

Reasons were offered for discounting results that were far out of line with previous findings. Many such results came from regressions that used the fixed capital measure, but "this was to be expected theoretically, due to the large random errors in the allocation of total capital between the categories of fixed and working capital." Also, "every case of an abnormally high k (above .85)" came from a sample that had failed to pass the stability tests, although the converse was not true – some statistically unstable estimates looked quite reasonable.

Standard error estimates were used selectively in the discussion of results. The authors commented on being troubled by the high standard errors of some parameters, but no explicit use was made of the 3-standard error tests of significance outlined earlier in the paper. Perhaps this significance rule was implicit in statements about the closeness of k

variable bias) may or may not have been intended by his statement that these effects had "a random distribution about the 'pure' effects upon P of L and C alone."

estimates to distributive shares ("never is the difference sufficiently large to furnish clear statistical evidence of exploitation"), but it was clearly abandoned in the discussion of tests of return to scale:

> Did increasing returns prevail in American industry in 1909? Apparently so, if one considers industry as a whole (using total capital figures, k+j= 1.06 ± 0.03). Apparently not, if one considers two of the subgroups in which one would expect increasing returns to be most in evidence a priori (Highly capitalized industries: k+j = .95 ± 0.07; metals and machinery: k+j= .97 ± 0.04, on the other hand, in monopolistic industries: k+j = 1.05 ± 0.08).
>
> (Bronfenbrenner and Douglas 1939, 776)

Since the numbers used in constructing the bounds in this passage were single standard errors, none of these estimates of k+j was more than three standard errors from 1. Standard errors were invoked to argue that k and j might be uniform across industries, even though the estimates of k and j varied, but both significance standards and stability tests were temporarily ignored to make the interesting point that it was the industries with a reputation for exploitation in which the k estimate fell the furthest below labor's share. However, it was admitted that this evidence of monopsonistic exploitation was "highly tentative."

The move to cross-section data had ameliorated some criticisms, and rendered others irrelevant. A cogent answer to Mendershausen's econometric critique had been developed. Durand's suggestion that the unrestricted equation be used and returns to scale measured had been embraced. But Durand's other chief criticism remained: the estimated Cobb–Douglas production function did not correspond in any way to the production function of economic theory. Indeed, the question had become more complicated, because there was now the possibility that the theoretical counterparts of coefficients estimated using cross-section data were something different from the theoretical counterparts of the coefficients estimated in the earlier time series studies.

The first answer to this criticism offered in the article was clearly Douglas's: "We do not see why the phrase production function cannot be applied as a normative term to all industries or to certain specific industries, nor why it must be confined to a single plant" (Bronfenbrenner and Douglas 1939, 779). But the simple assertion that there were several different, but equally interesting, types of production functions one could estimate did not satisfy Bronfenbrenner, and he returned to the topic a few paragraphs later:

> Durand insists quite correctly on sharp distinctions between the type of production function exemplified by the Cobb–Douglas (we christen this type "distributive" or

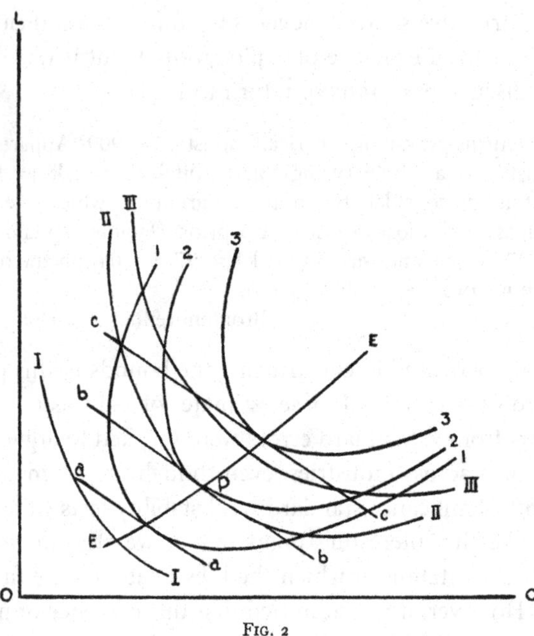

Figure 2.2 Martin Bronfenbrenner's illustration of the relationship between Douglas's estimated production function and the production functions of individual firms

"distributional") and the ordinary ("general") production function of mathematical economics. He does not attempt to show the relationship between the two types of functions, relations which make the "distributive" function a legitimate member of the economic Noah's Ark.

(Bronfenbrenner and Douglas 1939, 780)[14]

Bronfenbrenner then offered an analysis of this relationship, with the help of an isoquant-isocost diagram, a type of graph that was subsequently to become part of the standard analytical tool kit of formalistic neoclassical economics. The curves numbered 1, 2, and 3 on the figure (Figure 2.2) were the iso-product (isoquant) curves, two dimensional contour lines of a firm's (or industry's) production function showing combinations of labor and capital that produced the same value of output. The lines a, b, and c

[14] I attribute this text and the analysis that follows it to Bronfenbrenner firstly, because the term "distributional production function" and the analysis itself did not appear in subsequent Douglas production studies, secondly because Bronfenbrenner continued to work on this problem, and thirdly, because the reference to an "economic Noah's Ark" is typical of Bronfenbrenner's style.

were the iso-cost lines, showing combinations of labor and capital of equal cost.

Bronfenbrenner stated without elaboration that tangencies between iso-cost and iso-product lines showed how proportions of capital and labor used by the firm would vary as levels of total output changed, and that the long-run, minimum average cost equilibrium would be one of these tangency points (labeled P in his diagram). In long-run equilibrium, only such points as P would actually be observed. Further, although the production function might not be homogeneous of the first degree throughout its domain, (and, as Durand had pointed out, could not be if the equilibrium were to be determinate), it would be approximately so at the point of long-run equilibrium.

Then the curves I, II, and III were introduced. These were loci of the long-run equilibrium points of different firms (or different industries). These were all observable points, and because they were long-run equilibria, they were all points on functions that were (approximately) homogeneous of degree one. Although Bronfenbrenner did not explicitly say so, this provided an explanation for why the cross-section Cobb–Douglas regression yielded estimates of k and j that summed to one. Note that this justification of the homogenous of degree one or constant return to scale assumption, which Bronfenbrenner supported with a reference to a proof by J. R. Hicks, differs from that used by Douglas in previous works, which relied on the *reductio ad absurdum* argument that decreasing returns to scale would lead to one-man firms, and increasing returns to scale would lead to a single firm.[15]

Thus, an estimated Cobb–Douglas production function was not a firm (or industry) level production function, but "since each point on the family (I, II, III) was also a point on the family (1, 2, 3), a point corresponding to an actual rather than a hypothetical decision, it should be clear that a distributive production function differs from a general one primarily in that each one of its points has relevance to the real world." Bronfenbrenner added that the distributive function's use of aggregated labor and capital as

[15] Bronfenbrenner's argument here is also consistent with the partial equilibrium models of perfectly competitive long-run equilibrium developed by Frank Knight (1921) and Jacob Viner (1952 [1931]), in which firms end up operating at the minimum point of their long-run average cost curves (which imply production functions for which returns to scale differ at different levels of output). It is not unreasonable to suppose that Bronfenbrenner became familiar with the argument as a result of his graduate training at the University of Chicago.

the input variables made it more convenient for studying the distribution of income between labor and capital.[16]

FIGHTING MENDERSHAUSEN ON HIS OWN TERMS: GUNN AND DOUGLAS (1940)

Douglas's second cross-section study, coauthored with Grace Gunn, appeared half a year later, with results reported for five cross-section samples of Australian census data.[17] Like the Bronfenbrenner–Douglas article, it began with a review of Douglas's previous production studies, although the purpose of the research program was described as measuring the marginal productivity curves of labor and capital, rather than verifying the marginal productivity theory of distribution. Again, several criticisms of previous studies were described, as was the way in which cross-section data could circumvent one of the most persistent of these criticisms. Reference was made to the remarkable agreement between the k estimates from the US time series study and the first cross-section study of US data. The authors then gave accounts of the construction of capital, labor, and value-added variables from five samples of data from Australia: three cross sections of 35 industries from the state of Victoria (1910–11, 1923–24, and 1927–28), a sample of 138 industries for the Commonwealth as a whole for 1934–35, and a sample of 127 industries in New South Wales from the same year.

In describing the details of fitting the Cobb–Douglas regression to the data, Gunn developed her rebuttal of Mendershausen, which was rather different from Bronfenbrenner's. She did so in the context of a review of what she called "three treatments of linear regression: (A) the classical method or R. A. Fisher's, (B) R. Frisch's (C) T. Koopmans'" (Gunn and Douglas 1940, 406) The basic problem was to estimate the coefficients of a true regression equation $c_1X_1 - c_2X_2 - c_3X_3 - c = 0$. The classical approach

[16] One question Bronfenbrenner did not address was why different firms would end up on different iso-product curves with different capital/labor ratios. Did different firms (or industries, in the empirical context of the cross-section studies) have different production functions, or did firms in different industries face different prices for their (aggregated) capital and labor inputs? Econometrically, the question is what sort of variation in the real world leads to the observation of different capital/labor ratios in the data.

[17] Grace Gunn was a graduate student at the University of Chicago at the time. She had received an M.A. from Northwestern University in 1928, but does not appear to have completed a Ph.D. Over her career she served as an economist in a number of federal government agencies.

assumed that a random sample of n observations of the three variables was available, and that only one of the variables was measured with error, an error that was normally and independently distributed with a zero mean and a constant variance. The correct estimation approach under these circumstances was the method of least squares, minimizing in the direction of the variable measured with error.

However, Gunn explained, Frisch had pointed out that if more than one of the variables were measured with error, the least squares standard errors could not be used as measures of significance, and, Gunn admitted, "for our data we cannot claim that any two of the three sets of observations, X_1, X_2, X_3, are completely free from errors of measurement, so we have no satisfactory test of significance using the classical method" (Gunn and Douglas 1940, 407). This led to Gunn's explication of Frisch's analysis of the regression choice problem, an analysis that began with the assumption that all of the variables might be measured with error, and supported the idea that in the two variable case, a diagonal regression provided a good estimate of the true regression coefficient. If Frisch had a recommendation for how to deal with the three variable case, Gunn did not share it. Instead, she moved to the topic of bunch maps. "The question of what variables are to be included is of primary importance in (Frisch's) analysis," and Frisch had developed bunch maps as a tool for answering this question. Although the question of what variables to include had never been a major issue for Douglas or his critics, Gunn then provided a two-paragraph summary of how bunch maps were constructed, and how they could be used to identify the variables that should be included in a regression equation, something Mendershausen had not supplied when he had introduced bunch maps to the English-language journal literature. She reported that bunch maps had been constructed for all the data sets, and those for the 138 observation Commonwealth sample were reproduced for readers. At this point, a second, perhaps more important, reason for bringing up bunch maps was revealed: "Dr. Mendershausen has criticized an earlier study by one of the authors and used Frisch's analysis exclusively. We wish to point out that our bunch maps for the present study show substantial improvement over those represented by Dr. Mendershausen from our previous time series for the United States" (Gunn and Douglas 1940, 409). This claim of substantial improvement was simply that: a claim. Readers were not told what problem in the data Mendershausen had detected with his bunch maps, or what it was about the bunch maps for the Australian data that indicated improvement. Readers were likely just as puzzled as they had been by Mendershausen's equally bare assertion that the serious problem of a "nearly multicollinear set" in the US time series data was "exhibited very well" by his bunch maps. In any case, Gunn concluded that Frisch's method of analyzing the regression problem did not lead to any definite conclusions, so that consideration of Koopmans' method was in order.

Koopmans' (1937) analysis of regression began with Frisch's assumption of a deterministic linear relationship between several variables, all of which were measured with error. He augmented it in two important ways. First, as Gunn noted, he attempted a synthesis between Fisher's and Frisch's analysis, conceptualizing the observed variables as the result of an explicit sampling scheme and introducing sampling error as well as measurement error as a reason for the failure of the deterministic relationship to hold exactly in the data. Second, his mathematical analysis of the problem was much more formalistic and rigorous than Frisch's (Morgan 1990, 238–40). Gunn presented pieces of the Koopmans' analysis, using Koopmans' notation, which differed from the notation that had been previously introduced, and of which only the most cursory explanations were given. Koopmans' points about sampling error were not alluded to, and it was difficult to see how the Koopmans' analysis differed at all from Frisch's analysis: the correct direction of minimization depended on the relative size of the measurement errors in the variables, and if only one of the variables was measured with error, least squares minimization in the direction of that variable was the appropriate estimation method. But Koopmans had come to one additional conclusion that Gunn and Douglas found useful. He showed that in the multiple-variable case, the correct direction of minimization (or the correct set of weights to be used when averaging results obtained from choosing different directions of minimization) depended on more than the relative variances of the measurement errors. It also depended on the relative sizes of the coefficients in the true regression relationship. A long passage from Koopmans (1937) was quoted with notation changed to reflect the three variable case being considered by Gunn and Douglas, to the effect that when the coefficient of a variable is relatively small, the results attained by minimizing in the direction of that variable were untrustworthy. The coefficient of capital was the smaller coefficient in the Cobb–Douglas regression, so results obtained by minimizing in the C direction, which had in Douglas's previous studies been the most problematic, should be ignored. This, combined with the assumption (shared by Mendershausen) that the L variable was the most accurately measured of the three, led to the conclusion that minimization in the P direction was the best choice.

Inserted somewhat awkwardly in the discussion of Koopmans' method was also a response to Mendershausen's pinhead graphs, and his accompanying argument that Douglas's US data traced out a line rather than a plane in three-dimensional space, leading to instability in the estimates. Gunn and Douglas divided their data into groups of industries with approximately the same level of capital, and then created two-dimensional scatter plots of L and P for each capital group. If, for each capital group, values of labor and product formed a tight bunch on the graph, they argued, then Mendershausen's instability criticism applied to their data. But if the labor-product scatter plot for each capital group traced out a line, then the data points in three dimensions would trace out a plane. Three such graphs were reproduced, all of which showed points scattered along a line in L-P space, and readers were assured that these were typical of graphs drawn for all capital groups in the two largest data sets.[18]

With the matter of direction of minimization thus dealt with, results were presented for the five samples. Estimates of k ranged from .59 to .74. For three samples k+j was .99, while for the other two, both from Victoria, there was evidence of decreasing returns to scale. Gunn and Douglas attributed this to the high protective tariff in Australia, which encouraged manufacturing industries to grow above their optimal size. In the three Victoria samples, k fell over time from .74 to .59, which was consistent, Gunn and Douglas believed, with the time series estimate of k from Victoria of .71. Likewise, the cross-section estimate of k from New South Wales was very close to Director's time series estimate for the same state discussed in *The Theory of Wages* (.664 and .654, respectively).

The comparison of labor's share to the k estimates for the various samples was prefaced with an assertion that under the theory of perfect competition, the difference between the two numbers would not exceed the standard error of k, and the table in which the comparison was presented included the ratio of the difference between labor's share and k and the standard error of k. In two cases this ratio was below one. For New South Wales, labor's share was over three standard errors below the k estimate. Gunn and Douglas noted that such a discrepancy between labor's share and the k estimate had also been found in Director's time series study of

[18] Gunn and Douglas (1940, 412) linked this graphical analysis to the discussion of Koopmans' method by claiming that it showed something about the relative error variances, but never explained what it showed. Instead, they argued that it "did indicate that the surface was approximately a plane" and that the coefficient of capital was relatively small.

New South Wales. They attributed it to the existence of "rigid regulation ... by both the state and the Commonwealth, which, despite all charges to the contrary, may, in conjunction with the price fixing activities of industry, have operated to keep labor's share below what it would have been in a perfectly competitive society" (Gunn and Douglas 1940, 420). No explanations were offered for the two cases in which the absolute value of the ratio was between one and two. In a summary assessment of these results, Gunn and Douglas argued that differences between labor's share and the k estimates could be explained by errors in the data, price fixing by Australian industries, and regulation of wages by the state. These two mentions of price fixing as a possible explanation of a measure of labor's share that was well below k indicate that Gunn and Douglas did not yet fully appreciate the point made in the Bronfenbrenner and Douglas article that when monetary value added was used as the measure of product, the regression could not distinguish value of marginal product from marginal physical product, so that imperfect competition in product markets alone would not, in theory, cause a properly measured k to deviate from labor's share of value added.

Gunn and Douglas also offered a novel response to those critics troubled by the apparent disconnect between the theoretical production function of the firm and the empirical production function estimated with aggregated data:

> In the analysis which has been made thus far we have used totals of labor, capital, and value product for each of a series of industries. The usual discussion of the way the increments of product diminish as the quantities of labor and capital increase is, however, couched in terms of individual plants and of what happens therein. To make our analysis more realistic, therefore, we carried it through for two cross sections in terms of the average quantities per plant of labor, capital, and product in each of the various industries
>
> (Gunn and Douglas 1940, 416–17).

In other words, values of P, C, and L for each industry were to be divided by the number of plants in the industry prior to the regression analysis. It was found that this adjustment made little difference in the results. Changes in the k and j estimates were less than one standard error. Gunn and Douglas concluded that "all the evidence indicates that the relationships which have been discovered when totals for industries are treated as the units hold also in terms of averages per plant"(Gunn and Douglas 1940, 418).[19]

[19] The procedure of dividing industry totals by number of plants in the industry prior to analysis does not accomplish what Gunn and Douglas believed it would. It actually adds nothing to one's knowledge of the relationships between capital, labor, and output in

It is interesting to compare the Gunn–Douglas (1940) article to the Bronfenbrenner–Douglas article with respect to how it deals with criticisms of Douglas's program, and more generally, how it handles the statistical issues associated with the move to cross-section estimation. To begin with, the Gunn–Douglas article specified no formal tests for statistical significance. Standard errors were reported for the coefficient estimates, but this was accompanied only by a rather casual use of a one-standard-error rule as a metric for closeness, something Douglas had been comfortable with since the Douglas–Handsaker article.

In dealing with the question of direction of minimization, Gunn, whom I assume was primarily responsible for this aspect of the paper, made no use of the theoretically indicated causal relationship running from C and L to P. She did mention that in the classical approach to regression, the impact of excluded factors that affected a variable was considered along with its measurement error, but gave no indication that this point could aid in the selection of the dependent variable. Douglas actually took issue with Gunn on this matter in a long footnote (Gunn and Douglas 1940, 407–8), with an argument that described an excluded variable of the sort that Bronfenbrenner had talked about, and implicitly invoked causality from labor and capital to product. The P variable, Douglas explained, measured value added, which included a price component. Although in long-run equilibrium, an industry's value added would be proportional to the physical increment it added to the total output, in the short run output demand curves would be shifting, leading to higher than equilibrium prices in some industries, lower than equilibrium prices in others. These shifts represented excluded factors that, along with capital and labor, would causally determine the value of P. The quantity theory of money suggested that they would average to zero over the full sample of industries. Thus, they should be considered along with measurement error, which provides reason for minimizing in the P direction. Gunn responded that the inaccuracy of the capital figures, due to both the difference between available capital and utilized capital and the need to make an approximate

individual plants. Technically, dividing the industry totals through by the number of plants, and then estimating the unrestricted Cobb–Douglas regression using the logs of these variables is equivalent to including the log of the number of plants in the industry as a variable in the Cobb–Douglas regression, and restricting its coefficient to be equal to 1 – (k+j). If the number of plants in the industry is uncorrelated with the level of industry output, after controlling for the industry totals of labor and capital, and if k+j=1, this restriction will be true, and estimating with plant averages will yield the results very similar to those obtained using industry-level variables.

adjustment for the inclusion of the value of land in the capital variable, potentially made the capital variable's error much more problematic than error from any source in P.[20] In the end, Gunn would clinch the argument for minimization in the P direction not by invoking economic theory, as had Bronfenbrenner, but by supplementing a traditional statistical argument about relative error variances with Koopmans' statistical argument about relative sizes of the coefficients, complete with a data-based, rather than theory-based, demonstration that the coefficient of capital was indeed the smallest.

Gunn also eschewed Bronfenbrenner's formal stability tests. Instead, she fought bunch maps with bunch maps, and graphs with graphs. On this matter, Douglas was clearly with her. Never again would samples used in a Douglas study be subjected to Bronfenbrenner's stability tests, nor would the Cobb–Douglas regression be represented as a valuable but temperamental plant, which could only survive in rarely seen data conditions. This simply did not fit with Douglas's strategy of establishing the regression's legitimacy by estimating it with data from as many times and places as possible.

Gunn and Bronfenbrenner's styles in dealing with the stability question exemplify the contrast between two different rhetorical approaches to using statistics in persuasive argumentation: the rhetoric of expert judgment vs. the rhetoric of mechanical objectivity.[21] When the rhetoric of expert judgment is employed, the persuader presents a statistical construct (a graph, a table of numbers, or a set of summary statistics) and tells the reader what it means, and the reader is asked to judge the credibility of that interpretation in part based on the evidence of the author's expertise and integrity, as provided in the text itself or indicated by the author's identity or affiliation. The rhetoric of mechanical objectivity attempts to avoid this apparent need for the reader to assess the quality of an author's subjective judgment by basing interpretation of statistical constructs in a set of rules or procedures which, regardless of who applies them, always yield the same answer, for example, one variable will be judged to have an impact upon another based on a calculated t-statistic; a sample is to be judged stable or not based on calculated correlation coefficients. In Biddle (1999) I argue that during the 1930s and 1940s, the rhetoric of mechanical objectivity was

[20] Gunn did not seem to appreciate Bronfenbrenner's point about the difference between systematic and random measurement error in the capital variable.

[21] These two rhetorical styles are described more fully in Porter (1995), building on the idea of mechanical objectivity introduced in Daston and Galinson (1992).

becoming more prevalent in the literature of empirical economics, and it would come to be the dominant rhetoric as the century wore on, expressed largely in the language and apparatus of Neyman–Pearson hypothesis testing.

Frisch's bunch map analysis relied heavily on a rhetoric of expert judgment. As Hendry and Morgan (1989) point out, with bunch maps "much depended on interpretation of results that could only be subjective. There were no precise rules of inference from the bunch maps such as were available in statistics based on probability theory."[22] So, readers simply had to trust Mendershausen's expertise when he stated that his bunch maps clearly displayed a problem with Douglas's data, and in not providing explanations of how he reached his conclusion from the bunch maps, Mendershausen was implicitly asking for that trust. Likewise, readers had to trust Gunn when she said that maps based on hers and Douglas's data showed substantial improvement over Mendershausen's map, and when the two later disagreed on what the same bunch maps said, readers had to decide whom to trust. The same can be said for the graphs presented by Mendershausen and Gunn and Douglas to show that data points did or did not provide sufficient support for estimating a plane. Bronfenbrenner, with his preference for objective tests of stability (and for formal significance tests) was seemingly more comfortable with the rhetoric of mechanical objectivity.

A final interesting divergence between Gunn and Douglas and Bronfenbrenner and Douglas is their reaction to the criticism that Douglas's estimated production functions were not the production functions of neoclassical theory. As we have seen, Bronfenbrenner sought, through theoretical analysis, to build a bridge between the neoclassical theory of the firm and the coefficients of the Cobb–Douglas regression estimated with cross-section industry data. Gunn and Douglas, on the other hand, attacked the problem statistically, by introducing an innovation to the cross-section methodology that they believed would produce an estimated production function corresponding to the plant-level production functions of theory. They concluded that the production function estimated with industry-level data revealed relationships between inputs

[22] This characteristic of bunch-map analysis is clearly a problem from the perspective of 1989, when the rhetoric of mechanical objectivity had come to dominate empirical economics. But in a different period, to interpret data using mechanical rules that are invariant to the context from which the data were generated, a context about which some experts might have deep knowledge, might have seemed equally problematic.

and outputs that existed in typical firms, but if this had turned out not to be the case, it would not in Douglas's eyes have undermined the value of the industry-level estimates. Bronfenbrenner, on the other hand, despite adopting Douglas's rhetoric about different kinds of production functions, still gave special status to the firm-level production function. For him, the value of the "distributive" production function estimated with industry-level data depended on the extent to which it could be linked to the general production function of neoclassical theory.

DOUGLAS ON THE OFFENSIVE: GENERATING NEW RESULTS AND DEBATING MENDERSHAUSEN

Douglas's offensive continued in the form of three more studies with Gunn that appeared in 1941 and 1942. H. Gregg Lewis also made important contributions to Douglas's project during this phase. He was at the time a Ph.D. student and was working with Douglas on another project, but had also recently been given responsibility for teaching the advanced statistics course at University of Chicago economics department.[23]

The first of these three studies (Gunn and Douglas 1941a) was published in the *American Economic Review*, and used data from the 1919 Census of Manufactures for the United States. An introductory section chronicled the economic situation in 1919: the war recently over, prices and employment levels fluctuating wildly, war-related industries shutting down while consumer-goods industries were ramping up production.

> It might be expected that the forces governing production in this tumultuous year would defy analysis, and that no quantitative laws of cause and effect could be found between the quantities of the so-called factors of production on the one hand and the quantity of product upon the other . . .. If any fairly clear relationship is found between the determining variables of labor and capital and the resultant product, then the belief that there are underlying laws of production will be strengthened. Moreover, if there is any appreciable agreement between the results for this year and those for others, the case for such basic laws will be still further strengthened. For if the unruly year of 1919 was still subject to basic economic forces operating beneath the surface, how much more then, would any ordinary year be subject to them?
>
> (Gunn and Douglas 1941a, 68)

[23] H. Gregg Lewis remained on the faculty of University of Chicago economics department for many years and was named a distinguished fellow of the American Economic Association in 1981. See Biddle (1996) for details on Lewis's career.

The data for 1919 had strengths and weaknesses: information was reported for 556 industries, the largest sample yet for a Douglas production study, but the capital variable was total capital including land, and Douglas saw no good way to estimate the portion that was fixed for each industry. He also found it "impossible" to produce industry-specific estimates of depreciation to subtract from the value-added numbers.

The paper followed the format of the previous Gunn and Douglas paper, including yet another lengthy response to Mendershausen's criticisms. Bunch maps were presented for the data set. Readers were referred to Frisch's (1934) book on confluence analysis for a full explanation of bunch maps, but were told that "the maps indicate that capital has not a strong effect, but they do not indicate that it must be discarded." The decision to minimize in the P direction was justified by noting that errors in the L variable were likely small, while the relatively small impact of capital on product indicated that minimization in the C direction would "give a very poor estimate," with readers referred to the previous Gunn and Douglas paper for a more detailed explanation (Gunn and Douglas 1941a, 74, 77).

An alternative statistical framework for understanding the role of least squares regression in production analysis was introduced, that is, it was a tool for estimating a causal, nondeterministic relationship between variables: "one could not reasonably expect these variables to be perfectly correlated even if the data were complete and accurate. This leads to the interpretation of our results as a description of the average change in products as a function of changes in factors of production" (Gunn and Douglas 1941a, 74–75). This way of thinking about regression analysis had been suggested to Gunn and Douglas by University of Chicago Ph.D. student John H. Smith, to whose doctoral dissertation readers were referred.[24]

To combat the multicollinearity/instability concern, Gunn and Douglas created yet another graphical construct, again based on the procedure of dividing the data into subgroups of industries with approximately the same levels of capital:

[24] John H. Smith's statistical approach to regression involved assuming that the linear regression equation represents a conditional mean function, showing the mean value of the dependent variable, conditional on any set of values taken by the independent variables (a point Gunn and Douglas mentioned in a later paper). Gunn and Douglas added to the linear conditional mean assumption an assumption about the direction of causality.

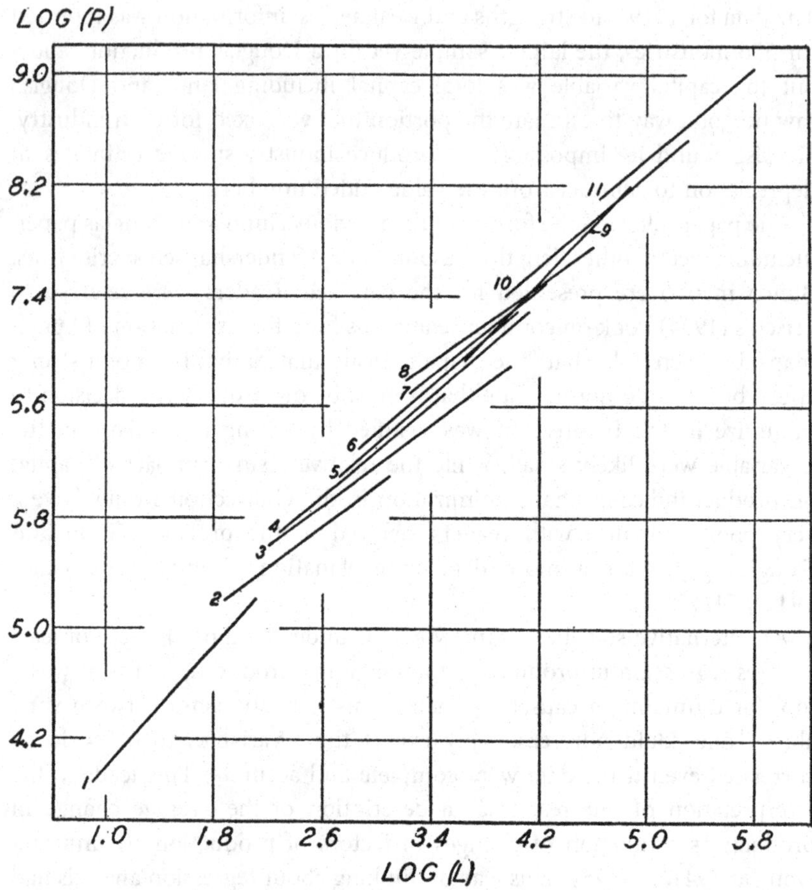

CHART III. Lines of Best Fit of Logs of P and Logs of L for Eleven Capital Groups. (Quantities of Capital Being Relatively Constant within Each Group)

Figure 2.3 Graph produced by Gunn and Douglas to show that multicollinearity was not a serious problem in their cross-section data

The graph showed the least squares lines fit to the labor-product scatter plots for each of 11 capital groups, with the length of each line showing the approximate length of the scatter plot (another graph showed a close-up for two capital groups of the actual scatter plots and their fitted lines). If the observations lay along a line rather than a plane in three-dimensional space, the authors argued, these scatters would be bunched rather than spread along lines. The authors pointed out that the lines did not coincide, that is, for a given value of labor, more capital led to more product. The production surface, they concluded, approximated a single plane.

The regression results provided Gunn and Douglas with both an affirmation and a puzzle. The k estimate for the unrestricted regression was .76, "truly surprising" in its proximity to both the US time series estimate and the estimate for 1909 from Bronfenbrenner and Douglas (1939). The puzzle lay in the fact that labor's share in manufacturing in 1919 had been .60. Gunn and Douglas (1939, 79–80) offered two possible explanations for this: first, it had not been possible to adjust the value-added figures for depreciation, thus pushing measured value product above actual value product. Second, 1919 was a year of rapid inflation, which raised value added without raising wages. The authors opined that the fact that W/P (labor's share) was so far below k in 1919 "may have accounted for much of the labor unrest of the year."

The article also introduced a new statistical test of the credibility of the Cobb–Douglas regression, one which Douglas attributed to Gregg Lewis. (Daly, Olsen, and Douglas 1943, fn. 11). It was a test based on the distribution of the regression residuals, and it became a standard element in the presentation of subsequent Douglas production studies. The test and its results were explained to readers with tables and graphs. One graph (Figure 2.4) plotted values of Log (P') against values of Log (P), where the Log(P') values were the regression predictions or "theoretical" values for Log(P). A bold line on the graph showed points where Log (P') equaled Log (P). The sets of two dashed lines parallel to the bold line on either side marked out zones for which Log (P') was within one and within two standard errors of Log (P), where the standard error referred to was the standard error of the regression equation.[25] The authors explained that roughly two-thirds of the observed values should be within one standard error of the bold line, and 95 percent of them within two standard errors. A second graph (Figure 2.5) was a histogram of the residuals, indicating that 48 percent took values between 0 and –S, (where S was a standard error), 34 percent were between 0 and S, and so on. "This indicates that the actual values in general were surprisingly close to what they should be according to the formula," which furnishes "added proof of the general reliability of the formula and its values for 1919" (Gunn and Douglas 1941a, 79).

This Gunn and Douglas article was the third Douglas production study to include an extended rebuttal of Mendershausen's original critique, and it drew a response from Mendershausen that was published in the *American*

[25] That is, the sample standard deviation of the variable Log(P') – Log(P).

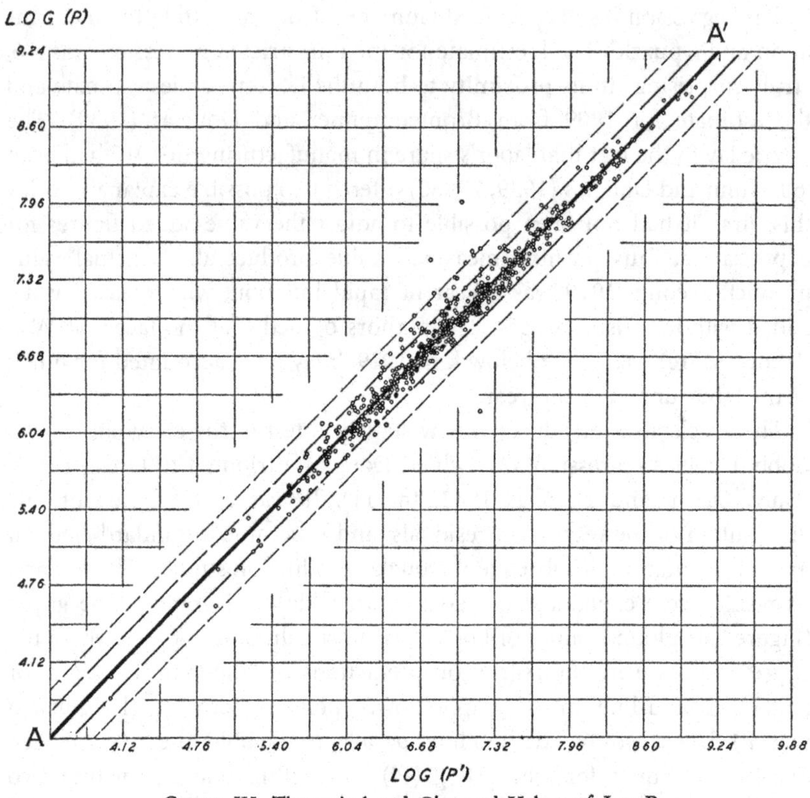

CHART IV. Theoretical and Observed Values of Log P
$P' = 2.39\ L^{.76}C^{.25}$

Figure 2.4 A graph used to illustrate a new statistical test of the credibility of an estimated production function, developed by H. Gregg Lewis

Economic Review seven months later (Mendershausen 1941a). Mendershausen argued that one could tell from the bunch maps presented in Gunn and Douglas (1941a) that there was multicollinearity, again illustrating the element of subjectivity involved in the interpretation of bunch maps. The graphs presented by Gunn and Douglas, based on the division of the data into capital groups (Figure 2.3), proved nothing, according to Mendershausen, because the linear spread of the labor-product scatter plots could be "reduced at will by reducing the width of the 'capital groups.'" Indeed, those graphs revealed a "high degree" multicollinearity, both in the closeness of the group regression lines to one another, and the fact lines for groups with higher levels of capital were uniformly above and to the right of lines for groups with lower levels of capital (Mendershausen 1941a, 563).

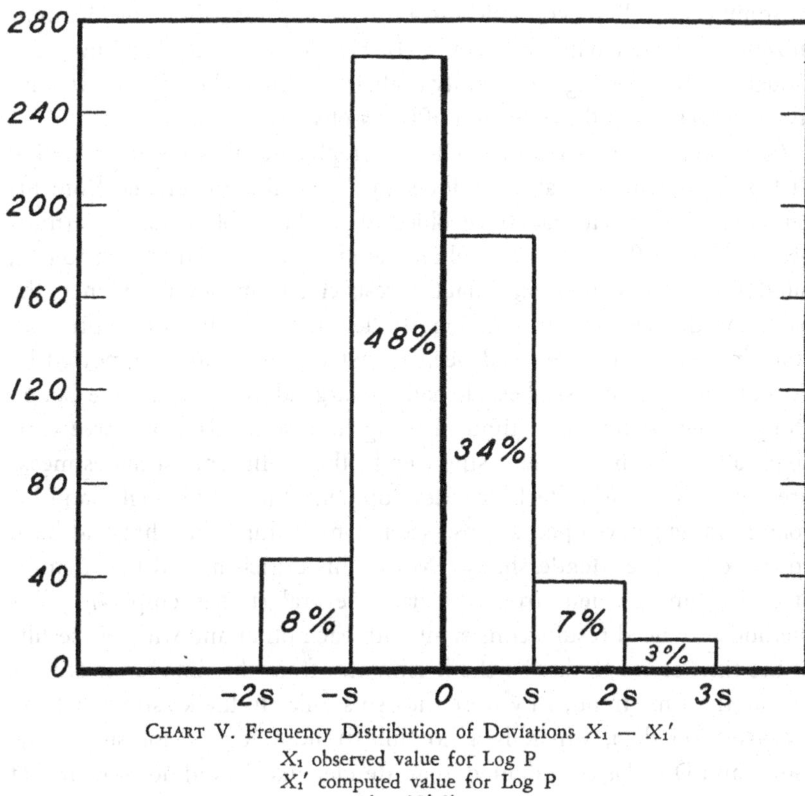

CHART V. Frequency Distribution of Deviations $X_1 - X_1'$
X_1 observed value for Log P
X_1' computed value for Log P
$P' = bL^kC^j$

Figure 2.5 A graph used to illustrate a new statistical test of the credibility of an estimated production function, developed by H. Gregg Lewis

Also, the entire discussion of the direction of minimization missed the point, according to Mendershausen. If "the choice of direction in which to minimize deviations is exerting excessive influence on the result," this is a warning to the researcher that none of the choices leads to reliable estimates.[26] To simply choose one of the directions and ignore the other two, quipped Mendershausen, was to act like "a man who stuffed his ears with wax in order not to be disturbed by the rattling of his alarm clock," thus dismissing the Gunn, Douglas, and Bronfenbrenner tactic of using a priori

[26] In this, Mendershausen was following one of the lessons Frisch had drawn from his confluence analysis, that least-squares regression was in general an unreliable approach to estimating economic relationships (Hendry and Morgan 1989).

reasoning, including economic theory, to choose one direction of minimization (Mendershausen 1941a, 563). He closed by chiding Gunn and Douglas for not testing the stability of their data by looking at the sensitivity of the results to the exclusion of a few observations.

Gunn and Douglas were permitted to reply, and they began by noting that Mendershausen's latest critique was "a significant retreat" from his earlier criticisms. He had once objected to the Cobb–Douglas formula because the coefficients of capital and labor were required to sum to one, but did not now acknowledge that this restricted formula was no longer the basis for the Douglas production studies, nor that the assumption of constant returns to scale had been repeatedly tested and supported by the data in these later studies. He had also argued that, because the Cobb–Douglas regression was estimated using time series data on three variables, all of which had increasing trends, the coefficient estimates measured only the trend in technical development. But now Douglas and his coauthors had developed a cross-section procedure, one that had been conceived before Mendershausen voiced his criticism, and that eliminated the time element from the data. Several studies employing this method produced results consistent with each other and with the results of the time series studies. If the k estimates from the time series studies captured a time trend, why were they so similar to the k estimates from cross-section data, which had no time trends? It was not surprising, Gunn and Douglas commented, that Mendershausen did not now repeat this criticism, but he could have at least mentioned that it had been addressed.

Instead, he "(fell) back to his last line of defense," criticisms related to instability and multicollinearity. Here, Gunn and Douglas reiterated the idea of the Cobb–Douglas regression as "a description of the *average* change in production as a function of the changes in the factors of production" (Gunn and Douglas 1941b, 566, emphasis in original), then pulled another idea from Smith's dissertation: that when the purpose of a regression is to estimate the value of a variable, the variable to be estimated should be the dependent variable, and it was correct to proceed as if there were no errors in the independent variable. They also argued that it was wrongheaded to think about collinearity without thinking about causality: "Certainly if there is any common-sense concept in economics it is that product (P) is a function of labor (L) and capital (C). To refuse to find parameters of the regression equation merely because the quantities of labor and capital are interrelated is to throw the baby out with the bath" (Gunn and Douglas 1941b, 566). Finally, they asked how one could reconcile the idea that the estimates from the Cobb–Douglas regression were unstable and indeterminate with the fact that estimates produced using many different data sets, both cross section and time series, were so consistent with one another, and that the k estimate tended to equal labor's share. It was hard to believe, Gunn and Douglas argued, that all this was merely due to chance.

The *American Economic Review* gave the final word to Mendershausen, who opened his rejoinder by asserting that Douglas and Gunn "seemed" to have accepted his criticism of their graphical analysis of multicollinearity (presumably he was assuming that their silence on the matter indicated consent to the criticism), then devoting three of his eight paragraphs to elucidating their misuse of a correct result from Smith's dissertation. Although multicollinearity between and measurement error in the independent variables did not adversely affect the ability of regression analysis to produce a good equation for estimating values of the dependent variable, he explained, the Cobb–Douglas regressions were intended to measure a structural relationship between capital, labor and product, not to forecast (i.e., estimate) values of output. Multicollinearity did cause a problem estimating structural coefficients, especially in the presence of measurement error in the independent variables.[27]

Both Bronfenbrenner and Douglas (1939) and the Gunn and Douglas papers had justified using P as the dependent variable on the basis that the disturbances in the P variable were more serious than those in the L variable. However, the important point, according to Mendershausen, was that using regression with P as the dependent variable to estimate structural coefficients could be justified only if there were *no* disturbances in either the capital or labor variables. He made no comment on the distinction these papers had made between measurement error and excluded factors as a source of "disturbances," but did note that Gunn and Douglas had ruled out the use of C as the dependent variable based on the relative size of its coefficient, a consideration that he dismissed as "entirely irrelevant."[28]

27 Mendershausen had, by this time, adopted Frisch's term "structural" to describe the deterministic linear relationships between variables assumed in confluence analysis, as well as the coefficients of those relationships.

28 Under the assumptions of both classical regression analysis and confluence analysis, Mendershausen was correct, in that linear regression can only produce unbiased estimates of the coefficients of an assumed linear structural (or population) relationship if there is no measurement error in the independent variables. This point is not directly

Mendershausen then took Douglas to task for a line of argument that Douglas had been employing in his production studies from the beginning. Menderhausen argued that one could not, as Douglas often did, both use the results of the Cobb–Douglas regression to measure whether factors were being paid in accordance with their marginal productivity and use the extent of agreement between the estimated k and labor's share as a test of the reliability of the estimates. One must either assume that the marginal productivity theory governed the actual distributive shares and treat the quality of the estimated coefficients as uncertain or assume that the coefficients reflect true marginal productivities, and use them to test the marginal productivity theory of distribution. "It is the old story of the cake one cannot eat and have too" (Mendershausen 1941b, 569). But Mendershausen finished with something of a concession. He recognized that the cross-section studies and time series studies had produced similar estimates. Although he thought the estimation methods dubious and the interpretations of the results incorrect, something noteworthy, an interesting empirical relationship that held across time and across industries at the same point in time, had been discovered.

related to the level of correlation between the independent variables (multicollinearity), the main impact of which is to cause the estimated coefficients to vary widely from sample to sample, or to be sensitive to small changes in the sample, although it also influences the size of the biases generated by any given amount of measurement error. However, Bronfenbrenner was also correct that the bias caused by measurement error was smallest when the chosen direction of minimization corresponded to the variable with the largest error variance, where this error variance included both measurement error and the impact of excluded variables. He had never claimed that bias was eliminated by choosing P as the dependent variable, as long as there was measurement error in the independent variables. Likewise, Gunn had been correct in following Koopmans' lead by considering the relative size of the coefficients as a factor in choosing the direction of minimization, in that when all variables are measured with error, the bias of the estimated structural coefficients produced by choosing a given variable as the dependent variable is decreasing in the relative size of that variable's true structural coefficient.

Under the assumption that measurement errors in the variables were uncorrelated with each other and with values of the three variables (an assumption accepted by all parties to this exchange) it is possible to estimate the relative error variances of P, C, and L in a sample. I have done this with the Commonwealth sample from Gunn and Douglas (1941a). If one then also assumes (as graphical analysis suggested) that the coefficient of C was one-half to one-third the size of the coefficient of L, it is possible to produce estimates of the biases associated with the three sets of regression estimates of k and j produced by minimizing in the three possible directions. This analysis shows that, at least for the Commonwealth data set, Douglas and coauthors had made a good decision. The biases associated with estimation in the P direction are markedly smaller than those associated with minimization in other directions, and lead to coefficients tolerably close to the assumed truth.

This was Mendershausen's last published comment on the Douglas research program, and Douglas's subsequent remarks on Mendershausen's criticisms treated them dismissively rather than seriously. Throughout the exchange Mendershausen followed the practice, established by Frisch in his confluence analysis, of treating all variables in a statistical analysis symmetrically. Collinearity between P and L or P and C was analytically identical to collinearity between L and C, and there was never a sense given of what an acceptable amount of intercorrelation between the variables might look like, only that all the graphical evidence that he had seen indicated that there was too much of it in Douglas's data. He never really engaged the arguments of Douglas and associates that combined statistical reasoning with assumptions about causality to make decisions about specification of the regression and interpretation of estimates.

A third production function study by Gunn and Douglas (1941c) once again used Australian data, this time four cross sections of industry data for the Commonwealth as a whole. The article began with a declaration that after many studies, Douglas and associates had finally determined that the unrestricted Cobb–Douglas equation was a suitable mathematical function for describing the production function for manufacturing. The function could be used to "test statistically some of the conclusions of the theory of production which are rather widely accepted." A noteworthy change in the article was a presentation of a formal statement of that theory of production in mathematical terms. It was based on R. D. G. Allen's mathematical theory of the firm (Allen 1938), and probably reflects the influence of Gregg Lewis, who was thanked in the acknowledgment footnote.

This was Douglas's most explicit move yet to link his production research program to the movement within the neoclassical econometric camp towards more rigorous mathematical representations of theoretical propositions and more explicit adherence to methodological individualism. The new mathematical model began with a general production function $x = f(a, b)$, a profit function $V = xp_x - ap_a - bp_b$, and the assumption that the entrepreneur maximized the profit function subject to the constraint given by the production function. Two cases were then considered, one in which the behavior of the "production unit" could not affect any of the prices, and one in which it could affect the output price but not the input prices. Setting the derivatives of the constrained profit function equal to zero led to the conclusion that "the price per unit of a factor is proportional to its marginal productivity. In the first case it is proportional to the price of the product; in the second it is the price of the product multiplied by one minus the price flexibility" (Gunn and Douglas 1941c, 110). This second proportionality factor was written $(1 - (1/\eta))$, where η was the absolute value of the elasticity of demand for the product and in theory had to take a value greater than one.

This general model was then restated in terms of the specific production function $P = bL^kC^j$, with a note made that when P represented value added rather than physical product, it stood for physical product times product price. The conditions regarding labor's share then became $(W/P) = k$ in the first case, and $W/P = k(1 - (1/\eta))$ in the second. These results, with their implication that imperfect competition in product markets would cause k to fall below labor's share, again contradicted Bronfenbrenner and Douglas's (1939) argument that when P was measured as value added, it was not possible to detect monopolistic exploitation, a contradiction that arose from an error in Gunn and Douglas's analysis of their model.[29]

The model was followed by an admission that the empirical measures available for estimating k did not correspond exactly to the theoretical terms in the model, particularly the capital term. Also, it was admitted that the model had not been specific as to whether the "producing unit" was a firm or industry. However, Gunn and Douglas again argued that even though there was no generally available data for individual firms, dividing the industry-level aggregates that were available by the number of plants in the industry would allow estimation of a production function that captured the production relations in a representative firm. Further, estimates derived using these average measures would correspond to the version of the model in which the producing unit's decisions had no impact on the product price, while estimates derived using the industry-level aggregate measures would correspond to the case in which the price of the product was influenced by the volume of output of the producing unit.

The four Australian cross sections used to estimate the production function came from years between 1912 and 1937, and included about 85 industries each. Gunn and Douglas avoided years of boom or recession, a point they demonstrated with a sketch of the recent history of Australian business conditions. A brief account of Commonwealth-level wage regulation was also provided to flesh out a claim that the years chosen were not those abnormally affected by sudden changes in wages. Although previous

[29] In equation (8') of Gunn and Douglas (1941c), the substitution of $p(\partial P/\partial L)$ for $\partial P/\partial L$ requires that product price p be unaffected by changes in L, which runs counter to the assumption of case (b) that product price is affected by output. Fixing this error leads to the result stated in Bronfenbrenner and Douglas (1939) that k will equal labor's share even in the presence of monopoly (i.e., "sensitivity of price to the output decision of the production unit").

Douglas studies had frequently made reference to Australian wage regulation in explaining the behavior of labor's share in Australia, in this paper wage regulation was represented as an aid to the attempt to estimate a production function. The model did, after all, assume that producing units regarded the prices of inputs as given, an assumption more likely to be met in an economy in which wages were set by the government.

The regression equation to be estimated was presented, and described as a conditional mathematical expectation. Explicit reference to Mendershausen was confined to a footnote that pointed readers to Gunn and Douglas's remarks in the *American Economic Review* exchange, and minimization in the P direction was justified by mentioning the lack of measurement error in L, and the presence in P of "the more important type of fluctuations . . . of somewhat the same nature as biological fluctuation," which were due to shifting product demand curves.

However, as we have seen, Douglas regarded the "instability problem" cited by Mendershausen and embodied in his pinhead graphs as something to be reckoned with. With Bronfenbrenner he had employed stability tests, and with Gunn he had developed graphical approaches to showing that his cross-section data outlined a stable plane rather than an unstable line in three-dimensional space. But Mendershausen had not budged, calling Gunn and Douglas's graphs a "faulty demonstration" of the absence of multicollinearity, which was apparent to him "even in the absence of a three-dimensional scatter diagram" (Mendershausen 1941, 563). So, Gunn and Douglas now offered what they likely considered a conclusive refutation of the instability charge: a photograph of a three-dimensional model of one of the cross-section samples, complete with pins, large white pinheads, and a plexiglass plane corresponding to the estimated production function. Readers were left to judge for themselves, but I doubt that many would have disagreed with the authors' assessment: labor, capital, and product did tend to increase together, but not uniformly, and there was sufficient scatter to determine a plane.[30]

The regression results were presented in the ordinary tabular fashion as well. When the regression was estimated using the plant average data, k values ranged from .5 to .6, while using the industry-level data yielded k values ranging from .49 to .59. Values of k+j were never more than .07 from unity, close enough on the whole to indicate to the authors an approximately linear homogenous production function. Since the k

[30] Douglas had wanted to make a three-dimensional model for the 1919 US cross section, but the sample size (>500) was prohibitively large (Gunn and Douglas 1941a, 75).

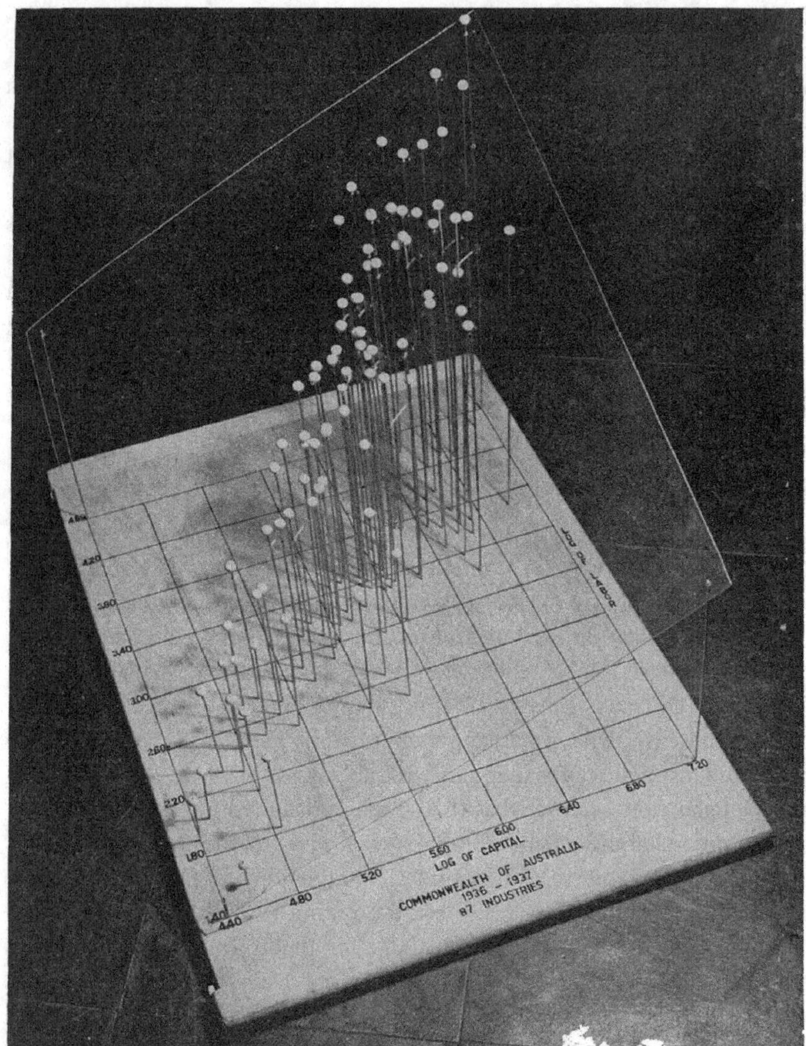

Figure 2.6 A three-dimensional model of a data set used in Gunn and Douglas (1941c), commissioned by Douglas to show that multicollinearity was not a serious problem

estimates were "appreciably" lower than those from other cross-section studies of Australian data (which averaged about .65), Gunn and Douglas did a thorough but inconclusive exploration of whether this was due to differences across studies in the way the variables were measured.

Measurement issues were also discussed in conjunction with the analysis of labor's share, or W/P. Unlike the Commonwealth cross section used in Gunn and Douglas (1941a), the current cross sections did not allow taxes, depreciation, and insurance to be deducted from the P measure, or the cost of workers' compensation insurance to be added to the W measure. Despite this, Gunn and Douglas found a level of agreement between the k estimate and labor's share that they considered "truly astonishing." Only once was the difference greater than a standard error of the k estimate. Gunn and Douglas concluded: "These results might be taken as an indication that for manufacturing industries in these particular years the elasticity of demand for their products was very high .... This would mean that the industries were operating under conditions which were approximately those of perfect competition in the markets for the factors (Gunn and Douglas 1941c, 127)." This shows an apparent continuing confusion over whether the cross-section Cobb–Douglas regression could detect monopolistic exploitation, as the specific reference to competition in factor markets, while consistent with the argument found in Brofenbrenner and Douglas (1939), does not really follow from the discussion of the elasticity of the industries' product demand curves.

Gunn and Douglas again presented a graph that plotted P against P', and associated graphs of the distributions of the residuals for all four cross sections, in order to show that the fitted equations "furnished a good description of production in the manufacturing industries" (Gunn and Douglas 1941c, 122). Douglas found supporting evidence in another aspect of the residuals as well. As mentioned in Chapter 1, in discussing his time series results Douglas had argued that large residuals could actually increase the credibility of the estimated production function (be "hewers of wood and drawers of water" for the function, as he once put it [Brofenbrenner and Douglas 1939, fn. 29]) if it were possible to identify reasons that the year associated with the large residual would be one in which the function would be expected to fit poorly. Douglas now introduced a cross-section version of this type of argument, again showing his tendency to use economic reasoning to interpret statistical results and defend the legitimacy of his procedure:

> If the point for a certain industry lies outside two standard errors of the estimate, it may be due to either of two causes. The production function for that particular industry may differ from the one we have used, or the price of the product may be extremely high or low in comparison with other products whose manufacture involves the same amount of labor and capital. We tabulated the industries which fell outside two standard errors and found:
>
> (a) arms and explosives, and shipbuilding were below 2S in two years,
> (b) tobacco was above 2S in two years,

(c) metal and ore reduction was above 2S in two years, lead mills and shot work in one year, and white lead paints, varnishes, etc. in one year.

It seems probable that arms and explosives and shipbuilding were subsidized in some fashion, that tobacco was a monopoly, and that the production function for mining and related processes differed from that for manufacturing. This is not surprising!

(Gunn and Douglas 1941c, 123)

The final paper coauthored by Gunn and Douglas estimated the regression using data from the 1914 US Census of Manufactures. By now the format of the cross-section studies had become routine. The k and j estimates were .61 and .35, which summed to a value sufficiently close to unity for the authors to declare that manufacturing was characterized by constant returns to scale. They went on to discuss the meaning and significance of the linear homogeneity of the estimated production function, including the point first made in Bronfenbrenner and Douglas's article about linear homogeneity of the production function as an equilibrium condition in a perfectly competitive economy. Based on this argument, they would later in the paper make the new move of citing the closeness to unity of the k+j estimate as evidence that the economy was operating under competitive conditions.

The graphs of P and P' and the residual plots were presented, and Douglas again used the large residuals as evidence of the quality of the regression: "Of the fourteen industries whose actual value of product differed from the computed by more than two standard errors of estimate, all but one were of a somewhat odd and esoteric nature and might be expected to display some eccentricity of behavior" (600). Readers were provided with a list of these industries, which included airplane parts, cordials and flavoring syrups, and fountain pens.

Labor's share for 1914 was within one standard error of the k estimate, and the authors inferred from this, combined with the k+j estimate, that "there was probably much more competition in the economy in 1914 than contemporary writers have sometimes assumed" (Gunn and Douglas 1942, 601), without specifying whether they meant competition in product markets or in factor markets. But the k estimate was well below the .75 estimates found for the United States in previous cross-section and time series studies. The authors attributed this to the depressed state of the economy in 1914, but their reasoning was tersely stated and difficult to follow.

The article ended with a mention of Mendershausen's criticisms, but with a significant shift in tone and style from respectful and technical to disdainful. The Mendershausen criticisms were "sterile." "This group" rejected any analysis that did not "show every conceivable point on a production surface." Then in a rather colorful passage, Douglas summarized the arguments about causality and acceptable versus unacceptable collinearity that he felt the stubborn Mendershausen had ignored:

> Enormous quantities of labor are seldom wedded to minute quantities of capital, any more than giants and pygmies are often mated in real life. It may be remembered that General Tom Thumb married the charming dwarf, Lavinia Warren, and not Barnum's other protégée, the giantess, Anna Swan. So it is in general. Even though there is a tendency for increased quantities of both labor and capital to be associated with increased product, it is surely the worst form of scholasticism to reason that it is the increased product which gives rise to the increased quantities of capital and labor. Because the statures of husbands and wives tend to be positively associated with each other and with that of their offspring, would the high priests of confluence analysis maintain that it was the stature of the children which helped determine that of their parents?
>
> (Gunn and Douglas 1942, 602)

But Douglas could be stubborn in the face of criticism as well, as he showed by quoting again the passage from Smith's dissertation about using regression to estimate a variable, even though Mendershausen had convincingly shown the point of the passage to be irrelevant to the issues that he and Douglas had been debating. It was not clear whether Douglas had accepted Mendershausen's criticism about having his cake and eating it too. However, he did not offer the closeness of k and labor's share as a validation of the production function estimates, only as a test of the theory of perfect competition. And the organization of the paper could be taken to imply a certain logical order in the empirical strategy: first one established the estimates as credible measures of the marginal productivity of capital and labor through the comparison to the results of earlier studies and the analysis of the residuals; then, implicitly maintaining the marginal productivity theory of distribution, these validated estimates were used to test for competition.

NEW RESULTS AND NEW INTERPRETATIONS: THE FINAL CROSS-SECTION STUDIES

In 1943, while Douglas was serving in the Marine Corps, two more production studies were published.[31] Daly, Olson, and Douglas (1943)

[31] Indeed, Douglas was still revising these papers while in the service. See letters from Douglas to Julia and Gregg Lewis, 9/ 17/42; "Friday," 1943; and February 28, 1943, Paul H. Douglas papers, Box 1, folders 1 and 2.

was a brief paper based on data from the 1904 US Census of Manufactures.[32] The k estimate was close to W/P, and of k+j was close to one. Implicitly maintaining the assumption that the production function had accurately measured the marginal productivities of labor and capital, the authors argued that this showed that labor received its marginal product, that there was "a greater degree of competition than is commonly believed," and that the production function was linear homogenous.

Daly and Douglas (1943) was a more substantial article published in the *Journal of the American Statistical Association.* It reported results of estimating the regression with four cross sections of Canadian industry-level data on manufacturing, with each cross section coming from an economically "normal" year. The first feature of the results highlighted by the authors was the proximity of k+j to unity in all four cross sections, similar to what had been found in "virtually all the other studies," which "corroborates the deductive conclusion drawn that under competition production is carried to the point of lowest cost on the average total unit cost curve which is the point of constant costs" (Daly and Douglas 1943, 179). This statement evidences a new perspective developing among the Douglas group on the significance of value of k+j. In *The Theory of Wages*, Douglas had represented the assumption k+j=1 as a good first approximation to the true law of production, one that could be defended with economic logic. In the subsequent papers, in which the assumption was relaxed, the estimated value of k+j was still described strictly in terms of what it revealed about production relations: were there constant returns to scale? Was the production function linear homogenous? The first hint that there was a relationship between the returns to scale of a production function and equilibrium in the competitive model had appeared in the theoretical part of Bronfenbrenner and Douglas (1939), as noted earlier; the link was mentioned more explicitly in Gunn and Douglas's (1942) discussion of the Euler equation, and in Daly, Olson, and Douglas (1943).[33] In the 1943 paper, this line of thinking was taken to its conclusion: in addition to measuring a characteristic of the production function, the estimated value of k+j was to be seen as a test of an equilibrium condition of the competitive neoclassical model. Although this was not mentioned, it

[32] Ernest Olson and Patricia Daly were graduate students at the University of Chicago. Olson's dissertation estimated something like Douglas's cross-section regression using nations as the unit of analysis (Olson 1948), and he went on to work for many years for the Board of Governors of the Federal Reserve System.

[33] The wording of this latter paper still left it a bit unclear as to whether a test of j+k=1 was a test for competition, linear homogeneity of the production function, or both.

also provided a test of competition in product markets that had been lost with the switch from physical value to value-added measures of P.

The values of k found for the Canadian cross sections were lower than those found for the United States, but Douglas reminded readers that he had never claimed that the value of k would be the same for all economies and periods. The authors speculated that the higher value of k for the United States was likely a consequence of the greater amount of capital per worker in the United States relative to Canada.

The Canadian data offered the advantage of explicitly reporting values for fixed capital and working capital. Douglas had always argued that fixed capital was the appropriate capital concept for production function estimation, but in the US data used for the cross-section studies, only total capital was reported. In Bronfenbrenner and Douglas (1939), an attempt had been made to estimate a fixed-capital variable on the basis of the reported value of total capital, but results obtained using this variable were less satisfactory than those obtained using the total capital measure. Daly and Douglas now reported two sets of estimates, one resulting from the use of the total capital measure and one from the use of the fixed-capital variable, but gave preference to the former. They offered no explanation for this decision, nor did they offer any explanations of why the k estimate tended to be lower when fixed capital was used, although they could have referred back to Clark's (1928) argument.

The now standard analysis of residuals was described, although this time it was accompanied by an explication that reveals the vision the Douglas group had developed of how the Cobb–Douglas regression extracted, from statistical data, the causal relationship portrayed in the Cobb–Douglas equation. The "modern theory of causation," the authors explained, did not require an exact identity of P and P' in every industry, only that the causal forces represented by the Cobb–Douglas equation expressed themselves in the data as "norms" or averages, as they are accompanied by a symmetric set of variations arising from several other sources. The first such source listed was measurement error, named without any elaboration or reference to the debate with Mendershausen. A second was movements of industry prices, due to the shifting of product demand curves. Differences across industries in the coefficients of capital and labor were listed as a third source of variation, a possibility not previously mentioned in the Douglas studies. "We have never maintained," the authors noted, presumably speaking for Douglas, "that labor and capital must have the same exponents in each and every industry." The estimated exponents were instead to be understood as averages of the differing industry exponents, which would be "more or less symmetrically distributed" around their average. Factors besides capital and labor that affected production were a fourth source of variation, while the fifth was "sheer chance." But if all these factors acted randomly, then the values of the exponents of labor and capital would be the main determinants of the level of product, and the estimated formula would be "descriptive and predictive" (Daly and Douglas 1943, 182,184). The finding that the estimated residuals were symmetrically distributed, and actually even closer to zero on average than the estimated standard error of the regression would predict, was said to strengthen the credibility of the estimated production function. The industries that generated residuals more than two standard errors from the mean were listed. Readers were told that the identity of these industries provided further proof of the "general reliability of the formula," but only in the cases of tobacco and breakfast foods, both known to be highly concentrated industries, were economic arguments presented to illustrate this claim.

The final table in the paper compared labor's share to both k and k/(k+j).[34] The authors called this a "test of the function," implicitly making marginal productivity theory and competition the maintained hypotheses, and the reliability of the measured marginal productivities the thing to be tested. Averaging over the four samples, labor's share was almost identical to k, but in 1935 labor's share was 10 percentage points above k, and in 1937 it was 9 percentage points below. In describing these differences, the authors seemed to be minimizing them, calling them "compensating" differences, and referring to them as differences of 10 and 9 "per cent."

By the time Douglas left Chicago for the Marine Corps, he was satisfied that he had successfully defended his program against Mendershausen's attacks. During the war, however, another set of critical articles would appear, raising new questions about Douglas's statistical method and revisiting old ones about the links between the coefficients he was reporting and key theoretical concepts of neoclassical theory.

[34] This was the first appearance in a Douglas study of the idea that labor's share should be compared to k/(k+j) as well as, or rather than, k, the explanation being that under perfect competition one would expect labor's share to be k, "or more properly k/(k+j); k/(k+j) being a more proper representation of labor's share of product under conditions of increasing or decreasing returns where k+j is greater than or less than one." This move gave Douglas an additional degree of freedom for his "labor's share" test of the function, and in the Canadian data k/(k+j) was indeed closer to W/P than was k. However, Daly and Douglas's justification of using k/(j+k) is puzzling in light of their earlier assertion that under perfect competition, j+k=1.

3

Theoretical and Econometric Challenges of the Early 1940s, and Douglas's Final Word

Paul Douglas's active work with the Cobb–Douglas regression was suspended while he served in the military during World War II and recovered from war-related injuries. He returned to his position at the University of Chicago in 1946, and was elected president of the American Economic Association in 1947. Douglas used the occasion of his presidential address to the AEA to offer a summary and assessment of his work with the Cobb–Douglas regression. Shortly after delivering the address, he began a successful campaign for a seat in the United States Senate, where he would serve for 18 years; his career as an economic researcher was over. Thus, Douglas's presidential address can be seen as his final assessment of what he thought he had accomplished, and what could be accomplished, using his regression technique.

Before turning to Douglas's valedictory, however, I discuss several important critical examinations of Douglas's research and of the Cobb–Douglas regression technique in general that had appeared in the journal literature of economics during the war. Douglas himself did not respond to or even mention these critiques in his presidential address. However, they would have an important influence on the life story of the Cobb–Douglas regression in the early decades of its diffusion.

THE TINBERGEN CRITIQUE

Early in 1942, Jan Tinbergen published a critique of Douglas's production function studies in the *Review of the International Statistical Institute*. Although there is little evidence that this article had any impact on discussions of the Cobb–Douglas regression over the next 20 years, it did raise important econometric issues about Douglas's cross-section regression that would soon be independently raised by others.[1] Tinbergen, like Douglas, accepted the concept of an aggregate production function,[2] believed that knowledge of the nature of that function was important "for the study of technical development and its influence on employment," and argued that for this reason Douglas's results warranted a critical examination (Tinbergen 1942, 37).

He began by deriving certain theoretical implications of the assumption that the production function took the Cobb–Douglas form. Some of the implications were familiar, such as the implied constancy of labor's share and the equality of labor's share with k under competition. Others were either new or had not received much attention in the previous literature. For example, if j+k=1 (which Tinbergen argued would approximately be the case for an aggregate production function in which the aggregate values of C and L used in the function were large relative to the optimal size of a firm), labor productivity could only increase if the capital-labor ratio increased. He also showed that the Cobb–Douglas function placed certain important restrictions on the possible values of the elasticity of labor demand, depending on what was assumed about the nature of the demand curves facing firms.

Tinbergen then turned to issues related to the "statistical testing" of the function. The Douglas group, he noted, had made "two series of investigations to test this formula," which he called the "historical" (i.e., time series) and the "geographical" (i.e., cross section). Tinbergen then raised a fundamental econometric issue regarding the Cobb–Douglas regression that heretofore had not been explicitly discussed:

> (We) may start with the general remark that there must be a certain variance in the figures if we are to find the values for λ and μ [Tinbergen's symbols for k and j]. How does this variance come about in the theoretical picture relating to the formula used? It is by the variations in the factors of production that it comes about. If, e.g. capital is scarce, its price will be high and this will induce the entrepreneur to use relatively little capital and relatively much labour. It is only by price changes that, in this theory, the relation between labour and capital used is changed"
>
> (Tinbergen 1942, 42).

[1] There is no citation to the article prior to 1962 in JSTOR or Google Scholar. More importantly it is not cited in Marschak and Andrews (1945) or Phelps Brown (1957), two of the most prominent critiques of the Douglas program.

[2] "We have to define which of all the possible production functions is the subject of our present investigation. As to the nature of the product, it is the combined product of all manufacturing industries that we will consider" (Tinbergen 1942, 37).

In other words, if one assumed that there were a single production function defining the amount of output that would be produced by various combinations of inputs, the statistical data needed to estimate this production function must include observations with different values of the capital-labor ratio, and these different values must arise due to differences in the prices of capital and labor associated with the different observations in the data. In the historical studies, Tinbergen explained, such price differences would exist due to the growing relative abundance of capital over time. But Tinbergen accepted Mendershausen's assertion that there was too much multicollinearity in the time series data to allow accurate estimation of separate j and k values, citing the large variation in the values of j and k produced when different directions of minimization were chosen. Only by estimating the restricted version of the regression could this problem be avoided.

For the geographical investigations, Tinbergen explained, the "theoretical picture" underlying the estimation of the production function required that the relative scarcity of labor would have to differ from region to region, leading to variation in wages from region to region. It would not be possible to estimate the coefficients of the production function "if there were free competition throughout the whole area considered," for under free competition the wage and the cost of capital would be the same in every region. Moving on to consideration of the unit of analysis that the Douglas team actually used in their cross-section studies, Tinbergen continued:

> Of course, the ratio between capital and labour varies very much from one industry to another, even if free competition between those industries exists. But this is not the type of variance for which our formula accounts. If the same wage and interest rate prevail in two industries, the formula cannot but give the same value for the ratio of labour to capital used. The variance remaining even under the conditions of free competition can only be accounted for by taking different production functions for different industries
>
> (Tinbergen 1942, 42).

Tinbergen presented these two graphs to further elucidate his point.

Tinbergen's Figure 1 (Figure 3.1) represented the case in which there was a single production function, and observed variation of the ratio of labor to capital occurred due to differences in the factor price ratio. The curved line was the unit production function, that is, the locus of combinations of capital and labor that would yield one unit of output. The straight lines were "cost lines," showing the locus of combinations of capital and labor having the same total cost, with line DF corresponding to one factor

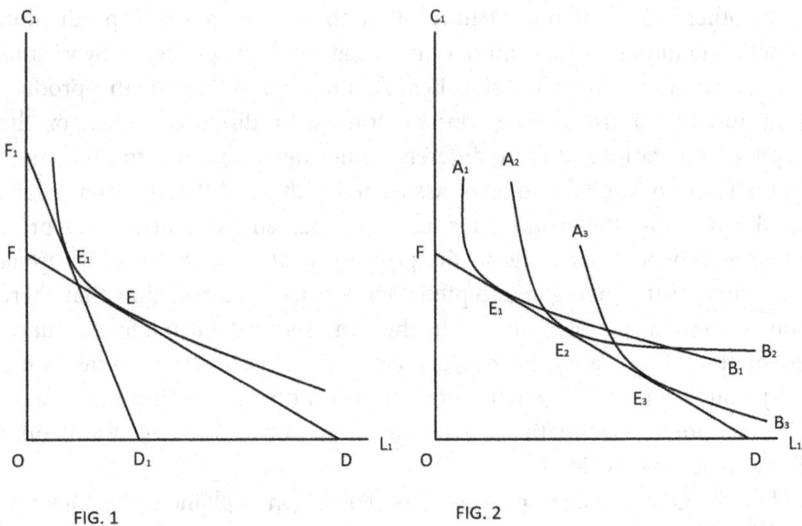

Figure 3.1 Graphs illustrating Jan Tinbergen's concerns about what the cross-section Cobb–Douglas regression might really be estimating

price ratio and line D_1F_1 corresponding to another. E would be the cheapest point of production (that is, the capital-labor ratio that would prevail under competitive conditions) if the factor price ratio were as represented by DF, while E_1 would be the observed capital-labor ratio if the factor price ratio were as represented by D_1F_1. If we observed enough different factor price ratios, the parameters of the single unit production function could be estimated, or, as Tinbergen actually put it, "The various points E, E_1, . . . realised in different conditions of relative scarcity of labour and capital, all ly [*sic*] on the unit production curve; this may be determined if only we are given enough points E, E_1, etc. (Tinbergen 1942, 43)."

Tinbergen's Figure 2 (Figure 3.1) represented the case in which the variation in capital-labor ratios across industries occurred because different industries had different production functions but competed in the same factor markets, and so paid the same prices for labor and capital. In this case, the three curved lines represented, for three different industries, the combinations of labor and capital that produced a quantity of output that would sell for some given price (e.g., the combinations producing \$1 worth of output in each industry). Under competitive conditions, each of the industries would have the same average cost, so, if DF represented the common factor price ratio faced by all, E_1, E_2, and E_3 would be the equilibrium values of the capital-labor ratio for the different industries.

In his cross-section studies, according to Tinbergen, Douglas thought in terms of one production function, so acted as if "the chart he obtains were no. 1."[3] But this could only be the case if there were no competition among the various industries for labor and capital, and they all had the same production function. Douglas "would ascribe the fact that in electricity power plants so much capital and so little labour was used to the cheap terms on which capital can be obtained by that industry and the high wages which it has to pay" (Tinbergen 1942, 44). Tinbergen believed that Douglas's data gave him something more like what was shown in his Figure 2 (Figure 3.1): a set of points along the cost line. Douglas could have obtained a much tighter fit to the cost line if he had measured the labor input with wages paid instead of employment, and had been able to use income from capital rather than a monetary valuation of the capital stock as his capital variable.

Tinbergen showed mathematically that if Douglas were actually estimating the cost line in his cross-section studies, the elasticity of output with respect to labor would equal labor's share. Tinbergen concluded that the cross-section studies did not yield production function estimates but instead were actually estimating the cost line. Only the "historical" studies were valid, and then, because of the multicollinearity problem, only when the restricted form was used. The similarity between coefficients from the cross-section studies and those from the time series studies arose only because the elasticity of output with respect to labor yielded by the Cobb–Douglas production function and the elasticity of value added with respect to labor along the cost line were both equal to labor's share.

But having pronounced as "valid" the results of a restricted Cobb–Douglas regression estimated with time series data, Tinbergen raised an objection even to that approach: it did not allow for technical change – a problem, Tinbergen pointed out, that Douglas himself had admitted in *The Theory of Wages*. Tinbergen suggested, as a simple approach to this problem, adding "time as an additional variable" to the restricted regression, that is, $\ln(P/C) = b + at + k\ln(L/C)$, where t is a trend term.[4]

[3] Recall that Douglas actually allowed that different industries could have different production functions, and that he was estimating average values for j and k.

[4] Tinbergen seems to have overlooked the estimates reported by Douglas produced by estimating the regression using trend ratios of the variables, but admittedly Douglas did not link these estimates to the problem of accounting for technical change.

Given Mendershausen's findings, however, Tinbergen worried about multicollinearity between time and the capital-labor ratio.[5]

Tinbergen's concerns about the importance of technical change and the collinearity between time and the capital-labor ratio were both confirmed by annual data on P, C, and L for US manufacturing covering the period 1919 to 1938, assembled by Spurgeon Bell (1939). The inadequacy of Douglas's function for explaining aggregate output over a long time period without some adjustment to allow for technical change was demonstrated by the fact that output in 1937 was slightly greater than the output in 1929, although smaller quantities of both capital and labor were employed in the latter year. Adding the trend term did not take care of the problem, however, as the k estimate was greater than one, implying a negative coefficient on capital. Either technological progress was uneven, or the production function was more complicated than the Cobb–Douglas function.

INTERFIRM AND INTRAFIRM PRODUCTION FUNCTIONS: REDER AND BRONFENBRENNER

The main point of Melvin Reder's (1943) "Alternative Interpretation of the Cobb–Douglas Function" was that the statistical finding that the coefficient of labor in a cross-section Cobb–Douglas regression was equal to labor's share was consistent not only with both monopoly and competition in product markets (as a result of the use of the value added measure of product) but also when labor was subject to monopsonistic exploitation. Because of this, Reder concluded, "Much of the economic significance of Douglas's empirical findings is lost" (Reder 1943, 264). Reder derived his result in the context of a partial equilibrium analysis of the firm's employment decision, illustrated on a single graph. His presentation was rather unclear, as evidenced by the fact that subsequent commentators offered differing accounts of what he was assuming and how he had reached his conclusions. He did, however, introduce new terminology for discussing the cross-section Cobb–Douglas regression, terminology that would be adopted by commentators on and users of the Cobb–Douglas regression. Building on the distinction between theoretical and distributive production functions developed in Bronfenbrenner and Douglas (1939),

[5] Tinbergen noted in passing, however, that if we believed that the production function were Cobb–Douglas, labor's share would provide a good estimate of the k coefficient, one that was actually very close to what Douglas had estimated.

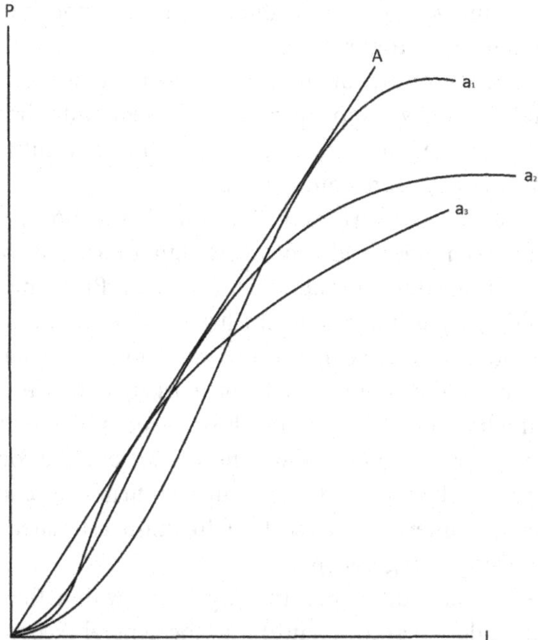

Figure 3.2 Martin Bronfenbrenner's second attempt to illustrate the relationship between Douglas's estimated production function (the interfirm function) and the production functions of individual firms (intrafirm functions)

he proposed that the "ordinary, theoretical concept" of the marginal value productivity of labor, that is, the partial derivative of the value of a single firm's output with respect to that firm's labor input, be called the *intrafirm* marginal value product of labor, while the rate of increase in the value of output "as we pass from one firm to another by varying the quantity of labor employed, but holding the quantity of the other factors . . . constant" be called the *interfirm* marginal value productivity of labor (Reder 1943, 261).

Martin Bronfenbrenner (1944) offered the first response to Reder's article, using it as an opportunity to return to the question of the relationship between the Cobb–Douglas regression and the production function of neoclassical general equilibrium theory, or, as he put it, "the basis of the [Cobb–Douglas regression] in economic theory itself," that he had first tackled in 1939. He complimented Reder for raising the question again, and for shifting the discussion of the Cobb–Douglas function away from the statistical debate over the direction of minimization, a debate that had "petered out, as do many economic controversies, without the conversion of the leading antagonists and without definitive conclusions for the interested spectators" (Bronfenbrenner 1944, 35).[6]

Bronfenbrenner's second attempt at understanding the relationship between what he was now happy to call interfirm and intrafirm production functions was embodied in a graph of P against L, representing a situation in which labor markets were competitive:

The curves a_1, a_2, and a_3 were "intrafirm" functions, showing the relationship between labor and product (holding constant capital) in the average firms of three different industries (although Bronfenbrenner noted that they could apply to three different firms within an industry as well). Each firm would equate the slope of this function to the single wage for labor determined in the competitive labor market, so that the slope of the "a" curve at the level of labor actually chosen would be the same for each firm. The line "A" on the graph showed how a tangent line could be drawn connecting the actually observed points on each firm's "a" curve. This "A" line would be the interfirm production function estimated by a cross-section Cobb–Douglas regression.

Bronfenbrenner also developed this argument within the context of a mathematical model, so as to "relat(e) it to the general theory of economic equilibrium," taking care to make the model formally complete by adding supply functions for capital and labor "necessary to establish equilibrium though unnecessary for the verbal or graphic argument of this essay." The interfirm production function, or "A" curve, was not one of the fundamental equations that determined equilibrium values of the variables, but was an equilibrium condition, "logically posterior to the determination of equilibrium" (Bronfenbrenner 1944, 38).[7]

So, starting with a mathematical, neoclassical model of factor market equilibrium, Bronfenbrenner had derived a relationship between the equilibrium levels of labor, capital, and output chosen by various industries (or firms) that, at least in theory, could be statistically estimated by a cross-section regression. However, he identified two difficulties that his argument raised for the Douglas production studies. First, Bronfenbrenner noted the suggestion of "a critic" that under long-run competitive equilibrium conditions, all firms would have the same "a" curve, and the interfirm

6 Bronfenbrenner added in a footnote that he continued to agree with Douglas's "economic justification" of preferring the P direction.

7 Bronfenbrenner did not say whether he was assuming that all firms (or representative firms within industries) had the same production function, or whether production function(s) took a Cobb–Douglas form. The "a" curves drawn on his graph could not have come from Cobb–Douglas production function, however.

production function would degenerate into a single point. Bronfenbrenner admitted that this seemed to follow from the assumption that there were only two factors, undifferentiated labor and undifferentiated capital, each with one market price, even if one assumed that different firms produced different products. But he argued to the effect that the success of Douglas's statistical studies showed that it was possible to consider labor and capital to be sufficiently heterogeneous across industries to avoid the coincidence of equilibrium points, while sufficiently homogenous to speak of their having single prices.

The second difficulty seemed to him more serious: his model led to the conclusion that the interfirm production function, his "A" line, would be linear in labor and capital, and this created "an interesting disparity . . . between the assumptions of the Cobb–Douglas function and the theory it is designed to verify" (39). Bronfenbrenner believed that this was an "insurmountable difficulty" for the Cobb–Douglas functional form, and argued that if one wished to fit an interfirm production function using cross-section data, the equation $P = b + kL + jC$ should be used. He explained that Douglas had originally rejected this functional form because it did not exhibit diminishing returns, but that this reasoning was based on a false analogy between interfirm and intrafirm production functions. Estimating an interfirm production function with a correctly specified regression could identify the marginal productivity of labor in equilibrium, thus providing the basis for a test of marginal productivity theory. It could not, however, be used to estimate the elasticity of the factor demand curves, since these were functions of the curvature of the interfirm production surface, which, as Bronfenbrenner's graph made clear, was not properly captured by the estimated interfirm production function.[8]

What of Reder's argument that the equality of k with labor's share was consistent with both competition and monopsonistic exploitation? Using his diagram, Bronfenbrenner showed that under monopsony, the slope of the "A" curve (which corresponds to marginal value product of labor estimated by the interfirm production function) would be below the actual marginal value product of labor measured along the "a" curves. Labor's wage would be below the actual marginal value product as well. As Bronfenbrenner understood it, Reder was arguing that it was possible, by

[8] This was a generalization of a point Bronfenbrenner had earlier made in a note, in which he argued that the fact that the Cobb–Douglas equation could not imply an inelastic demand curve for labor made it an inappropriate functional form for estimating the elasticity of labor demand (Bronfenbrenner 1939).

pure chance, for the negative bias in the estimate of labor's value marginal product to equal the extent to which monopsonistic exploitation depressed the wage. Such a coincidence was possible, Bronfenbrenner allowed, but certainly not likely enough to explain the finding, in study after study, that the interfirm estimate of k was very close to labor's share. It seemed much more likely that the frequent equality of the estimated k with labor's share was evidence that factor markets were competitive and that the Cobb–Douglas regression generally provided accurate estimates of k.

Bronfenbrenner had been recruited as a coauthor by Douglas while a graduate student, and in the succeeding years had independently pursued a deeper understanding of the relationship between the statistical results of the production studies and the basic concepts of the formalistic neoclassical value theory being standardized in works like Hicks's (1939) *Value and Capital.* By 1944 Bronfenbrenner still defended the Douglas research program, but more from the position of a friendly critic than a participant: He had determined that the Cobb–Douglas functional form was inappropriate, and that the Douglas methodology could not recover the elasticities of factor demand from cross-section data. There was no indication, however, that he had lost enthusiasm for the program of using statistical methods to estimate the fundamental parameters of production and distribution theory.

MARSCHAK AND ANDREWS: THE COWLES COMMISSION'S PRESCRIPTION FOR PRODUCTION FUNCTION ESTIMATION

In the fall of 1944, *Econometrica* published "Random Simultaneous Equations and the Theory of Production" by Jacob Marschak and William Andrews. Running over 60 pages in length, it was the most comprehensive critical examination of the Douglas program yet published. Marschak (1936) had earlier commented on Douglas's *The Theory of Wages*, enthusiastically endorsing the empirical sprit of the effort, but suggesting that Douglas and those who would follow him should be more attentive to the statistical issues being debated in the empirical literature on demand and to the methods being developed by top econometricians in response to those issues. In a sense his paper with Andrews was in the same vein, as it was in part an assessment of the Douglas program using a sophisticated econometric framework. A more complete understanding of the intent and significance of the Marschak–Andrews article, however, requires some additional context.

Marschak had been appointed director of the Cowles Commission for Econometric Research in 1943. Under his direction, the commission was becoming an agency for building an econometric program consistent with the "probability approach" to econometrics laid out in Haavelmo (1944), unpublished versions of which had been circulating since 1941. In keeping with the idea of econometrics as a synthesis of economic and statistical theory, the Cowles approach embodied a set of methodological heuristics to guide both the creation and the empirical testing of economic theory. The task of understanding economic activity began with the analysis of the choices of individuals acting in their capacities as consumers, producers, and owners of productive factors. Economic theory constituted an explanation of these individual choices and their social consequences, and the propositions of such theory could best be represented as a system of simultaneous equations expressing relationships between potentially observable economic variables. This approach to economic theory, with its emphasis on methodological individualism and mathematical formalism, was exemplified by the Walrasian model of general equilibrium. For the purposes of empirical analysis, these simultaneous equations were to be regarded as probabilistic relationships, that is, the actual relationships between the variables were subject to random fluctuations, although they fluctuated about a central tendency. This was in contrast to the view underlying confluence analysis, in which theory identified deterministic relationships between economic variables that were obscured in the data by measurement error. Haavelmo began, and his Cowles Commission associates continued, the development of statistical techniques that were appropriate to estimating these sorts of simultaneous stochastic relationships.

The Cowles econometricians achieved much in the area of statistical theory, and their contributions have been discussed at length elsewhere. The Cowles program also had a missionary aspect that should not be overlooked. The Cowles associates were enthusiastic about offering Haavelmo's probability approach and the accompanying simultaneous equations framework as a blueprint for reorganizing existing empirical research programs in economics, often at the same time as they used it to undermine the credibility of previous work in those programs. Koopmans' (1947) "Measurement without Theory" essay is an obvious example of this, arguing that the research strategies and empirical methods employed by the National Bureau of Economic Research's much respected business cycle research program were of questionable value, while offering methodological individualism and simultaneous equations modeling as the foundations of a more fruitful approach to understanding and ultimately attenuating economic fluctuations. In Koopmans (1945) and Girshick and Haavelmo (1947), the simultaneous equations framework was portrayed as the culmination and resolution of longstanding debates in the literature on the empirical estimation of demand curves. Haavelmo's (1947) paper for the *Journal of Farm Economics,* explaining the Cowles approach to the statistically sophisticated and policy-oriented audience of agricultural economists, exemplifies another element of the Cowles message during this period: the promise that Cowles methods would lead to empirical results more useful for policy than those of previous empirical research programs.

The Marschak and Andrews article should be seen as part of this effort. Douglas's production studies constituted a well-known, well-established empirical research program. They had attracted the attention of young, energetic neoclassical econometricians (including Douglas's coworkers Bronfenbrenner and H. G. Lewis), who saw it as part of the larger effort to provide empirical content to the theoretical system they favored. This made the Douglas program a promising target for assimilation into the Cowles program: Those who responded favorably to the Douglas program could be more easily convinced than, say, supporters of the National Bureau of Economic Research (NBER) business cycle program that the Cowles researchers shared Douglas's goals, and had developed means to reach them more effectively.

Marschak and Andrews began their article with a tutorial on the basic premises of the Cowles statistical worldview: economists wanted to estimate causal relationships, but could not perform experiments. They could only observe uncontrolled variables produced by a set of interacting economic forces that was well represented by a system of simultaneous equations. The statistical consequences of this were illustrated by comparing the task of an econometrician who wished to estimate a production function to that of the agricultural experimentalist who wished to estimate the relationships between fertilizers and crop yields. Through text and equations, Marschak and Andrews argued that the two researchers were operating in very different statistical environments, with the main difference being the need for the econometrician to take account in his research design of several interrelated random relationships, even if he were primarily interested in only one of them.

This led to a discussion of the "pioneering work" of Douglas and his associates, and how it raised many important issues that had also been raised in the statistical literature on supply and demand curves. In that literature, there was a debate over whether various estimated relationships between price and quantity really represented the supply or demand curves of theory, or whether they were "mongrel curves" that represented the combined action of the supply and demand functions, but revealed little about either. Now authors such as Reder and Bronfenbrenner were raising doubts as to whether the input-output relationships Douglas had estimated revealed anything about the "production functions of theory," by which Marshack and Andrews meant the production functions associated with individual firms. Readers were told that the work of Haavelmo had clarified the debate over statistical demand and supply curves, and that the lessons learned from that controversy (lessons that were explicated with four more pages of equation-laden text) could be fruitfully applied to Douglas's problem. One important conclusion was that "production functions" estimated by application of least squares to a single equation were not the production functions of economic theory, and were of limited value. Only estimates of the production functions of theory would allow the econometrician "to act like an engineer, i.e., to advise upon the likely result of some deliberate action of a government or a firm," and these estimates could only be obtained using statistical methods appropriate to a simultaneous equations setting.

Marschak and Andrews next embedded the production function in a system of 10 equations describing the behavior of an individual firm. The system included behavioral equations describing the firm's demands for the two inputs, derived from the assumption of profit maximization subject to the constraint of the firm's production function. The model was general enough to describe firms operating in both perfectly and imperfectly competitive product and input markets, with specific values for certain parameters indicating the presence of perfect competition. For "statistical manageability" the production function was assumed to take the nonrestricted Cobb–Douglas form, and the output and input supply equations were assumed to have constant elasticities. The system was specified as if it were to be estimated with a data set describing individual firms, each potentially observed in more than one time period.

As the model was intended to be stochastic rather than deterministic, Marschak and Andrews enumerated reasons why their equations would not be expected to hold exactly for each observation in the data. These included unmeasured differences across entrepreneurs in ability, drive, or luck, differences across firms or over time in production function parameters or technical efficiency, and so on.[9] After the model was

[9] Marschak and Andrews (1944, 159) attributed to Douglas the assumption that his j and k parameters were constant across time and space, leaving the additive term log(b) as the only variable parameter in his production regression. As noted above, Douglas had specifically denied assuming this in Daly and Douglas (1943).

"stochasticized" in this way, it yielded three random simultaneous equations, one based on the production function and two representing the firm's demand for the labor and capital inputs. The exact form of the three-equation system depended on whether one's data included variables measuring the physical quantities of inputs and outputs or total expenditures on inputs and outputs, but all equations were linear in the logarithms of the variables, that is, they took the form $X_0 = a + bX_1 + cX_2$, with X_0, X_1, and X_2 being the logarithms of observable variables and a, b, and c representing model parameters or functions of model parameters. The authors allowed that in general, one would want to assume that parameters varied across time and space, with the set of parameters applying to each observation modeled as a draw from a well-defined multivariate distribution. "The limitations of statistical tools available," however, required that the problem be simplified. Parameters that multiplied variables (like b and c) had to be regarded as constant, meaning that estimates of parameters like Douglas's j and k had to be considered "average" values whose variances and covariance could not be estimated (Marschak and Andrews 1944, 159). Additive parameters (like a) could be assumed to vary, and the deviations of these variable parameters from their mean values provided a zero mean additive "random term" for each equation.

Marschak and Andrews then provided a rather cumbersome demonstration of how the parameters of the system might be estimated, and why least squares estimation of the parameters of the production equation would produce a "mongrel function." The main exhibit was a graph, showing, in the authors' words, how "the same pair of 'single equation' least squares estimates [of k and j] is compatible with very different combinations of true values" (Marschak and Andrews 1944, 166). An appendix described in more detail how a maximum likelihood method might be used to estimate the parameters of the system. The explications in both the main text and this appendix were complicated by the fact that the system under discussion was not identified, to use the language later popularized by the Cowles econometricians, so that points about how the values calculated from the hypothetical data set were to be used to pin down the values of parameter estimates were interspersed with comments about how various external assumptions based on "economic considerations" or "knowledge additional to the observations" would affect the estimation procedure. There was no intuition provided as to why single-equation estimation of an equation that was part of a system could lead to what later came to be known as simultaneous equations bias, nor any distinction made between this problem and the identification problem. The debate on the estimation of supply and demand curves had provided templates for graphs that would convey this intuition very clearly, but Marschak and Andrews chose to construct a much more complex graph to make their point. In my opinion, their critique of single-equation estimation would have been very difficult to comprehend for anyone who did not already understand the Haavelmo framework.

The model and methods presented by Marschak and Andrews were designed to be used with a sample of firms drawn from a single industry. However, the authors pointed out, neither they nor Douglas and his coauthors had access to such data. Douglas had instead, out of necessity, used aggregate variables – either the totals for the entire manufacturing sector or totals from industries consisting of many firms. This raised further problems. In keeping with the Cowles' commitment to methodological individualism, Marschak and Andrews argued that production functions were characteristics of individual firms, and the "production function" for an aggregate of firms was not even a meaningful concept, unless it was a stable function of the production function parameters of individual firms. One could make an assumption that implied such a stable relationship, and Marschak and Andrews chose to assume that each firm in the industry had the same level of capital, labor, and output. This implied that for estimation purposes, all industry-level variables should be expressed as averages per industry, and weighted by the number of firms in the industry. But they made it clear that this "makeshift" assumption necessitated by data limitations undermined the credibility of the estimates, and that even were data to be available on individual firms, it would be unadvisable to work with a sample that included firms from many different industries, given the assumption that j and k were the same for all firms.

Having built a bridge, however tenuous, between their stochastic simultaneous equations model and production functions that were estimated with aggregate data, Marschak and Andrews presented a table summarizing the results of Douglas's previous studies, noting various ways in which Douglas's methods had fallen short of the procedures they had just outlined for estimation with aggregate data: trends had not been included in the time series studies, k and j had often been restricted to sum to one, industry aggregate variables had often been used instead of per-firm averages, and when per-firm averages were used, they had not been weighted by number of firms. A second table showed the results of reanalyzing the 1909 data used by Bronfenbrenner and Douglas (1939) to show the effects on the estimates of various improvements to Douglas and

Bronfenbrenner's methods, including a redefinition of industries designed to make each industry a more homogenous collection of firms. All of these results were generated using single-equation ordinary least squares regression – no attempt was made to implement the maximum-likelihood technique described in Marschak and Andrews' appendix. These two tables of results were meant to provide a backdrop for a theoretical and statistical critique of the two of the main claims of the Douglas program: that the sum of the estimates of j and k was always close to one, and that the estimated k coefficient tended to be close to labor's share.

The Cowles duo pointed out that Douglas and his colleagues had made various claims about what these findings revealed about the prevalence of perfect competition in markets. Rather than reviewing these claims in detail (which would have been a complicated task, given that the set of claims made was not consistent from study to study), Marschak and Andrews chose to use their simultaneous equations model to determine exactly what one could conclude about competition from these two empirical findings, assuming that they were indeed true. In that model, given that the measure of product was value added, the estimates of j and k were not the coefficients of labor and capital in the production function unless firms were operating as price takers. Otherwise, the estimates represented the production function coefficients multiplied by a factor related to the elasticity of product demand. Thus, to draw conclusions about the returns to scale of the production function required an auxiliary assumption about the extent of competition in product markets.[10] Marschak and Andrew's model also rendered problematic the practice of drawing strong conclusions from the equality of the k estimate and labor's share in total value added. Douglas's original arguments concerning this equality had been based on the fundamental result of J. B. Clark's marginal productivity theory that under competition, labor's wage would equal labor's value of marginal product. In the Marschak/Andrews model (as in some of the models presented in later Douglas studies) the relevant marginal productivity condition was that, for a profit-maximizing firm, k (multiplied by a factor reflecting competitiveness in the product market) equaled the wage (multiplied by a factor reflecting competitiveness in the labor market). This allowed them to conclude that if the k estimate equaled labor's share for each firm (and each firm was maximizing profit), the labor market was

[10] Although one could have derived this conclusion from the model of Gunn and Douglas (1941a) or the discussion of Bronfenbrenner and Douglas (1939), it had never been explicitly stated in any of the Douglas studies.

competitive. However, the equality between the k estimate and labor's share in aggregate output to which the Douglas studies pointed might mask great inequalities at the level of individual industries, already assumed to be made up of identical firms. The data indicated that labor's share did vary considerably from industry to industry, while (by assumption) k was identical across industries, suggesting that the degree of monopsony in labor markets must vary from industry to industry. Marschak and Andrews summarized the actual significance of the two major Douglas findings thusly:

> Provided that there is no monopoly in product markets (1) all production functions are homogenous of first degree; (2) if there is no monopsony in the resource markets, there is "free entry and exit"; (3) either the degree of labor monopsony varies strongly from industry to industry (and firm to firm), fluctuating around unity [or perfect competition]; or profits are not maximized
>
> (Marschak and Andrews 1944, 178).

Of course, one might alternatively conclude that the estimates produced by the Douglas studies were unreliable. To underscore this point, Marschak and Andrews reviewed the various strong assumptions required to link the estimates derived from aggregate data to the parameters of theoretical production functions, and argued that when one really looked at all the Douglas estimates taken together, there were quite a few instances in which the sum of j and k was rather far from one, and the k estimate rather far from labor's share. They gave additional attention to the problem of simultaneous equations bias. Given that in their model, unbiased estimates of j and k could not be identified by the data alone, they described how various alternative assumptions about the values of certain other model parameters could place bounds on the true values of j and k implied by any pair of single-equation estimates of j and k.

The Marschak and Andrews paper can be read as a devastating criticism of Douglas's work, a laundry list of problems and misunderstandings, both theoretical and empirical, that fatally marred the program. But the authors' tone undermined such an interpretation. They proclaimed Douglas a pioneer. They hinted that many of the problems they had identified with the Douglas estimates were due mainly to the inadequate data Douglas had been forced to work with: "(a) limitation, not of statistical tools, but (a more accidental one) of available published data, has made it necessary, in the studies of Douglas as well as our own illustrations, to assume that all firms within an industry are identical" and "with the type of data used here (and also used by Douglas and his collaborators) the discussion was necessarily critical and illustrative" (Marshcak and Andrews 1944, 179, 182). Douglas's results were still important, and revealed that the program itself was a worthwhile and promising one:

> Douglas's estimates . . . exhibit a stability from one year to another which presumably would not be much affected by applying corrections such as in Table 3. Since the least squares estimates are functions of the parameters of the joint distribution of output, labor, and capital, i.e., functions of the [j and k parameters] as well the variances and the covariances of the random components . . . the stability of Douglas's estimates suggest that those parameters change only slowly. This promises significant results as soon as better data are available for the estimation of those parameters
>
> (Marschak and Andrews 1944, 182).

Marschak and Andrews' tempering of their criticisms of Douglas stand in contrast, for example, to Koopmans' tone in his review of the NBER business cycle program. If the grand strategy of the Cowles econometricians was to absorb and restructure the existing fields of empirical economics, then their tactic with respect to the Douglas program was that of the friendly takeover.[11]

The Marschak and Andrews article included several appendices, two of which explored theoretical issues that had been raised in the more recent Douglas articles, particularly Bronfenbrenner and Douglas (1939), and in the exchange between Reder and Bronfenbrenner. One appendix sought to clarify the relationships between several issues that had "played a role in the theory and statistical study of production": the returns to scale in production, perfect competition, profit maximization, and free entry and exit. As discussed earlier, the Douglas team had come to embrace a position with respect to these matters that was rooted in the work of Chicago economists Jacob Viner and Frank Knight: the returns to scale faced by firms may differ at different levels of production, but in long-run competitive equilibrium (with free entry and exit), profit-maximizing firms would operate at a point where production was characterized by constant

[11] Marschak and Andrews' decision not to speak more harshly of Douglas's work may also have been related to circumstances in the University of Chicago's economics department, where at this time there was an "intense struggle" underway between faculty aligned with Frank Knight and faculty aligned with the Cowles Commission (Reder 1982). Differences over matters like the role of empirical work in economics and the potential for economic research to inform interventionist economic policy led to fights over hiring and resources. In Marschak's eyes, Douglas, with his strong record of empirical economic research and his progressive political views, was clearly on the right side of this struggle. To undermine Douglas would have been to alienate a potential ally.

returns to scale, and would earn zero profits. Marschak and Andrews acknowledged in a footnote that this was a theoretically coherent position to take, but the case emphasized in the text was that of a production function that was linear homogenous throughout its range (as was the Cobb–Douglas, if viewed as an "intrafirm" function), which led to an indeterminate long-run competitive equilibrium. Perhaps more interesting, however, was their opinion on the relevance of this debate for empirical research into production:

> Finally and probably most important: the whole problem of reconciling perfect competition, profit maximization, and the instantaneous wiping out of profits hardly arises in reality. A workable empirical hypothesis must not be based on any of these three. It is especially hard to believe that the functions involved would "adjust themselves" to the appropriate shapes with such rapidity, or that profits and losses would vanish so quickly that the statistician's survey would record "long-run" functions and the absence of profits and losses
>
> (Marschak and Andrews 1944, 191).

The empirical approach being rejected in this passage by the Cowles econometricians is arguably the one that Reder (1982), in his history of the University of Chicago's economics department, labeled "tight prior equilibrium." This approach, which by Reder's account emerged at the University of Chicago in the mid-1930s, used models of long-run competitive equilibrium as the framework for the interpretation of statistical results. That is, it was assumed that observed economic variables were, to a good approximation, long-run competitive equilibrium positions, and that deviations from equilibrium positions could be regarded as transitory and random, allowing the economic relationships embodied in the long-run competitive equilibrium model to be expressed in stochastic form.[12] This is clearly the approach used by Bronfenbrenner in his attempts to interpret the results of the cross-section Cobb–Douglas regressions, both in his 1939 paper with Douglas and in Bronfenbrenner (1944). It is also manifest in Gunn and Douglas's (1941c) use of a long-run equilibrium model. There are no formal mathematical models of long-run equilibrium in the earlier Douglas studies, but there is much to indicate that Douglas was comfortable thinking of his estimates in terms of a long-run normal relationship that was obscured in the observed data by random

[12] "In applied work, adherents of [tight prior equilibrium] have a strong tendency to assume that, in the absence of sufficient evidence to the contrary, one may treat observed prices and quantities as good approximations to their long run competitive equilibrium values" (Reder 1982, 12; see p. 11 as well).

disturbances to equilibrium. One can point, for example, to his argument that one source of the error in the cross-section Cobb–Douglas regression equation was the transitory shifting of product demand curves,[13] or his method of explaining deviations from his fitted functions or differences between labor's share and the k estimate in terms of deviations from the conditions required for long-run competitive equilibrium.

Marschak and Andrews' distaste for this "tight prior equilibrium" approach to econometrics was apparent in their second appendix as well. This appendix examined the Reder–Bronfenbrenner discussion of interfirm and intrafirm production functions. Marschak and Andrews found Reder's argument difficult to understand, but opined that his analysis "seem(ed) to point in the right direction" (192). Turning to Bronfenbrenner (1944), they determined that Bronfebrenner's "interfirm production function" was actually a zero-profit condition/budget constraint: "Thus, perfect competition is assumed, not only in the sense of the prices being independent of any single firm's action; but also in the sense of instantaneous free entry of exit of firms, instantaneously destroying profits and losses" (Marschak and Andrews 1944, 192, 193). They then criticized Bronfenbrenner's failure to add firm-specific random terms to the equation that described the interfirm production function, and his use of the "tight prior equilibrium" approach:

> Hence, the empirically fitted function must exactly coincide with [the theoretical interfirm function]. We do not think this is realistic. Entry and exit of firms . . . can hardly be regarded as rapid enough to ensure, at any time, actual absence of profits and losses among statistically observed firms. If therefore, the "zero-profits" equation can be included at all in the system of equations describing a firm, with a random term to denote a profit (or loss), that random term is certainly subject to strong fluctuations from firm to firm. There is therefore, little likelihood that a function fitted, e.g., by the least squares [*sic*] would give even an approximation of [Bronfenbrenner's interfirm production function]
>
> (Marschak and Andrews 1944, 193).[14]

13 "In a state of perfect equilibrium the P's would be determined by L and C alone. But economic society is virtually never in equilibrium, though always moving towards it. One of the chief disturbing factors is the shifting of demand curves, which is not invariably accompanied in the short run by corresponding changes in labor and capital . . .. In other words, forces outside the formula, notably alterations in demand, cause the observed P values to shift from the normal plane of relationship . . .. These departures, however, might be expected to cancel each other out" (Gunn and Douglas 1940, 408).

14 Marschak and Andrew's criticism of Bronfenbrenner's failure to add random terms to his equations seems disingenuous; it would be hard to read the discussion of the direction of minimization question in Bronfebrenner and Douglas (1939) and still assert that

In a footnote to the above passage, which was itself in an appendix, Marschak and Andrews pointed out that if the very unlikely long-run equilibrium assumption were granted, what Bronfenbrenner was really demonstrating was that Douglas's cross-section regressions were actually estimating budget constraints, that is, the necessary identity of value added to the sum of labor costs and capital costs. This, of course, was the point made by Tinbergen (1942), and in retrospect one can see the obvious resemblance between Bronfenbrenner's key graph (Figure 3.2) and Tinbergen's diagram of three isoquants tangent to a single cost line (in Figure 3.1). In any case, Marschak and Andrews attributed to Bronfenbrenner the technically correct position that his interfirm production function was, under the assumption of a zero-profit equilibrium, a restatement of the zero-profit condition, that is, a budget constraint. If this was really what Douglas's cross-section studies were estimating, claimed Marschak and Andrews, an approximate equality of the k estimate and labor's share would be observed whatever the state of competition in product or factor markets, since the budget constraint implied an elasticity of value added with respect to labor that would approximate labor's share of value added.

Victor Smith's Production Function for the Automobile Industry

In 1941 Victor Smith had completed a dissertation at Northwestern University entitled "An Application and Critique of Certain Methods for the Determination of a Statistical Production Function for the Canadian Automobile Industry, 1917–1930." It was not until 1945, however, that material from the dissertation was published, with a description of the application appearing in *Econometrica* (Smith 1945a), and the critique in the *Quarterly Journal of Economics* (Smith 1945b). Smith's application is interesting in that it came from outside the Douglas group, was the first published Cobb–Douglas regression using industry-level data from a single industry, and was the first time series application to be published since Douglas had introduced his cross-section approach.

Smith was particularly interested in what he called the "degree" of the production function, by which he meant the value of k+j. His input and output variables were in value terms: the value of production, the reported book value of capital, and wage bill, and he contrasted the "value function"

Bronfenbrenner thought that a statistically fitted equation "must exactly coincide" with his theoretical equation.

that characterized the relationships between such variables with the "physical functions" estimated in previous time series studies, "in conformity with the practice of theorists" (Smith 1945a, 262).[15] Differences between the estimates from the two types of function could arise due to imperfect competition and fluctuations over time in relative prices of inputs and output. The "value" production function, Smith argued, better captured the economic problem faced by business. He also noted that an estimated value function would likely have a lower degree than an estimated technical function, as expansion of the industry would depress prices.

Smith reported results from twelve regression specifications: minimizing in the P, L, and C directions, with and without a quadratic time trend (that is, the addition of year and the square of year as independent variables), using contemporaneous or lagged capital. Smith justified the use of the lagged value of capital by noting that the reported capital values were end-of-the-year estimates. Smith concluded that a bunch-map analysis, which he did not show, indicated that the specifications using lagged capital were more "stable." Smith did not report the standard errors of the estimated coefficients, but he did indicate their significance levels, and made a distinction between coefficients that were insignificant and those that were "useless," by which he meant smaller than their standard errors.

Smith's many specifications produced a wide range of estimates. Indeed, in an unusual editor's note at the beginning of the article, *Econometrica* editor Ragnar Frisch commented that the main contribution of the article was not its numerical results, but the demonstration of their sensitivity to "peculiarities of statistical techniques" (Smith 1945a, 260).[16] Given his particular concern with the "degree" of the function, Smith tested in each specification whether the value of k+j was significantly different from one, using the formulas for the standard error of the k+j estimate reported in Bronfenbrenner and Douglas (1939). He found that it almost always was; and that the sum was less than one for specifications that included a trend, and greater than one for those that did not.

It is easy to imagine that Smith's search for explanations of the variability of his results contributed to the length and severity of the "critique"

[15] Smith termed Douglas's cross-section regressions "hybrid" functions, mixing value capital with physical quantity of labor.

[16] Frisch's note also pointed out that the relation estimated by Smith was "between values of output, labor, and capital, while the Cobb–Douglas Function, as usually understood, deals with the relationship between the corresponding physical quantities." Frisch's sense that there was a "usual" understanding of the function at this time is contrary to my own, unless he is speaking only of the function as comprehended by theorists.

portion of his dissertation. He opened by criticizing the Douglas team for making claims "beyond the evidence" provided by their statistical results regarding returns to scale and the extent of competition in the economy. These arose from a failure to fully appreciate the size of the gap between the production functions of economic theory (by which Smith seemed to mean the production functions of individual firms) and the "statistical production functions" produced by their data.[17] The sources of this gap and its consequences for economists' ability to draw conclusions from statistical production functions became the organizing theme for the rest of the critique.

Smith did not make use of a mathematical model. He mentioned in a note that he had only become aware of the Marschak and Andrews article after having written his paper. Two of his main points, however, were similar to points made by Marschak and Andrews. He made the first of these by describing a hypothetical experimental procedure for producing data that would allow the statistical estimation of the production function of economic theory: an experimental variation of quantities of capital and labor used in production, without alteration of the technological methods used. Least squares analysis, he pointed out, had been designed for use with such experimental data. In the statistical data actually available, however, changes in the amount of labor and capital used were the results of management reactions to changes in expectations and passing events. "Under such circumstances the method of least squares will not give us results analogous to those from experiment" (Smith 1945b, 546).[18]

Next, Smith allowed that perfect competition and long-run equilibrium could substitute for experiment, explicitly accepting Bronfenbrenner's (1944) argument that under such circumstances the cross-section statistical production function would produce the intrafirm marginal value products of theory. But, Smith went on, the available data did not come from an economy in a long-run competitive equilibrium. They came from a dynamic economy in which changing conditions led to continual changes in the optimal choices of inputs, managers made mistakes, short-run optimality differed from long-run optimality, and adjustment took time

[17] Smith also correctly observed that the Douglas studies had at times contradicted one another regarding whether their procedure could test for both monopolistic and monopsonistic exploitation, and about how often labor's share turned out to be approximately equal to the k estimate.

[18] Smith did not elaborate further on this point; in particular, he did not develop the "simultaneous equations bias" argument that was so important to the Cowles researchers.

and cost money. Like Marschak and Andrews, Smith argued that statistics reflecting such short-run, imperfect, and incomplete adjustments were not useful for testing propositions associated with a theoretical long-run competitive equilibrium.

Almost half the paper was devoted to discussing problems of measurement that would cause statistically determined production functions to deviate from theoretical production functions. By far most of this dealt with the problems of producing a measure of capital that corresponded to the theoretical concept, reiterating the criticisms of Slichter (1928), and arguing that many of the problems with the cross-section industry-level data that Douglas and his coauthors had identified were more serious than they had been willing to admit.

Most of Smiths's points were not new by the time they were published in 1945, but their potential impact was increased by the fact that they had been collected in one place, and published in a widely read journal. Also, Smith's nonmathematical presentation of the criticisms of Marschak and Andrews made them more accessible to the average academic economist. However, in his concluding remarks, Smith took a position much like that taken by Durand (1937) in his critique of *The Theory of Wages*: Douglas's estimates may not reveal anything about the production functions of theory, nor about the extent of competition, but this was not a reason to stop producing statistical production functions:

> But it is well to emphasize that the argument is not intended to suggest that the statistical production function is of no importance. The statistical function represents relationships that prevail in a dynamic, disequilibrium economy, an economy in which time is consumed in making an investment, and in which value capital must be invested before physical capital is ready for use, and remains invested even though the physical capital is not fully used. The statistical function would be more useful if its meaning could be more precisely defined, and if we had more varied experience with it . . .. With the accumulation of experience and knowledge the time may come when we shall be able to interpret these functions with confidence
>
> (Smith 1945, 562).

Victor Smith thus belongs among the group I have called friendly critics, neoclassically oriented economists like Henry Schultz, Marschak and Andrews (and by implication, the other Cowles econometricians), Wassily Leontief, and J. M. Clark who, though convinced of the existence of deep flaws in the Douglas studies, still believed that the program of estimating "production functions" by regressing measures of output on measures of input was well worth pursuing.[19] I would argue that although they did not believe the claims Douglas made for what could be learned from his statistical procedure, they remained captivated by his vision nonetheless. And I would argue that this was rooted in a more fundamental belief in the importance of transforming economics into a progressive empirical science. If even some of what Douglas promised for his procedure could be achieved – a test for competition, empirical estimates of key concepts of neoclassical theory, the discovery of stable empirical relationships between inputs and outputs that would allow economists to replace theoretical possibilities with empirical realities in their reasoning – how wonderful that would be for economics! Douglas may have failed, but to argue for abandoning his program would be giving up on his – and their – dream. So they instead chose the alternative of believing that with better data, more careful analysis, and modified technique, it might yet be made to come true.

"ARE THERE LAWS OF PRODUCTION?": DOUGLAS'S OWN UNDERSTANDING OF THE COBB–DOUGLAS REGRESSION AND WHAT HE HAD ACCOMPLISHED WITH IT

While Bronfenbrenner, Reder, Marschak, Andrews, and Smith puzzled and argued over the meaning of estimated Cobb–Douglas production functions, Douglas served in the US Marine Corps. On May 9, 1945, he was hit by gunfire during the battle of Okinawa and seriously injured, and as a result was sent back to the United States. His recuperation took over a year, and he never regained the use of his left hand. By late 1946 he was teaching again at the University of Chicago, and was elected president of the American Economic Association, then, as now, one of the highest honors that American economists could award to one of their peers. He gave his presidential address in December of 1947. This address, which he later called "the best piece of economic work I had ever done" (Douglas 1971, 129) was a review and assessment of his production research entitled "Are There Laws of Production?"

Since writing *The Theory of Wages*, Douglas had worked with coauthors, to whom he gave considerable latitude in writing into the articles their own views on both theoretical and statistical issues raised by the estimation of

[19] J. M. Clark is often considered an institutionalist, and for good reason. However, he was neoclassically oriented in the sense that he used marginalist tools in his analysis of both individual behavior and the emergence of market-level or aggregate outcomes.

the Cobb–Douglas regression. It should be apparent by now that these coauthors often brought new ideas and approaches into the research program, and that they sometimes, but not always, changed Douglas's own views of what his production studies were revealing. As one reads over the research from "A Theory of Production" to "Are There Laws Of Production?," it is possible to pick out themes, interpretations, rhetorical strategies, and arguments that persist through many articles, those that change with changing collaborators, and those that appear with a new collaborator and still appear in later articles written with others.[20] This suggests that in the presidential address, we see Douglas's own views – as distinct from those of his coauthors – as to what he had accomplished with his production research: how it fit into the development of economics, the implications and significance of the results, and the agenda for future research that it created.

It is worth mentioning, to begin with, two things that were missing from the presidential address. First, there was no direct mention of Mendershausen or Frisch, or the problems of multicollinearity and instability. This might indicate, as argued earlier, that Douglas believed that he had won that particular battle. Second, there was no direct reference to the important articles by Bronfenbrenner, Reder, and Marschak and Andrews. Of course, these had appeared after Douglas had joined the Marines, and the months between his return from the war and the drafting of the address had been crowded ones: medical procedures and rehabilitation relating to his war injury stretching over a year, his increasing involvement in political affairs, and, once he learned of his election as president of the AEA, the considerable amount of statistical work required in the preparation of his address. It is likely that he just did not have time to give careful attention to new questions about his work that had been raised during his absence.

The title Douglas chose for his address harkened back to the beginning of his production research, as it speaks of "Laws of Production" rather than

[20] For example, the examination of large residuals to strengthen the credibility of the estimated function (using the exceptions to prove the rule) is a tactic employed throughout the production studies, and is identified in Samuelson (1979, 929) as a favorite Douglas tactic in the classroom. The difference between Bronfenbrenner and Douglas (1939) and the Grace Gunn and Douglas articles with respect to Mendershausen's criticisms, the use of standard errors for statistical inference, and the problem of relating estimated production-function parameters to theoretical production parameters has already been discussed. The analysis of the distribution of residuals, suggested by H. G. Lewis and introduced in Gunn and Douglas (1941a) was part of every subsequent study.

a production function. As I discussed earlier, Douglas had embraced the phrase production function after 1935, and in so doing linked his program to a Walrasian neoclassical approach to economics. Arguably, however, the choice of the phrase "Laws of Production" reveals an attachment to an earlier conception of economics, one that involved the search for general laws governing the production, distribution, and consumption of wealth; laws which, like those of classical economics, govern economic activity in its broad aggregate movements. At a minimum, it invokes something more substantial than a "production function" describing a relationship existing at the level of the individual firm, and potentially differing from firm to firm.

Douglas's first task, a fitting one for an AEA presidential address, was to provide historical context for his production research. He began with a reference to the classical theory of rent, which introduced the idea of diminishing marginal productivity and first proposed a link between the marginal productivity of a factor and the payment it received. He then moved to von Thunen, who had generalized this marginal productivity principle to explain the payments to labor and capital, thus becoming the "real discoverer" of the marginal productivity theory. A place of pride was given to John Bates Clark for "rediscovering" the marginal productivity theory. A paragraph was devoted to the history of the assumption that the relationship between inputs and outputs could be characterized by a "homogenous linear function of the first degree," which closed by endorsing (and attributing to Wicksell) the idea first introduced to the Douglas program in the 1939 article with Bronfenbrenner: that although constant returns to scale might not apply over the whole range of output a firm might produce, under perfect competition all firms would produce at a point characterized by constant returns to scale. Douglas then added this gloss: "Since industries were merely aggregates of firms and the economy as a whole was an aggregate of industries, it was presumed that the linear function tended, therefore, to be true of society as a whole at its growing points" (Douglas 1948, 3–4).

Douglas argued that since the development of the marginal productivity theory, a "scientific schizophrenia" had developed in the economics departments of the United States. Classes in economic theory would teach "the principles of marginal productivity ... uncontaminated by the idea that there might be imperfect competition" so that "labor received its full marginal product under conditions of full employment," while classes in labor economics explained wages and employment as the outcome of bargaining between workers and employers, and stressed the need for union and government action to insure that workers had sufficient bargaining power to secure fair wages. He also criticized modern marginal productivity theorists for eschewing any attempt to estimate the slopes of their theoretical curves, or to test empirically the predictions of their theory. They defended this negligence with the argument that the appropriate statistical data for such inductive research were not available, but this was just an excuse for "intellectual slovenliness" (Douglas 1948, 4–6).

Douglas's identification of these problems in the profession in the early decades of the twentieth century implies a certain narrative of Douglas's 1927 innovation: a young researcher, with an interest in the problems of labor and a record of realistic (i.e., statistically based) studies of those problems, develops a way to introduce the "valuable theoretical scaffolding" of the marginal productivity theory into the empirical study of wage determination, and at the same time provides a much-needed inductive test of that theory. Douglas did not explicitly contextualize his initial production study in this way, but he did offer his audience a brief synopsis of the high points of his twenty-year research program. He began with the story of showing his friend Charles Cobb a graph of the data series he had constructed for labor, capital, and product, and suggesting the idea of developing "a formula which would measure the relative effect of labor and capital upon product." He described the excellent fit of the resulting Cobb–Douglas regression, and the way in which the analysis of the years for which the equation fit badly actually enhanced its credibility. He recounted the "striking bit of evidence" that the estimated k value of .75 was almost precisely equal to labor's average share over the period, as the marginal productivity theory would predict, and how, in *The Theory of Wages*, he had reported results from other studies that showed a similar correspondence between labor's share and the k estimate. "We then introduced two important new features into our investigations," Douglas explained: implementing the suggestion of David Durand ("an able young American scholar") that the exponents of capital and labor be estimated separately, and "broaden(ing) our fields of investigation" by conducting cross-section analyses. After explaining and defending the cross-section methodology, Douglas announced that his "Chicago group" had now completed 21 cross-section studies, to which could be added four additional studies by non-Chicago researchers. There were many differences across the studies with respect to data and method, but, Douglas announced, he and his associates had recently begun redoing the older studies, hoping to put all the studies on as comparable a basis as possible (Douglas 1948, 7–8).

This set the stage for the central exhibit of the address – a summary presentation and analysis of the results of all these production studies. First, Douglas presented the production function estimates themselves. In three tables he showed k and j estimates from studies of US data, from studies using Australian data, and from studies based on data from other British Dominions. Results from both the restricted and unrestricted versions of the Cobb–Douglas regression were included. At the end of his address, Douglas would summarize these tables by saying that "within each country for the periods studied there is a substantial and indeed a surprising degree of agreement in the values of k and j which we obtain for various years" and "a surprising degree of agreement between the results for the United States, Australia, and Canada" (Douglas 1948, 40). Even allowing for the admitted imprecision of the concept of a "surprising degree of agreement," I do not believe that this is the conclusion that most of Douglas's audience would have drawn from an examination of the tables alone. But Douglas added considerable commentary to the tables in order to bring listeners around to his view.

For example, the time series estimates of k for the United States ranged from .63 to .81, and the cross-section estimates from .51 to .76. In keeping with the position that he had maintained from his first cross-section study on, Douglas first commented that one should not expect cross-section and time series estimates to line up, as a cross-section production function was "somewhat different" from a production function estimated with time series data. He then set about reconciling the results from the two types of studies. The different time series results actually came from four different versions of the 1899–1922 US time series data compiled for "A Theory of Production" and *The Theory of Wages*. The .81 estimate of k resulted from using the unrestricted regression with the data from the 1927 paper with Cobb. "Improved" versions of the series (better measures of labor and an updated index of output) led to k estimates of .78 and .75, and when a detrending procedure was applied to the improved series prior to estimation, the k estimate fell to .63, which was exactly equal to the average of the k values for the US cross-section studies. Moreover, argued Douglas, there was a systematic downward bias in the product series. It was an index based mainly on statistics for the output of raw materials, but over time the amount of processing and reworking of raw material going on in the manufacturing sector was increasing, leading to an increasing gap between the true value of output and an output index based on raw materials. Also, the index did not include statistics on new products developed over the period, for which demand was likely to be growing at the expense of old products. The downward bias led to a higher estimate of the exponent on labor.[21] This problem was not an issue for the cross-section estimates, and indeed they produced lower values of k. Douglas also pointed out that the estimate of k from the detrended series would be less affected by this problem, which is why it was quite comparable to the cross-section estimates of k. It is worth noting that aside from this brief mention of increasing fabrication in manufacturing and new products, Douglas made no reference to the questions raised for the time series studies by technological change, questions over which he had puzzled inconclusively in *The Theory of Wages*, and which had played a part in motivating his switch to cross-section analysis.

Douglas did not try to explain away the differences in the cross-section estimates; four of the six were within 2 percentage points of the average value of .63. Careful readers of the earlier Douglas studies might have noticed a significant change in the estimates for at least one of the cross sections. In Bronfenbrenner and Douglas's article, the k estimate for the 1909 cross section was .74, eye-poppingly close to the time series estimate reported for the United States in *The Theory of Wages*, and Bronfenbrenner and Douglas had made much of this fact at the time. The reworking of the 1909 data, however, had lowered the 1909 k estimate considerably, to .63. A finding that was once offered as a major piece of evidence in favor of the cross-section approach had disappeared without comment. The new estimate did resolve what had been a puzzle for Bronfenbrenner and Douglas, as labor's share for 1909 had been close to .63 as well.

Using the cross-section average k and j estimates of .63 and .34 Douglas explained the economic meaning of the k and j parameters both as elasticities of output with respect to input and in terms of the elasticities of the marginal productivity curves. And while pointing out that k+j was usually close to unity, he was willing to speculate that its average value of .97 for the cross-section estimates might indicate that American manufacturers

[21] From the beginning of his production research, Douglas had thought about the impact of biases in his series in terms of a time series graph displaying all three indexes. On that graph, the labor series grew the most slowly and capital most rapidly, with the product series rising in between the two. If the product line was roughly the same distance from the labor and capital lines, the k coefficient (the only one estimated in the original studies) would be .5. As the product line moved towards the labor line, the k estimate would rise. Douglas used the same method of reasoning in his presidential address to explain why the downward bias in the product series led the estimated coefficient of labor to be higher than it should be.

during this period, driven by a desire for power and prestige, pushed their firms to operate on a larger scale than was justified by the most efficient combination of factors.

As was the case for the United States (and for the same reasons, Douglas opined), the k estimates from Australian time series data were higher than the k estimates from the Australian cross-section studies. These cross-section estimates ranged from .52 to .74. Douglas directed his audience's attention to the low standard errors of these estimates, but no explanation was offered for their large range, only an admission that the k estimates for the Commonwealth as a whole were noticeably below the k estimates for individual states. He instead moved quickly to talking about the average values of k and j from the cross-section estimates, and what they implied about the elasticity of the marginal productivity curves for capital and labor in Australia.

Douglas highlighted two features of his results from Canada, South Africa, and New Zealand: First, that four Canadian cross sections produced very similar k estimates (he did not mention or try to explain why their average value of .47 was so much lower than the k values from the other studies); second, that a study of South African data had treated black and white labor as separate factors of production, an example of expanding the Cobb–Douglas regression beyond the two variable case.

A summary of the production function estimates was now offered that began in a somewhat more guarded fashion than the one (quoted earlier) with which Douglas would close his address. While he believed that there was "relatively close agreement" between the cross-section k and j estimates for the United States, Australia, and South Africa, those for Canada and New Zealand were different from those for the United States, and there were differences "between years within the same country." As had become standard when faced with variation across data sets in production function estimates, Douglas pointed to his 1934 assertion that variance in k and j over space and time was to be expected. But he then proceeded to argue that there was less to the variation of estimates than might first appear:

> (U)nderneath all these differences, it is submitted that there has been, *for the period studied*, a substantial core of stability within countries and that differences in technique, differences in the relative importance of different industries, and differences in the ratios of capital to labor may account for such deviations in the values of the exponents that do exist.[22]

[22] I assume that by "differences in technique," Douglas meant differences across studies in statistical methodology, rather than differences in production technique. Otherwise, the

It is submitted that the results are, on the whole, corroborative. If they were purely accidental, as some have charged, they would show widely varying results. The fact that on the basis of fairly wide studies there is an appreciable degree of uniformity, and that the sum of the exponents approximates unity, fairly clearly suggests that there are laws of production which can be approximated by inductive studies and that we are at least approaching them

(Douglas 1948, 19–21).

There had been some "negative results" in the research program, Douglas admitted. Attempts to refine Cobb's Massachusetts data led to nonsensical results. Time series estimates were often very sensitive to the exclusion of certain years, and "interspatial" cross-section studies based on state-level data "had no success." Douglas pointed hopefully, however, to the "comparative success" of an interspatial study by his former coauthor Ernest Olson (1948), who used a cross section of countries to estimate a version of the regression that included four inputs.

At this point, Douglas turned to the question of the relationship between theoretical production functions and the empirical production functions that he and his associates had estimated using aggregated data. He acknowledged that some theorists "probably believe that we are starting at the wrong end and that we should begin instead with the individual firm rather than the whole manufacturing sector of the economy and that we should consider the production function within these units rather than deal with inter-industry and aggregate functions." Such theorists were "accustomed in their *a priori* reasoning to start with the theory of production for the individual firm and . . . move to a model for a given industry but . . . shy away from developing a theory of production for the economy as a whole" (Douglas 1948, 22).

Douglas explained (as he had in *The Theory of Wages*) that he would be eager to estimate production functions for individual firms, if the data were available. He praised the recent work of a University of Chicago colleague who had estimated the production function for a meat-packing firm (Nicholls 1948), and called on the Census Bureau to release data that would allow for studies of individual industries based on samples of firms in order to "connect the theory of the firm and industry with that of the economy" (Douglas 1948, 22, 41). But it would be wrong to stop investigations of production until the ideal data were available. He then added this observation:

statement would approach being a tautology, that is, production function estimates are the same, except when the production function is different.

> I see no reason why we cannot approach this problem from either end and study the macrocosm as well as the microcosm. No one, for example, in the physical sciences would propose that we give up using the telescope because the microscope had not yielded all its secrets. Why should we not therefore study the economy as a whole as well as speculate about the individual firm, particularly since a knowledge of the former throws a great deal of light upon the latter?
>
> (Douglas 1948, 22–23)

This comment, particularly the last sentence, along with his statement that time series and cross-section estimates revealed different sorts of production functions, both "worthy of consideration," points back to his comment in *The Theory of Wages* about the importance of studying the general relationships that exist at the level of society as a whole because of the conditioning influence they exert on individual industries, and shows a consistency through the years on an important methodological issue. Despite the arguments of various friendly neoclassical critics, despite having allowed a coauthor to argue that the cross-section production function estimates were legitimately interesting only to the extent that they could be related to firm production functions (Bronfenbrenner and Douglas 1939, 780), and despite having in another paper adopted an individualistic neoclassical model as a framework for interpreting his production function estimates, Douglas's methodological position remained at odds with the exclusive commitment to methodological individualism for which Cowles was evangelizing and which was emerging as a defining feature of Chicago economics.

Douglas had been persuaded, however, that estimating the cross-section Cobb–Douglas regression with variables expressed as per plant averages was a way to learn something about plant (or firm) level production functions that could not be inferred from estimates based on industry aggregates, and his presentation included a table of such estimates. He had little to say about them, however, beyond pointing out that the method of plant averages led to consistently lower k estimates for the US cross sections, and to lower values of k+j.

The residuals from the US cross-section studies were next called up in support of Douglas's program, first in the form of the charts that plotted residuals on the Log(P)/Log (P') axes. Douglas explained what the distribution of these residuals would look like, in theory, if they were due only to "random errors of measurement and sampling." Upon demonstrating that actual residuals were grouped more closely around zero than theory would predict, Douglas told his audience that "belief in the reliability of the formula as a description of production is, therefore, strengthened rather than weakened." He further argued that it was likely that values of j and k varied from industry to industry, and that the distribution of deviations about the regression line revealed something about the distribution across industries of k and j values.

Making further use of the residuals, Douglas reviewed his hypotheses concerning the characteristics of industries associated with large positive or negative residuals: Industries characterized by monopoly and imperfect competition would tend to have value product higher than what their levels of capital and labor would predict, as would industries experiencing rapidly increasing demand. Such industries would therefore have positive residuals. Industries that were known to rely on large supplies of cheap labor ("sweated" industries) would have lower than average production costs, which would lead, in the presence of normal competition, to lower prices and thus negative residuals. Expressing regret that he did not have time to discuss all 87 of the industries associated with residuals more than two standard deviations from zero, he reeled off over 20 examples of industries with large negative residuals that were known to be "sweated" or on the decline, and almost 30 examples of large positive residuals associated with monopolistic and/or expanding industries. Because so many of the major deviations from the regression line were "precisely what we would expect on a priori grounds," Douglas argued, "belief in the function as a description of normal relationships should be . . . still further strengthened" (Douglas 1948, 35).

The final matter discussed by Douglas was the relationship between labor's share and the estimated value of k. This relationship had been of central importance to the research program from its beginning. However, as has been discussed, it was not always clear what conclusions Douglas believed that one could draw from the comparison of k to labor's share, or on what basis one could draw them. Sometimes Douglas seemed to take the accuracy of the k estimate as being well established, so that the closeness of k to labor's share was a test in some sense of the marginal productivity theory or of the presence of competition in factor markets. Other times the closeness of k and labor's share was pointed to as evidence of the credibility of the production function estimates, so that, at least implicitly, it was being assumed that the economy (or the labor market, at least) was approximately competitive and the marginal productivity theory correct. Since Douglas often argued that consistency of his results from study to study showed that they were unlikely to be due to "accident" or "chance," perhaps he had in mind a sort of argument from probabilities: the simplest and most obvious explanation for the consistent correspondence of the k estimate and labor's share was that the production function was correct and the economy was competitive. If the Cobb–Douglas regression produced biased estimates of k, and/or if wages were determined by relative bargaining power, monopsonistic exploitation, or other factors unrelated to productivity, what would be the odds that the estimation bias and/or the wage determining factors would be exactly such as to bring k closely into line with labor's share in several different data sets from different times and places?

Standing before the AEA convention, Douglas stated the matter thusly: "We would expect, under conditions of (1) true constant returns where the sum of the exponents is equal to unity and (2) perfect competition, that each factor of production would receive that fraction of the total product which is indicated by its exponent" (Douglas 1948, 36). He then presented two tables of comparisons between k and labor's share, one for the US cross sections and one for the non-US studies. At the end of the address, Douglas summarized this evidence by saying that "taken in the large, there is an almost precise degree of agreement between the actual share received by labor and that which, according to the theory of marginal productivity, we would expect labor to obtain" (Douglas 1948, 41), but I do not believe that this was self-evident from the tables alone, and again Douglas offered a fair amount of explanation to take his audience from his tables to his conclusion.

Each table showed, for each study, the value of k, of k/(k+j), of W/P (labor's share), and of the differences between W/P both k and k/(k+j) expressed in terms of the standard error of k.[23] Averages of k, k/(k+j), and W/P were also presented for relevant subgroups of studies. The table for the United States is reproduced in Figure 3.3.

The first feature of this table pointed out by Douglas was that "in five of the six years there was a very close agreement between the values of k and of W/P" (Douglas 1948, 37), thus implicitly employing a three standard error rule for determining closeness. He then added three observations. The first was to note that 1919 was a year of rapid inflation, so that we would expect wages to lag behind. The second was that the average value for the six cross sections was very close to the average value of W/P. To prefer a comparison of these average values of k and W/P to comparisons of values from individual years was consistent with Douglas's view that the

[23] Douglas now described k/(k+j) as "a rough measure of what we would approximately expect to occur if the total product were to be divided so as to eliminate either the net residual profits or losses."

TABLE VIII.—A COMPARISON BY YEARS OF THE VALUES OF THE EXPONENTS OF LABOR AND CAPITAL IN THE PRODUCTION FUNCTION FOR AMERICAN MANUFACTURING (k AND j) WITH THE UNWEIGHTED AVERAGE OF THE SHARES OF THE NET VALUE PRODUCT RECEIVED BY LABOR (W/P)

Year	N	k		$\frac{k}{k+j}$	$\frac{W}{P}$	Degree to which W/P differs from k and $\frac{k}{k+j}$ in terms of standard errors: $\frac{\frac{W}{P}-k}{\sigma_k}$	$\frac{\frac{W}{P}-\frac{k}{k+j}}{\sigma_k}$
1889	363	.51	.43	.54	.60	+ 3	+ 2
1899	332	.62	.33	.65	.58	− 2	−3–4
1904	336	.65	.31	.68	.64	−0–1	− 2
1909	258	.63	.34	.65	.63	0	− 1
1914	340	.61	.37	.62	.59	−0–1	− 1
1919	556	.76	.25	.75	.59	−8–9	− 8
Average	—	.63	.34	.65	.605	—	—

Figure 3.3 Douglas's table comparing US estimates of k to labor's share

marginal productivity theory held only in the sense that the equality of wages with marginal productivity was a "normal" or long-run average tendency, although he did not say so at this point. A third observation was that the values of W/P in the table were probably understated because, due to inadequate data, P had not been adjusted for depreciation. A long footnote explained why it would be reasonable, based on estimates from a recent NBER study by Solomon Fabricant (1938), to adjust labor's share upward by 3 percentage points, and allowed Douglas to conclude that, for the United States, "the degree of agreement between the values of k and W/P is most striking, and that the results conform to what normally would occur under competitive productivity theory. Hence, this constitutes a still further reinforcement to the productivity function itself" (Douglas 1948, 38).

After this statement, which seemed to offer competition and marginal productivity theory as maintained hypotheses, Douglas added a qualification. It was well known, he asserted, that large parts of the economy were characterized by monopoly and oligopoly, making it puzzling that labor's share was approximately equal to what one would expect under competition. Douglas suggested that oligopolists had shared with workers the excess profits they earned at the expense of consumers.

This passage invites comment for two reasons. First, Douglas was offering an argument based on unlikely coincidence, the sort of argument he dismissed when he believed it was being made by opponents. Second, it is pertinent to a question on which the Douglas team, through the years, had taken conflicting positions: Did imperfect competition in product markets lead labor's share to be below the value of k estimated with a cross-section Cobb–Douglas regression? As we have seen, Douglas and his coauthors had sometimes implied that a value of labor's share equal to k indicated competition in product markets. At a couple of other points, a distinction had been made between failures of competition in the product markets and imperfect competition in factor markets (i.e., monopoly vs. monopsony), along with the argument that only monopsony would lead to a depression of labor's share below the value marginal product of labor. And finally, in Gunn and Douglas's article the result that labor's share would be lower when the "producing unit" could influence the price of output was (incorrectly) derived from a mathematical model. Now Douglas was again taking the position that the "perfect competition" that led to the equality of labor's share with the k estimate included perfect competition in product markets.

The case for the equality of labor's share and the k estimate was stronger in the table of results for the British Dominions. In almost every individual study, the k estimate was within one standard error of W/P, and when averages were taken over the multiple cross sections for Canada and Australia, the difference was 1 and 2 percentage points, respectively. He was willing to speculate that the finding of a k estimate considerably above labor's share in South Africa was due to the presence there of a "highly monopolized set of industries which are largely run by foreign employers or by men whose cultural interest lie elsewhere, (and) do not give to the laborers that which in a competitive society they would obtain" (Douglas 1948, 40).

Douglas closed the address by discussing the great deal of work that remained to be done on the questions he had opened up.[24] "Is it too much to hope," he had then asked, "that if the older generation finds it impossible to carry on such studies, the younger economists may find such lines of inquiry a challenge to their ingenuity and abilities?" (Douglas 1948, 41)

[24] In a footnote to the published version of the address, which was probably not in the original, Douglas mentioned estimating the regression for long series of annual cross sections for the same country, for nonmanufacturing sectors of the economy, and for single firms or single industries using firm-level data.

One member of that older generation preparing to leave the field was Douglas himself. On the same evening that he delivered his address, he learned that he had been chosen by the Illinois Democratic Party as its candidate for the US Senate in the 1948 election. He would win this election, and would serve in the Senate for 18 years. His career as a research economist was essentially over, and the work of exploring and developing the Cobb–Douglas regression as a tool for empirical economic research was in the hands of others.

But this process was already underway as Douglas spoke. As we have seen, since the mid-1930s a number of econometricians, while expressing enthusiasm about Douglas's vision of using statistical data to estimate the fundamental equations of the neoclassical theory of production and distribution, had voiced reservations about Douglas's specific empirical strategies and suggested alternatives of their own. By the time of Douglas's address, alternative approaches to estimating the Cobb–Douglas function were being implemented. Victor Smith's (1945) study of the Canadian automobile industry has been mentioned above, and Douglas himself had cited William Nicholls' study of a single meat-packing plant. Lawrence Klein (1946) alluded to the existence of a number of other firm-level studies, commenting that "in many particular firms, statisticians have found that the Cobb–Douglas function (or simple modifications of this function) fit the output-input data very well." In 1944, Gerhard Tintner of Iowa State University estimated three agricultural production functions – two using cross-section data on individual farms, and one using national time series data (Tintner 1944a,b; Tintner and Brownlee 1944) – inaugurating what would become a fairly substantial literature on agricultural production functions. Within a few decades, the Cobb–Douglas equation, both in its regression form and as a building block for theoretical modeling, would be ubiquitous in the economic literature, while economists pursuing Douglas's vision of estimating production relationships would develop an array of more flexible and general production function forms to be applied to an accumulating body of larger and more accurate data sets. As Douglas himself put it near the end of his life, "A seedling that I had planted long ago, but left untended, had been cared for by younger men and … bec[o]me a sturdy tree" (Douglas 1971, 614–15).

PART II

THE DIFFUSION OF THE COBB–DOUGLAS REGRESSION

In the two decades following Douglas's presidential address to the AEA, the Cobb–Douglas regression came to be a familiar and widely used tool in empirical economics. Part II of this book explores this diffusion process, mainly by means of two case studies: the first describing how the regression was adopted by researchers in agricultural economics and the second looking at the uses to which the regression was put by economists seeking to measure and explain economic growth. First, however, I provide some necessary background for the case studies by reviewing three general developments that affected economists' perception and use of the regression in the 1950s and 1960s.

4

Three Important Developments in the Life of the Cobb–Douglas Regression, 1952–1961

During the 18 years that Paul Douglas was Senator Douglas of Illinois, the Cobb–Douglas production function became a widely accepted tool for empirical research in economics, being applied by increasing numbers of researchers to a broadening array of questions. Chapters 5 and 6 are case studies of the adoption of the technique in two research areas: the study of agricultural production processes and empirical investigations of the causes of economic growth. First, however, I recount three general developments in the period that had an important influence on the spread of the Cobb–Douglas regression and Douglas's larger idea.

THE COBB–DOUGLAS REGRESSION IN THE FIRST ECONOMETRICS TEXTBOOKS

Prior to the early 1950s, there were no adequate textbooks covering the new approach to econometrics being promoted by the Cowles Commission, at least in the opinion of those enthusiastic about Cowles-style econometrics. No one was teaching the material in any way to graduate students at Harvard or Yale; interested Harvard students studied Cowles monographs on their own (Biddle 2017). The first two textbooks teaching the new econometrics were Gerhard Tintner's *Econometrics*, published in 1952, and Lawrence Klein's *Textbook of Econometrics*, which appeared the following year. Both Klein and Tintner had been affiliated with the Cowles Commission in the 1940s, and each of their books included discussions of the econometric estimation of Cobb–Douglas production functions.

In Tintner's book, the first several chapters offered students a nontechnical introduction to the field of econometrics, discussing the relationships between econometrics, economic theory, and the theory of statistics, and offering examples of how econometric techniques had been applied to answer important questions in economics. One such example was production function estimation. Tintner explained why production function estimation was of "paramount importance" for economics, and he praised Douglas as "one of the great pioneers of econometrics." Tintner described the original Cobb–Douglas paper, but also two recent studies (one of which Tintner had coauthored) in which cross-sections of data gathered from hundreds of farms had been used to estimate agricultural production functions.[1] Footnotes made students aware of several other production function studies, and also of "an extensive critical literature" related to production function estimation, including Menderhausen (1937) and Marschak and Andrews (1944). Later in the book, Tintner took students step by step through the estimation of an aggregate time series Cobb–Douglas production function to illustrate the technique of "weighted regression," and compared the results of this procedure to findings of other studies estimating Cobb–Douglas regressions (Tintner 1952, 51–57, 134–43). The overall impression given by Tintner's book was that the estimation of Cobb–Douglas production functions was an important and active research field.

In Klein's book, the Cobb–Douglas production function first appeared as an example of how economic theory could be a source of the hypotheses used in econometrics. Klein reminded readers of the theoretical prediction that under competitive market conditions, the marginal productivity of labor would equal the wage rate. The concept of marginal productivity, he argued, implied a production function showing the technical relationship between inputs and outputs. Given an assumption about the mathematical form of the production function, and data on input, output, and wages, the econometrician could test the theoretical prediction. "One useful type" of production function, Klein noted, "is that estimated in so many cases by C. Cobb and P. H. Douglas," and Klein provided an equation of a Cobb–Douglas production function with three inputs, identifying for his readers the symbols in the equation that were the parameters to be estimated (Klein 1953, 3–5).[2]

Klein's chapter III on "Estimation of Aggregative Models" specified a Keynesian-flavored macroeconomic model meant to be estimated using

[1] These two studies are described in more detail in Chapter 5.

[2] Klein, of course, erred in saying that *Cobb* and Douglas had estimated the function "in so many cases," and in implying that Douglas had ever estimated a Cobb–Douglas regression involving more than two inputs.

time series data from the national income accounts. One of the equations of the model, labeled (3.1.3), was written

$$W_1 = \gamma(Y + T - W_2) + u_3$$

in which W_1 was the private-sector wage bill. W_2, Y, and T were defined such that the term in parentheses was the output of the private sector, and u_3 was a random disturbance. This meant that γ was the (average) ratio of wages to private-sector output; Klein had noted already the "remarkable stability" of this ratio over time in the national income accounts. He then remarked that

> if (3.1.3) were merely the accident of income distribution phenomena, we might not have confidence in it as an autonomous equation of economic behavior that would hold outside of special circumstances that have produced the observed income distribution. On the other hand, if physical output is related to physical inputs by the production function known as the Cobb–Douglas function and if markets are competitive, then a relation of the form given in (3.1.3) holds (Klein 1953, 76).

After demonstrating this mathematically, Klein reiterated that "equation (3.1.3) can be interpreted fundamentally in terms of economic behavior and is not merely an accidental product of the income distribution" (Klein 1953, 77).

The Cobb–Douglas production function appeared again in the chapter on "Methods of Sector Analysis." Assuming the availability of time series data on inputs, outputs, and prices for a single industry, Klein specified a model in which the industry production function was Cobb–Douglas with the three inputs labor, capital, and raw materials. The model also included three equations expressing the relationship between input marginal productivity and input price implied by the assumptions of profit maximization and competition. Klein explained that each of these marginal conditions suggested estimating equations of the form

$$\log x_t = \log \alpha + \log u_t$$

where x_t was the share of the total value of output represented by the cost of a factor of production (the factor share), α was the coefficient of the factor in the industry production function, and $\log u_t$ was a random variable with a zero mean. This meant that the best linear unbiased estimator for the factor's coefficient in the production function was the geometric mean of x_t (Klein 1953, 191–93). The method of estimating the parameters of a Cobb–Douglas production function using information on factor shares was demonstrated by Klein using a cross-section, firm-level sample of railroad data.

The discussions of Cobb–Douglas regressions in Tintner's and Klein's textbooks are significant for two reasons. First, for at least ten years these were the leading textbooks teaching "econometrics" to economics graduate students.[3] Through these books, several cohorts of economics graduate students were exposed through concrete examples to the nuts and bolts of estimating both cross-section and time series Cobb–Douglas regressions. More generally, the books gave these students a positive impression of the importance and potential of empirical production function research, while making little mention of the econometric critiques of empirical production function studies raised in the 1930s and 1940s.

Perhaps more important, however, was Klein's demonstration of how factor share data could be used to estimate the exponents of a Cobb–Douglas production function. As discussed in Part I, Douglas had mentioned this possibility in *The Theory of Wages*, but had not pursued it, probably because doing so would require one to assume competitive conditions and the correctness of the marginal productivity theory, and these were propositions that Douglas preferred to view as hypotheses that could be tested using his estimated production functions. In Klein's book, however, the idea appeared again, analyzed and operationalized in the context of a full-blown probabilistic multi-equation model in the Cowles style. And, his demonstration showed that a willingness to assume competitive conditions and marginal productivity theory allowed the researcher to cut through a Gordian Knot of potential problems surrounding the direct estimation of a Cobb–Douglas production function. Later in the 1950s, production researchers would begin to refer to "Klein's method" of estimating production function parameters using factor share data, and, as will be discussed, in the 1960s, the developers of the Constant Elasticity of Substitution (CES) production function and others would show how to use these assumptions as a lever for estimating the parameters of assumed production functions that were more complex, and more general, than the Cobb–Douglas.

THE PHELPS BROWN CRITIQUE OF 1957

In 1957, "The Meaning of the Fitted Cobb–Douglas Function," by E. H. Phelps Brown, appeared in the *Quarterly Journal of Economics*. Phelps Brown's thesis was that neither the time series nor the cross-section

[3] It was not until 1963 that another two econometrics texts destined for wide adoption, by Arthur Goldberger and J. J. Johnston, appeared on the market (Biddle 2017).

versions of the Cobb–Douglas regression had produced coefficients of an actual production function.

Phelps Brown began by acknowledging that Douglas's production function studies, if they accomplished what Douglas claimed they accomplished, were of great analytical significance. He noted four features of the collected results surveyed in Douglas (1948) that seemed to offer evidence in favor of Douglas's claims: The good fits of the regression to a variety of data sets; the considerable agreement across studies in the values of the estimated coefficients, the consistent result that the sum of the exponents is close to one, and the close agreement found in the various studies between labor's share and the estimated value of k. Phelps Brown also mentioned the independent evidence of stability over time of labor's share in total output, which was an implication of the aggregate Cobb–Douglas production function. The remainder of the article laid out Phelps Brown's reasons for rejecting Douglas's interpretation of his results.

According to Phelps Brown, "a production function shows what quantity of a given product will result from given intakes of factors, and its derivatives show the marginal productivity of those factors," and he granted that "there is reason to believe that differential contributions of broadly inclusive factors such as "capital" and "labor" may be estimated from the data of a large number of firms or farms, operated in the usual way of business, when these are making similar products by similar processes and in similar environments" (Phelps Brown 1957, 558–59).[4] Thus, Phelps Brown accepted that there were production functions in the actual world, that it made sense to talk about estimating the production function of an industry, and that it made sense to speak of and attempt to estimate the marginal productivity of the abstract aggregates "capital" and "labor."[5] His critique was focused, then, on the methods and data employed by the Douglas team in producing such estimates.

Phelps Brown offered separate assessments of Douglas's time series and cross-section studies. His first criticism of the time series studies was the a priori assertion that "it is improbable at first sight that one unchanging

[4] Appended to this is a footnote citing Heady (1955), a study based on farm-level data and discussed further in Chapter 5, and Lomax (1950), a study based on time series data from the British coal industry.

[5] It is also arguable that Phelps Brown accepted as sensible the idea of an aggregate production function, as his statement that "it is improbable at first sight that one unchanging production function should fit a growing, changing economy over a run of years" can be read to imply that one unchanging production function could fit the economy over a short period of time.

production function should fit a growing, changing economy over a run of years" (Phelps Brown 1957, 548–49). Why, then, did Douglas's regression fit the time series data so well? Here, Phelps Brown turned to Mendershausen's algebra showing the relationship between the estimated k coefficient in a time series Cobb–Douglas regression and the slopes of linear trend lines fitted to log C, log L, and log P.[6] The good fit of the Cobb–Douglas regression resulted from the fact that labor, capital, and product "are all likely to follow constant growth trends." Further, Phelps Brown argued, "These rates are historical. The differences between them will not directly have the significance of exponents in a production function" (Phelps Brown 1957, 550). Note that by itself, this is a question-begging argument. If the relationship between capital, labor, and output were determined by a stable, constant-returns-to-scale Cobb–Douglas production function, then the historical growth rate of output would be determined by the historical growth rates of capital and labor, and the three rates would be related to labor's coefficient k by Mendershausen's equation $k = (\alpha - \gamma)/(\beta - \gamma)$. The strength of Phelps Brown's argument that the "relative historical growth rates" interpretation of k is an *alternative* to the production function coefficient interpretation of k, rather than an *implication* of it, rested mainly on the strength of his a priori argument that the time series data could not have been generated by a single, constant-returns-to-scale Cobb–Douglas production function. He did, however, offer another reason for doubting Douglas's interpretation of his k estimates as production function coefficients, asserting that they implied an implausibly rapid rate of decline in the marginal productivity of capital with the growth of the capital stock.

Phelps Brown pointed out that in some historical periods (not those covered by Douglas in his studies), capital, labor, and output had grown in such a way as to imply nonsensical values of k, and he touched rather briefly on Mendershausen's multicollinearity and direction of minimization arguments. He did not, however, offer alternative explanations for the consistency of the k estimates produced by the time series studies, and ultimately attributed the close relationship in those studies between the values of k and of labor's share to "coincidence" (Phelps Brown 1957, 558).

Phelps Brown's discussion of the cross-section studies began with a graphical representation of one of Douglas's cross-section samples, which

[6] That is, $k = (\alpha - \gamma)/(\beta - \gamma)$, where γ is the growth rate of capital, β the growth rate of labor, and α the growth rate of product.

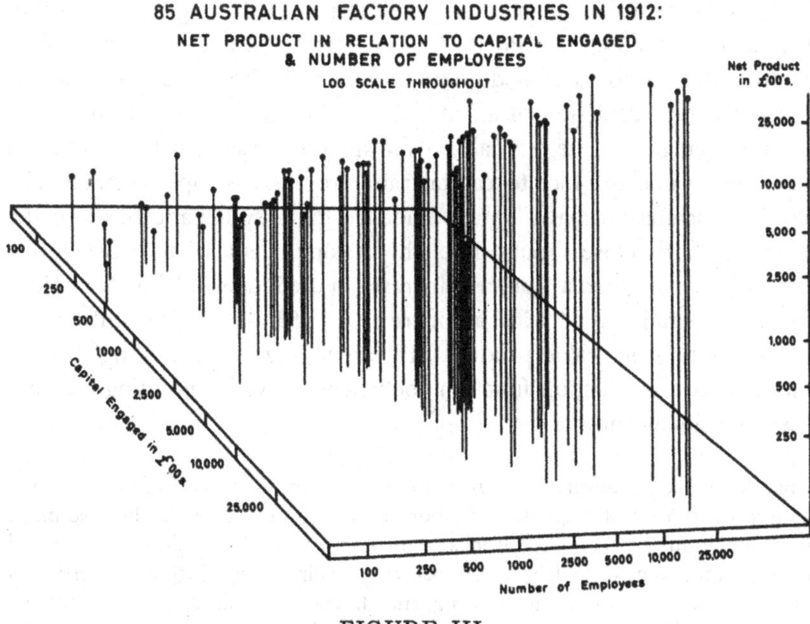

FIGURE III

Figure 4.1 E. H. Phelps Brown's illustration of the multicollinearity problem in Douglas's cross-section data

he used to help explain how Douglas's procedure produced estimates of j and k from such data (Figure 4.1):

He remarked first on the "striking" fact that "the points fall within one narrow cylinder, or tube, inclined at 45 degrees to each coordinate plane," which "simply expresses the tendency of L, C, and P all to change in much the same proportion between one industry and another." There was reason to believe that "this tendency would obtain widely," "subject only to deviations independent of size of industry." Given that, "we can regard the fit of the Cobb–Douglas plane as made up in effect of two elements: it will be hinged on the tube, and will be rotated around it to a position governed by the scatter." He showed mathematically that if the tube had a 45-degree slope, the j and k estimates would sum to one, so that Douglas's consistent finding that j+k was close to unity was "the outcome not of an analytical relation really governing the associated variations of L, C, and P, but simply of the fact that between one industry and another these variates change for the most part in proportion to one another" (Phelps Brown 1957, 553–54).

The relative sizes of k and j were determined by the angle of rotation of the plane around the tube. Phelps Brown displayed this angle of rotation by plotting the data on a second graph, in which the horizontal axis showed the percentage deviation of an industry's labor to capital ratio from the sample average, and the vertical axis showed the percentage deviation of an industry's value product to capital ratio from the sample average. The resulting scatterplot gave "much evidence for a systematic relation: the points lie fairly close about a line whose slope tells us that, between one industry and another, a 1 percent increase in the intake of labor per unit of capital generally went with an increase of .53 of one percent in the corresponding net value product." He argued against accepting this .53 estimate as a production function coefficient, however, pointing out that the .53 estimate showed

> what difference in net value product per unit of capital we generally find associated with a difference in the amount of labor used per unit of capital, when we move from one industry to another: it tells us only about the kind of difference we find between industries in which, by the nature of their processes, that proportion is relatively low – sugar refining, brewing, and chemical manufactures, for example – and those in which, by the same token, it is relatively high – jam-making and fruit-preserving, cabinet-making, and tailoring, for example. These differences do not necessarily throw any light on what will happen when we vary the proportion of labor to capital within one industry, with its given product and given technical requirements. But it is on this sort of analytic variation that the measurement of marginal productivity depends
>
> (Phelps Brown 1957, 555–56).

This is essentially Reder's intrafirm-interfirm critique. Put another way, Phelps Brown was rejecting a priori Douglas's implicit assumption that the production of value product from capital and labor in all of the heterogeneous industries represented in his cross-section data sets was governed by the same Cobb–Douglas function.

What then of the close agreement, in Douglas's various cross-section data sets, between the estimated k coefficient and the share of wages in value added? Phelps Brown argued that this resulted almost automatically from the fact that Douglas's output measure in the cross-section studies was the (monetary) net value product of an industry. Although wages and returns to capital faced by each industry in a cross-section data set would differ within a narrow range, it would be approximately true that for each industry i, $P_i = wL_i + rC_i$, where P_i was value added in industry i, and w and r were the sample average values of the wage and the rate of return to capital. This means that in k we have a measure of the percentage change in net product that goes with a 1 per cent change in the intake of labor, when the intake of capital is constant; but when we try to trace such changes by comparing one industry with another, and the net products of the two industries approximately satisfy $P_i = wL_i + rC_i$, the difference between them will always approximate to the compensation at the wage rate w of the difference in labor intake. The Cobb–Douglas k, and the share of earnings in income, will be only two sides of the same penny

(Phelps Brown 1957, 557).

This is similar to the critique presented in Tinbergen (1942) and Marschak and Andrews (1944), but whereas these earlier writers had limited the critique to a situation in which long-run competitive equilibrium led to the condition $P_i = wL_i + rC_i$, Phelps Brown was arguing that this equation would always be approximately correct as an accounting matter in the sort of industry census data used by Douglas.

In the conclusion of his article, Phelps Brown allowed that it might be possible in principle to learn about marginal productivities of capital and labor from interindustry comparisons, contending that his critique was based on statistical difficulties created by the combination of Douglas's data and methods – in particular, the high multicollinearity in the industrial census cross sections and the fact that product was measured as net value added, leading to the approximate identity $P_i = wL_i + rC_i$. But arguably, Phelps Brown's statistical arguments by themselves were not decisive. As with Phelps Brown's argument about historical trends being responsible for the good fits of the time series studies, the rhetorical power of the statistical difficulties identified by Phelps Brown lay in providing alternative explanations for the compelling features of the Douglas findings, once an a priori reason had been offered for believing that Douglas's estimates were not likely to be related to marginal productivities.

To see this point, recall that Phelps Brown appealed to a "predominating tendency" towards proportionality between labor, capital, and output across industries to explain the fact that most of the observations on his diagram were in a "tube" inclined at 45 degrees (creating multicollinearity). A reader with a predisposition to accept Douglas's interpretation of his findings could simply respond that this is what one would expect from a set of competitive industries sharing the same constant-returns-to-scale production function, and maximizing profits subject to the same input prices. Phelps Brown's repeated assertion of a tendency towards proportionality of capital, labor, and product was simply another way of saying the production function is characterized by constant returns to scale. Supporters of the production function interpretation could point to optimization errors as an explanation of the deviations from the tube, or propose that different industries faced different wage rates and/or returns to capital – something that Phelps Brown himself had suggested.[7] Phelps Brown's point about the necessary (near) equality of k and labor's share was undeniably correct, and it effectively refuted the claim that Douglas's cross-section studies had proven the existence of competition, or the validity of the marginal productivity theory. But if one were willing to assume profit maximization in competitive markets, labor's share simply became an alternative measure of the true coefficient of labor in the production function, not an alternative interpretation of the estimated coefficient of labor in a Cobb–Douglas regression. As Klein's textbook had shown, one could use the assumptions of competition and optimization to make Phelps Brown's "two sides of the same penny" into two methods for estimating a production function parameter. By implicitly questioning the assumption that the same simple production function described the way that capital and labor combined to produce product in dozens of heterogeneous industries, Phelps Brown had raised a compelling a priori reason for rejecting the production function interpretation of Douglas's cross-section results, but he wavered on this point in the end, and chose to rest his case against Douglas's regression on the "statistical difficulties" he had identified.

In some ways, Phelps Brown's entire article was behind the cutting edge of the empirical production function literature, in large part reiterating criticisms from the 1930s, especially those of Mendershausen, with no references to the articles by Bronfenbrenner, Reder, Marschak and Andrews, or Smith. Phelps Brown's versions of Mendershausen's arguments were less jargon laden and thus probably more clearly understood by readers than the originals, and appeared in a journal more widely read than *Econometrica.* He also brought to this wider audience Reder's intrafirm/intefirm critique, and offered a more robust version of the argument that Douglas's cross-section method would necessarily produce a k estimate that was close to labor's share. But however effective Phelps Brown's criticisms might have been against Douglas's work and his particular claims for what he had accomplished, they were much less effective against

7 As will be seen in subsequent chapters, by the end of the 1950s economists were beginning to propose optimization errors as an explanation of why the capital labor ratio would vary across firms/industries with the same production function facing the same input prices, and Zvi Griliches would propose differences across regions in wages as another source of this variation in his production function studies.

the production function literature of the late 1950s, particularly since Phelps Brown granted that production function estimates based on firm-level cross-section data or industry-level times series fell outside of his criticism. Although Phelps Brown's article did become a standard reference in the literature surrounding the production function estimation, with over 50 citations in JSTOR journals between 1957 and 1970, I suspect its impact on that literature could be described with words similar to those used by Martin Bronfenbrenner in the early 1940s with reference to the debate between Mendershausen and the Douglas group: it did not convert the antagonists and provided no definitive conclusions for interested spectators (Bronfenbrenner 1944, 35).

GOING BEYOND DOUGLAS'S REGRESSION IN PURSUIT OF DOUGLAS'S IDEA: THE CES PRODUCTION FUNCTION

As has been discussed in Part I, during the early years of his work with the Cobb–Douglas regression, Douglas had mentioned the desirability of exploring other mathematical functions for estimating "laws of production." He never seriously pursued this, however, and eventually came to conclude that the unrestricted Cobb–Douglas form provided an adequate representation of production relations in manufacturing (Gunn and Douglas 1941c, 108). J. M. Clark (1928) tested a more general functional form in 1928, and agricultural economist Earl Heady also worked with alternative functional forms for production function regressions during the 1950s. Such experiments did not attract imitators, however. Although economists during the 1950s would estimate production function regressions for a variety of purposes with a variety of types of data, almost every such study used the Cobb–Douglas form.

This changed in the early 1960s with the introduction of the Constant Elasticity of Substitution (CES) production function, which became the first generalization of Cobb–Douglas to be quickly and widely adopted by empirical researchers. As A. A. Walters (1963a, 1) would note in a survey of empirical production function estimation, "The Cobb–Douglas function has had a long and successful life without serious rivals. But recently it has been strongly challenged by a new function," that is, the CES production function.

The CES production function was first introduced to the economics profession in 1961, in the paper "Capital-Labor Substitution and Economic Efficiency," written by Kenneth Arrow, Hollis Chenery, Bagicha Minhas, and Robert Solow, which I will subsequently refer to as Arrow et al. (1961).

In this paper, the new production function was named and subjected to detailed analysis. The function's parameters were estimated using three data sets, and those estimates used to draw conclusions related to a variety of economic phenomena, from technological change to the distribution of income to the sources of comparative advantage in international trade. While Arrow et al. (1961) was awaiting publication, Murray Brown and John DeCani also derived the function and estimated its parameters (Brown and DeCani 1961), but the Arrow et al. (1961) presentation of the function was far more influential, and for that reason this section will be focused almost entirely on that paper – the circumstances that gave rise to the paper, the way the authors used the new production function as an empirical tool, and the paper's subsequent influence on empirical production function estimation.[8]

Background and Origins of the Project

Paul Douglas acknowledged from early on in his production research program that the Cobb–Douglas form placed limits on the behavior of important economic variables; these restrictions were a cost of the function's tractability for both theoretical and empirical analysis. By the late 1940s, it was well understood that one of the more serious limitations of the Cobb–Douglas form was that it constrained the "elasticity of substitution" between labor and capital to be equal to one. The elasticity of substitution, as a characteristic of a production function with two factors of production, had been first defined in print by Hicks (1932), who used the definition to derive a compact mathematical expression for the demand function for a factor of production, and in his discussion of the impact of economic growth on distribution. Hicks's conclusion that the effect of a relative increase in the supply of a factor on that factor's distributive share would depend on the whether the elasticity of substitution was greater than or less than one led to immediate controversy over the meaning and significance of Hicks's new elasticity measure.[9]

More broadly, the elasticity of substitution came to be an important parameter in a new mathematical representation of neoclassical value and

[8] The story of both the Arrow et al. paper and the other "discoveries" of the Constant Elasticity of Substitution (CES) production function is told in more detail in Biddle (forthcoming), from which this account draws heavily.

[9] Hicks (1936) reviews the initial discussions of the proposition and attempts to clarify his position.

distribution theory being developed by Hicks, R. G. D. Allen (1938), and a handful of others. Although this literature did not influence the research of most American economists during the 1940s and 1950s, it did attract the attention of several young, mathematically oriented economists whose work would ultimately have an important impact on the direction of economic research in the United States. The functions and associated elasticities of the new mathematical framework became the components used by these economists in the construction and analysis of theoretical models of production and distribution. To the extent that the analysis of such models revealed the value of the elasticity of substitution to be a determinant of important economic outcomes, a method of estimating production relations that constrained the value of that elasticity to one, as did the Cobb–Douglas regression, had a serious limitation.

Wassily Leontief's input-output analysis represented another framework for the conduct of theoretical and empirical research that attracted the attention of mathematically oriented economists in the 1940s and 1950s. Leontief's input-output model represented the economy as a system of relationships between several industries, with each industry assumed to have a production function characterized by "fixed coefficients of production," that is, a production function with an elasticity of substitution of zero (Leontief 1951 [1941]). Leontief's work showed that much could be gained by this assumption in terms of both theoretical tractability and feasibility of empirical implementation, and use of fixed-coefficient production functions spread in both theoretical and empirical analyses.

So it was that Arrow et al. (1961) opened with the observation that when it came to the making assumptions about possibilities for capital-labor substitution, theorists had typically chosen one of two alternatives: an elasticity of substitution of zero or an elasticity of substitution of one. "From a mathematical point of view," the authors noted, "zero and one are perhaps the most convenient alternatives," but "economic analysis based on these assumptions ... often leads to conclusions that are unduly restrictive." Further, they argued, direct observation gave "every indication of varying degrees of substitutability in different types of production" (Arrow et al. 1961, 225).

The authors went on to explain that they had derived a mathematical production function with a constant elasticity of substitution between capital and labor that could take on any positive value, and which contained the Leontief and Cobb–Douglas production functions as special cases. The authors promised to present tests of the validity of this production function using international cross-section data and aggregate time series data. In particular, their time series results would show an "over-all elasticity of substitution between capital and labor significantly less than unity" (Arrow et al. 1961, 225).

Each of the four authors of Arrow et al. (1961) came into the project by a different path and for different reasons. Three of them, Arrow, Solow, and Chenery, were already prominent figures in the profession. Solow and Arrow would go on to win Nobel Prizes, while Hollis Chenery would come to be considered one of the leading development economists of his generation, eventually securing a position at Harvard University and serving for ten years as the vice president for development policy at the World Bank (Page 1994). When the collaboration began, Chenery and Arrow were both on the faculty at Stanford University, and Bagicha Singh Minhas was a graduate student working under Chenery's supervision. Minhas would soon return to India and begin a successful career as an academic and civil servant (Parikh et al. 2005).

The starting point for the collaboration was Minhas's observation of an empirical regularity in the data he was analyzing for his dissertation: "that the value added per unit of labor used within a given industry varies across countries with the wage rate" (Arrow et al. 1961, 225). Minhas had been unsuccessfully trying to square this finding with the assumption that the industries for which he had data had Cobb–Douglas production functions, but Arrow, discussing the regularity with Chenery and/or Minhas, suggested that it actually proved that the production functions were not Cobb–Douglas. Arrow, intrigued, then "set out to find" the production function implied by the regularity. He spent two weeks on the task before producing a production function that "could be described as having a constant elasticity of substitution," that is, the CES production function. Arrow circulated a paper describing the function and its derivation, and his colleague Hendrick Houthakker pointed out to him that the same function had appeared in an important paper on growth theory by Robert Solow (1956) (Minhas 1963, vii–viii; Arrow 1985, 51).

Kenneth Arrow and Robert Solow had a close friendship dating back several years,[10] and after learning that Solow had already "found" the CES function, Arrow wrote to Solow in May of 1959 describing Minhas's data and his own derivation of the function.[11] Solow quickly responded with a

[10] Solow also had a lifelong friendship with Chenery dating back to their time together in graduate school.

[11] Arrow to Solow, May 29, 1959, Box 52, "A" folders. Robert M. Solow Papers, David M. Rubenstein Rare Book & Manuscript Library, Duke University (cited subsequently as "Solow papers").

brief history of his own work with the function. He had developed it as one of two specific functional forms employed to illustrate possible growth paths of key variables in his general growth model under alternative assumptions about production relations; the other was the Cobb–Douglas (Solow 1956). He had later realized that the function had the "constant elasticity of substitution" property.

Solow's response, while encouraging Arrow to continue the work, did not ask or offer to be part of the project.[12] In 2017, responding to an open-ended question of how he became involved in the project, Solow mentioned that "As for me, I had long been very suspicious of Cobb–Douglas's cross-section estimates of a production function . . .. So I was antsy when I saw the Minhas-Chenery data." But what Arrow had worked out "was at least a new and different way of estimating some parameters. I was also at the time (and still am) unhappy about the profession's romance with Cobb–Douglas."

Although later chapters will show that Solow, in the 1950s and early 1960s, had a pragmatic willingness to work with the Cobb–Douglas function to create empirically estimable models to embody his theoretical ideas, there is also ample evidence of his "unhappiness" with the function.[13] One area of economics that Solow believed to have been adversely affected by the profession's "romance with Cobb–Douglas" was the empirical analysis of the functional distribution of income. As noted above, it was already known that the path of labor's share in a growing, competitive neoclassical economy characterized by an aggregate production function F(K, L) was in part a function of the elasticity of substitution between capital and labor, and if the production function was Cobb–Douglas, labor's share would be constant over time. The measured share of labor appeared to vary little over time in the national income statistics, and the idea that it could be regarded as constant for practical and theoretical purposes was reinforced by Douglas's evidence that a Cobb–Douglas production function provided a good fit to data on the US manufacturing sector. Solow, however, was skeptical, arguing in Solow (1958a) that the apparent stability of labor's share in national income was perhaps an artifact of aggregating across sectors with different and time-varying labor shares. He emphasized that

12 Solow to Arrow, June 5, 1959, Box 52, "A" folders, Solow Papers.

13 At a National Bureau of Economic Research (NBER) conference in 1960, Solow expressed strong skepticism towards the cross-section approach to estimating Cobb–Douglas production functions, even dismissing it as "nonsense" (Stigler 1961, 64–65). The Solow quotes in this paragraph are from email communications with the author, February 15–16, 2017.

the response of the aggregate share to rising supplies of capital and/or labor would depend "on the elasticity of substitution, or rather on the distribution of [industry-level] elasticities of substitution on either side of unity." (Solow 1958a, 629). Prior to learning of Arrow's independent derivation of the function, Solow had tried to persuade Melvin Reder to use Solow's new production function to analyze labor's share; perhaps the opportunity to do such an analysis himself helped to convince Solow to join the Stanford team's project.[14]

Hollis Chenery, as B. S. Minhas's thesis supervisor, had suggested to Minhas the collection and analysis of the data with which the project originated, but that alone does not explain why Chenery decided to take an active role in the project. However, a review Chenery's activities in the late 1950s suggests reasons why Chenery would have been enthusiastic about research that led to a production function that was analytically tractable, empirically estimable, and allowed for a range of substitution possibilities between capital and labor.

At the time he began working with Minhas, Chenery was the director of the Stanford Project for Quantitative Research in Economic Development. In discussing the activities of the project, Chenery emphasized the importance of employing "interindustry methods" that allowed analysis of the changing relationships between sectors or industries of a nation's economy as both a cause and a consequence of the growth process (Chenery 1960a). He also stressed the policy relevance of the work: growth models developed by the project would facilitate exploration of the consequences for growth of various government-promoted investment strategies, and empirical evidence on the changing patterns of resource allocation that had historically accompanied the process of economic growth would help the leaders of developing nations guide their economies smoothly along the path already followed by the developed nations (Chenery 1960a, 650–51; 1960b, 650).

Chenery himself was working with a model he had developed to explain the historically observed tendency for a nation's manufacturing sector to grow relative to other sectors as per-capita income increased. Chenery's results pointed to the importance of import substitution as a driver of the growth of manufacturing in developing nations, and he speculated that changes in comparative advantage as relative factor supplies changed might be one important explanation of changing import substitution

[14] Solow to Arrow, June 5, 1959, Box 52, "A" folders, Solow Papers.

patterns. But the state of his model (and the available data) as of the late 1950s did not allow him to explore this possibility. Better data on factor supplies and factor prices in various nations at various stages of development would certainly be helpful, and Minhas's dissertation research began with an effort to compile such data. The industries in Chenery's model were assumed to have fixed coefficient production functions, and when data were available, Chenery would construct Leontief-style input-output models for the economies he wished to analyze (e.g., Chenery and Watanabe 1958). But he would also mention the inability of such models to capture the role played by factor substitution as relative commodity prices changed in response to changing factor scarcities. It is thus easy to imagine that Chenery would be excited by the possibility of a tractable production function that allowed labor-capital substitution. And in the published version of the Arrow et al. paper, the implications of the CES production function model for patterns of international trade was a point of emphasis.[15]

The Debut of the CES Production Function

As already mentioned, Arrow's derivation of the CES production function was based on an empirical regularity observed in data collected by Minhas; this regularity became exhibit A in the Arrow et al. (1961). The data in which Minhas observed the regularity first appeared was industrial census data from 19 countries, collected in years between 1949 and 1955. There were 24 industries for which observations from at least 10 countries were available, resulting in a cross-section data set of 349 industry-by-country observations. Value added (V), labor in man-years (L) and wages per man-year (W) were recorded or calculable for all observations, while the value of capital and/or information sufficient to estimate the return to capital was available for a small subset.

These data were used to estimate the following regression for each industry:

$$\log(V/L) = \log(a) + b\log(W) + \varepsilon \tag{4.1}$$

The regression fit the data well: "In 20 out of 24 industries, over 85% of the variation in labor productivity (was) explained by variation in wage rates alone." After promising to show that the b coefficient estimated the

[15] See point (ii) in the introduction, Sections II-B-4, II-B-6, and IV-C, and paragraphs 1, 3, and 5 of the conclusion.

elasticity of substitution for an industry, the authors noted that the value of *b* was significantly different from 0 in every industry, and significantly different from 1 in over half of the industries. Thus, the data seemed to reject both of the conventional assumptions about the elasticity of substitution.

Section II of the paper presented a model developed to "rationalize" this empirical finding. In the model, each industry consisted of firms operating in competitive labor and output markets. Within an industry, firms shared a constant-returns-to-scale production function consistent with the relationship between V/L and W observed in their data, that is, log(V/L) = log (*a*) + *b* log(W). The authors then derived the form that this production function must take.[16] The authors offered several ways of representing the production function; two versions that expressed value added (that is, output) directly as a function of quantities of capital and labor were

$$V = (\beta K^{-\rho} + \alpha L^{-\rho})^{-(1/\rho)} \tag{4.2}$$

$$V = \gamma[\delta K^{-\rho} + (1 - \delta)L^{-\rho}]^{-(1/\rho)} \tag{4.3}$$

And they gave this type of production function a name: "a constant elasticity of substitution production function (abbreviated to CES)."

The parameter ρ was dubbed the substitution parameter; it equaled $(1 - \sigma)/\sigma$, where σ was the elasticity of substitution; ρ could take on values from −1 to positive infinity, corresponding to elasticities of substitution ranging from infinity (straight-line isoquants) to zero (right angle isoquants, or constant input coefficients). It was shown that in the case of $\rho=0$ ($\sigma=1$), the CES production function became the Cobb–Douglas production function. In the equation (4.2) version of the production function, differences in the α and β parameters represented differences in the efficiency with which labor and capital, respectively, were converted into output. Equation (4.3) was derived from equation (4.2) using the definitions $\delta = \beta/(\alpha+\beta)$ and $\gamma^{-\rho} = \alpha+\beta$, so that equation (4.3) had a "(neutral) efficiency parameter" γ – a change in γ "change(d) the output for any given set of inputs in the same proportion" – as well as a "distribution" parameter δ, the value of which would determine the distribution of income between labor and capital given any value of σ.

[16] The full derivation is on pp. 229–230 of Arrow et al. (1961).

After the derivation and description of the CES production function came several pages identifying "testable implications of the model" accompanied by descriptions of a number of alternative methods of estimating the CES parameters, and then three full sections presenting the results of estimation and testing. A few examples help to illustrate the authors' eclectic approach to this phase of their project.

A first is the authors' method of testing their assumption that the values of the CES production function parameters were constant across countries within each industry. The authors derived a test statistic $c = (V/K)\ (1 - \alpha(V/L)^{\rho}\ )^{-1/\rho}$ that could be constructed for each observation for which capital data was available, using values of ρ and α implied by the regression coefficients of equation (4.1).[17] The authors argued that a finding that c was not constant within industries "may be read as suggesting that β varies across countries while α and ρ are the same," that is, that efficiency in the use of capital varied across countries, while the efficiency of labor did not.

It seemed more plausible, the authors suggested, that any international differences in efficiency would affect both capital and labor equally, so that within industries, γ varied across countries, while β/α (and thus δ) did not. Their model implied that $\beta/\alpha = (r/w)(K/L)^{1+\rho}$. For those countries with K and r data, an estimate of the right-hand side of this equation, and thus of δ, could be constructed for each country-industry observation using the industry's estimate of ρ. Then, estimates of δ and ρ could be plugged into the production function equation along with data on capital and labor to produce an estimate of γ for each observation.

There were four industries for which the authors had or could construct capital data for between three and five countries, and they calculated the values of α, β, δ, and c for each industry-country combination for which the necessary data were available. Eyeballing the resulting values for c was enough to lead the authors to "abandon the idea that efficiency is the same among countries and look for constancy in either α, β, or δ," and they ultimately concluded that "the constancy of δ, implying neutral variations in efficiency, is much the closest approximation .... Constant σ and δ characterize an industry in all countries, and differences in efficiency are assumed to be concentrated in γ_i."

A second example of estimation and testing involves the authors' treatment of the possible phenomenon of "reversals" in factor intensity implied by their model. They illustrated the phenomenon by proposing two hypothetical industries operating in the same competitive factor and output

[17] The regression provided estimates of b and log(a), and in the derivation of the CES production function, the authors had made the substitutions $\alpha = a^{-(1/b)}$ and $\rho = (1/b) - 1$.

markets. If one assumed that both industries operated with fixed coefficient production functions, or both with Cobb–Douglas production functions, the same industry would be the more capital intensive of the two regardless of the factor price ratio. However, if the two industries had CES production functions with different elasticities of substitution, the industry that was the more capital intensive of the two when wages were relatively high could be the less capital intensive when wages were relatively low. This possibility of factor intensity reversals was important, as "the relative factor-intensity ratio plays an important role in discussion of the tendency of international trade in commodities to equalize factor prices in different countries."

To determine whether the possibility was an empirical reality, the authors turned to a collection of industry-level data from the United States and Japan.[18] The data were used to construct "two-point estimates" of the CES parameters for each industry. The relationship $(K/L)_J/(K/L)_U = [(w/r)_J/(w/r)_U]^{\sigma}$ was used to estimate σ, where subscripts J and U denoted Japan and the United States. The resulting estimates implied that reversals in factor intensity were a real occurrence.

A third example of the diversity of approaches to estimation and testing found in Arrow et al. (1961) is provided by the authors' application of the CES production function model to aggregate time series data, in order to analyze technical change and the evolution of labor's share.[19] They first noted that given competition and profit maximization, the CES production function implied a path over time of the ratio of labor's share to capital's share that was independent of γ, that is, $(wL/rK) = ((1\text{-}\delta)/\delta)(K/L)^{\rho}$, so that if technical progress were neutral, this relationship would hold fairly well in the time series. If one were willing to accept the hypothesis of neutral technological change, the relationship implied an approach to estimating ρ and δ using the regression

$$\log(wL/rK) = \log((1-\delta)/\delta) + \rho\log(K/L) + \varepsilon \qquad (4.4)$$

The authors also described other approaches to estimating the CES parameters using a time series. The elasticity of substitution could be estimated using any two observations in the series, based on the relationship

[18] The data, which included quantities and prices of inputs and outputs for numerous industries, had been compiled for the purposes of constructing input-output tables, and were different from the industrial census information on the United States and Japan in the data used in previous sections of the paper.

[19] The data used was the time series for US aggregate non-farm production, 1909–1949, also used in Solow (1957), to be discussed in Chapter 6.

$(K/L)_1/(K/L)_2 = [(w/r)_1/(w/r)_2]^\sigma$. Or, one could begin with the assumed relationship that had motivated the derivation of the CES production function, $V/L = aw^b$. This relationship implied a time path for labor's share: $(wL/V) = (1 - \delta)^\sigma \gamma^{\sigma-1} w^{1-\sigma}$. Given estimates of σ and δ, the values of K, L, and V could be plugged into the production function to construct an estimate of γ for each time period. Alternatively, one could assume that γ grew at a geometric rate λ, such that $\gamma(t) = \gamma_0 10^{\lambda t}$, and could estimate λ and σ with the regression

$$\begin{aligned}\log(wL/V) = {} & [\sigma\log(1 - \delta) + (\sigma - 1)\log\gamma_0] \\ & + (\sigma - 1)\log(w) + \lambda(\sigma - 1)t \qquad (4.5)\end{aligned}$$

This regression also allowed straightforward tests of the null hypotheses $\sigma = 0$ and $\sigma = 1$; both these hypotheses were easily rejected.

These three examples reveal only a subset of the topics touched upon in Arrow et al. (1961); another matter receiving considerable attention was the relationship between efficiency, substitutability, and international differences in commodity prices. The variety of topics covered in the paper suggest that the production function regression was coming to be seen as a "general purpose empirical tool," one that might aid the exploration of a wide range of research questions in economics. The authors themselves noted the paper's broad scope in their concluding section, commenting that it reflected the "fundamental economic significance of the degree of substitutability of capital and labor." In the summary of empirical findings, they chose to emphasize the "evidence that the elasticity of substitution between capital and labor in manufacturing may typically be less than unity," and that international differences in efficiency within industries existed, but were "approximately neutral in their incidence on capital and labor." In the period immediately following the publication of Arrow et al. (1961), the authors' empirical claims did attract notice and generate controversy, but of course it was the CES production function itself that was the paper's most lasting legacy.

The Profession's Reaction to Arrow et al. (1961)

Arrow et al. (1961) had an immediate impact on economic research. By the end of 1966, around 70 articles citing the paper had been published in the leading economics journals.[20] Some merely referred to the existence of

[20] This citation count is based on a search of JSTOR indexed, English-language journals in economics and statistics. I did a full text search for "Arrow" and "Chenery" and "Minhas," then examined each article containing these three names. A benchmark for

the function as an alternative way of representing production relations, or cited an empirical result from the paper, but there were many substantive uses of the function as well. As an empirical tool, the CES was applied in its cross-section form to interstate and international data. Researchers exploring the impact of technical change on growth, or of the evolution of labor's share, applied it to time series data. Critics identified potential sources of bias in the estimation procedures of Arrow et al. (1961), for example, Fuchs (1963) and Ferguson (1963). Trade economists argued over the credibility of authors' claim to have demonstrated the importance of factor reversal.

In the years 1967–1969, another 70-plus journal articles cited Arrow et al. (1961). It was becoming more common for researchers to use the function as an element of an applied theoretical model, or to illustrate properties of a more general theoretical model. But by this period, the function was moving into the public domain – in 1969, the number of articles I found that mentioned or used the CES production function without citing Arrow et al. (1961) was about equal to the number that did cite it.

The presentation of the CES production function as a tool for empirical research in Arrow et al. (1961), and the profession's reaction to it, began an important transformation of the research program of estimating production functions using regression analysis that had developed out of Douglas's production research program. First, as already noted, the CES was the first generalization of Cobb–Douglas to be quickly and widely adopted by empirical researchers. I believe that one reason for the CES function's success in this respect was the growing popularity among the emerging leaders of the profession during the 1950s of Hicks and Allen's mathematical representation of the neoclassical theory of value and distribution, in which the elasticity of substitution was a key parameter. The generalization of Cobb–Douglas offered in Arrow et al. (1961) allowed this parameter to take on any value and to be estimated directly. Given the significance that had come to be attributed to the elasticity of substitution for important questions of value and distribution theory, this feature made the CES production function immediately attractive in 1961. This supposition is supported by the fact that a highlighted feature of several

assessing the citation counts reported in the text is provided by Hamermesh (2018), who reports that in a sample of all articles published in 1974–75 in the top five journals of economics, the mean (median) number of citations to an article over the ten years following publication (as recorded in the Social Science Citation Index) was 22 (11); the article at the 95th percentile was cited 82 times.

subsequently proposed and successful production function forms was that they placed even fewer restrictions on the behavior of the elasticity of substitution than did the CES (e.g., Lovell 1973, Christiansen et al. 1973).

Second, in order to derive an "indirect" procedure for estimating the parameters of the CES using factor price data, Arrow and his coauthors had assumed a neoclassical competitive equilibrium, that is, competition in output and input markets, cost minimization, and a resulting equality of marginal products and input prices. As we have seen, Klein had demonstrated in 1953 how to use these assumptions to specify a Cowles-style simultaneous equations model featuring a Cobb–Douglas production function, and estimate the parameters of that production function using data on factor shares. As of 1961, few researchers had implemented his suggestion. But after the publication of Arrow et al. (1961), using assumptions about competition, optimization, and equilibrium to develop strategies for the indirect estimation of both CES parameters and the parameters of other new production function forms became a widely accepted approach in empirical research. The most thoroughgoing manifestation of this method was the rigorous use of duality theory to infer production function parameters from the coefficients of estimated cost functions (e.g., Christiansen et al. 1973).

Obviously, one reason that Arrow and his coauthors developed their indirect approaches to estimating the CES production function was that the nonlinearity of the CES function almost precluded the use of a direct approach to estimating its parameters. The point is, however, that other researchers did not have to follow their lead. Yet many did, implicitly deciding that the new research results that could thus be obtained would have value in spite of any problems that might be caused by the failure of the necessary assumptions of competition, optimization, and equilibrium. My argument is not that Arrow et al. (1961) created among economists a willingness to employ estimation techniques based on these assumptions. Instead, I am pointing to the production function estimation strategies employed in Arrow et al. (1961) and the transformation of empirical production function research that followed it as evidence of an important change going on in the late 1950s and early 1960s with respect to the assumptions that economists were willing to make in order to facilitate empirical research.

I would also argue that these two changes in empirical production function research – the introduction of new functional forms and the increased willingness to assume the existence of a competitive neoclassical equilibrium – helped to immunize the larger research program of estimating production functions via regression against two of the more serious criticisms of the Douglas's methods and results. The project of developing new and more flexible production functional forms for empirical production function research that generalized the Cobb–Douglas responded to one obvious and important criticism of the previous attempts by Douglas and others to estimate production functions – that the Cobb–Douglas function was too simple to capture the reality of production relationships in the economy. After the introduction of the CES form, the proposition that the production function was "Cobb–Douglas" became something that could be tested, rather than something that had to be assumed. The increased willingness of economists to assume the existence of a neoclassical competitive equilibrium (an assumption which facilitated the estimation of the parameters of the new functional forms), represented something of an end run around another serious criticism of Douglas's research – that his methods of testing for competition or the accuracy of the marginal productivity theory were fatally flawed. A willingness to assume the existence of the competitive equilibrium of neoclassical theory implied a belief that testing whether such an equilibrium obtained was no longer a very important goal for empirical production function research, so the fact that Douglas's method did not allow for such testing was not a serious problem. As empirical production function research developed in the 1960s and beyond, the dominant attitude governing most applications was that the competitive equilibrium assumption was not problematic, provided that it allowed the estimation of the parameters of a production function that could be shown, through statistical testing, to satisfy certain basic implications of neoclassical production theory and to be a good fit to the observed data.

5

The Cobb–Douglas Regression in Agricultural Economics, 1944–1965

A. A. Walters, in his 1963 *Econometrica* survey of empirical production and cost functions, reported results from 103 Cobb–Douglas regressions that had been published since the original Cobb–Douglas article. Twenty-six of those had been estimated by Douglas and his coauthors. Over a third of the remainder were the work of agricultural economists. Walters chose not to report the results of what he called "engineering" or "process" production functions, that is, production functions estimated using data from a narrowly defined technological process, but noted that this method of production function estimation had also been "extensively used in agriculture" (Walters 1963a, 12).

Writing in 1962, Zvi Griliches, who would go on to become one of the most influential users of and commentators on the Cobb–Douglas regression, commented that in the years following Douglas's retirement from economics, empirical research on production functions, while "out of fashion on the national level," had "led a very vigorous life among agricultural economists" (Griliches 1962, 280). Griliches would later attribute the first aspect of this observation to the "withering attacks by critics" on the work of the Douglas group, and the second to the fact that the agricultural economists were able to apply the regression to microeconomic data for which "the necessary assumption for estimating something sensible appeared to be more plausible" (Griliches and Mairesse 1999).

As these contemporary sources indicate, agricultural economists were early and enthusiastic adopters of the Cobb–Douglas regression, and there are good reasons why one would expect this to be the case. First, agricultural economics was one of the most empirically oriented fields of economics in the mid-twentieth century, and agricultural economists were more comfortable than economists in general with advanced statistical techniques. Second, agricultural economists saw the production function regression as a means of addressing some long-standing questions specific to their field, and as a potential improvement over the empirical methods already being used to explore those questions.

Most of this chapter is devoted to a detailed examination of how the agricultural economists applied the Cobb–Douglas regression from 1944 through the early 1960s, what they understood themselves to be doing and discovering in those applications, and some of the critical reactions to their efforts. As in Part I, the story involves an energetic and influential advocate of the new method, as well as friendly critics, who, though believing there to be serious problems with the method, described and implemented strategies for ameliorating those problems. As was the case with Douglas's production research program, developments and debates in the literature related to estimation of agricultural production functions reflected broader trends in the use of statistical methods by economists. And in one important instance, a statistical innovation introduced in the context of estimating the Cobb–Douglas regression with agricultural data had a major impact on the subsequent course of what was by then commonly known as "econometrics."

The chapter ends with some speculation on why the Cobb–Douglas regression flourished more vigorously in agricultural economics than in other fields of economics in the decade or so following Douglas's 1947 appeal to the profession to carry on his work. Griliches's brief explanation, quoted earlier, hits on one very important reason: the data used by the agricultural economists seemed more likely to conform to the assumptions required for the Cobb–Douglas regression to produce useful and sensible results. The agricultural economists were the first to estimate the regression using data reported at the level of individual firms, as opposed to the more highly aggregated data used by Douglas and his coauthors, and agricultural economists also had access to experimental data on agricultural production processes. I also believe it important that the questions the agricultural economists sought to answer with the regression were different from those upon which Douglas had focused. As a result, their discussions of the method, and the criticisms they attracted from their colleagues, while drawing on the prewar literature surrounding the Cobb–Douglas regression, had noticeably different emphases. The agricultural economists saw the Cobb–Douglas regression as a means of estimating production relationships and diagnosing resource-allocation decisions by farmers, so that claims about the efficacy of the method as a test of the marginal productivity theory or the extent of competition, which had served as something of a lightning rod for critics of the Douglas program, became irrelevant.

BACKGROUND: WHY AGRICULTURAL ECONOMISTS WERE INTRIGUED BY DOUGLAS'S PROGRAM

During the interwar period, the field of agricultural economics was a hotbed of empirical research. The US Department of Agriculture and the state supported land-grant colleges employed economists with the expectation that they would conduct research into issues of interest to farmers and agricultural policy makers. These economists had access to the relatively rich agricultural data collected by the government, and to funding for the collection and analysis of experimental data and survey data on the activities of individual farmers. A further bias towards empiricism was created by the principle that their research should help create knowledge that was practically useful for farmers (Fox 1989). As a result, training in statistical methods was emphasized in graduate programs in agricultural economics, and, as Fox (1986) has pointed out, many of the pioneering econometricians of the interwar period came out of the field of agricultural economics. So, when Douglas's production studies, with their innovative use of regression analysis, began to appear, agricultural economists were in a better position than economists in general to understand them, and were more likely to be intrigued by the statistical issues that they raised.

In addition, Douglas's vision of statistically estimating the production function(s) of neoclassical economic theory was salient for two related and long-standing research areas in the field of agricultural economics. Banzhaf (2006) provides an excellent account of the emergence of agricultural economics in the early twentieth century, as economists first contributed to, and then came to dominate, the preexisting research area of farm management.[1] In the early 1900s, farm management encompassed the work of applied scientists from a variety of fields – plant genetics, soil science, entomology, and so forth – whose research was intended to help farmers solve practical problems and ultimately make more money. The early agricultural economists envisioned a central role for themselves in this field, as the experts who could teach farmers how to apply the scientific knowledge from several disciplines to keep their farms profitable in the

[1] This and the next two paragraphs are based on Banzhaf (2006), who describes some of the major figures behind the trends described. Additional references are to papers illustrative of the type of research described in the text.

face of shifting economic forces. Their claim to this role was based on their possession of a general analytical framework for thinking about the business decisions faced by a farmer: the neoclassical theory of the firm. A few basic concepts like opportunity cost and the equation of marginal cost and marginal benefit could be used to analyze the dizzying array of choices faced by a farmer seeking to maximize profits. To a greater extent than the average economist of the time, then, these economists were well versed in and convinced of the usefulness of neoclassical theory, although, as Banzhaf explains, it was a commitment to neoclassical economics as a normative tool to guide resource allocation, not as a positive description of economic activity. Indeed, they believed the agricultural sector to be rife with inefficiency and misallocation, thus justifying the need for farm-management research.

As economists moved into the field of farm management, they found a very empirical and practical, but rather atheoretical, literature in which common sense notions of economy were applied in what to the economists seemed haphazard and sometimes conflicting ways. Over the interwar decades, they set about trying to bring order to the field through the application of neoclassical theory, generating a body of research and knowledge they called production economics.[2] Research in production economics included the application of the logic of maximization to a variety of situations arising in farming, such as the allocation of laborers of varying efficiency to cooperating inputs of varying efficiency (Waite 1936), or the "multi-enterprise farm," which produced more than one output requiring the same type of input (Benedict 1932a). Empirical research included the development of better empirical counterparts for the cost and return concepts of neoclassical theory, for example, opportunity costs rather than accounting costs, and marginal rather than average returns (Benedict 1932b). As the neoclassical agricultural economists pushed this agenda forward through the 1920s and 1930s, there was continual tension between the desire for analytical concepts and empirical measures that were theoretically correct, and what was possible and practical given the resources and tools available for the collection and analysis of data.

A few examples serve to illustrate these tensions. One line of empirical research in the traditional farm-management literature involved the collection of detailed accounting records from samples of farms, and then the

[2] Ezekiel (1926) gives a good sense of the agenda of these economists.

calculation of input-output ratios (e.g., pounds of feed per hundredweight of cattle) or efficiency ratios (crop acres per man). The values of such ratios on more profitable farms were offered as guides or standards for farmers in general. Economists objected that such observed ratios on any given farm were a function of particular characteristics of that farm, and thus might not reflect an optimum for any other farm. Also, the calculation of ratios as guides for farmers often implicitly assumed away the core economic principle of diminishing returns. A good deal of experimental research, often conducted by noneconomists, was devoted to finding the most profitable mix of inputs to maximize a particular output, whether it was the mix of grain and hay in feeding cattle or the allocation of labor and machinery to maximize the value of a corn crop. Economists came to argue, however, that such information was potentially misleading to the many farmers on multi-enterprise farms, who had to allocate inputs between competing outputs. They pushed for additional data collection and analysis that focused on measuring the profits of the farm as a whole, and the correlation of those profits with the input and output choices of these multi-enterprise farmers (Black 1932, 250–62; Hopkins 1930).

It is thus easy to see why economists involved in farm management research in the early 1940s would be excited about Douglas's estimation of production functions. In principle, a properly estimated production function could provide a wealth of theoretically appropriate information to guide farmers in their input and output decisions. The regression would yield not just ratios but functions relating inputs to output, thus quantifying the action of the law of diminishing returns; it would also reveal input-substitution relationships. If applied to financial data of the sort typically collected in farm management studies, production function estimation could reveal the value productivity of expenditure on various types of inputs for multi-enterprise farms. Indeed, during the 1930s some agricultural economists had already produced estimates of the production relationships implied by neoclassical theory, in the form of two-way cross tabulations or bivariate regressions involving one input and one output (Hopkins 1930, Warren 1936, Menze 1942), and a few studies calculating partial correlation coefficients between several inputs and an output (e.g., Jensen 1940), but Douglas's approach offered clear advantages over these earlier efforts: his functional form easily handled several inputs and parsimoniously captured the key assumption of diminishing returns, and when estimated as a regression it produced coefficients that were directly and easily interpretable as elasticities of output with respect to inputs.

The normative neoclassicism that characterized economic research on farm management also found its way into discussions of national agricultural policy, although it was only one perspective among many. During the interwar years, a number of agricultural economists believed that misallocation of social resources within agriculture and between agriculture and the rest of the economy was a major contributor to the perennial problem of low farm incomes. Too much land was being cultivated by too many laborers, and in many areas agricultural resources were being devoted to the wrong outputs. This point of view was prevalent enough that it came to be embodied in the Agricultural Adjustment Act of 1933 (Barber 1994), and among those who shared it, some argued that the neoclassical principles that guided the farmer towards maximum profits also provided the best tools for analyzing the social misallocation of resources and for designing measures to address it (Heady 1948, 205; Johnson 1944, 635–36). These agricultural economists saw Douglas's production function as a tool for diagnosing misallocation of social resources, as it could detect situations in which the marginal productivity of inputs in agriculture varied across regions, or differed from the return those factors might earn in other sectors of the economy.

INITIAL APPLICATIONS OF THE COBB–DOUGLAS REGRESSION TO AGRICULTURAL DATA

Prior to 1950, most applications of the Cobb–Douglas production function to agricultural data were the work of a small number of researchers associated with Iowa State College, where future Nobel laureate Theodore W. Schultz had assembled a remarkably talented and energetic group of economists committed to using neoclassical reasoning and advanced empirical methods to help solve the problems of agriculture.[3] The first two applications appeared in *Econometrica* in 1944, in articles by Gerhard Tintner.

Tintner (1944a) estimated the Cobb–Douglas regression using data from a sample of 609 Iowa farms. Tintner pointed out the advantages of the Cobb–Douglas form, including the interesting elasticity interpretation of

[3] Burnett (2011). Schultz left Iowa State College for the University of Chicago in the fall of 1943. Of the economists whose work is discussed below, Tintner came to Iowa State in 1937 and remained after Schultz's departure, while Johnson and Heady were attracted to Iowa State College graduate program by Schultz, with Johnson accompanying Schultz to University of Chicago and Heady remaining at Iowa State.

its coefficients and its embodiment of the law of diminishing returns. Tintner's "product" variable was gross farm profits, and he grouped inputs into six categories: land, labor, improvements (farm buildings and other structures), liquid assets (e.g., livestock, feed, and supplies), working assets (tractors, other machinery, and work animals), and a residual category of cash operating expenses. Land was measured in acres and labor as months of hired and family labor, while the remaining inputs were measured in monetary terms. In "An Application of the Variate Difference Method to Multiple Regression," Tintner (1944b) used annual time series data to estimate an aggregate production function for the US agricultural sector, including a linear time trend in the regression along with capital and labor variables.

Tintner was first and foremost an econometrician, and his interest in Douglas's regression was motivated more by the econometric issues it raised than by its applications for agricultural policy. The "variate difference method" employed in the time series paper was a method he had developed for estimating the coefficients of a deterministic linear relationship between variables when all the variables were measured with error, that is, the same statistical model underlying Frisch's confluence analysis and Mendershausen's attack on Douglas's production studies. Tintner estimated the agricultural production function simply as a means of demonstrating this method. He made no effort to interpret his results, including the incredible estimate of 2.7 for the elasticity of output with respect to labor.

Likewise, Tintner's estimation of a cross-section Cobb–Douglas regression using farm records was aimed at addressing two important econometric shortcomings of Douglas's program. First, the use of a sample in which the farm was the unit of analysis was responsive to Marschak and Andrews' demonstration that a Cobb–Douglas regression was quite unlikely to recover the parameters of a true theoretical production function if it was estimated with data aggregated above the level of the individual firm.[4] Also, the paper was the first to explicitly and rigorously apply a probability-based theory of statistical inference to the estimates from a Cobb–Douglas regression, including several pages devoted to describing and conducting a statistical test of the hypothesis that the estimated coefficients of the inputs summed to one. Again, having presented his

4 Tintner did not explicitly refer to this issue, but he was clearly aware of the relevance of his paper to it, as Marschak and Andrews (1944) referred to Tintner's paper, and Tintner's acknowledgement footnote thanked Marschak for his advice and criticism.

results, Tintner had almost nothing to say about their implications for farmers or farm policy.

The role that the Iowa State College economists saw for the Cobb–Douglas regression in farm-management research became clearer in Tintner and Brownlee (1944). This time, the regression was estimated for a sample of 498 Iowa farms, and with five subsamples of distinct farm type. The paper followed the pattern of Tintner's earlier study in its definitions of input and output variables. However, after reporting the coefficient estimates, the authors presented a table of marginal productivities they had calculated from the coefficient estimates, indicating "the returns which might be expected from the addition of one dollar's worth of the various productive agents." Fiducial limits for the marginal productivities were presented as well.[5] In a section on "economic interpretation of the results," it was noted that most farm types showed decreasing returns to scale, although the authors warned that this might be because no measure of the management input had been included. Marginal productivities of different inputs were compared within farm types, leading to conclusions like "additional inputs of liquid assets and working assets, and additional cash expenditures on equipment repairs, fuel, oil and feed will probably yield higher returns than additional improvements" (Tintner and Brownlee 1944, 571). Indications that the marginal productivity of some inputs differed considerably across farm type were also pointed out, but no firm conclusions were drawn from this.

In both the studies just discussed, the sample data had been compiled by farmers participating in an agricultural extension program that encouraged them to keep more detailed financial records. This, as Tintner and Brownlee pointed out, led to a nonrepresentative sample favoring relatively large farms that "may represent the upper part of the production function" (Tintner and Brownlee 1944, 571). Tintner and Brownlee's colleague Earl Heady (1946) addressed this problem by estimating the Cobb–Douglas regression with a random sample of Iowa farms surveyed in 1939. Although he followed pretty closely the format and methods of the two previous studies, he gave a more a thorough account of the strengths and weaknesses of the method, and a more extensive discussion of the practical implications of the results for farm management.

Heady's sample had over 700 farms, and he estimated production functions for subsamples based on geographical area, type of farm, and

[5] Fiducial limits were a concept taken from R. A. Fisher, serving a similar purpose to (and in this case numerically identical to) confidence intervals.

farm size. Generally, the estimates indicated decreasing returns to scale. This surprised Heady, given the prevalent belief that larger farms were more efficient, and he presented a careful analysis of the circumstances under which this finding could be attributed to the omission of a variable measuring the "management" input. He observed that the marginal productivity of machinery was higher in those areas of Iowa known to be least mechanized. The uniformly low estimates of the marginal productivity of labor he attributed to the impact of the Depression in keeping people on the farms, and the tendency of farm operators to report working full time even during the inevitable slack periods associated with agricultural production. He cautioned about comparing marginal productivities of inputs within farm types: some input variables were the money values of stocks and others were the money values of flows, so assumptions about depreciation rates would have to be made before comparing the marginal impact of a one-dollar increase in a stock variable vs. a flow variable.

Heady voiced several concerns about the limitations of the Cobb–Douglas method, but presented his study as a first step in a better direction for farm-management research: with refinement, "the general type of analysis . . . might serve as a useful tool in studies concerned with the productivity and allocation of resources" (Heady 1946, 1,000). For example, he pointed out, it had become standard to assess the relative efficiency of farms with a measure of net farm profit (or loss) created by subtracting from total revenue a measure of the value of inputs used, including the imputed values of service flows from stocks of land, buildings, and machinery. Unfortunately, the farms ranked as most efficient by this measure during the years when output prices were high could end up being ranked as least efficient when output prices were low. Heady proposed as an alternative efficiency measure the difference between a farm's actual output and the output predicted, based on its input levels, by a well-specified production function estimated with a sample of similar farms.

The pioneering farm-level production function studies just described all made reference to Douglas's production studies, and evidenced a solid knowledge of the debates surrounding those studies. However, there are several interesting differences in approach and emphasis between the Douglas studies and the applications of the Cobb–Douglas regression to cross-section agricultural data by Tintner, Brownlee, Heady, and the researchers who would follow their lead over the next ten years. First, as noted above, the views of Douglas and his coauthors as to the statistical assumptions to make in thinking about their data, and thus the correct procedures for estimation and inference, evolved over time and never really stabilized. By contrast, the agricultural economists who used the Cobb–Douglas regression from the beginning thought about their estimation problem using the framework of statistical assumptions and procedures developed by Ronald Fisher.[6] They discussed as a matter of course the extent to which their samples were representative of a population of interest. Their least squares coefficients were regarded as estimates of population parameters, and they drew inferences from the estimates by using standard formulas to calculate fiducial or confidence intervals or determine levels of statistical significance. Thus, these agricultural economists brought to the empirical production function a higher level of mathematical formalism as well as Porter's (1995) "mechanical objectivity," in the form of a standardized set of inferential procedures. Also, while the agricultural economists shared with Douglas the goal of statistically determining the relationship between inputs and outputs and "the probable elasticities of the curves of marginal productivity," they did not see the Cobb–Douglas regression as a tool for testing the theory of marginal productivity, which they were already certain did not apply in the settings they were studying (e.g., Heady 1946, 1001).

Finally, the problem of actually specifying the Cobb–Douglas regression, in particular defining how inputs were to be categorized and measured, had a much greater significance for the agricultural economists than it did for Douglas. As noted above, Douglas worked with a conception of a law of production linking social capital and social labor to social output, which identified a two-input aggregate production function as an important relationship to estimate. He gave lip service to the existence of heterogeneity of capital and labor inputs and the desirability of developing measures to reflect this, but he regarded these issues as matters for future consideration rather than pressing items on his own research agenda (Douglas 1934, 60–61). Agricultural economists involved in farm management research could not comfortably take such a position, however. They were interested in production function estimation as a tool for diagnosing and prescribing actual agricultural practices, and the effectiveness of the method in this role depended on their ability to specify regressions that captured the possible production technologies and feasible input combinations found in the many different types of farming.

[6] Because agricultural researchers had access to experimental data, and because Fisher, in his widely read textbooks, explicated his methods in the context of agricultural experiments, it is not surprising to find that agricultural economists were trained in and willing to adopt this framework.

EARL HEADY: EVANGELIST FOR THE COBB–DOUGLAS REGRESSION

Cobb–Douglas regressions continued to appear sporadically in the agricultural economics literature in the later 1940s. Harries (1947) estimated the function using data from Canadian farms, and despite Harries' emphasis on the limitations of the method, a discussant of the paper at the conference at which it was presented was enthusiastic about its potential to advance the field of farm management (Sinclair 1947). Lomax (1949) estimated an aggregate production function using time series data from the UK. During the 1950s, however, Earl Heady was the most active user and promoter of the Cobb–Douglas regression.

Earl O. Heady, born in 1916, grew up on a farm in western Nebraska. He received both a B.S. and master's degree in agricultural economics from the University of Nebraska, and came to Iowa State University in 1940 as a Ph. D. candidate and instructor in agricultural economics. Within a few years of Heady's arrival, the Iowa State College economics department was shaken up considerably when department chair T. W. Schultz left for the University of Chicago, to be followed over the next few years by several of his Iowa State College colleagues. However, Iowa State College still had high quality faculty members with whom Heady could interact. Gerhard Tintner remained, and William Snedecor, one of the world's leading statistical theorists and practitioners, was head of the statistics department. Kenneth Boulding and future Noble laureate Leonid Hurwicz joined the faculty shortly after Heady received his Ph.D. in 1945.

In some ways, the departure of Schultz and others in the early 1940s created opportunities for Heady, in that funded research projects were left without senior investigators, and graduate students without supervisors. Heady had the ambition and ability to fill this vacuum, and by 1949 he was a full professor with a large and active research program and a number of graduate students working under his tutelage (Beneke 1994; Murray 1994).

Heady was the quintessential normative neoclassicist. In a 1948 article that was something of a manifesto on the appropriate future direction of the field of farm management, Heady took the position that farm management research was the study of the productivity of farm resources and efficiency in their use, making it a branch of "production economics," with an analytical framework provided by neoclassical theory. Economic theoretical models identified the conditions that characterized optimal resource use in any particular situation. Whenever actual patterns of resource use deviated from that ideal, a "problem" existed for the purposes of farm management research, which should aim both at identifying the reason for the deviation and developing a plan of action for eliminating it. And Heady repeatedly emphasized that the "problems" motivating farm-management research included both those associated with the practices of individual farmers and those created by public policy towards agriculture, as the two types of problems were related, and could be analyzed within the same theoretical framework.

The adoption of neoclassical definitions of efficiency and optimality indicated the empirical agenda for farm management research: optimization required reliable forecasts of future prices and knowledge of "production functions or input-output ratios." In particular, there were "countless production functions yet to be discovered." But it was important that the research techniques used to estimate these functions "correspond with known and established economic models and technical relationships." Heady underscored this point with explanations of how several existing empirical procedures designed to produce guidelines for farmers seeking to maximize profits failed to meet this standard (Heady 1948).

As has been discussed, by the late 1940s normative neoclassicism had become a familiar conceptual framework in the field of farm management. But Heady was presenting it in a particularly uncompromising form. He identified neoclassical theory with the formal mathematical models of R. D. G. Allen's (1938) *Mathematics for Economists*, insisted that empirical procedures be firmly grounded both in these models and in modern statistical theory, and essentially reduced farm management to a field of applied microeconomics. It is perhaps for these reasons that his ideas initially met some resistance.[7] Heady's colleagues later recalled the confident young professor presenting his methodological views to dubious if not hostile audiences in a series of professional meetings during the late 1940s, attempting "missionary work" and seeking "converts" to his way of thinking.[8] But Heady was on the right side of history. In 1952 he published *Economics of Agricultural Production and Resource Use*, a lengthy text that carefully elaborated the concepts, models, and analytical techniques required to execute the approach to farm-management research he had laid out in the 1948 article. One admiring review hailed it as the

[7] Heady's identification of agricultural economics as a branch of applied neoclassical theory is quite clear in Heady 1949, p. 837.

[8] See the essays by Beneke (especially fn. 4) and Murray (especially p. 25–26) in Langley et al., 1994, both of whom use the language of evangelism to describe Heady's efforts at persuasion.

culmination of a "revolution" in agricultural production economics, "led by a small group of able and venturesome workers in farm management," and it came to be a standard text for graduate programs in agricultural economics.[9]

The 1948 article also formed the blueprint for Heady's own research program, a substantial component of which involved the estimation of agricultural production functions. In a 1952 paper prepared to explain and justify his work with empirical production functions to the Association of Farm Economists, Heady argued that knowledge of production functions was "the partial basis for the majority of recommendations by agricultural economists," including "recommendations for (1) the quantity and combination of resources to be used by farmers and (2) the manner in which the national policies can facilitate a more efficient use of the nation's agricultural resources" (Heady 1952, 775).[10] The importance of understanding input-output relationships had long been appreciated by agricultural economists, he granted, but the empirical techniques employed to estimate those relationships often implicitly assumed that the production function was linear and/or characterized by constant returns to scale. Heady held that input-outputs relationships were best measured through regression analysis, using a functional form that allowed for diminishing marginal productivity, the dependence of the productivity of each input on the levels of other inputs employed, and substitutability between inputs. Heady noted that input-output relationships could be estimated "for a single technical unit (an animal or an acre of land), for a farm as an economic unit, or for an agricultural region or other aggregative unit" (Heady 1952, 775), but in the paper he only discussed the regression approach in connection with production functions for single technical units or farms, and in subsequent work these are the two types of production functions that he estimated.

Heady's first published production function for a "single technical unit" or agricultural process was an estimated Cobb–Douglas regression relating

[9] In 1987, the Fellows of the Association of Agricultural Economics were asked to identify the books that had made the largest contribution to their field. *Economics of Agricultural Production and Resource Use* received the most votes. The "revolution" quote comes from MacFarlane (1953). Two somewhat critical review essays by Glenn Johnson (1963, 1987, reprinted in Langley et al., 1994, pp. 158–92), place the book in the larger historical context of the development of the field of farm management

[10] Heady noted in the paper that he would use the phrase "production function" interchangeably with "input-output relationships," a phrase more common in the literature of agricultural economics at the time (pp. 775, 777).

the volume of milk produced by dairy cattle to the amounts of grain and hay that they were fed. Heady used the estimates to draw a three-dimensional production surface that provided concrete illustrations of theoretical concepts like the marginal rate of substitution and the marginal productivity of one input holding constant the other. The data for this production function were drawn from a previously published agricultural experiment, but Heady soon began conducting his own experiments in conjunction with graduate students and agronomists (i.e., physical and biological scientists) engaged in farm-management research, studying crop yields as a function of different combinations of soil nutrients, and animal growth as a function of different mixtures of feed and feed supplements.

Heady saw great potential in such joint research. Agronomists, with their understanding of the chemical properties of soils and fertilizers and of the growth processes of plants and animals, could provide qualitative knowledge concerning the likely relationships of soil and animal nutrients to plant and animal growth. This knowledge would help economists choose an appropriate algebraic form for the production function regression. But economists brought something to the table as well. Agronomists' experiments on fertilization or animal feed were typically designed to test the relative efficacy of a few discrete input combinations, with the data analyzed using Ronald Fisher's analysis of variance techniques. This, Heady pointed out, revealed only a few points on the production surface, and did not provide the information, like the marginal rates of substitution between inputs, that farmers needed in order to maximize profits. It also led to inefficient experimental designs. For experiments meant to be analyzed using analysis of variance, agronomists typically budgeted for a large number of treatments at each of a small number of input combinations, so as to obtain precise estimates of both the variation in the output level associated with a single combination, and the differences in the average output levels associated with different combinations.[11] What the farmer really needed to know, however, was the entire function relating inputs to outputs, so the experiment should be designed to reduce the standard errors of the regression coefficients, with a small number of treatments at each of a large number of input combinations (Heady et al. 1953; Heady 1957a).

Heady boasted to his fellow agricultural economists of his success at Iowa State College in convincing agronomists of the value of using

[11] That is, in the analysis of variance framework, experiments were designed to provide precise estimates of the within-treatment variance and the between-treatment variance.

economic models as the basis of their experiments. He claimed that after being exposed to economic models through graduate classes or informally organized seminars, physical scientists would enthusiastically take part in cooperative research (Heady 1957b). Heady et al. (1953) reported on an early experiment intended to demonstrate the possibilities for this sort of cooperation. The team designed an experiment in which pigs were fed with different levels of grain, protein supplement, and antibiotics, and used the resulting data to estimate Cobb–Douglas and quadratic production functions with weight gain as the output variable. By 1957, Heady was able to publish in *Econometrica* accounts of 14 experiments on crop fertilization and five involving the feeding of chickens, turkeys, hogs, or dairy cattle. More, he reported, were underway.

Certain features of these production function experiments are noteworthy. First, they were indeed controlled, randomized experiments, and Heady was aware that the use of experimental data neutralized many of the criticisms aimed at Douglas's and other empirical production function studies.[12] In the experimental setting, the researcher could ensure that there were no significant errors in the input data, which "fulfills one of the basic assumption of least squares multiple regression." The problem of multicollinearity, emphasized by Menderhausen, was avoided by the experimenter's control over the combinations of inputs to tested. As Heady and Dillon (1961) presented it, this advantage translated into the experimenter's ability to obtain information about a larger portion of the production surface than might be possible in a study using observational data from an area in which "tradition and other institutional circumstances" led farmers to use inputs in roughly the same proportions.

Heady and Dillon (1961) made another point about the advantages of experimental data using a formal model. The assumed production function was $Y = f(X_1, X_2, \ldots, X_k)$. In a nonexperimental setting in which only factors X_1 through X_g could be observed, the estimated production function would be $Y = f(X_1, X_2 \ldots, X_g) + \varepsilon$, where ε arose due to the omission of X_{g+1} through X_k. Some of these omitted factors would be fixed in the observational sample, and some would vary, a situation that could be represented by the equation

[12] Heady's most complete explanation of the strengths and weaknesses of experimental vs. nonexperimental data for production function estimation are found in the textbook Heady coauthored with John Dillon, *Agricultural Production Functions* (Heady and Dillon 1961), and the next three paragraphs are based on pp. 127–31, 144–50, and 214–15.

$$Y = f(X_1, X_2 \ldots, X_g/X_{g+1}, \ldots, X_h//X_{h+1}, \ldots X_k) + \varepsilon \qquad (5.1)$$

where X_{g+1} through X_h represented the fixed omitted factors, and X_{h+1} through X_k those that varied. Under these circumstances, the estimated production function would be "unreliable," although Heady and Dillon were not specific as to whether that unreliability was due to bias in the coefficient estimates, high standard errors of the coefficients, a large prediction error for the regression, or all of these. If experimental data were being used, however, along with "normal experimental procedures aimed at curbing the effects of 'extraneous' variables," the number of variables observed (that is, the number of X's before the / in equation [5.1]) would be larger, as would the number of relevant variables fixed in value (that is, the number of X's between / and //) due to control of the experimental setting, leading to a reduction of the number of unobserved variable factors. To the extent that this was true, the production function estimated with the experimental data would be "more reliable and tell more of the working of the production process" than the production function estimated with nonexperimental data.[13]

Another feature of Heady's work with experimental production functions was his use of functional forms other than the Cobb–Douglas form, for example, the quadratic form ($Y = \beta_0 + \beta_1X_1 + \beta_2X_2 + \beta_3X_1^2 + \beta_4X_2^2 + \beta_5X_1X_2$ for the two input case). The Cobb–Douglas form was parsimonious – a three-input Cobb–Douglas production function required the

[13] It is interesting to note what Heady and Dillon's analysis did not claim for experimental data. Over the subsequent decades, it would come to be accepted that a major advantage of the use of experimental data in regression analysis was that experimental design could ensure the absence of correlation between the independent variables and the error of the regression equation, thus eliminating an important cause of bias in least-squares estimates of the coefficients of the observed independent variables even if important variables affecting the dependent variable were not included in the regression, and even if the regression equation represented a relationship that was, outside of the experimental setting, part of a simultaneous system. This point is not even implicit in Heady and Dillon's analysis, as evidenced by their comment that if the number of observed and fixed but unobserved variables were the same in both the experimental and the nonexperimental data, the production function estimated using experimental data would be "as reliable and useful" as the one derived from nonexperimental data. Also, in an analysis of the bias in estimated production function coefficients caused by the omission of variables from the regression equation, which included the point that the bias will tend to be positive as the levels of observed inputs are likely to be positively correlated with the levels of unobserved inputs, Heady and Dillon (1961, pp. 214–15) commented that the analysis "applies equally to the derivation of production functions from experimental and nonexperimental data."

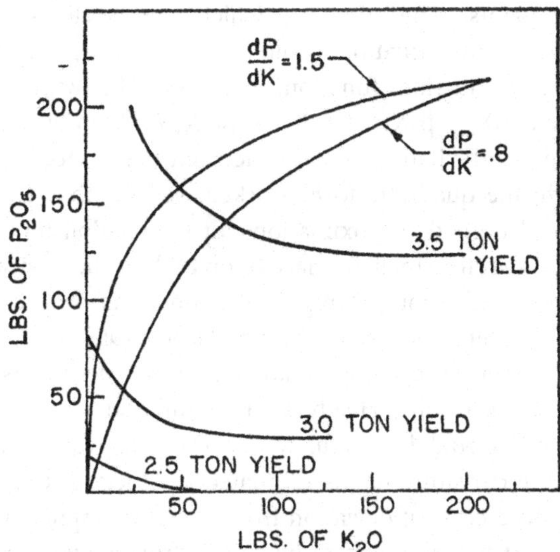

FIGURE 3.—Isoquants and Isoclines for Alfalfa from Equation (6)

Figure 5.1 Earl Heady's illustration of the need for experimentation with empirical production function forms other than the Cobb–Douglas

estimation of four coefficients, while a three-input quadratic production function with cross products required the estimation of nine coefficients – but the Cobb–Douglas form embodied restrictive assumptions that simply did not hold in many agricultural applications. The input of the agronomists regarding the biology of the phenomenon being studied was a key factor in the choice of functional form, but one also had to consider the computational and other costs associated with alternative functional forms, as well as the prediction errors associated with more parsimonious and therefore more approximate functional form choices (Heady 1952, 779; Heady 1957a).[14]

For example, fertilizer production functions were characterized by marginal rates of substitution functions that depended on the scale of output, and a point of maximum yield at which the marginal productivity of any additional nutrient was less than or equal to zero, a situation illustrated in Figure 5.1, from Heady (1957a).

The curved lines running from southwest to northeast, called isoclines by Heady, connect points of equal marginal rates of substitution on the

[14] Beneke (1994) described Heady's quest, in the 1950s, for greater computing resources, and his resort to more complex functional forms as those resources became available.

successive isoquants. The point at which the isoclines meet is the maximum yield. This situation could not be well approximated by a Cobb–Douglas production function, but could be with the function $Y = \beta_0 + \beta_1 X_1 + \beta_2 X_2 + \beta_3 X_1^{.5} + \beta_4 X_2^{.5} + \beta_5 (X_1 X_2)^{.5}$. Production functions for feeding dairy cattle had to take into account the limited capacity of the cow's stomach; the quadratic form worked well for this. Cobb–Douglas functions provided good approximations for the relationship of feed mixtures to weight gain for small animals, but based on the advice of agronomists, different Cobb–Douglas regression functions were fitted for the same animal at different stages of growth (Heady 1957a).

Thirdly, in designing his production function experiments and in the presentation of his results, Heady kept in mind the goal of providing information that would be useful to farmers. He would, for example, discuss what the curvature of the estimated production function implied about the financial costs of deviation from optimum input mixes – sometimes there might not be much to be gained from moving from "rule of thumb" practices to optimal practices. He paid particular attention to isoclines, both in choosing the functional form for the regression and in deriving the implications of his estimates, because a profit-maximizing farmer would want to combine inputs so that their marginal rate of substitution matched the ratio of the input prices, and an isocline function showed how the input combinations associated with any given marginal rate of substitution varied with different scales of production. And, as Heady (1957a) noted, one aspect of his production function research program was the development of devices "allowing farmers to equate derivatives or marginal quantities with price ratios." Figure 5.2 shows one such device, the "Pork Costulater":

As Heady explained to *Econometrica's* readers, the Pork Costulator

> includes data on both sides of a disc for determining the least cost ration in the different weight intervals and in predicting optimum market weights. In effect, it allows the farmer to equate the derivative with respect to soybean oil with the soybean oilmeal to corn price ratio. This is accomplished by turning the disc until the current prices of corn and protein supplement are in mesh at the edge of the wheel. Within slots are data showing the amount of feed which meet the mathematical conditions for optima. The data also indicate the amount of time for marketing under each ration, since the rate of growth varies with rations. If the farmer expects a price break, he may wish to feed protein in excess of that for the least-cost gains, in order to take advantage of higher prices before the market break
>
> (Heady 1957a, 265–66).

FIGURE 10.—Pork Costulator for Determining Least-Cost Rations

Figure 5.2 Although Heady's methods and results were understandable only to a small number of technically sophisticated economists, he believed that they would soon produce practically useful knowledge for farmers

Heady's production function research also included the estimation of farm-level production functions, or "farm-firm" production functions, as he sometimes called them. Heady estimated these farm-firm functions using cross-section data collected from random samples of individual farms. The use of nonexperimental data was a decision based on practicality – "it would be possible, but surely infeasible, to set up a farm or a region as an experimental unit from which production function data could be generated at the researchers' discretion" – as was the use of the

Cobb–Douglas form, which provided "a compromise between (a) adequate fit of the data (b) computational feasibility and (c) sufficient degrees of freedom unused to allow for statistical testing," the third consideration being especially important "where research resources are limited and collection of farm-firm data is expensive" (Heady and Dillon 1961, 150, 328).

Heady admitted that, unlike experimental production function studies of narrowly defined agricultural processes, farm-firm production functions could not be the basis for detailed technical advice to farmers, not least because the input variables used were highly aggregated. The results might, however, indicate to a farmer that he was using too much or too little capital, or that he could gain by shifting capital from livestock to crop production. They could also be used to inform or evaluate government policies that affected the allocation of agricultural resources. And, unlike experimental production functions, farm-firm production functions could be used to diagnose the presence and extent of disequilibrium in actual agricultural markets, and to test behavioral hypothesis derived from economic theory (Heady and Dillon 1961, 258, 554–55).

For example, by the late 1940s a number of agricultural economists had used neoclassical models and reasoning to derive hypotheses regarding how different farm tenure arrangements (e.g., sharecropping lease, cash lease, farm ownership) would affect farmers' resource-allocation decisions, demonstrating that some lease arrangements would lead farmers to choose socially inefficient allocations (Heady 1947). Heady (1955) was an account of a study designed to test some of these hypotheses. Heady drew random samples of farms from each of two homogenous farming areas in Iowa. In one sample, 140 farms were evenly divided by design between those whose operators paid cash rents ("cash lease" farms), and those whose operators paid a predetermined share of the value of the crop ("share lease" farms). The other sample of 142 farms included share lease farms and owner-operated farms. Separate Cobb–Douglas production functions for the value of annual crop production were estimated for farms under each tenure arrangement in each sample.

Neoclassical theory predicted that farmers with share leases would invest less in labor and capital than owner operators or farmers on cash leases, leading to higher marginal products of labor and capital and lower marginal products of land on share lease farms. Using his production function estimates, Heady calculated the marginal products of each of the three inputs under the different tenure arrangements and observed, without exception, the patterns predicted by theory. However, based on t-tests, the observed differences in marginal products between share lease farms and other farms were only statistically significant in the case of land. Heady also used his results to compare the estimated marginal productivities of land with the average rental rates – rental rates were below productivities, and significantly so, for all farm types in both samples. He speculated that this may reflect a discount for the risks faced by farm operators and expectations of falling prices at the time the samples were collected.

As noted earlier, one important stream of thought in the agricultural economics literature of the time saw resource misallocation in the agricultural sector as a major cause of low farm incomes, and pushed for public-policy measures that would help to correct the misallocation. During the early 1950s, Heady procured data from farm surveys conducted in Montana and Alabama, and used them to estimate production functions for crop production and livestock production. He used the estimates, along with similar production function estimates for two Iowa farm samples, to get some indication of the extent to which inter- and intra-regional allocations of agricultural resources in the United States satisfied neoclassical efficiency criteria. In Heady and Shaw (1954), the estimated production functions were used to calculate marginal productivities of inputs, which were then compared across different farm types in the same region, across farms of the same type in different regions, and to the appropriate within-region factor prices. The authors concluded that the size of the differences (and the extent to which they were statistically significant) suggested a less serious misallocation problem in agriculture than had been indicated by previous writers using simpler measures, such as ratios of output per worker.

In Heady and du Toit (1954), the estimated production functions for Alabama, Montana, and Iowa were compared to production functions estimated for crop and livestock farms in South Africa. The authors stressed the importance of such comparisons for both theoretical and policy purposes: international trade models were often based on assumptions about the relative labor productivities in trading nations, and since World War II, the United States had been spending increasing sums of money in attempts to increase resource productivity in "underdeveloped" areas. The estimates indicated that labor productivity was almost twice the wage rate in South Africa, and that the marginal productivities of land and capital exceeded their rental rates as well. The authors found these differences very hard to explain, but conjectured that risk, uncertainty and lack of knowledge were important contributing factors.[15] In comparing the estimated production functions for South Africa to those for the US regions, the authors pointed out that the very low labor productivity in South Africa resulted largely from low capital/labor ratios, that is, if US farms operated with the levels of labor and capital employed on South African farms, the marginal labor productivities in the two nations would be comparable. A policy conclusion derived from the comparison was that transfers of agricultural capital from the US regions to South Africa would augment world output.

Heady's production function papers displayed a command of statistical theory and technique well beyond that of the average economist publishing empirical research during the period. He was frank about the limitations of his data and his methods, presenting the work as exploratory research meant to demonstrate a potentially fruitful method that he hoped would be improved by others. He had studied the critical literature surrounding Douglas's production function work, so was aware that his use of non-experimental data for his farm-level studies posed a particular set of problems. The issue that concerned him most was what he called the problem of "hybridity," which he discussed using diagrams like Figure 5.3:

Curve ABC in Heady's Figure III represented an isoquant for one type of farm, and the goal of a production function study would be to estimate such an isoquant, so as to learn the tradeoffs between corn and protein in feeding pigs. Curves A, B, and C in Heady's Figure IV illustrated the isoquants associated with the same amount weight gain for three different types of farms that might be found in the same sample. If, as seemed almost certain to Heady, farmers who used relatively little protein in feeding tended to be those with other problems like vitamin-poor feed or disease in their feedlots, an isoquant estimated from this sample would look like the dashed line abc in Figure IV. The estimated isoquant was a "hybrid" derived from three different production functions, and a C-type

[15] In general, when Heady encountered evidence of disequilibria in these farm-firm production function studies, he offered theoretically grounded conjectures for what might lie behind them. For example, on finding the measured return to an additional dollar's worth of capital on the highly mechanized farms of Iowa was less than a dollar, he pointed to possible nonmonetary benefits of mechanization, such as the role of machinery in reducing the drudgery associated with farm work (Heady 1955, 503). Such speculation was in keeping with the tenet in his 1948 manifesto that farm management research should search for explanations for the deviations from equilibrium uncovered by empirical research, as farmers would often have "important and sound reasoning" for decisions that appeared suboptimal (Heady 1948, 224–25).

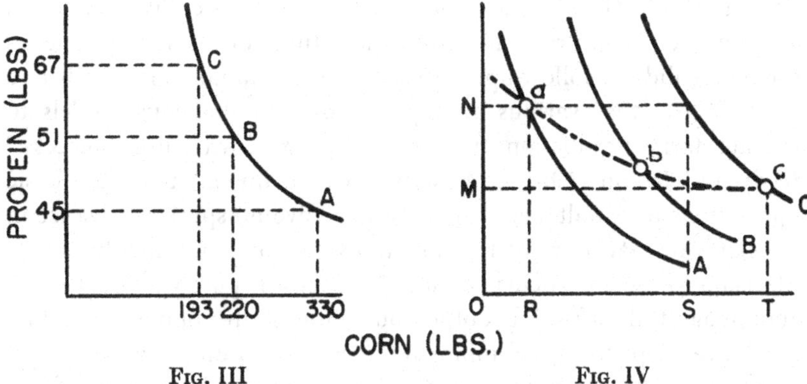

Figure 5.3 Heady's illustration of the problem of "hybridity," a potential source of bias when the Cobb–Douglas regression was estimated with nonexperimental cross-section data. Figure 5.3 is taken from Heady (1948), and is used to critique nonproduction function methods of estimating input-output relationships. For a similar diagram making the identical point with respect to production function estimation, see Heady and Dillon (1961, 191).

farmer would be poorly advised if he were told that he could replace corn of the quantity RT with protein in the amount MN without affecting the rate of weight gain for his pigs. Heady linked the hybridity problem with the "rather confusing" intrafirm/interfirm discussion initiated by Reder (1943) and Bronfenbrenner (1944), and explained that hybridity was due to the action of variable factors that affected output but were not included in the production function regression (Heady and Dillon 1961, 196).

According to Heady, the best approach to mitigating the hybridity problem when estimating a production function with farm survey data was to use a sufficiently homogenous sample. For example, when estimating a crop production function, the sample should include only farms growing the same crop in the same region on the same type of soil, preferably as identified by agronomists. Separate functions should be estimated for separate products (e.g., livestock vs. crops). And so on (see e.g., Heady 1952, 782).

Heady (1952) mentioned that production function researchers should at least consider a simultaneous equations approach, since actual input decisions on farms are made by entrepreneurs, and may be "determined simultaneously by a system of structural (functional) relationships of which the production function is only one and the estimational procedure should be set up accordingly." This required much careful thought and effort, but "may be of extreme importance in isolating a non-hybrid production function." Heady promised to soon present production function coefficients resulting from the estimation of a simultaneous system. He did not follow up on this, however, and noted in Heady and Dillon (1961) that various attempts to use simultaneous models to estimate farm production functions had "met with little success." Heady and Dillon (1961, 584) went on to comment that "the basic suppositions of simultaneous models may have no special relevance in terms of whole farm production functions," as "once a farmer has made a decision to use a particular input, the process is purely physical, with input magnitude affecting output but without the opposite holding true ... (e)xcept for a few minor interyear exceptions, it appears that inputs can be considered purely as exogenous variables in their effects on outputs."

By 1961, Heady had become aware of the argument that if all firms had the same production function, and all were in profit-maximizing equilibrium, all would use the same input combinations and the production function could not be estimated. In response to this, he cited an argument of Konijn (1959) that this was not likely to be a serious problem when estimating farm-firm production functions. H. S. Konijn set up an econometric system in which farms shared the same Cobb–Douglas production function up to multiplicative error term (additive when the function was logged) and farmers made input choices that maximized profits "on average," though each farmer deviated from the profit-maximizing levels by an amount that could be represented as an additive error in the (logged) input demand functions. Konijn was willing to assume that the production function error had a relatively small variance – production functions were very similar across farms – but that optimization errors in choosing inputs were likely to be large in the farm business, due to farmers' inaccurate forecasts of output prices and actual yields. Also, there was likely to be little correlation between the production function error and the optimization errors. Under these circumstances, the estimates of the Cobb–Douglas coefficients would be "approximately" unbiased.[16]

[16] This is a correct analysis within the standard simultaneous equations framework of the time. Further, a sufficiently homogenous sample would lend credibility to the assumption that farms shared production functions up to a (relatively small) error term, and, with cross-section data, (shared) weather shocks that both affected yields and created (shared) deviations from optimal input choices would not create bias-causing correlations between individual farmers' production function errors and optimization errors.

CRITICISM, FRIENDLY AND UNFRIENDLY, SPURS ECONOMETRIC INNOVATION

By the mid-1950s agricultural economists outside of Iowa State College were responding to Heady's evangelism, publishing experimental and nonexperimental production function studies in journals and in the agricultural bulletins that were the main vehicle for communication of research results among agricultural economists (Johnson 1955). However, articles criticizing the method, in particular its application to nonexperimental farm survey data, also began to appear in the *Journal of Farm Economics*. Some of their authors drew on the literature that had criticized Douglas's work (e.g., Redman 1954). Several pointed out the interfirm-intrafirm problem, although some were willing to accept Heady's argument that the problem could be minimized if farm-level data were used, with a sufficiently homogenous sample of farms. The exclusion of a variable measuring the management input seemed a serious problem to some of the doubters (e.g., Wheeler 1950). Jones (1952) questioned the theoretical framework, empirical methods, and policy recommendations of the researchers he dubbed the "Schultzeans" or the "Ames School," expressing particular concern with the likely mismeasurement of the labor input.

The most common arguments of the critics in the early 1950s, however, revolved around a belief that the Cobb–Douglas form and the regression method were insufficiently flexible to capture the variety and complexity of the technological processes involved in agriculture. Older and newer technologies might be simultaneously employed by different farms in the sample or even on the same farm. Inputs were too numerous to all be included in a single regression equation, and too idiosyncratic to aggregate. Plaxico (1955) offered the most thorough and rigorous critique along these lines. Among other things, he showed that whatever functional form was used in a regression study of the production function, different decisions about aggregating some inputs would lead to different estimates of marginal productivity of others. He explained that there were optimal aggregation rules for different classes of inputs (perfect substitutes, perfect complements, imperfect substitutes), should one already know of these relationships, but the assumptions required for the rules to hold seemed unlikely to be met. Likewise, aggregation of a number of farm outputs into a single monetary product variable would bias the marginal productivity estimates except under very unlikely circumstances, for example, if the different outputs were produced in the same proportions on all farms. In a summary assessment that took aim at the entire range of applications for which the new method was being promoted, Plaxico opined that "extreme caution should be exercised in suggesting intrafarm adjustments on the basis of Cobb–Douglas functions. Also, since it is not clear just how an estimating equation which is not suitable for guiding individual farm decisions can suggest optimum area shifts, the validity of policy recommendation arising from Cobb–Douglas analysis is quite questionable" (Plaxico 1955, 675).

Plaxico was an unfriendly critic of the empirical production function research, to be sure. However, there were friendly critics of the farm-level production function literature as well. In the late 1950s and early 1960s, Zvi Griliches, Irving Hoch, and Yair Mundlak published analyses of the problem of estimating production functions with cross-section, firm-level data. Their work differed from that cited in the previous paragraph in two ways. First, their identification of problems facing the production function researcher were accompanied by concrete proposals for dealing with those problems, which, in the case of Mundlak and Hoch, involved the development of an innovative econometric technique. Second, they developed their analyses within the formal statistical frameworks found in the latest textbooks on statistical methods for economists, now almost universally termed "econometrics," leaving behind the statistical frameworks used by Gunn and Douglas or even Mendershausen and Tinbergen to interpret the estimates produced by the regression. Indeed, none of these papers contained references to the original Douglas studies. Instead, they contextualized their own research with references to Marschak and Andrews (1944), Klein's (1953) econometrics textbook, the interfirm/intrafirm debate of Bronfenbrenner and Reder, and each other's articles.

Zvi Griliches's Analysis of Specification Errors

In 1957 Zvi Griliches was still a graduate student in agricultural economics at the University of Chicago when he published his analysis of "Specification Bias in Estimates of Production Functions." His paper on the topic opened with a clear explanation of his motivation:

> It is common in empirical work to compromise and use second best methods or variables. Sometimes we may know what we want, but even then it might be impossible to get it. Either there are no pertinent data, or the variables are non-measureable, or our budget or computational facilities are limited. Hence we exclude variables, accept approximations, aggregate, and commit various other sins of omission and commission .... In this note, I shall attempt to describe a

method of ascertaining the consequences of some of these compromises. If we know their effect on our results, we may better be able to interpret out results (Griliches 1957, 8).

In Griliches's model, presented using matrix notation, y = Xa + u was the "true" regression relationship, where y was a column vector containing the observations of the dependent variable, X was a matrix of observations of the independent variables, u was a column vector of the regression residuals with zero expectation, and "a" was the vector of regression coefficients that "we" wanted to estimate. However, we could not observe X, but only the matrix X*, which could differ from X for various reasons. A column of X* might be the sum, product, or other combination of two or more columns in X (an aggregation problem) and/or X* might be missing one or more of the columns included in X (an omitted variable problem). In any case, the regression actually estimated was y = X*a* + u*. Estimating this regression by least squares would produce a vector of coefficient estimates $b = (X^{*\prime}X^{*})^{-1}X^{*\prime}y$, with expected value $(X^{*\prime}X^{*})^{-1}X^{*\prime}Xa$, or as Griliches wrote it, E(b) = Pa, where P was the matrix $(X^{*\prime}X^{*})^{-1}X^{*\prime}X$. Thus, it was possible to express the expected values of the coefficients actually estimated in terms of the coefficients we wanted to estimate.

Griliches then explained that the elements of the ith column of the P matrix would be the coefficients produced if i^{th} independent variable of the true regression were regressed on all the observed independent variables of X*, that is,

$$x_i = p_{1i}x_1^* + p_{2i}x_2^* + \ldots p_{hi}x_h^* + v$$

This meant that each coefficient we estimated was a weighted average of all the true regression coefficients, with weights given by elements of the P matrix. He concluded that "(i)f it is possible ... to use some outside knowledge and specify the sign and the magnitude of the various p's, it is then possible to arrive at conclusions about the sign and magnitude of the bias in our estimates" (Griliches 1957, 10).

Griliches first applied this model to the case in which input x_k was excluded from a Cobb–Douglas regression, so that the X* matrix was simply the X matrix with one column missing. Then, the expected value of estimated coefficient of the ith observed input was given by $E(b_i) = a_i + p_{ik}a_k$, meaning that, assuming $a_k > 0$, whether b_i would tend to overestimate or underestimate the true coefficient a_i depended on whether the excluded input tended to vary positively or negatively with input x_i, holding other inputs constant. Griliches applied this result to "(t)he specification error most often conceded by estimators of production functions," the omission of a measure of entrepreneurship or managerial services. Common sense suggested to Griliches that "a farmer who farms on twice the scale of his neighbor is not twice as good an entrepreneur, nor does he do twice as much managerial work," so that the omission of a managerial variable would lead to an underestimate of the returns to scale of the production function. Also, farmers with more managerial or entrepreneurial skills were probably less subject to capital rationing, so that omission of the managerial variable would lead to an overestimate of the capital coefficient (Griliches 1957, 10–13).

Griliches went on to analyze the situation in which workers of different quality or ability were aggregated into one labor input, showing that this would lead to an overestimate of the capital coefficient and a downward bias of the labor coefficient. He also examined the consequences of aggregating several categories of spending into a single capital input. Probably more important than any particular result of Griliches's analysis, however, was that it provided researchers with a way to think systematically about how to adjust for biases caused by some of the common problems encountered in the estimation of production functions, and its overall message that one could reasonably proceed with production function estimation even in an imperfect data environment, rather than giving up the attempt. Heady and Dillon's (1961) text incorporated Griliches's analysis into its discussion of omitted variables and aggregation, ensuring that the rising generation of agricultural economists would be exposed to it.

Hoch, Mundlak, and the Development of Methods for the Analysis of Panel Data

The 1955 issue of *Econometrica* included a brief account of a paper presented at the Econometric Society's 1954 meeting in Montreal, in the session on agriculture. The paper, by Irving Hoch, was a "report on research in progress with the goal of estimating production functions and testing for efficiency using combined time series and cross section data" (Hoch 1955). Hoch was working with what would now be called a panel data set of 63 Minnesota farms, from which data had been collected annually from 1946 to 1951. He had used the data to estimate an "extension" of the Cobb–Douglas regression that could be written in log form as $\log(Y_{it}) = k_0 + k_i + k_t + \alpha_1\log(X_{1it}) + \ldots + \alpha_p\log(X_{pit}) + u_{it}$, where Y_{it} was the output of farm-firm i in year t. The X variables were measured inputs, as usual, and the α's were the conventional Cobb–Douglas elasticities. The k parameters constituted Hoch's extension of the Cobb–Douglas function: k_i was a "firm constant," or a farm-specific factor representing the assumption that some farms would tend to produce more each year than others given the same inputs, while k_t was a "time constant," representing the assumption that farms on average would produce more in some years and less in others, given the same inputs.

Hoch's note indicated that he used "analysis of covariance" to estimate the α and k parameters.[17] Inputs were labor, real estate, machinery, and feed and fertilizer, all measured in dollar terms, as was output. He reported four sets of estimates of the α's and of the corresponding marginal (monetary) return per one dollar of each input. The first set of estimates was obtained with Klein's method of using the sample mean of a factor's share as the estimate of that factor's Cobb–Douglas coefficient. The second resulted from conventional least squares estimation that implicitly assumed all k_i and k_t coefficients to be equal to zero. The third set resulted from introducing the "time correction," allowing k_t to vary across years, while the fourth set came from the analysis of covariance model that introduced "both time and firm correction," allowing a separate k_i for each farm. Hoch also reported F tests of the hypotheses that the k_i coefficients were all equal to 0 and that the k_t coefficients were all equal to 0, and rejected both hypotheses. He speculated that the "striking" change in the estimates caused by adding the firm correction occurred because the firm correction controlled for the effect of entrepreneurial ability.

In 1954 Hoch was a graduate student at the University of Chicago. His dissertation would not be completed until 1957, and the two major papers Hoch derived from his dissertation would be published in 1958 and 1962. But the 1954 paper presented in Montreal already contained Hoch's major innovation: recognizing how "combined cross section and time series data" could be used to estimate an econometric model of a production function that could change over time and also differ across firms (albeit only in a particular way).[18]

[17] "Analysis of Covariance" is a least-squares procedure originally developed as an extension of the analysis of variance in order to allow one to control for the possible influence of continuous independent variables on a dependent variable while making the standard "analysis of variance" comparisons of the mean value of the dependent variable conditional on different values of a categorical independent variable. The procedure is equivalent to estimating Hoch's production function by ordinary least squares, but including as independent variables along with the X's a set of dichotomous variables indicating the year of the observation and a set indicating which farm the observation came from.

[18] As shall be discussed, Hoch's econometric production function model (and the similar one introduced by Mundlak's [1961]) was offered and accepted as a solution to a number of the problems believed to plague existing approaches to production function estimation. But because these problems Hoch and Mundlak were attempting to address were specific

In Hoch's dissertation, one sees vocabulary, rhetoric, and style of presentation very much like what one would see in a Cowles Commission publication, for example, his three-step characterization of the "theoretical development" that preceded his empirical application "to a set of firms in agriculture": "(a) construction of an equation set – or economic model – that describes the behaviour of the competitive firm; (b) derivation of a statistical model from the economic model by the introduction of disturbance terms and by the specification of characteristics of those disturbances; (c) further development of the statistical model, calling for the use of combined time series and cross-section data" (Hoch 1962, 34). This is in contrast, of course, to the Douglas studies, but the style of mathematical formalism introduced by the Cowles researchers, and adopted by Hoch, was also distinct from the still quite technical presentations of Heady, or of Griliches (1957) for that matter, who combined mathematical formalism with a rather informal explicatory style, and seemed to want to keep technical notation to a minimum.

Hoch's first published paper from his dissertation, "Simultaneous Bias in the Context of the Cobb–Douglas Production Function" (1958), was an exercise in econometric theory, highlighting the problem that his novel empirical technique was intended to solve: that of estimating a production function for firms operating in a competitive industry.[19] His theoretical model consisted of a Cobb–Douglas production function with q inputs, and the q additional equations defining the optimal (profit maximizing) input demand functions of a competitive firm operating with that production function and facing constant prices for inputs and output.[20] Hoch allowed that R_q could vary across firms in a sample, but given estimates of the production function parameters, the sample average value of R_q and its values for individual firms could be calculated, providing a test of unrestricted profit maximization.

manifestations of general problems facing empirical researchers in a number of fields (e.g., simultaneous equations bias, omitted variable bias), their models are seen as seminal contributions to the history of econometrics broadly considered, as discussed in Dupont-Keiffer and Pirotte (2011).

19 He acknowledged that his problem was a special case of the more general problem of production function estimation examined by Marschak and Andrews (1944), who had not assumed competition, but Hoch noted that he had derived some results that they had not.

20 Hoch also introduced a parameter into his model, Rq, that would allow him to test whether firms were choosing the profit-maximizing levels of inputs.

However, if the investigator used the "traditional single equation, least squares procedure" to estimate the production function parameters, there was a danger of simultaneous equations bias. Or, as Hoch explained,

> Single equation estimates are biased when the equation is a member of a system of equations in the following way: the system is such that some of the independent variables, as well as the dependent variable, are functions of the disturbance in the given equation. This contradicts the assumptions underlying single equation regression since the presumed independent variables are in fact correlated with the disturbance. The resulting bias may be called the simultaneous equation bias (Hoch 1958, 568).

To analyze formally the potential problem of simultaneous equations bias Hoch moved to the research step of converting his theoretical model into a statistical model, adding a multiplicative disturbance "U" into the production function and multiplicative disturbances "V_q" into the input demand functions. After logging, the statistical model included the Cobb–Douglas regression with an additive disturbance term u= Log(U), and the q input demand functions of the form $\log(X_q) = k_q + \log(X_q) + v_q$, where X_0 and X_q were the quantities of output and input q, v_q was the log of the V_q disturbance to the qth input demand function, and $k_q = \log(a_qP_0/R_qP_q)$.

Hoch then presented a thorough Cowlesian analysis of the circumstances under which single-equation least squares estimation of the statistical model would lead to simultaneous equations bias, and factors that would affect the seriousness of the bias problem. A point he stressed was that the sum of the estimated coefficients, the traditional measure of the returns to scale of the production function, would typically be biased towards one.

Hoch's definitive results of estimating his extended Cobb–Douglas production function with his sample of Minnesota farms appeared in his 1962 *Econometrica* article. The article began with a review of the economic and statistical models of Hoch (1958) – now with "i" subscripts indexing firms added to the X's and the U and V_q disturbances – along with a verbal review of why the least squares estimates of the system's production function would be biased. While Hoch's 1958 paper had made no specific mention of farms or agriculture, speaking only of "firms" as the decision-making units to which his models referred, the 1962 paper included comments on what the U and V elements of his statistical model might represent in agricultural data. In agricultural production, Hoch argued, the U_i disturbance probably included the effects of weather, and it was reasonable to argue that inputs were chosen on the basis of average or "anticipated" weather conditions, and were unaffected by weather conditions that caused output to be more or less than expected. If this were all there was to U_i in agricultural production function, Hoch explained, single equation estimation would be unbiased. But U_i probably also included differences across farms in "technical efficiency" that would affect output and also influence input choices, thus causing simultaneous equations bias, and a similar source of simultaneous equations bias could occur in time series data if there were increases in productivity over time.

"A way out of this difficulty," Hoch claimed, "is suggested by the use of the analysis of covariance if combined time series and cross-section data are obtained; that is, if data on a set of firms over a period of years are obtained." He then presented a revised version of his statistical model, amenable for use with panel data, that included the production function from his 1954 note along with input demand functions. The production function was now written as

$$X_{0it} = K_0 K_t K_i^* \prod_q^Q X_{qit}^{a_q} U_{it}$$

and expressed in log form as $x_{0it} = k_0 + k_i + k_t^* + \sum a_q x_{qit} + u_{it}$.[21] The "i" subscripts on the variables and disturbances indexed firms, and the t variables indexed time periods, for example, x_{0it} was the log of output of farm i in period t, and u_{it} was the disturbance to the production function of farm i that occurred in period t. Hoch described, with words and formulas, how the analysis of covariance could be used with panel data to estimate the k and a_q parameters. He also offered various explanations of what was represented by the K_i and K_t^* factors, and of how their inclusion in the model "avoided or reduced" the problem of simultaneous equations bias in estimating a production function:[22]

[21] Hoch added the assumptions that both the k_i terms and the k_t^* terms summed to zero, that there was no correlation between the disturbances of the production function and the disturbances of the input demand functions, and the standard Gauss Markov assumptions on the residuals of the production function and the input demand functions.

[22] The type of statistical model proposed here by Hoch has since been the subject of a great deal of analysis and discussion by theoretical and applied econometricians. To avoid the risk of reading into Hoch's presentation some of the subsequently explicated and now well-known ideas of what such models accomplish, and what their various elements can be held to represent, I have chosen to present only Hoch's own words on these matters. Additional insight into how Hoch understood his model is provided by a footnote in which he discusses Marschak and Andrews' (1944) definition of "technical efficiency" as depending on "technical knowledge, will, effort, and luck of a given entrepreneur in a given year," and commenting that his own usage of technical efficiency, that is, that which

Basically, K_i will reflect differences in technical efficiency between firms; that is, given the same bundle of inputs, the more efficient firm obtains more than average output (K_i greater than one), the less efficient firms obtain less than average output (K_i less than one). The time constant, K_t^*, will reflect change in technical efficiency over time and differences in weather between years. If unadjusted money values of variables are used, K_t^* will also reflect changes in both relative prices and the general price level (some caution must be exercised in this application, however)

(Hoch 1962, 39).

... The disturbance term u_{it} does not enter into the observed values of x_{qit}. Differences between firms and time periods affecting x_{qit}, as well as x_{0it}, are accounted for by the k_i and k_t^* terms. Hence, simultaneous equations bias does not occur in this model; and the single equation analysis of covariance is appropriate for [the production function]

(Hoch 1962, 40).

It should be noted that bias arising through the differences in technical efficiency is a special case of bias arising because of differences between firms or time periods or both. In general, if such bias exists, unbiased estimates can be obtained using the analysis of covariance. (Footnote: Thus, say $u_{it} = u_i^* + u_t^* + u_{it}^*$ and assume, for example, that $\bar{x}_{pi} = c_p u_i^*$, that is, for some unspecified reason, the firm average x_p is related to the disturbance component u_i^*. Then, ordinary least squares will be biased because of this, but analysis of covariance estimates will not be biased.)

(Hoch 1962, 41)

As noted earlier, Hoch measured all his variables in monetary terms. Farm output was the total dollar value of crops and livestock produced, plus family consumption of farm produce, minus a 5 percent allowance for inventory. In the course of writing the dissertation, Hoch had decided to work with two alternative specifications of the inputs. The first input list included labor (measured as wages paid to hired work, plus imputed wages for the labor of the operator and his family, plus 20 percent of expenditures on "custom work hired"), real estate (measured by real estate taxes paid, on the assumption that they would represent a constant fraction of land value), machinery (repairs, fuel, 80 percent of custom hired work, and depreciation and interest on the value of machines) and "feed, fertilizer and related expenses." Hoch was worried about the real estate variable because

was captured by his K_i term, did not include "luck," which instead was "a component of a residual random disturbance," or the model's u_{it}.

of lags in assessed value, and because he had no measure of building repairs. He was also particularly worried about his machinery variable, because it combined the stock value of machinery purchased in past periods with the flow value of repairs and fuel purchased in the present period. Hoch explained how the k_t terms could control for the changes in relative and general price levels if all variables in a period's observation were expressed in the same period's prices (allowing the investigator using panel data to skip the step of deflating variables expressed in nominal terms), but that a bias would be caused if a variable combined monetary values expressed in the prices from different periods. This is what motivated him to develop his second input list, in which the labor and "food and fertilizer" inputs from the first list were joined by a "current expenses" variable, including maintenance, fuel, repairs, and real estate tax, and a "fixed capital" variable, which represented the value of real estate and machinery, converted to a service flow variable using price-index numbers and standard assumptions about depreciation.[23]

Hoch reported six sets of estimates of the a_q parameters: three for each of his input lists, corresponding to three different assumptions about the k factors: all the k_i and k_t^* factors equal to zero (the conventional assumption), only the k_i assumed to equal zero, and both k_i and k_t^* factors potentially different from zero (the analysis of covariance estimates). He also reported the six corresponding sets of estimated marginal returns to increasing an input. Based on F-tests, Hoch could reject, at the 95 percent level, the hypothesis that the k_i were all equal to zero and the hypothesis that the k_t^* were all equal to zero for both input lists, leading him to accept the analysis of covariance estimates as the best estimates.

The sum of the estimated Cobb–Douglas coefficients yielded by conventional least squares was very close to one, while for the "best" estimates it was much lower. Most of the decline in the sum (which occurred for both input lists) was due to a decline in the coefficient of labor, and for the second input list some of the other coefficients actually rose, though not significantly, when the firm effects were allowed to differ from zero. In trying to explain this disproportionate decline of labor's coefficient caused by including the "firm correction," Hoch first considered measurement error in the labor variable, due to the imputation of a salary for the operator and his family. But when he split the labor variable into two,

[23] Hoch devoted a page to explaining the construction of this variable, particularly the method of calculating depreciation. He did not explicitly mention whether he had information on the year that each asset was purchased, but the discussion suggests that he did.

one for operator and family labor and one for hired labor, and reestimated the models, the decline occurred for both labor variables. Another possibility was that farms that employed more labor were more efficient. If efficiency differences were not controlled for in the regression, this would bias upward the coefficient of the labor input. To test this hypothesis, Hoch divided the sample farms into groups based on the values of their estimated k_i values. Firms in the higher k_i groups, that is, those presumed to be more technically efficient, did indeed use more labor on average over the six sample years. The puzzle remained, however, because the use of other inputs also rose with k_i values at about the same rate as the use of labor, so that by the logic of the hypothesis, all the Cobb–Douglas coefficients should have declined by about the same amount when the analysis of covariance was applied.

Notwithstanding this puzzle, Hoch saw evidence that the analysis of covariance estimates had eliminated simultaneous equations bias. He referred to the result of his 1958 paper that simultaneous equations bias from any source would bias the sum of the Cobb–Douglas coefficients towards one in a conventional production function regression. The 1958 paper had also derived relationships between the sample moments that would have to exist if input levels were correlated with the u_{it}. When applied to estimates from the procedures that assumed the k_i to be equal to zero, this test indicated the presence of simultaneous equations bias; when applied to the analysis of covariance estimates, it did not.[24]

The "best" estimates of the marginal (value) productivities of the inputs allowed Hoch to look at the question of profit maximization and resource allocation. An additional dollar invested in labor on the sample farms returned significantly less than one dollar; the estimated returns for a dollar more of the other inputs were in all cases above one dollar, sometimes significantly so. This confirmed the "presumption" of a misallocation of resources in agriculture such that the marginal returns to nonhuman factors were higher than optimal, and those to labor lower than optimal.[25]

Hoch's 1962 paper contained a reference to a "similar analysis of covariance study carried out for a set of farms in Israel" published the previous year by Yair Mundlak in *The Journal of Farm Economics.*

[24] It is not clear to me how Hoch meant for this test to be conducted, as in Hoch (1958) it is stated in terms of the variances and covariances of the input and output variables, which could be estimated using sample moments that would be the same regardless of what method was used to estimate the production function.

[25] This presumption was particularly strongly held among the "Schultzeans" at University of Chicago, with whom Hoch had studied.

Mundlak's econometric model of the Cobb–Douglas production function and his method of estimating it with panel data were essentially identical to Hoch's, as Mundlak recognized, and his paper included discussion of the results reported in Hoch (1955). However, Mundlak's motivation in developing an improved procedure for production function estimation differed from Hoch's. Mundlak was searching for a solution to the problem of omitted-variable bias due to the lack of a variable measuring managerial ability. He made no mention of simultaneous equations bias, nor was his production function presented as one part of a system of simultaneous equations. He did not refer to Marschak and Andrews (1944), but discussed the bearing of his procedure on the debate over interfirm vs. intrafirm production functions. As a result of this difference in motivation, Mundlak also differed from Hoch with respect to some of the interpretations he gave to his estimates and the uses to which he put them.

Mundlak wrote his production function (with variables in logs) as

$$Y_{it} = B_0 + B_1X_{1it} + \ldots + B_kX_{kit} + CM_i + e_{it}$$

M_i was "management," e a disturbance, and the Bs and C "true coefficients to be estimated." The i subscript indexed firms, and the t subscript time periods. The management variable had only an i subscript because "whatever management is, it does not change considerably over time; and for short periods, say a few years, it can be assumed to remain constant" (Mundlak 1961, 44). This was a key assumption for Mundlak.[26]

To discuss the issues arising when such a production function was estimated using cross-section data, Mundlak used a graph like the ones Heady used to illustrate "hybridity":

The lines f_1 and f_2 were the actual production functions of two firms with different levels of M (leading to different Y intercepts). Their common slope was the B coefficient of an "intrafirm" production function. A cross-section regression would lead to a line like DF, which would be the "interfirm" production function. Further, without assumptions about competition and equilibrium, one could not infer the slope of the intrafirm

[26] Mundlak used this production function in the formal description of his model, in deriving the formulas for his estimates, and in describing auxiliary procedures. However, in the empirical section, he explained that he would add a term A_t to the model, a "year effect" to "catch changes in the level of productivity which occur in time." With this addition, his statistical production function model was identical to Hoch's.

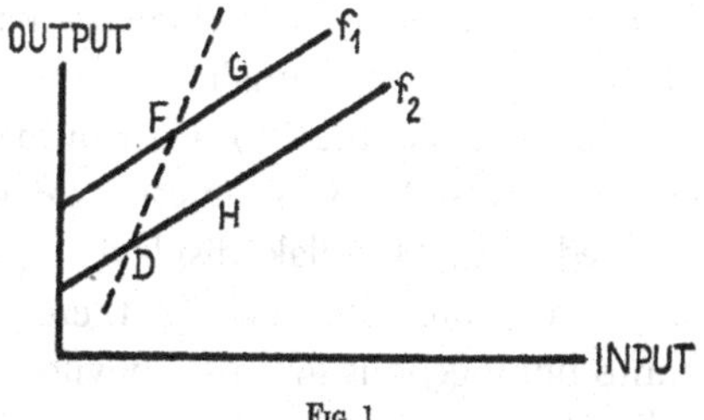

Figure 5.4 Mundlak's graph showing "hybridity," a problem he proposed to solve by using panel data to estimate the Cobb–Douglas regression

function f_i from DF.[27] Mundlak was proposing a way around this problem, and gave this concise and intuitively clear explanation of how his empirical procedure accomplished this: "The key to the estimation of the slope of the intrafirm function is to have at least two points on each f_i. In this case it is possible to get the slope of each of the lines f_i, average them and get the final estimate. That requires a combination of time series and cross-section data."

There followed a presentation of the sum-of-squares equation to be minimized by the procedure and the resulting equations to be used to calculate the estimates (b_j being used to signify the estimate of B_j, and a_i an estimate of $A_i = CM_i$), with Mundlak pointing out that the b_j would be estimated by averaging within-firm covariations. The least squares procedure provided only an estimate of the amalgam CM_i. But if one were willing to assume that a "complete" production function would exhibit constant returns to scale, it followed that C, the coefficient of management, was equal to $1 - \sum B_j$, so that an unbiased estimate c could be constructed as $1 - \sum b_j$. Then, one could create a measure of the management variable $m_i = a_i/c$. Mundlak noted, however, that for some purposes the a_i would serve as well as the m_i as an index of management.

There was one serious concern, however, with this interpretation of the estimates, and that was the possibility that some other input was fixed for individual firms over the period of observation. The regression coefficient of such a factor would necessarily be zero, and a_i would capture the impact of that input as well as management. In the agricultural setting, the obvious

27 The diagram was drawn under the assumption that better managers used more of the input. Mundlak also explained the case in which better managers used less of an input, so that the interfirm production function would have a flatter slope than the intrafirm, and perhaps even a negative slope.

candidate for such a fixed input was the particular environmental conditions of the farm (including, e.g., soil quality). Should such things vary across farms, "this would not affect the b_j or their properties, but it would change the meaning of a_i. It would now be an estimate of the management and farm effect combined." But Mundlak, displaying considerable empirical ingenuity, went on to comment that "if there is a possibility of grouping the farms into homogenous groups, say villages, and if management is randomly distributed over these villages, an introduction of a parameter to represent the village effect may eliminate some of the farm effect" (48).

Referring to Griliches's (1957) analysis of omitted-variable bias in the Cobb–Douglas production function, Mundlak explained that the bias in the cross-section estimate of Cobb–Douglas coefficient B_j (still assuming that the only omitted input was management) could be written as Cd_j, where d_j was the coefficient of input j in an auxiliary regression of the unobserved management variable on the observed inputs, that is, $M_i = d_1X_{1i} + \ldots d_kX_{ki}$. The difference between a b_j produced by a cross-section regression and a b_j produced by Mundlak's method would serve as an estimate of the bias Cd_j, which could be divided by c to produce an estimate of d_j. The d_j values would indicate the relationship between management quality and input levels, and could be used to predict the size of the management variable for other farms in the population from which the estimating sample was drawn.

Mundlak applied his method to a sample of 66 family farms in Israel observed annually from 1954 to 1958. Input and output variable descriptions were rather brief: Y was "value of output"; land was measured in dunams (quarter acres), with one irrigated dunam considered equivalent to four nonirrigated dunams; the labor variable was "number of labor days," other inputs were "variable expense," value of livestock at the beginning of the year, and value of livestock and poultry barns. All monetary variables were deflated to 1954 values. At this point Mundlak explained that a "year effect" term A_t could be added to the model, creating what he called the "unrestricted function," and that four versions of the model had been estimated: one with no firm or year effects (all A_i and $A_t = 0$); one allowing firm effects only, one allowing year effects only, and the unrestricted version that included both firm and year effects.

In both versions of the model that allowed the firm effects to differ from zero, those effects were jointly statistically significant. He calculated two estimates of the bias of each b_j from the model with no time or year effects by comparing them to the corresponding estimates from the two models that included firm effects, and then did similar calculations using the results reported in Hoch (1955). He also reported the implied coefficients of the auxiliary regression of M on the observed X's, both for his results and Hoch's, and explained how the coefficient of determination for these auxiliary regressions could be calculated. This was useful because in order to establish that the conventional regression (without time and year effects) produced biased estimates, one needed to show both that management had an effect on output (reject the hypothesis that the firm effects were jointly equal to zero) and that management was correlated with the measured input variables (reject the hypothesis that coefficient of determination of the auxiliary regression was zero). This turned out to be the case.

Hoch and Mundlak had constructed and demonstrated an econometric model of the Cobb–Douglas production function, one which they claimed could address two of the more serious concerns with the existing approach to production function estimation: simultaneous equations bias and omitted-variable bias. Their claims were accepted by a significant number of economists, and the empirical production function research program in agricultural economics and in other fields was thereby given a significant boost.

Hoch's and Mundlak's papers had a much wider impact than this, however, for the problems of simultaneous equations bias and omitted variables were faced by empirical researchers working in a number of areas of economics. A substantial econometric literature grew up analyzing models of the type proposed by Hoch and Mundlak and developing extensions of those models. The message of this literature, that the analysis of panel data could throw light on a number of pressing questions on the agenda of empirical economics, in turn helped fuel an explosion in the number of panel data sets collected and constructed over the next two decades.

Mundlak and Hoch were both trying to deal with a problem created by a variable for which no good direct measure existed, call it managerial ability, technical efficiency, and so forth. Unmeasured concepts are a perennial problem in empirical economics, whether the empirical economist wants to analyze the unmeasured concept, or, as in the case of "managerial bias," the lack of a measure for the concept stands in the way of measuring some other concept or relationship of interest. One response to the problem is direct data collection – devote the resources necessary to directly measure the concept. Another is to develop an indirect measure of the concept by using assumptions, expressed in the form of an economic theoretical model, about the relationship between measured variables and the unmeasured variable, as when changes in worker productivity are measured using changes in the wage, under the assumption that the marginal productivity theory of distribution is valid. I would argue that Hoch and Mundlak were pursuing a third strategy, that of using statistical modeling to create an indirect measure of the unmeasured concept, or at least "control" it so that it no longer created a problem. They built their econometric production function model around a statistical assumption that the unmeasured concept "management" did not change over time for a given firm, while other unmeasured variables that affected output did vary over time and across firms in a way that was uncorrelated with the variations in the measured inputs. Given these assumptions, they used statistical theory to show that the management input could be "controlled" and arguably even measured using currently existing statistical methods, provided that the data on the observable variables had been collected in a particular way, that is, by measuring the same variables for all members of a cross-section sample at more than one point in time. Of course there was economic theory involved in Hoch and Mundlak's measurement method, not least of all the theory that there was a stable production function relating inputs to outputs. But that theory did not solve their problem; indeed, the problem had in a sense been created by the acceptance of a body of theory that pointed to the existence of difficult to measure factors that affected both levels of output and choices about inputs. The innovation that Mundlak and Hoch designed to solve the problem was statistical in nature.

The methods of statistical experimentation, such as those developed by R. A. Fisher and employed, as we have seen, by agricultural economists, can arguably be seen as a similar example of the use of statistical methods to solve a problem created by unmeasured concepts, a problem similar to that faced by Hoch and Mundlak. In both cases, the attempt to learn about the relationship between a measurable "independent variable" and a measured "dependent" variable was hampered by the existence of a number of unmeasured variables that also influenced the dependent variable. Fisher used statistical theory to justify the use of certain statistical methods for estimating and making inferences about relationships between observable variables without measuring the problematic unobservable variables, provided the data on the observable variables were generated in a certain way, that is, through a properly designed experiment.

Articles using the Cobb–Douglas and other regression specifications to estimate production functions appeared with increasing frequency in the *Journal of Farm Economics* between 1955 and 1960, written by authors from a variety of institutions, and often referring to agricultural bulletins or Ph.D. theses in which the method was also employed. Some agricultural economists were convinced of the shortcomings of the early agricultural production function regressions, but, unwilling to abandon the research goals that had motivated their authors, turned to the newer technique of linear programming as better suited for the estimation of agricultural production relationships. Even Earl Heady came to conclude that, at least for the analysis of activities on a multi-enterprise firm, linear programming was superior to the production function approach (Dillon 1996, 54). Still, by the mid 1960s the Cobb–Douglas regression was well on its way to becoming ensconced in the toolbox of agricultural economists involved in farm management research, as is reflected in this comment in a 1986 agricultural economics textbook: "The Cobb–Douglas type of production function has been estimated by agricultural economics for virtually any production process involving the transformation of inputs into outputs in an agricultural setting. To review scientific application of the Cobb–Douglas type of function would be to review a large share of the literature in which empirical attempts have been made to estimate production functions" (Debertin 1986).[28]

CONCLUSION

In 1927, Douglas had presented his new empirical procedure as a tool with the potential to shed light on a broad range of questions in economics, and in his AEA Presidential Address of 1947, he intimated that there were still numerous fruitful fields of application for the regression as yet unexplored. But in the body of empirical research Douglas left behind, he had concentrated on demonstrating and defending the regression as a means of accomplishing a specific set of tasks, albeit tasks of great interest to the profession: estimating the marginal productivity curves of capital and labor conceived of as two broad aggregate inputs, testing whether factor markets and possibly output markets were competitive, measuring the returns to scale of production in manufacturing, and determining whether the wages of labor corresponded to labor's marginal product. In the late 1940s, Earl Heady, motivated by a desire to contribute to important research programs

[28] Or this much earlier observation in Fuller (1962, 82): "The estimation of production functions and the use of empirically derived functions to estimate optimum levels and combinations of resource inputs has become quite common in agricultural economics research."

in agricultural economics, had promoted and employed Douglas's regression for a different set of tasks than those for which Douglas had used it. And in the fifties, economists began to develop additional novel applications for the Cobb–Douglas regression and the production function regressions that developed out of it.

It was in the roles created for it by Earl Heady, however, that the Cobb–Douglas regression first gained widespread acceptance. At a time when production function estimation in the Douglas style seemed to have more critics than imitators, a significant number of agricultural economists came to view the Cobb–Douglas regression as a tool that produced credible evidence on an interesting set of questions, and a technique that should be taught to graduate students as a matter of course. In part this was, as Griliches argued, because of the data used by the agricultural economists to estimate the regression. But it was also because of the questions they chose to explore with the regression, and the conclusions they were willing to draw from the results. For the agricultural economists, the data used to estimate the regression combined with the purposes for which it was estimated in such a way that many of the "withering criticisms" aimed at the Douglas studies did not apply, or applied with much less force, to the body of empirical results produced by the agricultural economists.

This is most obvious in the case of the experimental production function studies. The use of experimental data avoided almost all of the statistical issues raised by critics of Douglas's methods of estimating production functions. Inputs and output could be measured very accurately, and the impact of unmeasured inputs could be "controlled" through the experimental design, so that the true marginal productivity of the measured inputs could be estimated. Heady explicitly made the point that experiments could be designed to avoid Mendershausen's multicollinearity critique. Concerns about simultaneous equations bias or bias due to the omission of a management variable simply did not apply. It is perhaps enough to mention again that Marschak and Andrews (1944) had proposed the hypothetical agricultural experiment as the ideal setting in which to estimate a true production function.

In addition to requiring fewer questionable statistical assumptions, however, the experimental production function studies, given their purpose, required fewer questionable economic assumptions. Indeed, since the data they used were not generated by actual economic activity, no assumptions about the nature of the economic system were required in order for the estimates to represent what they were claimed to represent – the maximum level of an output obtainable by any given combination of inputs. By contrast, Douglas and his coauthors had, in interpreting and defending the credibility of their results, often relied implicitly or explicitly on contentious assumptions about the economic system: that producers were actually achieving the maximum possible output that could be squeezed from their inputs, that the marginal productivity theory actually held (at least Douglas was perceived to be assuming this when he defended his method by pointing to the closeness of labor's share to the estimated labor coefficient), or that the economic system was consistently in equilibrium (assumed in Bronfenbrenner and Douglas's [1939] model relating the estimated Cobb–Douglas regression to the production functions of theory). It is of course true that because the experimental production function studies were based on data generated under idealized experimental conditions, there were obvious limitations on the range of potentially interesting questions they could address.[29] But it is also true that this research was perceived by the agricultural economics community to be producing credible evidence on questions they cared about.[30]

The so-called "farm-firm" production function studies were also insulated from criticisms directed at Douglas by a combination of the data they employed and the questions they were designed to address. As noted already, several critics of the Douglas studies had allowed that a believable set of production function estimates might be obtained from firm-level data, and the agricultural economists were working with firm-level data. Further, these economists could plausibly argue that, with the help of expert advice from agronomists, they were creating homogenous samples of farms, thus lessening the interfirm/intrafirm or "hybridity" problem.

The farm-level data were observational data generated by actual economic activity, but even so, the economic assumptions made by the agricultural economists to establish the validity of their method were less

[29] This was not actually a commonly voiced criticism of the experimental production functions. The only good example I could find was Kanel (1957), who argued that the experimental production function studies will never answer questions about the importance of the managerial input, which he considered to be a crucial matter in farm-management research. More technically, he argued that the marginal productivity of agricultural inputs likely depended on the level of the managerial input, so that marginal productivities estimated under conditions in which managerial ability was experimentally "fixed" were not those for any real farm.

[30] See Johnson (1955) for the uses to which the experimental estimates were being put even by the early 1950s. The experimental production functions did attract criticism, but the criticism usually involved technical matters of experimental design that were recognized by the critics as correctable, rather than arguments questioning the general validity or value of the research area.

controversial than those made by Douglas. It was not assumed that the agricultural sector as a whole was competitive, only that farmers were price takers, an assumption to which few economists of the time would have objected. Farmers were not assumed to be in the unconstrained optimum positions identified by neoclassical models, but only to be doing their best given the constraints placed upon them by ignorance, uncertainty, and institutions. This assumption actually offered a way around Tinbergen's criticism that if all firms with a common production function faced the same input prices, all would choose the same input combination, so that the production function could not be estimated. And recall that the argument that farmers' errors of optimization were very large compared to the impact of unobserved factors on the production function was advanced to minimize concern with simultaneous equations bias. Another plausible assumption about farmer behavior, that most input decisions were made well before actual output was observed, also helped to counter the simultaneous equations criticism.

The agricultural economists estimating the Cobb–Douglas regression with farm-level data did not need to make the assumptions about economic behavior made in the Douglas studies because they were not trying to answer the same questions about the economic system. But they could still make a case that the method, as they used it, did produce valuable information about the economic system. Measures of the deviations from efficient allocation in agriculture were of interest to policy makers, and Heady's (1955) study of the resource allocation decisions of farmers working under different farm-tenure arrangements was a model of how the Cobb–Douglas regression could be used to test behavioral hypotheses derived from a simple neoclassical model.

I would argue that there is another link between the fact that the agricultural economists were using the regression to explore questions different from those that were the focus of the Douglas studies, and the lower level of resistance their work provoked from fellow economists. I think that Douglas's work with the regression attracted more criticism because the things that he said he was proving with it were much more controversial. The questions on which he claimed to have produced evidence, such as the extent of competition in the manufacturing sector and the validity of the marginal productivity theory of distribution, were questions that had long been the subject of contentious argument among professional economists, with answers that had implications for high-profile political and ideological debates. For that reason, Douglas's studies attracted criticism from people who might not have devoted a lot of effort to examining a study that employed an innovative empirical procedure to explore more mundane matters. Simply put, a study claiming to have good empirical evidence that there was too much labor in the agricultural sector or that farmers under share leases allocated resources differently than farmers under cash leases was just not going to attract as much critical scrutiny as one claiming to show that labor did receive its marginal product, or that competitive conditions prevailed in the US manufacturing sector.

Admittedly, the agricultural research involving the Cobb–Douglas regression in the 1940s and 1950s was provincial in nature, that is, written for a relatively small group within the profession as a whole, usually published in the specialized outlets of that group, and addressing issues of importance to that group but not of great interest to economists in general. This did limit the impact of the work on the ongoing development of empirical research in the profession. I believe that in spite of this, however, the Cobb–Douglas regression's "vigorous life" in agricultural economics in the initial years following Douglas's election to the Senate was an important phase in the process through which the production function regression came to be a standard tool of empirical economics.

To begin with, it meant that examples of successful applications of the Cobb–Douglas regression (i.e., applications resulting in published articles, approved dissertations, etc.) continued to accumulate, creating a literature that went beyond Douglas's studies. It was a progressing literature, in the sense that contributors were identifying shortcomings of the method but also responding positively to them with statistical innovations, more nuanced theoretical arguments, and further applications. Also, as noted earlier, it was a literature in which the Cobb–Douglas regression as an empirical method was presented and discussed in the context of a formal theory of statistical estimation and inference, first the more classical framework created by Fisher, and then the econometric framework popularized by the Cowles Commission researchers. So, in the 1950s and 1960s there was a literature to which general economists could turn should they see a potential application of the regression in their own research, one that looked more up-to-date than the original studies of the Douglas group, and which signaled that economists still believed in the validity of the method.

Perhaps more importantly, the continued use of the method by agricultural economists meant that it was being taught to a rising generation of economics Ph.D. students who were taking classes in statistical methods/ econometrics in agricultural economics programs or in joint economics/ agricultural economics departments, such as those that existed at Iowa

State College. Mundlak, Hoch, and Griliches are leading examples of such students, and also illustrate the importance of the phenomenon for the diffusion of the regression beyond agricultural economics. As mentioned already, Hoch and Mundlak's econometric model for estimating the Cobb–Douglas production function with panel data was widely adopted by subsequent researchers working with firm- and industry-level data from all sectors of the economy. Griliches became one of the profession's most high-profile users of the Cobb–Douglas regression, developing a role for the method that transcended agricultural economics. His work with the regression is part of the larger story of how production function estimation came to be part of the twentieth-century research program concerned with measuring and understanding the nature of economic growth and technical change, which is the subject of Chapter 6.

6

The Cobb–Douglas Regression as a Tool for Measuring and Explaining Economic Growth

The 1950s saw a tremendous upsurge in interest among economists in the analysis of economic growth, interest that manifested itself in new theoretical models of the growth process and novel empirical investigations of the causes of economic growth. An important component of this research effort was the discussion and evaluation of various actions the government might take to increase the rate of economic growth, as during the same period faster economic growth emerged as a public policy goal of the first importance. In the closing years of the 1950s, several researchers hit upon using modifications of the time series version of Douglas's regression as an empirical tool for explaining the causes of economic growth, and about the same time Zvi Griliches introduced an empirical framework for explaining economic growth that involved estimation of Cobb–Douglas regressions very much like those in Douglas's cross-section studies. This chapter of the book, divided into three parts, tells the story of this second major field of application for Cobb–Douglas regressions in the postwar decades.

A proper understanding of how and why the Cobb–Douglas regression became a tool in the effort to measure and explain economic growth, however, requires a retelling of the broader story of that effort. My account begins in the second decade of the twentieth century, with the development of credible measures of the growth of the nation's economy, followed a few years later by the development of measures of labor productivity. The new measures revealed that the US economy had indeed been growing at a healthy pace since the late 1800s, and that this growth was largely due to dramatic increases in the productivity of the typical American worker, findings that stimulated a new empirical research by economists into the causes and possible consequences of economic growth.

As described in Part I, Paul Douglas originally imagined that the regression technique that he and Cobb developed could be employed in this research, mentioning in introduction of "A Theory of Production" that the paper's statistical work might help determine the extent to which recent increases in output had been "primarily caused by technique," rather than changes in the quantities of labor and capital employed. The results described by Cobb and Douglas, however, threw no light on this matter, a fact that troubled both Douglas and other economists who commented on his novel empirical procedure. Douglas never adjusted his procedure to either measure or control for the impact of technological change on growth, instead sidestepping the problem by developing his cross-section method.

However, economists working in the research program that grew up around the creation and analysis of national income measures started attacking the problem from another angle. In the mid-1930s, one of the leading researchers in this area, Morris Copeland, suggested a procedure for performing the basic decomposition of growth into growth due to increases in capital and labor, and growth due to "changes in technique." Implementing the procedure would require the development of a reliable time series measure of aggregate capital and separate price indexes for deflating the capital measure and the measure of net national product. Over ten years passed before economists were confident enough in a constructed series measuring the "real capital stock" to actually implement Copeland's suggestion. When they did, the conclusion of one study after another was that the overwhelming majority of the economic growth in the United States had been due to "technical progress," which all economists involved in the research readily admitted was a euphemism for "factors we have not quantified and know very little about." The portion of economic growth due to as yet unidentified factors came to be known as "the residual," and the attempt to shrink the residual by more accurately identifying and quantifying causes of growth became the central purpose of an area of research dubbed "growth accounting."

A pivotal event in the story is Robert Solow's 1957 article, "Technical Change and the Aggregate Production Function," which offered an empirical operationalization of a conceptual division of measured economic growth into "shifts in the production function" and "movements along a production function," an operationalization that included as one step the estimation of a Cobb–Douglas regression. As Griliches (1996) pointed out, the Solow article led to the merger of two streams of research, one building on the time series version of the Cobb–Douglas regression, the other involving the increasingly sophisticated measurement of the residual using Copeland's approach. It also made a convincing case for adopting a particular conceptual framework for thinking about the ongoing research on the measurement of productivity/technical change, one rooted in an aggregate version of the marginal productivity theory of production and distribution.

The widespread adoption of this framework led to a process in which a number of hypotheses about sources of economic growth offered over the previous decades came to be represented as a series of modifications to Solow's basic neoclassical production function, which in turn led, not surprisingly, to attempts to test empirically these hypotheses using production function regressions. It was also a process, however, during which empirical research into the causes of growth and the consequences of technological change was coming to be more standardized and more narrowly focused: more standardized in the sense that an aggregate version of the neoclassical theory of production and distribution was widely adopted as the framework used to develop and discuss the concepts, methods, and measures used in that research; more narrowly focused in that adoption of this framework pointed the research away from some of the questions, hypotheses, and methods found in the growth research of the previous decades.

The third part of this chapter gives particular attention to two of the empirical research programs that moved this standardizing and narrowing process forward, and which made use of variants of Douglas's regression procedure: the literature on "embodied technical change" touched off by Robert Solow in the late 1950s and early 1960s, and Zvi Griliches's work measuring the causes of economic growth, which commenced at about the same time. From the 1920s onward, empirical growth researchers who worked towards a decomposition of aggregate economic growth into that which was caused by increases in the quantities of inputs and that which was caused by technological change understood that this was only a first step towards a more nuanced empirical analysis of a complex phenomenon, and they hypothesized that output could increase due to improvements in the quality of labor, that growth in the quantity of capital might be the way in which much technological improvement manifested itself, and that scale economies might be important. Griliches and Solow proposed empirically tractable ways of testing these venerable hypotheses. Their proposals proved attractive in part because they made use of an empirical procedure, production function estimation, that involved statistical methods that were coming to be the foundation of graduate training in econometrics and because they were expressed in terms of the mathematical neoclassical theory that was becoming central to graduate training in economic theory. However, expressing a concept like "improving input quality" or "capital embodied technical change" in a way that can be measured with existing data using a particular statistical technique means choosing one out of a number of possible meanings of the concept. Thus, after 1960, economic research into causes of growth was more standardized, but also more narrowly focused, than the prewar research had been.

EMPIRICAL RESEARCH ON THE EXTENT AND CAUSES OF ECONOMIC GROWTH, 1920–1950

Measuring Economic Output and Growth: the 1920s

By the second half of the 1800s, there was broad agreement among economists that steady, if not astounding, growth in productive capacity had become a standard characteristic of modern, or "civilized" nations, and that a major factor driving this growth was what would today be called technical change.[1] The view could be found at mid-century in both *The Communist Manifesto* and J. S. Mill's *Principles of Political Economy* and, a few decades later, in Alfred Marshall's *Principles of Economics* as well as the opening pages of Henry George's *Progress and Poverty*.[2] It was not until the early decades of the twentieth century, however, that enough statistical material had been accumulated to allow economists to confidently attempt to measure this growth and empirically investigate its causes.

Measuring the growth of a nation's output required consistent and repeated measures of that output, and by the early 1920s, two basic approaches to constructing such measures were being employed. One, which I shall call the physical-index approach, proceeded in three steps. The first was to gather several time series measured in physical units, each intended to represent the activity of a well-defined industry or sector of the economy. A series might measure one of the outputs of the industry or a key input used by the industry: for example, the leather industry might be represented by both cattle hides consumed and leather gloves and mittens produced. The next step was to express all the values of each series relative to the value of that series in a common base period. The third step was to average these series of ratios using a set of weights that reflected the relative

1 Writers of the time used words and phrases such as "invention," "changes in technique," "improvements in the industrial arts," or "increases in man's command over nature."

2 Mill (1987 [1848], 696–97); Marx and Engels (1992 [1848], 7–8); George, (1981 [1879], 3); Marshall (1948 [1890] 671, 674–45).

importance of the industries they represented, as measured, for example, by total sales, employment, or value added.

An early example of such a measure was the Index of the Physical Volume of Production constructed by E. E. Day and Warren Persons of Harvard's Committee on Economic Research (Day and Persons 1920a, 1920b, 1920c, 1920d, and 1921). This index combined series representing the three sectors of agriculture, mining, and manufacturing, with manufacturing further divided into 14 industry groups. The agriculture component of the index, for example, included the annual production of 12 "important" crops, while the manufacturing component included such series as gallons of distilled liquors and tons of pig iron.

During the 1920s new indexes of this type were being introduced and old ones revised as more and better data became available. In "A Theory of Production," Cobb and Douglas used as the "product" or dependent variable in their regression the manufacturing component of the Day-Persons index (as revised in Matthews (1925)), but only because a better index being constructed by Woodlief Thomas was not available in time (Cobb and Douglas 1928, 150). In 1922 the Federal Reserve Board began issuing a monthly index of production, with coverage going back to January of 1919 and composed of 22 series. In 1927, the index was broadened and several refinements were introduced into its construction:

> The new index of industrial production ... is made up of two component indexes, one of manufactures and the other of minerals, and is computed from 60 series of monthly figures representing average output per working day and adjusted for typical seasonal variations. The average of three years 1923, 1924, and 1925, was adopted as the base. The weights for the various industries in the manufactures index were derived from figures showing value added by manufacture, as reported by the Census of Manufactures for 1923 and 1919, and those of the minerals index were derived from the values produced ... An aggregative formula was employed to combine the individual series into a composite index. From 1919 to 1922 the final index was the average of the two separately combined indexes, one with 1919 weights and the other with weights for 1923 (1923–25 in the case of minerals) ...
>
> (Thomas 1927b, 316–317).

This passage only begins to hint at the many challenges and decisions that faced economists creating these indexes. The conversion of the data from monthly totals to average output per working day in the revision of Federal Reserve Board index, for example, was a response to spurious fluctuations in the monthly totals caused by changes in the number of working days per month. Numerous options were available in choosing weights, and series could be averaged arithmetically or geometrically, before or after being converted into relative form. Day and Persons developed a method for "anchoring" their annual manufacturing index based on 33 series to a far more comprehensive index built from materials reported in the quinquennial US Censuses of Manufactures. And the maker of each new index was expected to offer tests and proofs of the credibility, if not the superiority, of his index, such as measures of the share of each industry's output comprised by the series used to represent that industry, or graphical and statistical comparisons of the consistency of the new measure with previously established indexes of production, accompanied by reasonable explanations of any important deviations. But there was fairly broad agreement across the indexes of physical production when it came to the question of economic growth: From 1900 to the mid-1920s, mining and manufacturing output had increased by 5 to 6 percent per year on average, while the index that included agriculture grew at a little under 4 percent per year. With population growing at about 2 percent over the same period, this implied a healthy annual rate of growth of per capita output.

The work of the National Bureau of Economic Research (NBER) on the measurement of national income in the early 1920s provided a second approach to measuring economic growth. The plan pursued by the NBER economists was to construct two alternative but theoretically equivalent annual measures of the national income, one based on statistics of incomes received by individuals and one based on statistics of the value of goods and services produced. In their initial report (Mitchell et al. 1921) the researchers constructed the two measures for each year from 1909 to 1919, expressing them in current-year dollars. Both series were also converted into constant-dollar terms using a process that divided each current dollar series into subcomponents, and deflated each subcomponent with a different price index (e.g., incomes received by employees were deflated using the Bureau of Labor Statistics (BLS) cost of living index, while incomes received as interest, dividends, rents, royalties, and profits were deflated using a special cost of living index based on the consumption habits of more affluent households). The two deflated series were averaged to create a third "final" series of what was deemed "real" national income, which was represented as a measure of "the serviceable goods available for use by the population," and "the aggregate of commodities and services which the current money income would buy," that is, a measure of total output (Mitchell et al. 1921, vol. 1, 73, 75). To further underscore the point that real national income represented a measure of the quantity of output, these real income series were compared to four indexes of physical production, including the Day-Persons Index. The NBER "final" real income measure showed an annual growth rate of 2.5 percent over the years 1910–1918, following, in the words of the NBER researchers, "an intermediate course through the field covered by the fluctuations of the physical production index numbers" (Mitchell et al. 1921, vol. 1, 80).

Measures of output and growth derived from national income estimates eventually came to supplant those based on physical indexes of production, at least for nations or broad aggregations of industries, but during the 1920s there was not yet consensus upon which measurement approach was superior. The statistical materials on which the real national income measures were based covered a broader range of economic activities, as they could include both series expressed in terms of physical units and those measured in monetary terms. However, the early national income accountants often encountered time periods and industries for which adequate data were not available, and like those constructing the physical indexes, resorted to extrapolation and proportionality assumptions to fill in the gaps. More importantly, the fact that each year's national income figure had to be deflated in order to measure changes over time in output gave rise to an additional set of reasons to doubt the accuracy of the "real" national income estimates, as a number of challengeable assumptions and estimation procedures went into the construction of any given price index.

The NBER's first national income study was well enough received, however, that the bureau continued to produce and refine annual national income estimates throughout the 1920s, and in 1929 another comparison between a real national income measure and a physical index of production appeared in a chapter by Morris Copeland in the NBER's volume on *Recent Economic Changes*.[3] Copeland chose to work with what he called realized income, a national income measure based on money incomes received, but made it clear that the ultimate goal driving his decisions about what to count and how to count it was the measurement of

[3] *Recent Economic Changes* was the outcome of an extensive research effort to provide a broad-based account of the US economy's development since the world war, with an eye towards understanding the causes and consequences of the major trends thus revealed. The project was commissioned by Herbert Hoover while he was the secretary of commerce and coordinated by the National Bureau of Economic Research (NBER), and reflected Hoover's belief (shared by NBER founder, Wesley Mitchell) that a key element of sound governmental economic policy was the acquisition and dissemination of objective knowledge of the economic system to both private and public sector decision makers. See Barber (1985).

"production of goods and services or our capacity to produce them." In deflating his realized income series into constant-dollar terms, Copeland used the NBER approach described above, and he compared the resulting series to a production index similar in coverage to the Day-Persons index. He was disturbed by some obvious divergences between the two series' verdicts regarding year to year changes in output, which is understandable given that the accurate documentation of cyclical fluctuations was a major purpose behind the development of both measures. Copeland noted as a potential weakness of the physical index of production that the industries it represented, being limited to those engaged in commodity production, generated only about a third of the nation's income. The national income measure had a serious weakness as well, however, as "deflation is a process that requires cautious use . . . (and) the method of deflation employed . . . is not well adapted to the particular purpose of comparing income with output" (Copeland 1929, fn. 8). When it came to longer term economic growth, however, the two series were in remarkable agreement, both indicating that between 1913 and 1926 there had been an increase of about 42 percent in the nation's output of goods and services..

Early Attempts to Understand the Causes of Growth: Studies of Labor Productivity

As time series measures of output were being developed and refined in the 1920s, they became inputs into measures of labor productivity. Woirol (2006) documents this first major productivity research program in the United States. He argues convincingly that the most important immediate consequence of the early attempts to measure labor productivity was a concern that rising labor productivity was generating technological unemployment, and that this concern provided a major motivation for pushing the research program into the depression years of the 1930s. However, it is also clear that many of those who wrote and responded to the early labor productivity studies viewed them as a first step towards understanding the causes of the economic growth revealed in the new output measures.

The basic approach to constructing a measure of changes in labor productivity was straightforward. One began with a measure of output at the level of an industry, sector, or economy, expressed in an index form. One then constructed an index number measuring the growth of the labor input, either hours of work or number of employees. For example, in the May 1927 issue of the *Monthly Labor Review*, BLS researchers reported that an output index for manufacturing had increased from 100 to 134 between 1919 and 1925, while an index of the number of wage earners employed in manufacturing had declined from 100 to 93.3 over the same period, indicating a growth in labor productivity, measured as output per wage earner, of 43.6 percent. (US BLS 1927, Woirol 2006). As Woirol describes, a research team headed by Ewan Clague produced a number of influential labor productivity studies in 1926 and 1927, releasing numbers first for individual industries like shoes and automobiles before providing the measure for manufacturing as a whole. Thomas (1927b) created measures of labor productivity growth from 1899 to 1925 in manufacturing, agriculture, railways, and mining, as well as a combined measure for all four sectors.

The productivity studies led to broad consensus on one point: labor productivity, whether measured per wage earner, employee, or man-hour, was growing dramatically. Put another way, the growth in output revealed by the physical indexes and the real national income was largely due to something other than growth in the labor force. Further, the growth in productivity had been particularly rapid since the end of the war. A number of economists proposed explanations for the dramatic increases in productivity, typically in the form of lists of possible causes. The lists often overlapped, but all gave a place of prominence to technical change, or, more accurately, to factors that would later come to be understood as falling under the broad rubric of technical change. Paul Douglas proposed three main causes of the measured productivity increases: increased quantities of capital per worker, "the rapid development of American technical methods, including as its most notable feature, the moving conveyor," and economies of scale both internal and external to firms, made possible by the nation's "large internal market in which free trade prevails." Interestingly, Douglas listed as a fourth factor the inability of unorganized workers to resist the introduction of new production methods. As to why productivity growth had markedly accelerated after the war, even though the factors he cited had been operative for some time before, Douglas pointed to changes in the willingness of managers to seek out and employ new and more productive techniques, a change driven, Douglas argued, by the restrictions on immigration and the increase in the real wages of workers, but also by "fifteen years of discussion of scientific management and of efficiency." Prohibition, Douglas noted, was another recent change to consider in seeking for explanations (Douglas 1927).

Woodlief Thomas (1928) thought it obvious that the main causes of productivity growth were the growing use of mass production, increased mechanization, and scale economies achieved through industrial consolidation. He was also willing to give credit to improved education and literacy, the organization of scientific research in universities, and the increasing use of statistics by business people. He, like Douglas, sought particular explanations for the postwar surge in productivity growth, finding them in the war experience, which accelerated the discovery and implementation of new technologies, as well as the easy availability of new investment funds, which led to the replacement of old capital equipment with new and better capital equipment.

Wesley Mitchell, writing the summary chapter of the *Recent Economic Changes* volume, sought to place the postwar economic trends in the United States in a larger historical context. When it came to explaining economic growth, he too put technical change at the center of his account, but portrayed the innovations that had revolutionized methods of production and distribution in the developed economies as a product of a more fundamental social trend, speaking of "the purposeful application of scientific knowledge to all aspects of production." In his view, the postwar spurt in US labor productivity was due mainly to an intensification of this longstanding tendency: "Since 1921, Americans have applied intelligence to the days' work more effectively than ever before. Thus the prime factor in producing the extraordinary changes in the fortunes of the European peoples during the 19th century is the prime factor in producing prosperity in the United States in recent years. The old process of putting science into industry has been followed more intensively than before; it has been supplemented by tentative efforts to put science into business management, trade-union policy, and Government administration" (Mitchell 1929, 844, 862).

It is not surprising that along with lists of possible causes of increasing labor productivity came attempts to develop a more empirically based understanding of them, if not quantify their relative importance. One approach to quantifying the importance of those causes that could be at least approximately measured was an extension of the index-number method originally used to ascertain the extent of labor productivity growth. Thomas (1928), for example, presented alongside of his indexes of output and labor input an index of "horsepower of installed prime movers," taken from the censuses of manufacturing. This index number had soared from 100 to 356 while the output per worker index had grown from 100 to 147. L. P. Alford (1929) took this approach further, adding to the conventional indexes of output, labor, and output per worker indexes of a number of other factors potentially related in some way to productivity, including the value of manufacturing buildings and of manufacturing machinery (taken from the original Cobb–Douglas paper), the cost of materials, and the average wage rate. Alford showed, graphically and in tables, how the growth paths and growth rates of these various factors compared with those of output per worker, but it was not made clear what the reader was to take from these comparisons: While dividing output measures by measures of labor input (or comparing the two indexes) led to a quantity of obvious significance, it was less obvious how these other series should be compared or processed to gain more insight into the sources of productivity growth.

Alford also reported large amounts of information, obtained via questionnaires and on-site investigations, on where and how "changes in technique" had been introduced into American manufacturing, making it an illustration of another strategy adopted during the period for gaining a more empirically grounded understanding of the nature and consequences of technical innovation. A survey by the National Research Council, for example, had yielded information from over 500 large firms on their organized, in-house "industrial research" activities. The Census of Manufactures provided detailed information on the types and sizes of nonhuman power sources used in the nation's manufacturing plants. The American Engineering Council and Traveler's Insurance had conducted investigations of safety procedures. Alford himself had sent questionnaires to firms asking about new processes being used, new materials and products being put on the market, and the installation of new machines and materials-handling equipment. Results from these and other information-gathering efforts were presented by Alford in numerous tables that revealed the incredible variety of cost-saving innovations recently developed or adopted in US manufacturing: Dewey and Almey Chemical had created a new latex-shoe cement and a new compound for sealing cans. American Linseed had installed a new process for pressing linseed that saved four cents per bushel. Manufacturers had begun separating aluminum scrap from other scrap and selling it separately at a higher price. Freeman Dairy Co. installed a coal conveyer and saved $2,500 per year. There were literally hundreds of examples like this going on for page after page.

The productivity research program at the BLS also included the collection of detailed information on recent changes in the production methods and processes of various industries under study. In most cases, this information was presented in narrative form, often with photographs, in bulletins and articles such as "Technological Changes in the Cigar Industry and their Effects on Labor" (US BLS 1931). In a few cases, however, the BLS economists attempted to use this sort of detailed descriptive information on specific innovations as a basis for a statistical analysis of the relationship between technological change and labor productivity, at least at the level of individual industries. The study of "Productivity of Labor in Merchant Blast Furnaces" provides a prime example (US BLS 1928). It was based on records from a large number of plants covering the years 1912–26, with many plants reporting for multiple years. A plant's productivity was measured in terms of tons per stack (i.e., furnace) per day and output per man-hour. The researchers used their detailed knowledge of the history of and production processes involved in the blast-furnace industry to construct meaningful empirical measures of technological and other changes that might have affected productivity, then compared the time series of these measures to the productivity time series. For example, they identified the two most important technological innovations of the period, the mechanization of the process of feeding material into the furnace and the "machine casting" of the iron coming out of the furnace, then constructed measures of the percentage of plants each year that had adopted each of these innovations. And, after a description of the relationship between the volume of a stack and its productivity, a cross-tabulation of stack volume in cubic feet and output of tons per cubic feet was presented, showing that volume affected daily output per cubic foot, but that other factors were also clearly at work. A look at data from plants that had switched from two twelve-hours shifts to three eight-hour shifts provided evidence that labor productivity was much higher when the latter system was used. On the whole, the study was a very impressive example of statistical analysis, particularly when viewed in the context of the empirical economics literature of time.

There were other BLS efforts to measure the impact of specific new technologies on an industry's productivity, including one that measured and compared the productivity and unit cost figures for a number of old and new technological methods that still coexisted in the glass industry (Stern, 1927) and another in which similar comparisons were made between past and present processes for printing newspapers, based on the historical production records of a variety of firms (Kjaer, 1929). The BLS decision to focus on explaining productivity growth at the level of particular industries allowed the researchers to identify a small number of key innovations and develop an understanding of the channels through which these innovations could influence a firm's output and demand for labor. This knowledge could then be used to craft sensible empirical strategies for quantifying the impact of the innovations on measured productivity. This is in contrast to the situation faced by Alford, who had on the one hand aggregate productivity measures from the manufacturing sector as a whole, and on the other descriptions of a multitude of innovations from the whole range of manufacturing industries. The task of developing useful aggregated measures of technological change in manufacturing out of the latter body of information certainly must have seemed daunting.

Harry Jerome posed the problem thusly in his 1934 book *The Mechanization of Industry*: "Can we state this tendency towards mechanization in a more generalized form than by describing the development peculiar to each industry, and in a form reasonably comparable from industry to industry and from period to period? . . . Can we measure it or at least delineate its main lines of advance" (Jerome 1934, 205)? Jerome's book was concerned with a broad subcategory of innovations that he described as "power mechanization" or "the increasing reliance on equipment driven by generated power, be it steam, electricity, compressed air, or gasoline that furnishes the motive power" (Jerome 1934, 41). Like Alford and the BLS researchers, Jerome provided extensive descriptions of a broad range of specific innovations, accounts based on fieldwork and interviews with business people. But he also proposed a number of general measures of mechanization that might be used to make comparisons across industries in the level or growth of mechanization, or quantify the increase over time in overall mechanization, including horsepower per worker, proportion of establishments with power, employment in the machine-producing sector, and the ratio of wages to value added in manufacturing. Jerome's chief purpose in developing these general indexes of mechanization, along with measures of mechanization specific to particular industries, was to explore more fully the impact of mechanization on unemployment, a matter which by this time, as noted earlier, had become a major focus of productivity research. Although he granted as a matter of course that mechanization had also increased productivity, he was not interested in quantifying that relationship.

Analytical Frameworks for the Empirical Analysis of Growth in the 1920s and 1930s

As was described in earlier sections, the development in the 1920s of empirical measures of the growth of output and labor productivity quickly led to attempts by economists to identify the causes of that growth, and to ascertain empirically the relative importance of those causes. It should also be clear from the earlier discussion that there was no widely accepted, well-articulated analytical framework upon which the economists based those efforts. The existence of a number of less-than-fully developed and sometimes conflicting sets of concepts, hypotheses, and categories for thinking about economic growth is reflected in Douglas's attempts to analyze the phenomenon. For example, early in *The Theory of Wages*, Douglas reiterated the basic framework for thinking about the causes of growth initially outlined in the introduction to "A Theory of Production," decomposing the growth in output into that which was due to increases in the quantities of the factors of production and that which was due to changes in technical knowledge (Douglas 1934, 18–19). This decomposition lined up with his statistical approach of constructing index numbers of the growth of labor and capital and using them to account for the growth in a production index, but had roots in classical economics, as in J. S. Mills's (1987 [1848]) chapter on the "Influence of the Progress of Industry and Population on Rents, Profits, and Wages" in which he traced the effect on distributional shares of increases in capital, labor, and "the arts of production," each considered separately while assuming the others constant. However, later in *The Theory of Wages*, Douglas also endorsed the argument of J. M. Clark that the quantitative accumulation of capital necessarily involved qualitative change in capital, that is, technological change, although that idea was incompatible with Douglas's earlier decomposition scheme. He also departed from the basic decomposition framework by acknowledging the possibility that an improvement in the quality of the labor force contributed to growth (Douglas 1934, 212–13). This position, shared by a number of others at the time (e.g., Thomas [1927a]) suggested that an attempt to account statistically for the causes of growth should include investigations of trends that might increase worker quality in general, such as improvements in education or nutrition, or even prohibition.[4] In addition, Douglas

[4] The idea that the growth of capital necessarily involved changes in technique could also be found in the classical canon. In Adam Smith's account of growth, technological change could be seen as a passive factor that occurred almost automatically as capital accumulation facilitated specialization and the division of labor; John Rae offered an alternative account that made technological change the active factor creating an impetus for capital accumulation, with the growing quantity of capital embodied in increasingly sophisticated and productive implements (Brewer 1991). The proposition that improved worker quality led to higher labor productivity is present in Mill (1987 [1848]), more prominent in Marshall (1948 [1890]), and gained an added boost in the early twentieth century as a result of the popularity of eugenics (Leonard 2016).

had argued in 1927 that one of the major causes of increasing productivity (along with increasing capital per worker and improved technology) was the exploitation of economies of scale by producers serving the growing US market. However, in *The Theory of Wages*, Douglas asserted, citing the authority of Knut Wicksell, that the relationship between inputs and outputs should by logical necessity be characterized by constant returns to scale, thus justifying his statistical procedure that forced this restriction on his estimated production function, but drawing criticism from economists like David Durand who believed increasing returns to be an important part of the growth process.[5]

Pluralism was also in display in economists' attempts to understand technical change and its consequences. Economists had not even settled on a common term for the phenomenon, which might be called "invention" by one economist, "changes in technique" by another; and various classification schemes for thinking about the phenomenon could be found. S. C. Gilfillan's four categories of inventions have already been mentioned. Harry Jerome proposed a number of ways of classifying technological change in his *Mechanization in Industry*. Although the book was mainly concerned with "Labor saving changes that take the form of increased mechanization," he acknowledged the importance of nonmechanical changes, which he divided into subcategories including better production control (such as those brought about by time and motion studies) and better knowledge of the order market and forecasting techniques (Jerome 1934, 23). Jerome explained that labor-saving changes could be classed as "productivity increasing" if they increased the number of units of output that a laborer could produce, or "labor displacing," if they lowered the number of workers needed "in a specific operation, plant, or industry," or could be of both types. This was a central analytical distinction in Jerome's book, with detailed explanations and hypothetical numerical examples provided to show how it could be applied in practice. Beyond this, labor-displacing changes could be classified by the means by which they reduced the labor requirement (e.g., eliminating hand operations or increasing machine speed) and labor-saving machines could be classified by the operation in which they were used (handling materials vs. changing their form), the degree to which they were automatic, and so on (Jerome 1934, chapter 2). Merton (1935), in an analysis of factors affecting the rate of invention, divided inventions into those embodied in industrial

[5] Douglas 1934, 55–56; Durand (1937).

technology, techniques of industrial organization and scientific management, and those embodied in consumer goods. Dennison (1930) asserted that a similar distinction between what he called "process" and "product inventions" was important in understanding the impact of technical change on unemployment.

In *The Theory of Wages*, John R. Hicks (1932) also introduced an analytical framework for thinking about technological change. Hicks's framework was a modification of an earlier schema of A. C. Pigou's, who had proposed that "inventions and improvements" could be classified as labor saving, capital saving or neutral according to whether they decreased, increased, or left unaltered the capital/labor ratio outside the industry affected by the invention (Pigou 1932 [1920]). Hicks kept the three categories, but redefined them in terms of ratios of marginal products: a labor-saving invention increased the ratio of the marginal product of capital to the marginal product of labor, a capital saving invention reduced it, and a neutral invention left it unchanged. In the course of discussing the differences between his and Pigou's definitions, Hicks also introduced a distinction between labor-saving and very labor-saving inventions, with the former referring to those that lowered labor's relative share of output, and the latter to those that lowered labor's share in absolute terms. Important for our purposes is that Hicks's definitions ran in terms of the concepts of marginal productivity theory, and, like Pigou's, were clearly designed to facilitate the use of a Marshallian/neoclassical theory of production and distribution for analyzing the impact of technical change, as was illustrated by both men's use of their definitions to discuss the impact of inventions on real wages and on labor's share of total output.[6]

There are few references to Hicks's labor saving/capital saving classification in the journal literature of the 1930s. Still, by 1946, one finds economist Gordon Bloom referring in the *American Economic Review* to Hicks's "well known chapter" in *The Theory of Wages*, where one finds "a partial theory of invention which . . . embodies the use of concepts that have so captured the economists' fancy that the theory of invention has achieved a certain fame of its own. Indeed the terms "labor saving"

[6] Hicks also introduced a distinction between induced inventions (those spurred by changes in relative prices) and autonomous inventions (all the rest), with the induced inventions further distinguished by whether they existed before the change in factor prices led them to be adopted, or whether they actually came into being as a response to the change in factor prices. Interestingly, this particular taxonomy of Hicks's is implicit in J. M. Clark's (1927) remarks on technical progress discussed earlier.

invention, "induced" invention and "autonomous" invention have become stock in trade to most economists" (Bloom 1946, 83).

Measuring Economic Growth and a Plan for Quantifying its Causes: the 1930s

During the 1930s, economists continued to refine and expand the coverage of physical production indexes, providing ongoing measures of output for narrowly defined industries and broad sectors of the economy engaged in commodity production. As of 1930, however, the NBER's program of producing annual estimates of national income faced an uncertain future. Willford I. King, who had been charged with producing estimates of the national income up to 1928, had left the bureau on the completion of that project, and in 1931, Simon Kuznets was given responsibility for the program. He planned to carry the work forward using concepts and methods significantly different from those employed by King, as well as revising King's estimates from earlier years. However, the NBER was uncertain at this time whether or how they would fund this ambitious plan, as their revenues had fallen dramatically due to the Depression. This funding problem was solved by a 1932 Senate resolution directing the Department of Commerce to produce national income estimates covering the years 1929–31 (Gay and Mitchell 1932, 1933). The work was carried out cooperatively by the NBER and Department of Commerce researchers, with Kuznets directing the project. Within a few years, the estimation of national income had been made a permanent function of the Department of Commerce, handled by the Department's Bureau of Foreign and Domestic Commerce (BFDC), and while Kuznets returned to the NBER, the BFDC researchers continue to employ his concepts and methods.[7]

Other economists were also working on estimating the national income and its major components during the 1930s, including Clark Warburton at the Brookings Institution and Lauchlin Currie at the Federal Reserve

[7] Willard Thorp, a former NBER researcher, was director of the Bureau of Foreign and Domestic Commerce (BFDC) at the time, and former Kuznets student Robert Nathan directed the national-income program during much of the late 1930s. However, during the war years, Department of Commerce researchers led by Milton Gilbert would part company with Kuznets on several important points as they created the conceptual framework that still underlies the modern National Income and Product Accounts of the United States (Carson 1975).

(Carson 1975), and not surprisingly, there was disagreement among these scholars on matters ranging from foundational concepts to what data sources to use and how best to use them. It was largely in response to the existence of such unsettled questions that in 1936 the NBER established the Conference on Research in Income and Wealth, made up of researchers "actively engaged in research relating to . . . the amount and distribution of national income and wealth," drawn from universities, government agencies, and private research institutions. Most notably, the conference organized and sponsored regular meetings in which researchers could share ideas and research results, with the proceedings of these meetings published in an annual volume entitled *Studies in Income and Wealth.*

The first meeting of the conference led to an "urgent recommendation" by organizers that a subcommittee be appointed to consider basic matters of definition and terminology, and at the second meeting subcommittee chair Morris Copeland presented a paper outlining areas of agreement and controversy related to "Concepts of National Income" (Copeland 1937). Among the seventeen summary points of Copeland's essay was that what he called the gross value product of a community (the total money value of goods and services produced), if deflated, "would give a broad production index number," that is, a measure of an economy's physical output. However, he warned, current deflation techniques were "in a very elementary stage, and one might rightly hesitate to describe as 'comprehensive' any existing attempt to correct for price changes in the estimates of the national income of any nation for any two years." In addition to endorsing, at least in theory, the idea that national income research could lead to a measure of economic growth, Copeland offered a pregnant suggestion of how the results of national income research could be used to measure technical progress, a suggestion that essentially operationalized what I have called the "basic decomposition" framework for thinking about the sources of economic growth: "Income derived from an area may be deflated to show changes in the physical volume of services of labor and wealth employed by the economic system ... the deflated distributive shares may be compared with the deflated consumed and saved income to show changes in the efficiency of operation of the economic system" (Copeland 1937, 11, 31, 33).

At the following meeting of the conference, in an essay with E. M. Martin more narrowly devoted to examining the use of deflation as "an indirect method of constructing an index of physical volume," this idea was fleshed out (Copeland and Martin 1938, 85, 87):

More than one deflation of the same dollar volume may be possible. The discussion up to this point has been of the procedures required to deflate national income in its credit aspect as the value of ultimate goods and services. National income may also be treated in its debit aspect as a set of primary distributive shares – payroll, interest, profits, etc. We may deflate national income in its debit aspect in order to measure changes in the physical volume of services of labor and wealth used by the economic system in the productive process. In other words, we may use deflation to measure in physical terms the 'input' that results in the 'output' of our economic system.

In terms of uncorrected prices, total national income in debit terms and in credit terms are necessarily equal. In general, the correction of national income for price changes over a series of years will make the two volumes unequal . . . Over a period of years the output curve will ordinarily increase more rapidly than the input curve, and this more rapid increase may be taken to measure the increased efficiency of the economic system

(Copeland and Martin 1938, 103–04).

Milton Friedman, a discussant of the Copeland and Martin paper at the conference, was probably not alone when he questioned the empirical feasibility of this proposal. He pointed out that the well-known biases inherent in the use of price indexes to produce measures of real output would also plague attempts to create measures of real input, and "the divergence of two indices, each of which is subject to a bias, can scarcely provide an accurate measure of changes in technology." Further problems were created by the difficulty of measuring the quantity of capital, or its price, or the quantities of other resources. (Friedman, in Copeland and Martin 1938, 126–27). In response, Copeland and Martin, reflecting the gung-ho attitude often found among empirically oriented economists of the time, remarked:

It must of course be conceded that measurements of the changes in the physical volumes of social input and output are certain to be rough under present conditions. However, those who insist on a high degree of precision had best choose some field of activity other than estimating national wealth and income.

The measurement difficulties about which Mr. Friedman is concerned do not seem to have deterred others to the same extent. Dr. Kuznets has already provided measures of deflated national income in an output sense . . .. Dr. Kuznets' measures of capital formation necessarily involve measurements of the quantities of all kinds of capital . . . (E)stimates of total man years of employment have been developed. Thus, the two main elements for measurements of changes in social input (except for non-reproducible wealth . . .) are admittedly at hand . . .

(Copeland and Martin 1938, 134)

Measuring Capital: the 1930s and 1940s

The measures of capital formation referred to by Copeland and Martin were part of an NBER research program that ultimately produced new time series for the real value of the capital stock for sectors and for the economy as a whole, the first such capital measures since Cobb and Douglas's (1928) time series for the real value of fixed capital in manufacturing. Recall that Douglas's series for 1899–1922 was based on periodic census of manufactures estimates of the money value of capital in manufacturing, only four of which separately measured the value of fixed capital. To fill in values for the years between census estimates, Douglas allocated the total increase over the period using an annual physical production index of a few important construction materials (e.g., pig iron and cement). The resulting measure embodied a high ratio of assumption and interpolation to actual data, and, as described earlier, Douglas's critics honed in on this capital measure as one of the weakest components of his original time series production study.

While Douglas's construction of a capital index in 1927 was a somewhat experimental adjunct to his main project of creating reliable time series of wages, employment, and unemployment, Kuznets's (1934) plan for measuring capital formation was clearly that of a researcher who anticipated devoting considerable time and resources to creating the best measure possible. Capital formation, as defined by Kuznets, was a flow measure of per period changes in "the nation's stock of wealth." Gross capital formation for a year consisted of the value, at prices paid by the ultimate consumer (firm or household) of all durable commodities produced in the year, plus changes in the value of firms' inventories, plus the value of construction, plus the value of repairs. To this was added "net changes in claims against foreign countries," defined as the value of exports minus the value of imports. Estimates were reported in both current and constant dollars. Net capital formation was obtained by subtracting from gross capital formation an estimate of consumption or depreciation of capital.

Kuznets's NBER affiliation gave him access to research assistants and perhaps the most extensive collection of privately and publicly collected economic data then in existence.[8] And, there was simply more data available for the postwar period covered by Kuznets's initial estimates than

[8] As Richard Stone noted in his review of Kuznets (1938), "All the arts of this branch of political arithmetic are combined with a degree of industry which is only possible to an investigator backed by a large institution like the National Bureau" (Stone 1939, 308).

for the earlier period covered by Douglas's index. So, where Douglas used a narrow production index to estimate annual additions to capital during five- and ten-year gaps not covered by the census of manufactures during his period, Kuznets's plan involved dividing all manufacturing output into over forty separate commodity groups plus construction materials, and using biennial censuses of manufacturing to estimate separately the contribution to the capital stock produced by each. In place of Douglas's single price index for deflating annual increments to capital, Kuznets, using mainly BLS wholesale price data, constructed separate price indexes for each commodity group and each of four types of construction. Among those economists willing to entertain the idea that aggregate capital could indeed be measured, Kuznets's numbers were of a nature to engender much less skepticism and concern than Douglas's.

Over the next two decades, Kuznets revised, refined, updated, and pushed further into the past his capital-formation estimates, building on the work of other NBER researchers, whose projects were designed in part to dovetail with Kuznets's project. For example, William Shaw's (1941) estimates of the value of commodity output prior to 1919 helped in the development of estimates for earlier years, and Solomon Fabricant's (1938) estimates of annual capital consumption were used to convert estimates of capital formation from gross to net form.[9]

However, capital formation was a flow measure of additions to the capital stock, while the estimation of a Cobb–Douglas regression or the implementation of the Copeland–Martin technique for estimating increases in technical efficiency required measures of the capital stock

[9] While Kuznets employed a "source-based" approach to measuring capital formation, based largely on measures of the output of durable-goods industries, George Terborgh (1939) developed a "user-based" measure, estimating annual expenditures for plant and equipment by broad sector, for example, railways, mines, utilities, and so forth. Terborgh relied mainly on annual sector-specific surveys of capital spending conducted by governmental and private agencies, although when it came to the broad, heterogeneous manufacturing sector, he had to fall back on Kuznets's source-based methodology. The difference in the two men's approaches is well illustrated by how each estimated the value of new construction. Terborgh estimated the value of new-factory construction in the manufacturing sector using statistics of contracts awarded for new-factory construction, assembled annually by the private statistical agency F. W. Dodge. Kuznets produced an estimate for total private-sector (nonresidential) construction first by estimating the total value of construction materials produced, then allocating a certain fraction of that to private, nonresidential construction based on past patterns of construction spending, then applying a multiplier, derived from the 1929 Census of Construction, representing the ratio of the value of finished construction to the value of construction material. It should also be noted that Terborgh's capital-expenditure series was not adjusted for inflation.

itself. Although Kuznets believed that statistical limitations and conceptual difficulties, particularly those related to the valuation of the various "instruments of wealth," made any allegedly comprehensive measure of the nation's capital stock dubious, other NBER researchers were not so pessimistic. Solomon Fabricant (1938) used direct measures of the "book value of capital" as reported to the Department of Treasury on corporate-tax returns to create annual series on the value of capital held by corporations in various sectors and subsectors, from 1926 to 1935. He deflated the series with a laboriously constructed capital-price index designed to account for the fact that the capital stock in any given year was made up of elements purchased at many different points in the past. And a few years later, Kuznets combined his capital-formation estimates with periodic Censuses of Wealth conducted between 1880 and 1922 to produce decadal, economy-wide measures of "reproducible wealth," defined as producer equipment plus new construction and improvements to real estate (Kuznets, Epstein, and Jenks 1946). He remained skeptical of estimates of other categories of wealth, and of the feasibility of creating accurate measures of the change in the capital stock over periods shorter than a decade.

By 1946, however, annual series of the real value of the aggregate capital stock and its major components (private plant and equipment, housing, inventories) covering the 1921–41 period had already been constructed by Lawrence Klein, for use in estimating the structural macroeconometric models he was developing at the Cowles Commission. He anchored these series with stock estimates for a single year (1934), filling in values for other years by adding or subtracting annual capital-formation estimates.[10]

Raymond Goldsmith was also undaunted by the hurdles that Kuznets saw in the way of developing annual capital-stock estimates and wealth estimates more generally. In Goldsmith (1951) he explained a procedure for creating what he called a "Perpetual Inventory of National Wealth," an annual measure of the value of national wealth (including, and especially, "tangible reproducible wealth," a term of art for capital among national income scholars) that could be expressed in current and constant dollars. The key to Goldsmith's strategy was to develop depreciation rules for each of a number of broad categories of capital expenditure, based on business behavior and accounting practice. This allowed the flow estimates of capital formation created by Kuznets and his collaborators to be built into

[10] See Klein (1947). The Klein series was circulating by 1946, as evidenced by its use in Tintner (1946).

stock estimates without relying on past Censuses of Wealth, which were considered to rest on a shakier statistical foundation than the Kuznets figures. Annual estimates of tangible reproducible wealth produced by this method were presented in Goldsmith (1952).

Of course, there was still disagreement among the most able economic theorists of the time over whether "aggregate capital" was a meaningful and coherent theoretical concept potentially susceptible to measurement, or whether it was, as Sumner Slichter (1928) had quipped with respect to Douglas's original capital estimates, "the stuff that dreams are made of." But for those economists committed to measuring and empirically analyzing key macroeconomic quantities, Goldsmith's work provided an annual, constant-dollar capital-stock series dating back to 1896, one that bore the imprimatur of the respected NBER Conference on Research in Income and Wealth.[11]

THE GROWING FASCINATION WITH ECONOMIC GROWTH AND THE DISCOVERY OF THE RESIDUAL, 1945–1960

Interest in economic growth – what caused it, and how it might be increased both in developed nations and in the newly independent nations of what would come to be known as the third world – increased dramatically among both research economists and economic policy makers in the two decades following World War II.[12] Simon Kuznets was in the vanguard of this movement within the economics profession. In his doctoral dissertation, published in 1930 as *Secular Movements in Production and Prices*, he had taken his first cut at analyzing the process of economic growth, examining long series of output and price data from a number of nations, identifying empirical regularities and offering tentative hypotheses about the causes of and relationships between these regularities. He was soon after put in charge of the NBER's national income accounting

[11] Raymond Goldsmith's estimates of the value of new-factory construction prior to 1920 were based on Kuznets's estimates, and Kuznets was relying on assumptions and conclusions used by Douglas in constructing his capital series. So, measures of aggregate capital used by empirical economists in the 1950s and beyond still bore marks of Douglas's statistical labors of 1927 (see, e.g., notes to table IV-2 in Kuznets, Epstein, and Jenks [1946]).

[12] A variety of economic, political, and social forces combined to push growth towards the top of the economic research and policy agendas, including the reality of postwar economic growth and the felt need to compete – both in actuality and in the propaganda war – with the Soviet Union. Yarrow (2010, chapters 1 and 2) gives a good account.

program, and the analysis of economic growth took a back seat to discovering what could be learned about business cycles from the new and more reliable national income estimates he was producing. This was in keeping with the central concern of both the NBER and the economic policy community at the time, as was his application of national income data to questions of wartime planning and production during the early 1940s. With the war's end, however, he turned his attention back to growth. In 1946 he published national income estimates for the United States going back to 1869, and in a companion summary volume, devoted a chapter to describing the long-run behavior of the rate of growth in the national income (Kuznets 1946; Kuznets, Epstein and Jenks 1946). In 1947, he contributed a paper on "Measuring Economic Growth" to a symposium on economic growth sponsored by the *Journal of Economic History*, making the case that the best empirical counterpart to the theoretical concept of economic growth was sustained increase in the measured national income (Kuznets 1947).

In 1948, in his capacity as chairman of the Universities-National Bureau Committee on Economic Research, Kuznets organized a conference devoted to "The Problems of Economic Growth."[13] The committee had decided in the previous year to sponsor a series of stand-alone conferences on single topics, each designed to summarize existing knowledge and identify important research questions related to that topic. By Kuznets's account, "In a review of the various topics or areas for survey and exploration via such special conferences, the field of economic growth, particularly of large aggregates such as nations or regions, elicited the keenest interest among members of the Committee and the university groups canvassed" (Kuznets 1949a). Kuznets may have had his finger on the scale when making this assessment, but it also may be an accurate reflection of the profession's growing interest in growth research, mentioned earlier. Kuznets's two papers for the conference focused on the statistical approach to growth research, and repeated the central points of his essay for the *Journal of Economic History's* symposium: economic growth was best understood as sustained increase in economic magnitude of "large, diversified aggregates such as national state units," and the best available

[13] The Universities-National Bureau Committee had been established by the NBER in 1935 to encourage interaction and coordination of research efforts between the in-house NBER researchers and economists based in leading universities. The continuing Conference on Research in Income and Wealth, discussed in the text, was an early initiative of the committee (Mitchell 1936, 16–17).

operational measure of this concept was the growth rate in the national income. Kuznets emphatically argued that future growth research must be rooted in a solid statistical base and have a strong quantitative component, if it were to produce something more than the "the vague and commonplace statements" of "Philosophies of History" (Kuznets 1949a, 12). Measurement of growth came first, followed by analysis of the causes of growth, concentrating on factors that could be measured, so as to strengthen the quantitative aspects of the inquiry. Kuznets offered a brief hint at the statistical form that he believed such research into the causes of growth should take: "Since economic growth is a continuous process, some index or total that permits the calculation of rates for comparison over time and space is essential. It should serve as the dependent variable, for which measurable factors would be sought as independent variables" (Kuznets 1949b, 127). Throughout the 1950s and 1960s, Kuznets would build his own growth research program on the principles outlined in these essays.

During the 1950s, changes in both the nature of research being done at the NBER and the organization's public statements of its research priorities in its annual reports also reflected the growing fascination with economic growth. NBER researchers had been involved in empirical labor productivity research since the early 1930s, and by 1938 the bureau had established a formal program devoted to the study of historical trends in output, employment, and productivity. In the program's early years, however, analysis took a back seat to building the bureau's collection of data on output and employment. When the program's researchers did offer tentative analyses or summaries of the productivity indexes they had constructed, the subject was as likely to be the impact of productivity increases on employment or income distribution as the role of technological change in increasing productivity, or the relationship of productivity to economic growth. This was, in part, a result of the industry- or sector-specific nature of the NBER productivity indexes. Fabricant (1942), for example, could draw solid generalizations from his data about the standard course of productivity over the industry life cycle or the relationship between productivity increase and employment growth at the industry level, but could make little more than descriptive statements about co-movements of labor productivity and the national income.

Also standing in the way of attempts at detailed analysis was the researchers' awareness of the crudeness of the labor productivity measure as an indicator of economic or technological development. It became standard for authors to warn readers against making unwarranted inferential leaps from the labor productivity numbers, as in this passage from Fabricant (1942, 7–8):

> Because the reduction in labor per unit of product reflects many diverse changes, it cannot be taken as a measure of the change in the efficiency, amount, or character of any one productive factor. Those who consider the figures cited to be indexes of labor efficiency or of invested capital and improvement in capital equipment are ascribing, in fact, to one or another factor in a complex situation the net result of changes in all factors.

By the early fifties, however, labor productivity's link to economic growth was eclipsing its link to employment as the central concern of the NBER productivity studies. Frederick Mills's (1952) report on his productivity research was entitled "Productivity and Economic Progress." It opened by pointing out that over the previous 50 years, national income had increased by a factor of five, while population had only increased by 80 percent. There followed a statistical decomposition of the gross national product (GNP) growth into that due to labor-force growth and that due to labor productivity growth. The bureau's 1954 annual report, penned by Fabricant, highlighted the theme of "Economic Progress and Economic Change." Fabricant claimed that the bureau had always been interested in research related to the nation's long-run economic progress, but that recent developments in the research program prompted him to "highlight what our work suggests of the rate and nature of this country's economic progress." "This emphasis on the long term growth," he explained, "is especially desirable when the public's attention is being absorbed by the problem of stability." Arguably, Fabricant had it backwards – previous annual reports portray a research organization still very concerned with business cycles at a time when the topic of economic growth was practically becoming an obsession among economic policy makers and other elites.[14]

Fabricant's account of the bureau's past and prospective contributions to understanding the causes of economic growth included a sketch of the research plans of John Kendrick, who took over the productivity research program in 1953 due to Mills's retirement. Kendrick had begun to use the

[14] See Yarrow (2010, chapters 3–4) for documentation of this growing obsession. Rutherford (2005, 121–22) describes the commitment of Arthur Burns, Fabricant's predecessor, to making business cycles the central focus of the NBER research program, and the tensions this caused within the organization. For example, differences between Burns and Kuznets over the bureau's research priorities led Kuznets to significantly reduce his involvement with the NBER in the late 1940s, and seek funding for his growth research from the Social Science Research Council.

capital-stock measures being developed at the bureau to combine measures of output per unit of capital with the existing measures of output per worker, leading to measures of productivity growth that could correct some of the misleading conclusions about the sources of economic growth that might be drawn from examining labor productivity indexes in isolation (Fabricant 1954, 10–11). In his first progress report on this research, Kendrick would speak of the "paramount importance" of productivity growth in raising living standards, strengthening national security, and providing for future economic growth (Kendrick 1956, 1).

The NBER's most emphatic proclamation of its commitment to growth research came in the 1959 annual report, entitled simply "The Study of Economic Growth." Fabricant did not waste any time getting to the point. Within a page readers understood that little was actually known about the causes of economic growth or how to promote it; that having such knowledge was very important while seeking it was uncertain, even risky; and that almost everything that NBER researchers were doing would contribute in some way to building that knowledge. If readers were not completely sure of why it was important for the nation to learn how to increase its growth rate, there was a long discussion of an NBER study on economic growth in Russia, which was "an important, if not the overriding, fact of our time." Fabricant explained how NBER research – Kuznets's work on national income and Kendrick's refinement of and additions to productivity data – had led to the by-then familiar finding that "a large part of the explanation of the rise in production remains to be determined." Fabricant went on in this vein, explaining how past and prospective NBER research projects were "gradually filling in the knowledge we need of the intricate process of economic growth" (Fabricant 1959, 13).

At the time that this report was written, the NBER was in something of a crisis. It had lost the support of the Rockefeller Foundation in the previous year, and was awaiting a decision from the Ford Foundation on a request for the large amounts of funding necessary to resolve an unsustainable budgetary situation. In the course of interacting with these two foundations, the NBER leadership received repeated signals that the bureau was losing its once solid reputation as "the foremost economic research institute in the world" among the leaders of the economics profession as well as the business and academic elites who ran and advised the major foundations.[15] That Fabricant would, at this crucial time, prepare an annual

[15] See Rutherford (2005, 126–30) for a detailed account of this period in the NBER's history.

report arguing that nearly every NBER project contributed in some way to an understanding of economic growth stands as another piece of evidence of the great importance that had come to be attributed to the subject by members of the two overlapping audiences that he needed to persuade: leading members of the economic profession and influential figures in the foundations. This steadily increasing concern with economic growth in the postwar period among both economists and their clients provided the context for the technical line of research that led to what Griliches (1996) called "the discovery of the residual," and to the adoption of strategies for using the Cobb–Douglas regression to explore the causes of growth.

Discovering and Measuring the "Residual": From Copeland–Martin to Solow

With the creation and refinement of capital-stock measures at the industry-, sector-, and economy-wide level during the 1940s and 1950s, it became possible to implement the Copeland–Martin procedure to construct what were coming to be called, by the mid 1950s, indexes of "total factor productivity."[16] It is not too surprising that the first application of the Copeland–Martin approach to data for the US economy as a whole appeared in the 1951 dissertation of one of Simon Kuznets's graduate students, Jacob Schmookler. The dissertation was, for the most part, devoted to an innovative experiment with using patent statistics to measure trends in "inventiveness" (Schmookler 1951).[17] One chapter, however, developed and reported a measure of "The Changing Efficiency of the American Economy, 1869–1938," and was published as an article in the

[16] A total-factor productivity (TFP) index is the now standard term for an index number reflecting the change over time in the ratio of a measure or index number of real output to a weighted average of measures or index numbers of the quantity or real cost of inputs (always capital and labor, sometimes other inputs as well). The phrase was coined to highlight the difference between such an index and the typical "single factor productivity" index, which involved the ratio between an output measure and a measure of a single input (almost always labor). John Kendrick (1956, 2), puts quotation marks around the term but does not define it, suggesting that it had become familiar by then, at least to NBER researchers; the only earlier appearance of the term in a JSTOR journal is in a 1951 letter to the editor of the journal *American Statistician*, in a manner that indicates that it was familiar at least to productivity specialists (Siegel 1951).

[17] Kuznets had suggested the analysis of patent statistics to Schmookler, and it follows from his comment at the 1949 conference on growth that exploratory research into the causes of economic growth should include studies of "the application of empirical science to technology" (Schmookler 1951, ii; Kuznets 1949a, 16).

following year (Schmookler 1952). The article carefully detailed the construction of an index of real output over combined real inputs, with an explicit reference to Copeland and Martin's suggestion of 1938.[18] And although Schmookler's title followed the linguistic usage of Copeland by referring to "efficiency," the article's first line made a more specific claim about what was being measured: "The index of output per unit of input discussed in this article is intended to describe the pattern and magnitude of technical change for the United States as a whole."

The numerator for Schmookler's series was Kuznet's measure of real GNP observed at the midpoints of overlapping decades (e.g., 1869–78, 1874–83). To construct the denominator, he divided the labor input into agricultural and nonagricultural, and each type of labor was weighted by an estimate of its 1929 wage. After an unsatisfactory attempt to construct separate series for agricultural and nonagricultural land, Schmookler settled on a single index of total acreage, weighted by a 1929 price per acre derived by dividing total land value in 1929 by total acres in 1929. His measures of the value of reproducible wealth were refined versions of the decadal estimates created by Kuznets. Then, to convert the sum of these stock measures of real land value and real capital value into measures of service flow, he multiplied them by a 5.2 percent "rate of return to property" for 1929, obtained by dividing an elaborately derived estimate of total property income in 1929 by the combined value of land and capital in 1929.

Upon examining his completed index, Schmookler observed that it grew more slowly than existing labor productivity indexes, and that about half of the increase in GNP over the period represented the effect of increased resources, the other half reflecting "the effect of increased efficiency in their use." Pressing his interpretation of his index as a measure of technical change, he argued that a good criterion for judging the plausibility of the index was that "the expansion of output per unit of input . . . be greatest for those periods when general knowledge leads us to anticipate that the existence of periods of unusually rapid technological change" (Schmookler 1952, 225–26). As one would expect from a student of Simon Kuznets, Schmookler left his readers with very few questions about how he had arrived at his estimates and what their weaknesses were, but he

[18] Griliches (1996) identifies two earlier published applications of the Copeland–Martin approach: Stigler (1947) and Glen and Cooper (1948). Neither paper cited Copeland and Martin, but both were clearly using the Copeland–Martin approach, with separate price deflators for nominal input and output measures.

also expressed the opinion that the broad trends indicated by his index were "too sharp to be erased by any reasonable refinements and corrections" (Schmookler 1952, 227).

Although it was not as detailed as Schmookler's, the total factor productivity index calculated by Moses Abramovitz in his 1956 paper on "Resource and Output Trends in the United States since 1870" pointed to a similar conclusion, and seems to have been more widely noticed. Abramovitz posed a question that harkened back to Douglas's basic decomposition of 1927: "How large has been the net increase of aggregate output per capita, and to what extent has this increase been obtained as a result of greater labor or capital input on the one hand and a rise of productivity on the other?" His answer was clear: "Almost the entire increase in net product per capita is associated with a rise in productivity."[19] While an index of capital plus labor utilized per capita had increased by 14 percent since 1870, the productivity of a "representative unit of all resources" had increased by 250 percent. Abramovitz also found this answer sobering, if not discouraging. Using a phrase that would frequently be quoted in the coming years, he commented, "Since we know little about the causes of productivity increase, the indicated importance of this element may be taken to be some sort of measure of our ignorance about the causes of economic growth in the United States" (Abramovitz 1956, 11).

In addition to being a "measure of our ignorance," Abramovitz believed his finding gave an "indication of where we need to concentrate our attention." His own starting point was to note two issues raised by his approach to calculating the separate contributions to output growth of the increased quantity of inputs and increased productivity. First, the growth of the quantity of capital and labor employed in production might itself have increased productivity. After all, he noted, there had been a tripling of total man-hours and a ninefold increase in capital over the period. If there was anything to the idea of increasing returns to scale, this increase in the scale of production would be associated with increased productivity. Second, the conventional approach to measuring the quantities of labor and capital probably understated the growth of these inputs. With regard to labor, Abramovitz argued that, because of the reduced share of the labor

[19] Abramovitz (1956, 5, 11). Because Abramovitz was attempting to explain growth in net national product (NNP) per capita rather than total GNP, his conclusion that "almost the entire" growth in NNP per capita was due to rising productivity is comparable to Schmookler's conclusion that about half of the growth in GNP was due to rising productivity.

force represented by teenagers and old men, the quality and intensity of each hour of labor had been increasing, even abstracting from such matters as rising average levels of worker skill. Also, the growth of capital was likely understated. Any current spending that helped increase output in future periods should be included as part of capital formation, including spending on health, education, training, and research. But even consumption spending not intended to increase future productivity, such as that for more and better food and clothing or leisure pursuits, might incidentally tend to increase future income. And these categories of spending would be expected to have increased along with the increasing surplus of output above minimal consumption requirements.

Robert Solow and the Emergence of the Aggregate Production Function as a Tool for Analyzing Growth

By far the most influential application of the Copeland–Martin approach to measuring technical change was that found in Robert Solow's (1957) article on "Technical Change and the Aggregate Production Function." Indeed, it would be difficult to exaggerate the impact of this article, along with Solow's 1956 article "A Contribution to the Theory of Economic Growth," on both the theoretical and empirical study of economic growth for the remainder of the twentieth century.[20] The main point to be made here, however, is the importance of these articles in helping to establish a new role for the Cobb–Douglas regression, and the production function regression more generally: that of a research tool for measuring and explaining economic growth.

The 1956 paper had no empirical component, but served as an impressive demonstration of what could be accomplished by building a theoretical model of growth around a neoclassical aggregate production function. Solow wrote the aggregate production function as $Y=F(K, L)$, where Y was aggregate output, K was capital, and L was labor; it was assumed that the production function exhibited constant returns to scale, and that capital and labor combined to produce output under "standard neoclassical conditions," by which Solow meant that there was substitutability between capital and labor. In the basic version of Solow's model, the labor force and the capital stock grew at fixed, exogenously determined rates, and the paths

[20] The essays in part 2 of Boianovsky and Hoover (2009) serve to place Solow's two articles in context of twentieth-century growth theory and discuss their subsequent influence on growth economics.

of the wage rate and the return to capital were determined in accordance with the marginal productivity theory. In particular, the wage was assumed to adjust to ensure full employment. Extensions of the model allowed growth rates of labor and capital to depend on the wage rate and the rate of interest, respectively, and introduced "neutral technological change" represented mathematically by a factor A(t) that multiplied the production function F(K, L) and could grow over time. Although Solow did not say so, this mathematical representation of technological change matched Hicks's (1932) definition of neutral technological change as change that did not affect the marginal rate of substitution between capital and labor.[21] With each version of his model, Solow solved for the time paths of key variables (output, wages, capital, etc.), often assuming that the model's neoclassical production function took the Cobb–Douglas form in order to derive equations and diagrams that illustrated some of the possibilities inherent in the model.

So, Solow's 1956 paper made a strong case for the aggregate neoclassical production function, and its Cobb–Douglas version in particular, as a tool for theorizing about economic growth. Similarly, Solow's "Technical Change and the Aggregate Production Function" would demonstrate the usefulness of the aggregate production function as a tool for thinking about the empirical analysis of economic growth. Solow identified as the "new wrinkle" offered by his 1957 paper the explication of "an elementary way of segregating variations in output per head due to technical change from those due to changes in capital per head," that is, of performing Douglas's basic decomposition (Solow 1957, 312). The paper also contained a second "new wrinkle," however, as Solow used this decomposition as a first step towards estimating a production function, that is, doing what Schultz and Douglas had referred to in the 1930s as "eliminating the time element" from the time series data before estimating the marginal productivities of labor and capital.

A first significant feature of the paper is Solow's defense of his use of the aggregate production function both as a theoretical concept and a construct for conducting empirical research, a defense offered in his frank and nonchalant style:

[21] It seems plausible that Solow's decision to add a multiplicative, time-varying factor to the production function to represent technical change was a borrowing from Hicks, and this is also suggested by his use of Hicks's term "neutral." However, Boumans (2009) makes a case that Solow's decision to represent technical change with a multiplicative factor had its origins in his work with Samuelson on balanced growth.

In this day of rationally designed econometric studies and super-input-output tables, it takes something more than the usual "willing suspension of disbelief" to talk seriously of the aggregate production function. But the aggregate production function is only a little less legitimate a concept than, say, the aggregate consumption function, and for some kinds of long run macro-models it is almost as indispensable as the latter is for the short-run. As long as we insist on practicing macro-economics we shall need aggregate relationships.

Before going on, let me be explicit that I would not try to justify what follows by calling on fancy theorems on aggregation and index numbers. Either this kind of aggregate economics appeals or it doesn't. Personally, I belong to both schools. If it does, I think one can draw some crude but useful conclusions from the results (Solow 1957, 312).

The sentiment that both the theoretical and empirical analysis of aggregate relationships is worthwhile, if not indispensable, even in the absence of justification in the form of "fancy theorems on aggregation," was not new to economics, as should be clear from previous chapters. It was embodied in Douglas's frequent assertion that an aggregate production function was something different from, but at least as worthy of study as, the production functions of individual firms. It is what led David Durand (1937, 754–55), after his detailed demonstration that the production function estimated by Douglas had absolutely no relationship to the production functions of Walrasian theory, to defend Douglas's research program as a means of understanding aggregate input-output relations in a growing economy. But the sentiment was not universally shared among the cutting edge neoclassical econometricians of the 1930s and 1940s. There is no trace of it in Marschak and Andrews' (1944) critique of Douglas's work, and all of their suggestions for improving empirical research on production functions were aimed at creating more plausible estimates of firm-level production functions. One can also point to Douglas's coauthor Martin Bronfenbrenner's two attempts to build a theoretical bridge between the estimated coefficients of a cross-section industry-level production function and the theoretical parameters of the production functions of neoclassical firms, along with the implication that building such a bridge was necessary to establishing the usefulness of the estimates (Bronfenbrenner and Douglas, 1939, 780; Bronfenbrenner 1944).

So I believe it is significant that Robert Solow, already a respected economist with strong bona fides as a master of neoclassical microeconomics in its mathematically expressed, Walrasian mode, one whose deep familiarity with the methodological intricacies and substantive contributions of the Cowlesian econometric research program could not be questioned, was arguing strongly for the aggregate production function as a legitimate concept for theoretical and empirical research. It is not just that Solow's opinion on the matter was influential in and of itself, although it would be wrong to downplay that possibility, but that it shows the opinion could be comfortably held by an economist in the vanguard of macroeconometric research in the 1950s.

In the 1957 paper Solow worked with many of the assumptions used in the 1956 paper. The paper's first equation was an aggregate production function, now written Q = F(K, L; t), with Q representing output and K and L standing for capital and labor, all measured in physical units. The letter t stood for time, and was meant to represent the impact of technical change, although, Solow cautioned, this was a broad definition of technological change as "*any kind of shift*" in the production function (emphasis in the original), including "slowdowns, speedups, improvements in the education of the labor force, and all sorts of things." Again Solow introduced the assumption of "*neutral* technological change" (emphasis in the original), now explicitly identified as technological change that left marginal rates of substitution between inputs unaltered, which allowed the aggregate production function to be written as Q = A(t)f(K, L) where A(t) measured the cumulative shifts in the production function over time. Solow had already informed readers that his decomposition method would rely on the assumption that "factors are paid their marginal products," which, Solow noted, was "an assumption often made"; this assumption along with some calculus and algebra allowed Solow to conclude that the percentage change in output would be equal to the percentage growth in the technological change factor A(t), plus the percentage growth in capital times capital's share in output (w_k), plus the percentage growth in the labor input times labor's share in output (w_L). Then,

> (a)n amusing thing happens here. Nothing has been said about returns to scale. But if all factor inputs are classified either as K or L, then the available figures always show w_K and w_L adding up to one. Since we have assumed that factors are paid their marginal products, this amounts to assuming the hypotheses of Euler's theorem. The calculus being what it is, we might as well assume the conclusion, namely, that F is homogenous of degree one
>
> (Solow 1957, 312).

This assumption led to the decomposition $\%\Delta q = \%\Delta A + w_K{}^*(\%\Delta k)$, where %Δ signifies percentage change, k is K/L and q is Q/L, which had the empirical implication that the change in A(t) between two periods could be calculated from information on capital's share in output, the change in the capital/labor ratio, and the change in the output/labor ratio.

Solow presented, in tabular form, "rough and ready" figures that would allow him to construct empirical analogues for q, k, and w_K covering the years 1909 through 1949. His capital series was "one that will really drive a purist mad." "Naturally," he used Goldsmith's capital estimates that included "land, mineral stocks, etc." These were stock measures rather than flow measures, the use of which created "(a)ll sorts of conceptual problems" but was necessary, as the idea of constructing a time series of the flow of capital services was "utopian." To account for the fact that "what belongs in a production function is capital in use, not capital in place," each year's capital stock estimate was multiplied by the percentage of the labor force employed that year (with estimates from 1909 to 1926 taken from Douglas's *Real Wages in the United States*). This procedure embodied the assumption that the unemployment of the capital stock in a year matched the unemployment of labor, which was "undoubtedly wrong" but "closer to the truth than making no correction at all." NBER researcher John Kendrick had calculated the necessary estimates of man-hours employed per year and GNP per man-hour. The measure of capital's share was "another hodgepodge, pieced together from various sources and ad hoc assumptions." From these ingredients Solow calculated annual values for the change in A(t), and, in a final column of the table, these annual changes were used to build up an index of technological change. The index rose from an assigned value of 1.00 in 1909 to a value of 1.809 in 1949. Readers were provided with graphs of both this index and the annual changes in A(t).

Solow confessed to having little idea of how to judge whether the technical-change series looked "reasonable." He was reassured by the strong upward trend of the series; dips after the two world wars could probably be easily rationalized, and an "unpleasant sawtooth character" in the early years was probably a statistical artifact. The production function seemed to have been shifting upward at a faster annual rate during the second half of the period. Over a comparable time period, Solow's estimate of the growth in output due to technical change was about equal to Schmookler's (1952), although the latter had included the agricultural sector in his analysis while Solow had not. Valavanis-Vail (1955), whose method, Solow noted, was "different and rather less general" than his own, had estimated a much slower rate of technical change.

Solow's estimates implied that 7/8ths of the increase in output per man-hour over the period was due to technical change, and 1/8th to increased intensity of capital per worker. This should not be taken to mean, Solow warned, that "the observed rate of technical progress would have persisted even if the rate of investment had been much smaller," as "most innovation must be embodied in new plant and equipment to be realized at all." In a footnote, he also mentioned discussions with T. W. Schultz, then in the early stages of formulating his ideas about human capital, that had led Solow to realize that the rising quality of the labor force represented an important type of capital formation. This would appear in Solow's estimates as a shift of the production function, but Solow proposed that this problem could be addressed by treating labor of different skill levels as separate types of input.

Solow compared his estimate that 7/8th of economic growth per capita since 1909 had been due to technical progress to Solomon Fabricant's (1954) conclusion that 90 percent of the growth since 1871 had been due to technical change. Solow noted that what he called the "output per unit of input" calculations employed by Fabricant, while seeming to be "assumption free," actually implicitly assumed, as did he, that technological change was neutral, that the production function was constant returns to scale and (as expenditure shares were used as weights) that factor markets were competitive. In addition, it implicitly assumed a linear production function.[22]

Solow reminded readers that the "unavoidable" assumption of constant returns to scale and the assumption of neutral technical change allowed the aggregate production function to be written as $q=A(t)f(k, 1)$, but also that a simple plot of q on k would give a distorted picture of the $f(k, 1)$ function because of the shift factor $A(t)$. Since, however, "we have provided ourselves with an estimate of the successive values of the shift factor … it follows … that by plotting $q(t)/A(t)$ against $k(t)$ … we can proceed to discuss the shape of $f(k,1)$ and reconstruct the aggregate production function" (Solow 1957, 317).

This plot showed "a remarkably tight fit," considering "all the a priori doctoring which the raw figures have undergone."[23] Solow fit the points with five different functions, all of which could be estimated using simple regression, including $q = \alpha + \beta k$, implied by a linear production function,

[22] This assumption is embodied in the use of fixed weights in constructing the index of inputs.

[23] Before estimating the production function, Solow actually omitted some "maverick observations" that lay well off the line. These observations were soon shown to be the result of a computational error. Correcting the error led to a slight increase in the share of growth attributable to technical change (Hogan 1958).

and $\log(q) = \alpha + \beta\log(k)$, implied by the Cobb–Douglas.[24] All the regressions produced r-squares above .99, although "for what it was worth," the Cobb–Douglas and the semi-logarithmic $q = \alpha + \beta\log(k)$ had the best fits.

Griliches (1996, 1,328) is correct in pointing out that in one sense, Solow's construction of an empirical measure of the contribution of technological change to economic growth was not very original: "not the question, nor the data, nor the conclusion was new." The method itself was simply the Copeland–Martin technique, with inputs averaged geometrically using weights that changed each period. Griliches goes on to argue, however, that this representation ignores Solow's important contribution of explicitly linking the Copeland–Martin approach to economic theory, which "clarified the meaning of what were heretofore relatively arcane index number calculations." I would state the case somewhat differently. Griliches's use of the word "clarify" suggests that Schmookler, Abramovitz, Kendrick, and other productivity researchers were thinking about their calculations, at least on some level, as being rooted in a J. B. Clark–style marginal productivity theory featuring an aggregate production function. This is not my impression. Instead I would say that what Solow did was to make a convincing case for adopting a particular conceptual framework for thinking about what Schmookler, Kendrick, and others were doing with respect to the measurement of productivity/technical change, one rooted in an aggregate version of the marginal productivity theory of production and distribution. The several-decade effort to perform an empirical division of measured economic growth into that which was due to growth in input quantities and that which was due to technical progress was, in Solow's hands, an effort to empirically separate shifts of the production function from movements along a production function – a production function that was neoclassical in nature.[25] This framework would serve to structure

[24] Thus, Solow was estimating a "restricted" version of the Cobb–Douglas. The resulting capital coefficient was .353. Later, in response to a criticism of his assumption of constant returns to scale (Hogan 1958), Solow estimated the "unrestricted" version of the Cobb–Douglas with his data. The capital coefficient was .338, the labor coefficient .618, and the standard error of the sum was .048. So, increasing returns to scale was not ruled out, but "not especially indicated" by his results (Solow 1958b).

[25] Interestingly, this transition seems to take place within the paper itself, as in the introduction, Solow announces that he will describe "an elementary way of segregating variations in output per head due to technical change from those due to changes in capital per head," while in the conclusion he states that he has "suggested a simple way of segregating shifts of the aggregate production function from movements along it" (Solow 1957, 312, 320).

economists' subsequent efforts to explore empirically several decades' worth of accumulated ideas about the sources of economic growth.

Solow was not the first economist to talk about the basic decomposition in terms of movements along and shifts in a production function (e.g., Smith 1945a, 266). But in the key contributions to the efforts to measure technical progress produced in the early 1950s – Schmookler (1952), Kendrick (1956), Fabricant (1954), and Abramovitz (1956), one does not find talk of measuring shifts in vs. movements along the production function, and only Abramovitz even comes close to invoking the marginal productivity theory as a justification for the weights used in constructing the index of total input.

One indication of the increasing importance of the production function concept in economists' discussion of productivity and growth can be found by looking at the changing role of the concept in the work of John Kendrick, the pioneer of total factor productivity measurement and leader of the NBER's productivity measurement program in the 1950s and 1960s. In a preliminary report of results from his program of constructing total factor productivity indexes for individual industries and for the economy as a whole, he described these indexes as measuring "net savings in real cost per unit of input"; "what inputs of a given period would have produced had their productive efficiency per unit remained the same as in the base period," and "chiefly the effect of technical innovation and changes in scale of output" (Kendrick 1956, 2, 5, 7). The phrase "production function" never appeared. However, in his 1961 book *Productivity Trends in the United States*, readers were told in the introduction that "underlying the estimation of input-output relations stands the concept of the production function, i.e., the notion that the physical volume of output depends on quantities of productive services, or inputs, employed in the production process and the efficiency with which they were utilized." He further explained that the same volume of output could be created with many different combinations of inputs, but "the actual combination used will tend to be the least cost combination, given relative prices." The observed combination of inputs could change due to changes in these prices, changes in technology, or changes in the scale of production if returns to scale were not constant. This made "single factor" productivity measures like labor productivity misleading as measures of changing productive efficiency. It was necessary to "relate output to *all* associated inputs." "Increasingly in recent years," investigators were attempting to measure productivity change in terms of a complete production function. But while "regression equations may be fitted to output and input data to reveal coefficients of technical progress," Kendrick had chosen to work with "productivity ratios," as they provided "greater flexibility for the analysis of movements and of relationships with other variables" (Kendrick 1961b, 6–8).

Kendrick's decision to introduce the production function as a fundamental concept underlying his approach to productivity measurement might have been influenced by the fall 1958 meeting of the Conference on Research in Income and Wealth, which was devoted to "Output, Input and Productivity Measurement". In his introduction to the volume of conference proceedings, Kendrick (1961a) explained that the goal of the conference was to "bring theoretician and statistician together in this important field to try to sharpen our concepts of output, input, and productivity, and to suggest needed improvements in methods of estimation and basic data." Solow was there as a commentator, and a number of the contributors to the conference had no problem following him in using marginal productivity theory and the concept of the production function as organizing principles for empirical work on technical change and economic growth. George Stigler's critique of labor productivity indexes and total factor productivity indexes as attempts to measure "economic progress" ran entirely in terms of the marginal productivity theory. Kenneth Boulding's contribution was mainly concerned with the ways that non-neutral technological changes complicated the interpretation of total factor productivity measures, but all of the discussions ran in terms of movements along and shifts in production functions.

However, there were some holdouts. Irving Siegel (1961) of the Council of Economic Advisors presented a paper "On the Design of Consistent Output and Input Indexes for Productivity Measurement." He advocated developing arithmetical tests for input and output index numbers, similar to the tests developed by Irving Fisher for price-index numbers. Those tests, Siegel argued, had been rooted in common sense and the rules of arithmetic, and the subsequent development of ideas about the proper construction of price indexes based on consumer theory and welfare economics had turned out to be of no use to practitioners who actually had to construct index numbers. Similarly, Siegel believed that the proper construction of input and output indexes was "closer to accounting than economics." He was dismissive of the idea that a static production function was of any use in designing productivity indexes, and also of "empirical dynamic production functions, from which time series are derivable for marginal as well as average productivity," and even "attempts to isolate the roles of labor, capital, and so-called 'technological change' . . . in explaining the difference between two values of a dynamic production function" (Siegel 1961, 23–24, 32, 36, fn. 17).

Siegel's paper was discussed by Carl Christ, a Cowles Commission–style econometrician, who saw much good sense in Siegel's guidelines on constructing index numbers, but objected to his argument that "the so-called economic theory of index numbers, dealing with indifference curves and production functions, is of no help at all in designing productivity indexes," going on to say,

> Of course he is right if he means that there are terrible problems involved in trying to aggregate indifference curves and production possibility curves, and that without quite severe simplifying assumptions we cannot easily interpret the results of such aggregation. Nevertheless, I feel that shifts of production functions are what productivity indexes are really about, and that in trying to measure productivity we will be ahead if we remember that production functions are in the theoretical background of what we are doing"
>
> (Christ, in Siegel 1961, 42).

Morris Copeland did not attend the conference, but was so troubled on reading the papers from the conference that he felt a need to add a comment to the conference proceedings volume. He began by noting that in the beginning, the Conference on Research in Income and Wealth had been intended as a forum that brought together producers and users of national income statistics to discuss issues of common interest. In the twenty-odd years since its founding, however, the scope of topics considered at the conferences had expanded to include "about everything that comes under the head of empirical aggregative inquiries." For the most part, this was to the good: the statistical measures underlying empirical aggregative economic analysis were the social accounting magnitudes with which the conference had always been concerned. But not all aggregative analysis was statistical. Some of it involved what Copeland called "*a priori* model analysis(,) because of the tenuous connection between the neoclassical models it investigates and the real world," and increasingly, he observed, contributions of conference participants consisted of such a priori model analysis. This was particularly in evidence at the 1958 conference, and worse, such analysis had been not been labeled for what it was, but instead, the "line between *a priori* analysis and empirical research had been distinctly blurred." Rather than going paper by paper to point out such transgressions, Copeland chose to focus on Stigler's paper, as Stigler was a careful neoclassical thinker who had a history of attempting to make a connection between his models and the real world, but was also was also annoyingly arrogant (Copeland in Stigler 1961, 69–70). Copeland proceeded with a detailed critique of Stigler's attempts to use theory to draw conclusions about biases in productivity indexes, and his attempts to measure some of those biases.

Reading Copeland's comments, it is apparent that he did not object to the use of the production function as a conceptual framework for thinking about growth and technical change or a tool for measuring them. He identified technical progress as a shift of the production function, to be distinguished from movements along it, and he spoke of the procedure of regressing output on capital, labor, and a trend as a "technique of sorts" to perform the basic decomposition of growth. The part of Stigler's (and Solow's) analytical framework to which Copeland did object is apparent in the last two lines of his comment: "The idea of a functional relation between output and inputs that represents the long run adjustment for various price situations and for a given state of the arts does not readily lend itself to statistical exploration. If Stigler has a way of exploring such a relation I wish he would tell us about it" (Copeland in Stigler 1961, 74). But that was exactly what Solow's 1957 paper, with its assumption of continuous equality between factor payments and their marginal productivities, had done.

Solow's use of what he called a "neoclassical" production function in his two seminal articles on economic growth also had repercussions for ongoing discussion of appropriate policies to encourage economic growth, both in the developed world and in the less developed nations of what had come to be called the third world. Solow's "Contribution to a Theory of Economic Growth" was, to be sure, written for other economic theorists, and presented by Solow himself as an exploration of a rather narrow theoretical matter: the consequences of relaxing certain assumptions in the growth models of Roy Harrod and Evsey Domar, one of those being the assumption of a fixed capital-output ratio. In the 1950s, however, this assumption was beginning to take on a significance beyond the world of formal economic theory. The developing historical statistics on the capital stock, capital formation, and national income were such that a case could be made that the capital/output ratio, both marginal and average, was constant over long periods of time within particular economies. Given the widely acknowledged imprecision of the capital data, the case was certainly debatable. But the evidence led some to consider the possibility that the ratio of capital to output was a technological datum, with the implication that the most direct, if not the only, means of increasing an economy's growth rate was through increasing the rate of capital accumulation, with either government-provided incentives to investment or direct investment by the government itself. This approach to thinking about policies to promote economic growth and development later came to be known as "capital fundamentalism." The Harrod–Domar model, along with the work of pioneering development economist W. Arthur Lewis (1955), had provided formal theoretical foundations for capital fundamentalism, and Solow's model, in which the capital-output ratio was not constant, responded to factor prices, and was independent of the long-term rate of economic growth, provided a foundation for arguments questioning capital fundamentalism.[26]

Likewise, Solow's 1957 paper stood as one more empirical demonstration that the rapid growth of the capital stock in the United States over the late nineteenth and early twentieth century had played only a small role in US economic growth over that period. This also called into question the idea that policies to encourage faster capital accumulation were a key to economic growth. Solow 1957, 316–17) recognized this, at least obliquely, when he noted that he did "not mean to suggest that the observed rate of technical progress would have persisted even if the rate of investment had been much smaller or had fallen to zero" as "much, perhaps nearly all, innovation must be embodied in plant and equipment to be realized at all," although "one could imagine this taking place without net capital formation as old fashioned capital goods are replaced by the latest models."

If capital accumulation did not explain economic growth, what did? If one took the Schmookler-Kendrick-Abramovitz-Solow results seriously, the "measure of our ignorance" on this question was stunningly large. Even if one believed that technical change was the most important component in the collection of unknown or unmeasured growth enhancers that Domar (1961) would soon dub "the Residual," the sense of ignorance was little assuaged, as there was nothing approaching a consensus among economists or any other body of social scientists concerning what policy levers to pull in order to reliably stimulate technological progress. The high priority that political and media elites had assigned to the issue of

[26] The case for a constant capital-output ratio is made by Kuznets (1952) for the United States, while Gordon (1956) is an example of one who did not see the US evidence as supportive of the constancy assumption. Gordon (1956) and Aukrust (1959) are contemporaneous references to perceived links between the belief in a constant capital-output ratio, the Harrod–Domar model, and discussions of policies to encourage economic growth. Yanatopuolus and Nugent (1976, 12) and Easterly (2001) include retrospective accounts of the origins of capital fundamentalism, the impact of the Harrod–Domar and Solow models on it, and its powerful influence on development policy in the 1950s and 1960s.

economic growth, not to mention the natural curiosity of economic researchers, led immediately to efforts to address this ignorance, giving rise to a literature devoted to what came to be known as "growth accounting." This imperative to better account for the causes of economic growth, combined with the growing consensus that the questions related to economic growth and technical change could be fruitfully explored, both theoretically and empirically, using the concept of the production function, stimulated new applications of the Cobb–Douglas regression, and further development of Douglas's idea.

THE COBB–DOUGLAS PRODUCTION FUNCTION AND GROWTH ACCOUNTING RESEARCH

Upon finding the large share of past economic growth that was unexplained by the growth of conventional measures of labor and capital, both Abramovitz and Solow had suggested directions that the empirical attack on this growth "residual" could take: exploring the possibility that the aggregate production function exhibited increasing returns to scale, properly measuring changes in the quality as well as the quantity of the labor input, operationalizing the idea that technical change was embodied in new capital equipment, and expanding the idea of capital to include spending on scientific research and increased individual investments in health. These were not new suggestions. As has been recounted earlier, all of these possible sources of economic growth and increasing productivity had been proposed in the 1920s by economists in response to the newly developed statistical evidence of high growth rates of manufacturing output and labor productivity in the early decades of the twentieth century. However, the growing acceptance of the idea of an aggregate production function regression as an appropriate tool for empirical research into the growth process created the possibility of a comprehensive strategy for operationalizing these old ideas, a strategy centered on the time series Cobb–Douglas regression.

The "residual" itself could be understood as the coefficient of a trend term in a time series Cobb–Douglas regression of aggregate output on aggregate inputs. The unrestricted version of the Cobb–Douglas regression allowed for increasing returns to scale, and provided a vehicle for a formal test of that hypothesis. Ideas about changes in the quality of capital and labor could be explored by developing new, quality adjusted measures of existing capital and labor series, and the potential contribution to growth of other "inputs," such as R&D expenditures or education, could be assessed by developing plausible time series indexes of those inputs and including them in the production function regression.

As it turns out, most of the contributors to growth accounting literature of the late 1950s and early 1960s did not follow this "comprehensive strategy." Indeed, Edward Denison (1962), who would become perhaps the best-known practitioner of growth accounting, made no use of production function regressions at all. He instead built on the Copeland–Martin inspired "index of real output over real inputs" approach of Kendrick and others, and concentrated on creating better measures of both the quantity and quality of the inputs, most notably by developing an approach to adjusting the labor input for secular increases in educational attainment. But the Cobb–Douglas regression did show up frequently in this literature, as a means of testing a single hypothetical explanation for the residual, as part of a hybrid approach to testing several hypotheses, or as part of a macroeconometric model of the type proposed by Tinbergen (1942), in which it provided an aggregate supply relationship to complement Keynesian-inspired equations representing factors influencing aggregate demand.

Augmenting the Aggregate Cobb–Douglas Regression: Two Scandinavian Production Functions

Arguably, something very close to the "comprehensive strategy" described above was adopted by Olavi Niitamo (1958) to explain the growth of output in Finland from 1925 to 1952. Niitamo began by making a distinction between measuring productivity with "simple ratios" and with "certain parameters indicating the interdependence of a change in output and the changes in input." He intended to conduct the second type of analysis using as a "point of departure" a "model of the Cobb–Douglas type" (30). It is fairly clear from context that Niitamo's goal was to create a regression model that would do a good job of explaining, in a statistical sense, past growth of output in Finland, and could also be used for forecasting (Niitamo 1958, 30, 39–40).

Niitamo's output variable was an index of value added in the mining, manufacturing, and public-utility sectors, and in most of his regression models, the labor variable was an index of man-years. After explaining the difficulties involved in creating an appropriate measure of the flow of capital services each period, he proposed two proxy measures: an index of kWh of electricity consumed by industry, and a weighted average of this variable and an index of horsepower of machine capacity in use in industry, with weights determined by estimating a Cobb–Douglas regression of output on labor, the machine capacity variable, and the electricity use variable. As a simple labor productivity index for Finnish industry revealed a trend "attributable to technical and other similar kinds of development," Niitamo proposed adding an exponential trend to the regression. A variable should also be added, he argued, to reflect the fact that productivity fluctuated in response to the business cycle. After some experimentation, he chose the trend ratio of Finland's exports for this purpose.

In response to the common suggestion that the general growth in productivity might be due to rising levels of knowledge, education, or technological know-how, Niitamo developed several variables to measure the level of knowledge in Finland to be used in the regression in place of the exponential trend, such as an index of the number of people who had graduated from lower secondary school.

His empirical strategy involved using measures of fit (multiple correlation coefficient [R] and standard deviation of the regression [S]) to make comparisons between specifications with more vs. fewer types of variables included, with his most elaborate specifications involving a capital variable, a labor variable, a business-cycle variable, and either an exponential trend or a "level of knowledge" variable. He explained to readers that because his aggregate-level data did not represent profit-maximizing choices of firm owners and otherwise "did not satisfy the conditions postulated in the theory of the firm," such as perfect competition, he had no intention of testing hypotheses underlying the marginal productivity theory, including that of constant returns to scale. Indeed, in all but one of his reported specifications, he constrained the labor and capital coefficients to sum to one. He also cautioned that because his data did not satisfy the "conditions of the methods of testing, the traditional methods of testing can merely be employed as analytical tools capable of giving possible suggestions."[27]

Niitamo ultimately presented the results of eight specifications out of a much larger number estimated. His preferred specification was

$$Q = 1.011\ L_m^{.779} K_{mx}^{.221} W_s^{.130} H_r^{.545} \quad R = .997 \quad S = .0127$$

where L_m was the man-hours index, K_{mx} the combined index of electricity use and machine horsepower, W_s the business-cycle measure, and H_r the

[27] By "methods of testing," it seems likely Niitamo meant comparisons of residual variance, because these were the comparisons upon which he seemed to place the most weight, and he did comment at one point that residual variances of two of the models did "not differ from each other significantly."

ratio of secondary-school graduates to working-age population. He made particular note of the fact that including all four variable types resulted in consistently lower S values, and that the K_{mx} variable improved fit relative to the measure of electricity use. Using a level-of-knowledge variable in place of a trend variable improved fit, but not significantly. However, while the exponential-trend variable "merely described, as it were, rather than truly explained the trend in productivity," in a model that used the level-of-knowledge variable "*the trend development in productivity now appeared to get a concrete and reasonable explanation*" (Niitamo 1958, 38, italics in original).

In Niitamo's preferred model, more of Finland's increase in output per worker was explained by growth in the level-of-knowledge variable than by growth in the machine-use variable. He urged caution, however, in using the models of his paper either to analyze the process of economic development or to make forecasts. The small residual variances could be due to multicollinearity, or to the correlation between the variables included in the model and variables that affected output but were not included in the model. Niitamo also noted that his decision to model changes in output as a result of changes in input ran against the grain of much modern theorizing on changes in output, which focused on demand side factors such as the multiplier and the accelerator. His hope was to see models like his embedded in a "system of equations in terms of which it would be possible to follow up various kinds of policy decisions and predict how they are going to affect, with different lags, the output" (Niitamo 1958, 41).

A second Scandinavian production function regression appeared in 1959 in two papers (Aukrust 1959; Aukrust and Bjerke 1959). Based on data from Norway covering the years 1900 to 1955, minus the war years, it was a basic, unrestricted Cobb–Douglas regression with a linear trend, using real net national product as the output variable. In terms of the life history of the Cobb–Douglas regression as an empirical tool, the Aukrust–Bjerke regression stands as an early and explicitly recognized demonstration that what came to be called the "residual" could be measured directly using a Cobb–Douglas regression. And, the authors pointed out, since the average annual growth rate of total output over the period was 3.4 percent, and the trend term accounted for over half of that, the regression also showed that the residual in Norway was on the same order of magnitude as that for the United States, as revealed by Solow, and for Finland, as revealed by Niitamo's basic specification with an exponential trend.

In Aukrust (1959) the regression results were made a key exhibit in an argument about economic policy. In particular, Aukrust was attacking the thesis that "the national product of a country will increase at about the same rate as the country's real capital," that is, that the marginal capital to output ratio is constant. According to Aukrust, this idea had "penetrated and gradually become accepted in the economic and political debate" (Aukrust 1959, 37), leading policy makers aiming at economic growth to concentrate on actions designed to increase investment.

Aukrust argued that the idea that the shape of an economy's production function would lead to a constant capital-output ratio "contradicted almost everything we have learned about economic laws of production" (Aukrust 1959, 39). An attempt to determine empirically a more realistic production function should instead start with the four traditional factors of production identified by economic theory: land, labor, capital, and organization, the last of which Aukrust preferred to call "the human factor." Aukrust admitted that it was necessary to assume some shape for the production function, and he chose the Cobb–Douglas form, which, he pointed out, implied diminishing marginal productivity. Since organization was unmeasurable, he also made the admittedly untestable assumption that it increased over the period at a constant rate, and thus its effect could be measured by adding a trend to the traditional Cobb–Douglas regression. The regression results showed that "better organization" accounted for more than half of Norway's growth over the period, and numerical examples showed that "the possibilities of accelerating economic growth by increased investment are considerably smaller than we have been used to assume." Although Aukrust at one point admitted that his identification of the estimated trend coefficient as a measure of organization or "the human factor" was "outside what is rigorously proved" by his results, this did not prevent him from concluding that the focus of growth policy should be shifted from investment to areas related to the human factor, such as research and education (Aukrust 1959, 48–50).

In the Aukrust and Bjerke article, by contrast, much more attention was given to statistical and econometric issues associated with the estimated production function, although a muted attack on the idea of a constant capital-output ratio remained. The first third of the article focused in detail on the process of creating the capital-stock series for Norway, with much discussion of the associated conceptual and practical problems: valuation, deflation, aggregation, depreciation, and so on. It serves as a reminder that as of 1960, although capital-stock and capital-formation estimates were being routinely used for a variety of purposes, even those who were strongly committed to the idea that capital could and should be measured believed that the existing data had serious shortcoming that all users should take into account.

The discussion of the production function specification included references to the previous uses of the regression by Douglas and others, with Smith (1945) and Tinbergen (1942) cited as authors who had added an exponential trend to the specification. In Aukrust and Bjerke (1959, 105), the coefficient of the trend was presented as a measure the impact of "technique," that is "the general level of technical knowledge, the efficiency of management and workers, the industrial structure, etc.," rather than organization or the human factor.

The estimated parameters of the production function were reported along with their standard errors, which the authors considered to be worrisomely large. The fit was announced to be good, based on comparisons, in percentage terms, between actual and predicted values of net national product. The authors also showed, however, that when the function was fit on four subperiods of the data, the estimates varied quite a bit, and that a regression based on prewar data gave a very poor fit for the postwar years.

On the whole, the authors argued, there were two viewpoints from which to judge their "computations": as "experiments in macroeconomic curve fitting" or as "an attempt to determine constants in a macroeconomic relationship." From the first point of view, they judged the experiment successful. The Cobb–Douglas with a trend gave a very good description of what had actually happened in Norway over the period 1950–55. The authors were rather ambivalent regarding their success from the second point of view. There were subtle theoretical issues to consider here. Although there was some justification for assuming that micro-level production functions took a Cobb–Douglas form, this did not guarantee that the macro-relationship took a simple form, or that it even made sense to try to explain trends in aggregate production only with changes occurring in other macro-level variables, without regard to, say, the industries in which those changes occurred. But, the authors reasoned, the basis of much macro-analysis was "presumably" that explaining aggregates with aggregates did make sense, and on that basis, the Cobb–Douglas assumption seemed reasonable, and there was little in their results to suggest that "a macro-type production function cannot be a useful hypothesis" (Aukrust and Bjerke 1959, 109).

Exploring Aggregate Returns to Scale with the Cobb–Douglas Regression

Two papers used the regression to explore the possibility that the aggregate production function was characterized by increasing returns to scale. In his contribution to the 1958 conference on Output, Input, and Productivity Measurement, described in Chapter 5, George Stigler had argued that if, at a given point in time, the production function were characterized by increasing returns to scale, then conventional total factor productivity measures, which assumed constant returns to scale, would attribute too little of any subsequent growth in output to increasing quantities of inputs, and too much to economic progress. According to Stigler, the argument for economies of scale at the level of the aggregate economy, "familiar since Adam Smith's time" was certainly valid, the only question being the quantitative importance of these economies.

To provide a framework for discussing the potential importance of the bias in question, Stigler estimated an unrestricted time series version of the Cobb–Douglas regression (without trend) using data from the manufacturing sector for six years between 1900 and 1948. The coefficients of capital and labor summed to 1.36. Stigler did not offer this result as evidence of increasing returns to scale, but as a summary of growth over the period, from which one could infer that a 248 percent growth in an input index led to a 435 percent growth in output, for a conventionally measured total factor productivity increase of 53.7 percent. However, if increasing returns were such that the true coefficients of labor and capital in the manufacturing production function summed to 1.1, the correct measure of economic progress would have been 35.7 percent; if the true coefficients summed to 1.2, the correct measure of economic progress would have been 19.7 percent.

Stigler rejected Douglas's cross-section studies as a source of valid evidence regarding the importance of economies of scale. Conceptually, he argued, such cross-section studies could only capture the economies of scale achieved by large industries compared to small ones at a point in time, and not those accruing to all industries as the total size of an economy grew over time. Further, since all the industry-level observations in Douglas's samples came from the same economy at the same point in time, the production functions he estimated were "essentially meaningless." If the economy were in a competitive equilibrium, the marginal value products of both labor and capital would be the same in all industries regardless of size. Douglas's functions, then, could only be measuring "monopoly returns or short-run disequilibria." However, Stigler (1961, 62) proposed that making international interindustry comparisons potentially offered a way around these problems, "for then the measure of the effects of scale would not be obscured by the forces of competition (unless mobility of resources between the nations were high), and the measure would not exclude the economies of scale of the entire economy which are shared by all industries." He illustrated his thinking by comparing industry-level data from the United States and Great Britain in 1948, compiled by Frankel (1957). Stigler assumed that "the production function (not technique) of an industry is the same in the two countries,"[28] with output in Great Britain given by $P_e = aL^{\alpha}C^{\beta}$ and output in the United States by $P_a = b(\lambda_l L)^{\alpha}(\lambda_c C)^{\beta} = k\lambda_l^{\alpha}\lambda_c^{\beta}P_e$, where λ_l was the ratio of labor in the US industry to labor in the corresponding British industry, and λ_c was defined similarly for capital. This led to $P_a / P_e = k\lambda_l^{\alpha}\lambda_c^{\beta}$, which could be logged to produce a linear estimating equation for α and β. Frankel's data allowed Stigler to create a sample of 23 industry pairs, with which he produced estimates $\alpha = .827$, $\beta = .444$, and $\alpha + \beta = 1.27$. Despite offering some reasons to believe that his estimate of $\alpha + \beta$ was probably upward biased, Stigler was willing to assert that economies of scale "are potentially of the same order of magnitude as technical progress," and certainly deserved further study, mainly because of their bearing on the theory of growth (Stigler 1961, 63).

Participants in the conference had even more concerns than Stigler himself about his attempt to measure scale economies. Solow agreed wholeheartedly with Stigler on both the likelihood that increasing returns were empirically important and the urgency of measuring their magnitude. He believed that, conceptually, time series data was the natural place to look for evidence of increasing returns, but because input quantities, output quantities, and technical know-how all trended upward over time, he saw no "sure and simple" way to disentangle the effect on output of increasing returns from that of technical change. Solow was completely dismissive of Douglas's cross-section approach, and although Stigler's method of using international comparisons to avoid the problem that competition equalizes factor returns was "ingenious," Solow did not believe that it "dodge(d) the nonsense in the cross section approach" (Solow in Stigler 1961, 65).

Solow illustrated his concern with a model in which all industries had Cobb–Douglas production functions, with values of α and β the same across countries within an industry, but differing across industries ("I am sure Stigler is under no illusions about the meaning to be attached to the

[28] Technique might differ across nations because of scale economies. Although he did not say so, Stigler's approach also assumed that within each country, each industry had the same production function, in particular, the same α and β.

single interindustry α and β in his cross section function" [65]). He assumed that approximate competition prevailed in both countries leading to the standard marginal productivity conditions, while commenting on the problem with this assumption in a model that allowed increasing returns to scale. The model implied that λ_c/λ_l would be the same in every industry, something that was clearly not the case in Frankel's data. Solow suspected several reasons for this: some industries may not have Cobb–Douglas production functions, and some may not have the same production function in each country. Frankel's fuel consumption may be a poor proxy for capital, and differing levels of skill and education across the two countries may make ratios of employment poor measures of the ratio of the labor input. The degree of monopoly may differ across industry.

Robert Eisner also believed that Stigler's method was biased towards finding increasing returns. Suppose, he argued, that some industries made use of specialized factors (land, skill) with which countries were differently endowed. An industry in the country with a better endowment of its specialized factor would have a higher marginal product curve for labor and capital in that industry, and, if factors were less than perfectly mobile, higher rates of remuneration for labor and capital in that industry. This, Eisner argued, would be enough to cause the upward bias: In each country industries with relatively high endowments of their specialized factors would produce more for a given labor and capital input, and would employ more labor and capital, than their counterparts in the other country.[29]

Stigler inserted a response to Solow's comments in the published conference proceedings volume, in which he offered an alternative approach to estimating returns to scale using the Great Britain-US comparison. Having secured from Frankel the price data that corresponded to his input and output data, Stigler estimated the regression log[US Price/UK

[29] Eisner's assumption of imperfect mobility seems unnecessary here, if not counterproductive. An industry in a country that was well endowed with the specialized factor would draw relatively more capital and labor *as a result* of perfect mobility (e.g., if the specialized factor raised the marginal product of labor curve, more labor would be required to drive wages down to the competitive level), and the industry would have higher output for the same quantity of labor and capital input due to the contribution of the specialized factor. There would essentially be an omitted variable (ratio of the specialized factor) that was positively correlated with labor ratio, capital ratio, and output ratio holding constant input ratios, biasing upward the coefficients on the labor and capital ratios.

Price] = 2.005 – .236log([US output/UK output], with a standard error of .075 for the slope coefficient. This, he said, implied a value of $\alpha + \beta$ of 1/(1 – .263) = 1.34, "substantially identical" to the value from his original regression.[30]

A. A. Walters was apparently unaware of Stigler's 1958 experiments with estimating returns to scale and the discussions thereof (all published in 1961) when he wrote his own "Note on Economies of Scale" (Walters, 1963b), in which he adopted the direct approach of estimating an unrestricted Cobb–Douglas regression with a trend.[31] His stated motivation for exploring the question of scale economies was concern that Solow's (1957) measure of the contribution of neutral technical change to economic growth, having been produced by a method that assumed constant returns to scale, could have also reflected the impact of increasing returns to scale. He mentioned the ample evidence for something very close to constant returns to scale in manufacturing presented by Douglas (1948), but also Burton Wall's (1948) estimates of the unrestricted version of the Cobb–Douglas regression, which had indicated strongly increasing returns in US mining and manufacturing.

Walters chose to analyze the same time period as had Solow, 1909–49. The output series was GNP from the private nonagricultural sector, and the labor series was private non-farm employment, measured by the corresponding employment series. Walters worked with three capital series: the Goldsmith's net capital series, the same series as adjusted for employment by Solow (1957), and Hogan's (1958) gross capital series. The three resulting versions of the production function were estimated by ordinary least squares, with and without a correction for first-order autocorrelation.

30 Stigler did not explain how he arrived at his estimating equation, but it can be derived by writing down the cost function associated with the Cobb–Douglas production function for each country, then using the long-run competitive equilibrium conditions that price equals average cost in each country and factor prices are the same across industries within each country.

31 It is also interesting to see Walters offering an apology for/defense of his use of the concept of the aggregate production function similar to Solow's of the 1957 article: "The theoretical foundations of the aggregate production function give one grounds for doubting whether the concept is at all useful. Nevertheless, the temptation to discuss movements in indices of input and output in terms of such a function is difficult to resist. And there is no doubt that it is useful to rationalize the data along these lines" (Walters 1963b, 424). One also can find other such (pro forma?) apologies during this period for assuming the existence of an aggregate production function. See, for example, the opening paragraph of Nelson (1964).

Walters's ordinary least squares results "discredited" the hypothesis of constant returns to scale, with the sum of the labor and capital coefficients ranging from 1.27 to 1.38, all significantly different from 1. The estimates implied that 27 percent to 35 percent of the technological change over the 41-year period was due to scale economies, and the annual rate of neutral technological change might be as low as 1 percent per year, rather than Solow's estimate of 1.8 percent. When the estimates were corrected for serial correlation, the picture became more ambiguous. Although the coefficient estimates did not change much, in only one of the specifications was the sum of the labor and capital coefficients significantly greater than one at the 95-percent level. The evidence, Walters concluded, was not overwhelming, but did cast doubt on the assumption of constant returns to scale.

Walters closed by noting that he was not exactly sure what it meant for the aggregate production function to display increasing returns to scale. It certainly did not necessarily imply, he asserted, that large numbers of firms in the economy enjoyed increasing returns. Marshallian external economies may be important, or the increasing returns in the aggregate production function may reflect the influence of scale economies in a few large industries, such as transportation and utilities.

The Cobb–Douglas Regression and the "Embodiment" Question

Aukrust (1959) had no trouble concluding from his results, and the similar results of Solow (1957) and Abramovitz (1956), that policies to encourage investment and capital formation would have very little impact on economic growth, and others at the time and after drew the same conclusion from this work. But Solow himself worried that his 1957 model "grossly understated the importance of old-fashioned capital investment as a vehicle for bringing new technology into productive operation," as "much, perhaps nearly all, innovation must be embodied in new plant and equipment to be realized at all." By 1958, he was working on an alternative model of the growth process, a "clean model in which all new technology had to be embodied in new gross investment before it could have any influence on production or productivity" (Solow 2001, 173; Solow 1957, 316). The model in question first appeared in a paper presented at a conference in 1959 (Solow 1960).

Solow opened that paper by citing the recent empirical studies, including his own, showing that growth in capital per head had very little impact on the growth of per capita output. Solow argued that these studies had all been based, implicitly or explicitly, on a production function of the form $Q(t) = B(t)f(K(t), L(t))$, with those who explicitly acknowledged their reliance on the production function concept assuming a Cobb–Douglas production function with an exponential trend. In this formulation, he pointed out, technical change is "disembodied," in that the rate of investment had no influence on the rate of technical change, and technical change affected the productivity of both old and new capital equally. Solow wished to reconstruct the model to account for the obvious fact that most innovations needed to be embodied in new capital equipment in order to be made effective. To do so in an empirically tractable way, he explained, he would keep the assumption of an aggregate production function with a Cobb–Douglas form, despite the many criticisms that could be leveled against it.

Solow's alternative model began with the assumption that "all technical progress is uniform and approximately exponential over time, and capital goods at their moment of construction embody all the latest technical knowledge but share not at all in any further improvements in technology." This assumption was operationalized by means of a production function for each "vintage" of capital, given by $Q_v(t) = Be^{\lambda v} L_v(t)^{\alpha} K_v(t)^{1-\alpha}$, where $Q_v(t)$ stood for the amount of output produced in year t using capital of vintage v, that is, created in period v; $K_v(t)$ was the stock in year t of capital of vintage v, and $L_v(t)$ was the amount of homogenous labor working with vintage v capital. It was also assumed that a competitive labor market led to a single wage, so that workers were assigned to capital equipment to equalize the marginal product of labor for each vintage of capital. The original quantity of capital of vintage v was equal to gross investment in year v, after which it depreciated at a constant rate of δ. With these assumptions, Solow was able to derive a production function of the Cobb–Douglas form, in which the traditional capital variable was replaced by a variable $J(t)$, which was essentially a weighted sum of past investment, with the weight of each period's investment determined by the quality of technology in that year, and depreciation since that year.

However, the $J(t)$ variable depended on the unknown parameters of the model, and Solow could see no "elegant" way to estimate his new production function. His response to this dilemma was to show that if one assumed values for α and δ, the model's relationships implied that one could use observed series on investment, output, and labor, to construct variables for estimating λ, the rate of technological change, via linear regression. This he did, using Kendrick's data on real private GNP and private sector man-hours, and Kuznets's most recent estimates of capital formation, 1919–53, assuming $\delta = .04$ and $\alpha = .67$ or .75. His preferred λ estimate was .025.

A section entitled "Economic Significance" included some illustrative calculations to show how the model of embodied technical change compared with the standard aggregate production function with "disembodied" technical change when it came to predicting the impact on growth of an increase in the rate of capital formation. Given reasonable parameter values, the conventional model implied that doubling the rate of capital investment would lead to growth of 28 percent over the next 10 years, while his model of embodied technical change would imply growth of 35 percent. The differences were not staggering, he concluded, but neither were they negligible. Also, in his model half of the growth in output was due to capital formation, and half to technical progress, and (by assumption) if gross investment fell to zero, technological progress would cease.

Solow applied his model of capital-embodied technical change to a specific policy question in a paper prepared for a session at the 1961 AEA meetings on "The Lagging U.S. Growth Rate" (Solow 1962). The question was "How much fixed investment is necessary to support alternative rates of growth of potential output in the United States in the near future?" and Solow emphasized that he was looking at potential output, and talking about the investment "necessary to support," not "sufficient to generate" alternative growth rates. He chose to approach the question by estimating an aggregate production function because, he commented, "I do not know any other way to go about it" (Solow 1962, 76).

Solow's path in this paper from the assumption that "*all* technological progress needs to be embodied in newly produced capital goods" to a production function for potential output was much shorter than that taken in the 1959 conference paper. He began by specifying an "equivalent stock of capital" equation

$$J(t) = \sum_{v=-\infty}^{t} (1+\lambda)^{v} B(t-v) I(v)$$

in which $I(v)$ was the original stock of capital of vintage v, $B(t-v)$ was a depreciation factor, and λ was, as before, the rate of technological improvement or "improvement factor." Potential output in year t was then P(t) = F(J(t), N(t)), where N(t) was the "available" input of labor, and F(.) was assumed for empirical purposes to take a Cobb–Douglas form with constant returns to scale. Solow also introduced an empirically implementable adjustment for the problem that an aggregate production function could only describe potential output. He wrote actual or observed output as A(t) = f(u(t),P(t)), where u was the unemployment rate, and specified the f(u) function as "what amounts to the half of a normal curve lying to the right of the peak," because "one would want, I think, to have a kind of diminishing returns to the reduction of unemployment after a point, and this occurs as the normal curve flattens out near its peak" (Solow 1962, 78). Then, actual output could be written as:

$$A = a10^{b + cu + du^2} J^{\alpha} N^{1-\alpha}$$

which led to the equation actually fit by Solow:

$$\log(A/N) = \log(a) + b + cu + du^2 + \alpha\log(J/N)$$

By assuming a value of .04 for "full employment," Solow could write b in terms of c and d, thus eliminating one of the constants from the equation.

Rather than assuming a value for α and estimating λ, as he had done in the 1959 paper, Solow chose to assume values for λ, construct alternative series for equivalent capital J(t) corresponding to the various assumed λ values, then estimate a, c, d, and α directly via regression using each of the alternative *J(t)* series. More specifically, Solow defined investment as the sum of national income account figures for "producers' durable goods" plus nonresidential construction, excluding educational, religious and hospital construction. J(t) for any given year was then a sum of past investment weighted using depreciation schedules developed by George Terborgh. Six alternative series for J(t) series were created, each corresponding to an assumed pair of λ values for plant (construction) and equipment (producers' durables), such as [λ Plant = .02, λ Equipment = .03]. The output variable, defined to correspond with the capital variable, was GNP minus product originating in government, households, other institutions, and the rest of the world, and minus services of houses. The labor variable was an estimate of "full employment man hours," and the unemployment rate was the percentage difference between actual man-hours and an estimate of "full employment man hours," rather than the official unemployment rate.[32]

[32] In the published paper, Solow never specifically indicated the dates covered by his data. A remark on page 80 suggests that the data covered the period 1929–61.

TABLE 3

INVESTMENT QUOTAS FOR ALTERNATIVE GROWTH RATES

Growth Rate	3%	3½%	4%	4½%	5%
J_3					
Slow growth in man-hours	9.9	11.2	12.4	13.8	15.0
Fast growth in man-hours	9.2	10.4	11.7	13.1	14.3
J_4					
Slow growth in man-hours	9.0	10.2	11.4	12.5	13.7
Fast growth in man-hours	8.5	9.8	10.9	12.0	13.2
J_5					
Slow growth in man-hours	10.1	11.3	12.6	13.9	15.3
Fast growth in man-hours	9.4	10.8	12.0	13.3	14.7

Figure 6.1 Solow's illustration of how different assumptions about the embodiment of technical change in capital led to different conclusions about the impact of capital accumulation on growth

Solow was satisfied with the resulting estimates. The estimated relationship between unemployment and output corresponded to what other researchers were finding using other data sources, and he believed that pattern of variation in the estimates produced by different assumptions about the capital improvement rates to be "obvious."[33] Solow also used the data to estimate a standard restricted Cobb–Douglas regression with a trend, producing an estimate of "disembodied" technical improvement of 2.5 percent per year.

The key issue, however, was what the estimates implied for the relationship between investment and economic growth, which, given Solow's data and methods, meant growth of potential output in the private sector. Solow's approach to exploring this issue is captured in Figure 6.1, taken from Solow's paper.

The two possible growth rates of potential private-sector man-hours were based on extrapolation of the potential man-hours series used in the analysis adjusted using future projections of labor-force growth. Three possible improvement-rate combinations were considered (J_3, J_4, and J_5) along with five possible target growth rates ranging from 3 percent to 5 percent. The entries in the table were the necessary investment quotas for reaching the target growth rates given the assumed rates of labor-force

[33] For example, lowering the assumed rate of technical progress led to larger values of the coefficient on capital.

growth and embodied technical improvement, with "investment quota" being a term then coming into vogue for the ratio of investment to output.

As Solow read them, the estimates suggested "that a necessary condition for increasing the rate of growth of output from about 3½ per cent annually to 4½ per cent annually may be a 20–25 per cent increase in the investment quota from the range of 10–11 per cent of business GNP to the range of 12–14 per cent of business GNP" (Solow 1962, 84–85). By comparison, the conventional production function with disembodied technical change, given its high time trend and its low estimated elasticity of output with respect to capital, implied that while growth could continue at 2.5 percent per year with no increase in capital or labor, lifting the growth rate to 4 percent per year would require an investment quota of almost 20 percent of potential output. This struck Solow as quite unrealistic, which suggested to him that the embodied model was more realistic. However, he was careful to point out that nothing in his analysis "proved" (his quotes) that his model of technical change embodied in new capital was a better model of production than the conventional model with disembodied technological change.

Solow closed his paper by reminding his audience that capital formation was just one of the prerequisites of growth, referring to ongoing research into the significance for growth of education, research, and public health. It was a standard call for further research, but the language in which it was expressed was consistent with a vision none too unusual among the leading macroeconomists of the early 1960s: one in which the government took responsibility for promoting economic well-being, and economists provided the knowledge and expertise required to carry out that responsibility:

> (W)hile economists are now convinced of the significance of these factors in the process of economic growth, we are still a long way from having any quantitative estimates of the pay-off to society of resources devoted to research, education, and improvements in allocative efficiency. Since such estimates must form the foundation for a national allocation of resources in the interests of economic growth, their provision by hook or by crook presents a research problem of great theoretical and practical interest
>
> (Solow 1962, 86).

Solow's model of technological improvement embodied in new capital had an immediate impact on both theorists of economic growth and on those with a practical interest in designing policies to promote growth – two groups, it should be noted, with significant overlap. Edmund Phelps, writing in 1961, called the idea represented by the model the "new view" of investment, and spoke in Hegelian terms of its influence on economists' thinking about technical change, capital formation, and growth:[34]

> In 1956 appeared the first in a series of papers disputing the traditional thesis that capital deepening is the major source of productivity gains and conjecturing that we owe our economic growth to our progressive technology.
>
> Thesis and antithesis were synthesized by 1960. Investment has been married to Technology. In the new view, the role of investment is to modernize as well as deepen the capital stock. Now investment is prized as the carrier of technological progress.
>
> (Phelps 1962, 548)

Abramovitz (1956) and Solow (1957) were among the papers cited as establishing the "antithesis," which Phelps termed "investment pessimism," while Solow's (1960) was the theoretical paper cited as the basis of the "new view" synthesis. Phelps went on to describe the impact of investment pessimism on economic policy advice, as reflected in Herbert Stein and Edward Denison's chapter on "High Employment and Growth" in the report of President Eisenhower's Commission on National Goals, and the subsequent embrace of the "new view" by the economists of the UN Economic Commission for Europe and by Kennedy's Council of Economic Advisors (on which Solow was serving).[35]

Reading Phelps's paper, one might conclude that the Solow-inspired "new view" of investment quickly spurred a widespread recommitment to "capital fundamentalism" on the part of economists and policy makers. As a matter of fact, however, Solow's model of capital-embodied technical change received considerable theoretical and empirical scrutiny over the next several years. Indeed, the purpose of Phelps's (1962) paper was to question whether the "new view" of investment really implied a more

[34] Phelps' paper, published in *the Quarterly Journal of Economics* in 1962, had appeared as Cowles Foundation research paper #110 (revised) in March of 1961.

[35] Phelps cited the following passage from a report by the Council of Economic Advisors to the Joint Economic Committee: "One of the reasons for the recent slowdown in the rate of growth of productivity and output is a corresponding slowdown in the rate at which the stock of capital has been renewed and modernized .... As has been confirmed by more recent research, the great importance of capital investment lies in its interaction with improved skills and technological progress. New ideas lie fallow without the modern equipment to give them life" (US Joint Economic Committee, "The American Economy in 1961: Problems and Policies," Council of Economic Advisers, Hearings on the Economic Report of the President, 1961, p. 338). The 1962 Economic Report of the President also explicated the embodiment hypothesis in laymen's terms in a section entitled "Investment as a Source of Growth" (pp. 127–129).

important role for capital formation in driving economic growth. Constructing and analyzing a model that enveloped both the old (disembodied) view and the new view, he concluded that the answer was "not necessarily": in particular, the long-run growth rate depended only on the rate of technical improvement, not on whether it was embodied in capital or disembodied. Denison (1964) made an empirical case that, given the facts concerning past rates of productivity growth and the historical evolution of the US capital stock, the question of what fraction of technical improvement is embodied in new capital goods was of little importance for policy.

Denison was responding to what he saw as a growing consensus that a determination of the share of technological progress that was embodied in capital was "an issue of first rate importance."[36] Despite Denison's skepticism on this point, however, two high-profile studies pressed the Cobb–Douglas production function into service to address just that issue.

Eitan Berglas (1965) used variations on Solow's (1962) restricted Cobb–Douglas regression to test several hypotheses regarding the relationship between investment, the rate of technological change, and growth. His basic data on output, investment, labor, and the capital stock were those used by Solow (1962); only the unemployment rate series differed. Berglas first created measures of "effective capital" in the manner of Solow (1962), assuming improvement rates ranging from 0 percent to 3 percent for both plant and equipment. He found that models that included both an effective capital measure and a trend term fit better than those without a trend term and that when a trend term was included, its coefficient was always significant. Among the models with a trend term, the one that used a conventional capital series fit no better or worse (statistically speaking) than models that assumed nonzero improvement rates for embodied technological change. Berglas took this as evidence that at least some important portion of technological improvement was disembodied, and that there were no statistical grounds for preferring a model in which some technological change was embodied in capital to one in which all was disembodied. Further, the model in which capital improved at a rate of 3 percent per year made about the same prediction regarding the impact of an increase in investment as the "all disembodied" model.

Berglas also experimented with specifications meant to capture alternative ways in which investment might stimulate technical improvement, but

[36] Denison (1964, 90) was actually quoting Moses Abramovitz's (1962) review of Denison (1962).

in the end concluded that "the model that works best for the business sector is the model in which technology is not embodied in capital goods, and in which technological change is approximated by a time trend." He believed that he had "failed to show that any part of technological change is related to investment," thus providing no grounds for overturning pessimistic conclusions about the efficacy of policies to increase growth through stimulating investment.

Michael Intriligator (1965) also attempted to differentiate between rates of embodied and disembodied technical change by adding a trend term to the empirical model of Solow (1962).[37] Unlike Berglas, he did not experiment with alternative ways of allowing investment to influence growth, but he did experiment with the labor variable, using indexes of employment, man-hours, and Edward Denison's index of man-hours adjusted for the age, sex, and educational attainment of the labor force. Given four different labor indexes, five versions of the effective capital stock index (calculated based on assumed rates of improvement ranging from 0 to 5 percent), and the need to estimate every specification with and without a trend, Intriligator reported results from 40 regressions. In the discussion of results, the most attention was given to the R values (multiple correlation coefficients) and the statistical significance of the estimated trends.

Not surprisingly, results were similar to those of Berglas's specifications of the embodiment model with a trend. Including the trend always raised the R value significantly. The model that simply used an index of employment as the labor variable fit significantly better than the those using the age-sex-education adjusted index, and this, along with the fact that models with no trend and an assumed improvement rate of zero had the worst fits, led Intriligator to conclude (a) that both embodied and disembodied technical change were important, and (b) that technical improvement embodied in capital was more important than technical improvement embodied in labor over the period of his data.[38] However, given insignificant differences in fits across the models that assumed different rates of embodied technical change, Intriligator was reluctant to make a definitive division of technical progress into the embodied and disembodied categories.

[37] Michael Intriligator's paper was a revised chapter from his 1964 dissertation, completed under Solow's supervision.

[38] By contrast, Eitan Berglas drew the conclusion that embodiment was unimportant by comparing across models with trends and noting the (insignificantly) higher r-squared value for the model assuming no embodied technical change.

At the time that the Berglas and Intriligator papers were appearing, however, other empirical growth researchers were questioning the credibility of any alleged estimate of the rate of embodied vs. disembodied technical change. The essence of these criticisms was that one could not, using the aggregate data on investment and output employed by Solow, simultaneously identify the rate of disembodied technical change, the rate of embodied technical change (that is, the rate at which the productivity of capital goods improved over time), and the rate of physical deterioration of capital.

One issue was that the depreciation rates used in the embodiment literature to convert the investment figures from past years into a measure of the quantity of capital of each vintage surviving in the current year included, along with an allowance for the decline in productivity of old capital due to physical deterioration, an allowance for "obsolescence," that is, the decline in the market value of old capital as new and better capital became available. But such "obsolescence" was just a manifestation of Solow's "embodied technical change": if capital of newer vintages was more productive than capital of older vintages because it embodied technical improvements, this would be reflected in the relative market values of old vs. new capital, which were typically one basis of estimated depreciation rates. Richard Nelson had shown in a footnote that "the Solow embodiment model reduces to the simple Cobb–Douglas model if capital net of obsolescence is used in the equation" (Nelson 1964, fn. 13), and Murray Brown (1966) developed the argument further, concluding that if a conventional Cobb–Douglas regression were estimated with a net capital-stock measure, both the embodied and the disembodied component of technical change would be captured in the coefficient of the trend term. But, Brown argued, since the analyst had already committed himself to an assumed rate of obsolescence when creating the net capital-stock measure, that rate could be subtracted from the coefficient of the trend term to estimate the rate of disembodied technical change.[39]

[39] By gross capital, both Murray Brown and Richard Nelson meant capital still existing from the past after allowing for physical deterioration, and net capital was gross capital adjusted for obsolescence. Thus, discussions involving separate measures of gross and net capital assumed that one had separate measures of the obsolescence and deterioration components of the overall depreciation rate, which Brown elsewhere implied ("a depreciation rate, consisting in the main of an obsolescence factor and a deterioration factor, is approximated from the available data" [Brown 1966, 88]). But Terborgh, whose depreciation schedules were used in constructing Solow's J(t) measures, did not make this separation. In 1966, the Bureau of Economic Analysis published new series of gross

Dale Jorgenson (1966) focused on a different problem in reaching his conclusion that whether one estimated an aggregate production function or constructed an index of output over inputs, "one can never distinguish a model of embodied technical change from a model of disembodied technical change on the basis of evidence such as that considered by Solow and Denison," (Jorgenson 1966, 2). Jorgenson laid out a model in which any set of aggregate time series on labor, capital, output, and investment implied a particular index of disembodied technical change (like that calculated in Solow [1957]) but also a single "corresponding" index of embodied technical change. Jorgenson's demonstration that the growth of total factor productivity between 1939 and 1959 was equally well explained as the result of an average annual rate of disembodied technical change of 2.5 percent or an average annual rate of embodied technical change of 10.1 percent implied that the regression methods employed by Intriligator and Berglas, even with the assumption of constant rates of technical change, could not separately identify those two rates.[40]

Robert Hall (1968) also argued that there was a "problem of identification" in a model of technical change that included "three basic notions of capital theory – deterioration of capital, capital embodied technical change, and disembodied technical change." Augmenting Solow's (1960) model of embodied technical change with a nonzero rate of growth of disembodied technical change, Hall showed that if disembodied technical change, embodied technical change, and capital deterioration were all assumed to proceed at an exponential rate, a given set of data on labor, and investment, and output was consistent with an infinite number of combinations of values for the three rates, although one could make alternative assumptions about the time paths of these three processes to partially solve this problem.

Both Jorgenson (1966) and Hall (1968) argued that a more promising strategy for empirical research into the role of capital in economic growth

and net capital, where gross capital was the sum of past investment adjusted for the retirement of old equipment and structures. Assumptions about when retirement occurred were based on estimates of the service lives of various types of equipment and structures. Net capital was created by adjusting gross capital for "depreciation," an adjustment that also used estimated service lives along with depreciation formulas like "straight line" or "sum of the year's digits." See Gross, Rottenburg, and Wasson (1966).

40 Dale Jorgenson did not refer to these two papers, but his model could have been offered as an explanation of why the r-squared values of their various specifications changed so little when different assumptions were made about the rate of embodied technical change to be used in constructing the J(t) series, once a trend was included in the model.

involved the creation of better price indexes for capital goods, with Hall concluding that "if data on the prices of used machines and the interest rate are available, then the index of embodied technical change and the deterioration function can in fact be calculated from these data (Hall 1968, 43)." That there was much data-construction work still to be done in this area was the theme of Griliches and Jorgenson (1966), who pointed out that existing price indexes for capital were based largely on changes in the prices of the inputs into capital-good production rather than the prices of the capital goods themselves, thus understating improvements in the quality of capital goods.

Nelson (1964) suggested another possible way around the identification problem that hindered attempts to identify the rates of embodied and disembodied technical change with aggregate production function regression. He pointed out that the rate of change in Solow's J(t) could be approximated as a function of the growth of the gross capital stock, the change in the average age of the capital stock, and the rate of embodied technological change, leading to a Cobb–Douglas regression of the form $\ln Q_t = \beta + (\gamma + (1-\alpha)\lambda_k)t + (1-\alpha)\ln K_t + \alpha \ln L_t + (1-\alpha)\lambda_k a_t$, where K_t was the gross capital stock, a_t the average age of the capital, γ the rate of disembodied technical change, λ_k, the rate of embodied technical change, and α the coefficient of labor in the production function. In endorsing Nelson's idea, Brown (1966) noted that this allowed the rate of embodied technical change to be estimated "within the model": the four coefficient estimates from the regression could be manipulated to produce estimates of α, γ, and λ_k.[41]

In subsequent years, some economists estimated Cobb–Douglas regressions to pursue Nelson's suggestion (see, for example, McHugh and Lane (1983)). However, the aggregate production function regression never became the workhorse tool for empirical research into the embodiment question. Instead, researchers interested in measuring improvements in the quality of capital (which came to be an alternative way of describing the phenomenon of "embodiment") followed the leads of Hall, Griliches, and Jorgenson and focused on creating better price indexes for capital goods. In 1990 Robert J. Gordon published new price indexes covering the postwar period for a wide variety of types of capital equipment. These new indexes, based almost entirely on data sources other than those used by the BLS to

[41] Since Nelson defined gross capital stock as capital adjusted for physical depreciation but not obsolescence, his proposed method required the problematic assumption that the rate of physical deterioration of capital was known.

create the official capital-price indexes, were widely accepted as being more accurate than the BLS indexes, which indicated a much higher rate of price inflation for capital goods than did Gordon's (Gordon 1990). The existence of this new and presumably more reliable price data, covering a significant portion of the nation's output of capital goods, reinvigorated research into the importance to overall economic growth of embodied vs. disembodied technical change.[42] This research did not, however, make use of aggregate production function regressions.

Growth accounting in general also remained a very active research field in the 1970s and 1980s, with attention focused on explaining a "slowdown" in economic growth in the United States and Europe that had commenced in the early 1970s. However, the leading contributors to that literature based their analyses of the growth record on indexes of real output over real inputs rather than aggregate time series production function regressions.[43] Robert Barro (1999), reflecting on this trend from the vantage point of the late 1990s, identified three major problems with what he called the regression approach to growth accounting, relative to the index approach: the implicit assumption that marginal productivities (that is, Cobb–Douglas coefficients) and the growth rate of total factor productivity were constant, the possibility of simultaneity bias, and possible biases due to measurement error in the input variables. These technical matters were indeed important considerations for the economists of the time, I think, but were further bolstered by the fact that the index-number approach was conceptually more robust than the regression approach, that is, consistent with a wider range of theoretical perspectives. Those committed to the idea that empirical analysis of growth should be firmly based in neoclassical theory, in particular, a neoclassical aggregate production function, could be comfortable with the index approach, as there could be shown to be a one-to-one correspondence between particular assumptions about the form of the aggregate production function and particular formulas for constructing the necessary index numbers. The use of factor shares as weights could also be justified by an appeal to neoclassical competitive equilibrium. And, as Barro pointed out, the index-number approach easily allowed the relaxation of the assumption that marginal productivities were constant over time. At the same time, for those who were agnostic or worse when it came to the validity of the idea of an aggregate production function, the typical

[42] See, e.g., Hulten (1992) or Greenwood, Hercowitz, and Krusell (1997).

[43] See, for example, the contributions to the "Symposium on Productivity Growth" in the *Journal of Economic Perspectives*, August 1988, and the studies cited therein.

index-number formulas could be derived from accounting identities (the value of inputs equals the value of outputs). Factor-share weighting of the input indexes could be likewise justified, so that the use of the index-number approach did not really require any commitment to the idea of neoclassical competitive equilibrium.

Given these advantages of the index-number approach to growth accounting, one might wonder why the use of aggregate time series production function regressions to measure and explain the rate of economic growth gained even the temporary popularity that it did. One possible explanation is that the regression approach represented what the economists of the time called an "econometric" approach to growth accounting.

The term "econometric" had, by the 1960s and 1970s, come to be associated with a certain approach to empirical economics, based on the methodological heuristics developed by the Cowles Commission in the mid-1940s, as discussed in Part I.[44] An approach was "econometric" if it involved using maximum likelihood or least squares methods to estimate the parameters of an equation or system of equations. The equation(s) and parameters were linked to, if they did not actually embody, a theoretical model of a Keynesian or neoclassical flavor, with the parameters representing important economic quantities or relationships. In the case of growth accounting, the implied or explicitly presented model was a model of the growth of the macroeconomy, including as a component an aggregate production function. The key parameters, as we have seen, were quantities like the marginal productivity of inputs, the rate of embodied technical change, and the rate of disembodied technical change. Further, the use of regression techniques resulted in estimates to which classical techniques of statistical inference could be applied, that is, hypothesis testing and the construction of confidence intervals. This inferential framework, which provided a means of conducting "formal" tests of important propositions related to growth theory (for example, the hypothesis of constant returns to scale) was often cited as the greatest advantage of the econometric approach. I suspect, however, that a tendency to favor "econometric" approaches to estimation, other things equal, was also a manifestation of an ongoing trend in economics at the time towards more and more technical mathematical methods, both in the expression of economic theory and the explication of and rationalization of statistical techniques.

[44] Examples of this usage of "econometric" in the empirical growth literature can be found in Griliches (1963a), Jorgenson (1988) and Barro (1999).

That is to say, estimating regressions was more fashionable than constructing index numbers.

These factors did not prove to be enough to establish the time series production function regression as a common tool for growth accounting. However, production function regressions, and even the Cobb–Douglas regression, did remain a part of research into the causes of growth and technical change in the last decades of the twentieth century. In the early 1960s, Zvi Griliches developed a new role in growth research for the Cobb–Douglas regression in its much maligned cross-section form. Over the next 30 years, he would become one of the most prominent practitioners and defenders of production function estimation and at the same time one of its most frank and careful critics.

Zvi Griliches, Growth Accounting, and the Cross-Section Cobb–Douglas Regression

Zvi Griliches was a Lithuanian Jew, born in 1930. Griliches was first exposed to neoclassical microeconomic theory and econometrics as a master's student in agricultural economics at the University of California in the early 1950s. He was attracted to the University of Chicago for his doctoral studies by a generous financial-aid offer, the presence of the Cowles Commission, and a strong program in agricultural economics led by Theodore Schultz and D. Gale Johnson. As a student in agricultural economics, he was exposed to the most up-to-date examples of the use of the Cobb–Douglas regression, and because of his interest in empirical applications of economics and his aptitude for mathematics, he took full advantage of the presence at the University of Chicago of some of the leading econometricians of the time. Thus, his graduate training left him with an appreciation for the potential of the Cobb–Douglas regression as an empirical tool in economics, but also an awareness of its limitations.[45]

Though trained as an agricultural economist, Griliches's chief research interest from his doctoral dissertation onward was the empirical investigation of the processes driving technical innovation and growth. During the late 1950s and throughout the 1960s, he published a series of influential papers based on what he called at the time an "alternative framework" for empirical research into the sources of economic growth, a framework based on the assumption that "changes in output are attributable to

[45] Further details of Griliches's early life and education are found in Krueger and Taylor (2000) and Nerlove (2001).

changes in the quantities and *qualities* of inputs, and to economies of scale, rather than 'technical change,' the production function itself remaining constant (at least over substantial stretches of time)." "The whole concept of a production 'function,'" he opined, "is not very useful if it is not a stable function, if there are very large unexplained shifts in it" (Griliches 1963b, 332, emphasis in the original).[46]

Griliches argued that the ever more carefully measured "residual" in the various studies of the sources of growth was actually the result of measurement errors: among other things, price indexes used to deflate input series were flawed and led to the understatement of improvements in input quality, important growth-enhancing inputs were left out of the calculations altogether, and inappropriate weights were used in aggregating inputs. Given correct identification and measurement of inputs and correct assumptions about the nature of the production function, the "residual" would all but disappear, and the sources of growth would be identified and quantified. As Griliches noted on at least one occasion (Griliches 1963b, 346), his emphasis on linking output increases to measurable improvements in the quality of inputs was an extension to all inputs of Solow's notion of the embodiment of technical improvement in new capital; however, Griliches had developed his research framework prior to the appearance of Solow's seminal articles on embodiment.[47]

In practice, Griliches's growth accounting exercises culminated in the calculation of a measure of total factor productivity growth that compared an output index to an index of input growth, in the manner of Kendrick or Denison. But for Griliches, the estimation of production functions played an important role in the design of the index of inputs, and he frequently defended his use of production functions for this purpose. In one paper, under the heading "Why Estimate Production Functions," Griliches explained:

> Econometric production function studies can be used to investigate the appropriate algebraic form for the assumed aggregate production function, the number and type of variables that should be included in the list of inputs and the appropriate way of measuring them, and what numerical values should be assigned to the coefficients to be attached to each of these variables. Even though these questions are basic to any attempt to allocate the observed growth in output to its various

46 Griliches's framework is developed formally in Griliches and Jorgenson (1966).

47 Griliches began to formulate his conceptual framework as a graduate student, following his first exposure to the phenomenon of the residual in one of Theodore Schultz's classes. See Schultz (1956, fn. 15), and Krueger and Taylor (2000, 181–82).

"causes," they are typically assumed away rather than investigated in most of the studies measuring productivity and technical change

(Griliches 1963b, 333).

And elsewhere he noted that:

Productivity, technical change, or "the residual" are usually computed residually, as part of some accounting framework. Because of the nature of the beast, it is impossible to test *accounting* frameworks statistically . . .. It is possible, however, to test some of the components of an accounting scheme separately if data which these concepts do not have to fit tautologically are used

(Griliches 1964, 371, emphasis in original).

So, for example, whether one should use arithmetic or geometric averaging in constructing the index of inputs depended on the elasticity of substitution of the aggregate production function, which could be estimated with a production function regression. The appropriate weights to use depended on the marginal productivities of the respective inputs. The conventional approach was to use factor shares as weights, which was correct if one assumed constant returns to scale and competitive equilibrium, but why not, instead, estimate these marginal productivities with a production function regression, which could also provide an estimate of the magnitude of any scale economies that might exist? Further, production function regressions could provide guidance concerning what additional inputs to include in an accounting framework and how best to measure them.[48] In short, Griliches was attracted to the fact that production function estimation was an "econometric" method, associated with a formal framework for using the numbers it produced to objectively "test" the sorts of assumption commonly used in growth accounting.

Griliches estimated his production functions using cross-section data, or in a few cases, panel data. He was not unaware of the many econometric criticisms of cross-section Cobb–Douglas regressions – indeed, quite the opposite. A master of econometric theory, many of his articles included careful analyses of how problems like misspecification of the form of the production function, errors in measuring the variables, or omission of variables would bias the estimated coefficients of production function regressions. Although these analyses often included treatments of such problems in general terms, using the algebraic derivations of the properties of estimators, they were almost invariably linked to particular applications,

[48] See Griliches (1967, 310).

with discussions of the likely seriousness and consequences of the problems in light of the data actually used in the application.[49]

While he pulled no punches in pointing out possible violations of the assumptions required for unbiased estimation of production functions, he clearly did think that applied econometricians should not let the best become an enemy of the good. As discussed in Chapter 5, a general message of Griliches's early article on "Specification Bias in Production Function Estimation" was that empirical work necessarily involved compromises and approximations, and the appropriate response to this reality was to attempt to understand the consequences of these compromises. A few years later, when discussing the potential for simultaneity bias in the estimation of production functions, he commented that "Given the data limitations and the special context of the problem, 'simple' least squares, while not optimal, may be 'good enough,'" referring readers to a recent discussion by statistician John Tukey of "the distinction between 'good' or 'useful' and 'optimal' procedures in data analysis" (Griliches 1963a, 421, fn. 2).[50] His goal was to aid rather than discourage those who would estimate production functions. Along with Griliches's willingness to tolerate deviations from the conditions required for unbiased estimation, however, came an insistence that results obtained under such circumstances be regarded as good but tentative steps on the way to something better. As he commented in summarizing the results of one of his production function studies, "None of these conclusions is very firmly established, and some may be subject to substantial bias, but the only known way of either confirming or disproving them is the slow and expensive but cumulative process of conducting additional studies of this type on different bodies of data" (Griliches 1964, 972).

In the early 1960s, Griliches presented a comprehensive application of his framework and methods designed to explain the sources of productivity growth in US agriculture between 1940 and 1960. Griliches's procedure had three main steps: (i) the individual time series measures of inputs used in the standard total factor productivity calculations were adjusted to better represent changes in input quality, (ii) an unrestricted cross-section Cobb–Douglas production function was estimated using the conventional list of

49 See, e.g., Griliches (1957), or the discussion of simultaneity bias in Griliches (1963a, 421–22).

50 Among other things, Tukey had advised that "if data analysis is to be well done, much of it must be a matter of judgment, and 'theory,' whether statistical or non-statistical, will have to guide, not command" (Tukey 1962, 10).

agricultural inputs, plus a measure of the educational attainment of the agricultural workforce, and (iii) the improved input measures were combined into an index of inputs, with weights taken from the estimated production function and an adjustment for scale economies of a magnitude indicated by the estimated production function.

Conventional growth accounting calculations indicated that total factor productivity in agriculture had increased by 48 percent between 1940 and 1960. Using Griliches's index of inputs reduced total factor productivity growth to 25 percent, and the adjustment for the scale economies indicated by his production function actually made it slightly negative, allowing Griliches to claim that "we may have succeeded in providing an explanation for what were previously unexplained increases in farm output" (Griliches 1963b, 346).

Griliches first presented his "Estimates of the Aggregate Agricultural Production Function from Cross-Sectional Data" in a separate article in the *Journal of Farm Economics*, opening the paper with a brief explanation of the role that production function estimation could play in the analysis of technical change and productivity growth. Has data set was based largely on information gathered in the 1950, 1945, and 1940 Censuses of Agriculture. Measures of the value of output, inputs, and wages were reported as averages per commercial farm for 68 "productivity regions," which were aggregations of contiguous counties judged to have relatively uniform farming conditions and practices. The output variable was the value of farm production in 1949. The census had reported information on the values of land and buildings in 1950, and estimates of the value of farm machinery came from the 1945 Census of Agriculture, adjusted for price change and the national increase in tractors per farm between 1945 and 1950. The value of livestock was the number of each kind of animal multiplied by its price. All these stock measures were converted to service flows using various assumptions about interest and depreciation. The United States Department of Agriculture (USDA) had collected data on expenditures on fertilizer and lime per farm, but for many states county-level data were not available, requiring the use of proportionality assumptions to create expenditure measures for the productivity regions in those states. These expenditures were added to an existing measure of expenditures on seed, plants, and irrigation.

To create a labor variable, state-level estimates of the average monthly agricultural wage were assigned to productivity regions, multiplied by 12 to put them on an annual basis, then divided into the total expenditure on hired workers reported in the Census of Agriculture, producing an estimate of man-years of hired labor. This labor variable was further adjusted to reflect the contributions of unpaid family workers and farm operators (who counted less if they were over 65 or also had off-farm jobs).

The 1950 Census of Population reported county-level data on the distribution of the rural farm population, aged 25 or over, across "years of education completed" categories. After aggregating these distributions to the "productivity region" level, Griliches created his average "education" per worker measure (quotes his) by weighting each "years of education completed" category by the average income in 1950 for all males 25 and over in that category, the assumption being that wage differences across these education classes roughly proxied productivity differences.

In a section on "Estimation Problems," Griliches defended his use of simple least squares and an unrestricted Cobb–Douglas regression of the log of value added on the logged input measures. It would have been possible to estimate the Cobb–Douglas coefficients using Klein's (1953) factor shares approach, he admitted, "but since this would have assumed equilibrium and constant returns to scale, it would have begged some of the most important questions we are interested in" (Griliches 1963a, 421). The directly estimated Cobb–Douglas regression was tractable, and fit the data – experiments with Constant Elasticity of Substitution (CES) and "transcendental" forms had led to no improvement in results. Griliches understood that least squares estimation could lead to simultaneous equations bias if farmers' input decisions were influenced by unmeasured factors that affected output, and were thus were part of the error term of the production function regression. He mentioned the argument that simultaneity was a minor problem for the estimation of agricultural production functions because weather shocks were the most important part of the error term, and were unrelated to the input decisions that had to be made well before harvest, but pointed out that this reasoning did not hold for harvest labor and for livestock and dairy farms in general. He placed more confidence in a defense of simple least squares based on the assumption that farmers tended to deviate substantially from profit-maximizing input choices (Griliches 1963a, 421).

Griliches also confronted one of the more persistent arguments against the use of cross-section Cobb–Douglas regressions. "If all firms faced the same prices, had the same production functions, and maximized profits, they would all be at the same point, and we could not estimate anything. Even if they are not all at the same point, it is important to explain why they are not" (Griliches 1963a, 422). Griliches argued that the cross-regional differences in agricultural wages found in the data reflected true

TABLE 1. AGGREGATE AGRICULTURAL PRODUCTION: 1949, U.S.—68 REGIONS (ALL VARIABLES ARE LOGARITHMS OF ORIGINAL VALUES UNLESS OTHERWISE SPECIFIED; UNITS—AVERAGES PER COMMERCIAL FARM)

Regression Number	Coefficients of								
	X_1 (livestock expense)	X_2 (other current expense)	X_3 (machinery)	X_4 (land)	X_5 (buildings)	X_6 (man-years)	E (education)	R^2	Sum of coefficients (excluding E)
U17	.169 (.023)	.121 (.032)	.359 (.048)	.170 (.033)	.094 (.044)	.449 (.072)		.977	1.362
R6	.140 (.025)	.111 (.031)	.325 (.049)	.167 (.032)	.075 (.042)	.524 (.076)	.431 (.181)	.979	1.352

The numbers in parentheses are the calculated standard errors of the respective coefficients.
X_1—log of (purchases of livestock and feed and interest on livestock investment)
X_2—log of (purchases of seed and plants, fertilizer and lime, and cost of irrigation water purchased)
X_3—log of (purchases of gasoline and petroleum fuels, repairs of tractors and other machinery, machine hire, and depreciation and interest on machinery investment)
X_4—log of interest on value of land
X_5 log of (building depreciation and interest)
X_6 log of average full-time equivalent number of workers per commercial farm
E—log of the average education of the rural farm population weighted by total U.S. income by education class weights; not per commercial farm but per man
Dependent variable—log of value of farm production per commercial farm

Figure 6.2 Zvi Griliches's estimates of an aggregate agricultural production function, produced using cross-section data

differences in the price of labor, and that deviations from profit-maximizing input choices likely occurred for different reasons in different regions. This would lead to differences in chosen levels of inputs that could accurately identify the production function coefficients.

Figure 6.2 shows Griliches's presentation of his "main results," of which he highlighted three features: the education variable had a statistically significant coefficient, the estimated coefficient of machinery was larger than the factor share of machinery, and the regression indicated substantial economies of scale. He interpreted the significant education coefficient as "a finding of an influence of the level of formal education of the labor force on the level of output holding other inputs constant."

The table reproduced above as Figure 6.2 appeared again a few months later in the article "The Sources of Measured Productivity Growth: United States Agriculture, 1940–1960" (Griliches 1963b), now as part of a comprehensive description and application of Griliches's "alternative" growth accounting framework. Though much of the article was devoted to other aspects of Griliches's framework such as constructing better deflators and more realistic measures of depreciation for the capital inputs, there was also further discussion of these cross-section Cobb–Douglas regression estimates, focused on those aspects of the estimates that were particularly important in the implementation of the new framework, and that showed the benefit of supplementing the index of output over inputs approach to growth accounting with information obtained from production function estimation.

For example, the estimated coefficients of the input variables, which were the theoretically correct weights to use in creating a combined index of inputs, did not line up that well with the factor shares of the inputs, which were the weights conventionally used under the assumption of competitive equilibrium. In particular, the labor coefficient was below labor's share, and the machinery coefficient well above machinery's share. But were the production function estimates reliable? Griliches pointed out that agricultural economists had long believed that the marginal product of labor in agriculture was well below the wage quoted in agricultural statistics, and the return to capital above conventional mortgage rates. He also cited empirical evidence from a variety of sources that was consistent with the message of his production function estimates. The majority of agricultural production function studies based on farm-level data produced estimates of labor's productivity substantially below the local agricultural wage. Migration out of agriculture in 1950 equaled 5.2 percent of the total farm population, and had remained high since. The ratio of power and machinery inputs to labor inputs increased by 74 percent over the 1950s, while the farm wage rose only 9 percent relative to machinery prices. Although this could be explained as the result of an incredibly high elasticity of substitution, it was more likely due to an adjustment to the disequilibrium situation indicated by his estimated production function for 1949.

Griliches also saw support in other data sources for his surprisingly large estimate of the scale economies in agriculture. He cited a survey of 43 production functions estimated with farm-level data, in which 36 had coefficients whose sums exceeded 1.0. The existence of economies of scale in agriculture in 1949 implied that the distribution of farms by size should have shifted in favor of larger farms since 1950, and a study of the distribution of farm sizes in 1959 showed that this was the case. Finally, economies of scale in agriculture should lead to a rise in the price of agricultural land, the agricultural input with the lowest supply elasticity, and since the late 1940s the price of land had risen substantially relative to the prices of other agricultural inputs.

In 1964 Griliches published the results of another Cobb–Douglas regression for agriculture, this one based on panel data. This paper reflected two important components of Griliches's blueprint for integrating production function estimation into research on the sources of growth: it used new data in order to check and refine the conclusions of his previous production function estimates, and it tested a hypothesis regarding a potential growth enhancing input not considered in previous growth accounting exercises.

Griliches adapted the model developed by Hoch (1962) and Mundlak (1961) for use with farm-level data to data aggregated to the level of 39 states or groups of states for the years 1949, 1954, and 1959.[51] To the list of inputs he had used in his cross-section regression, Griliches added the new, experimental, variable, "public expenditures on agricultural research and extension." He compiled it from the budgets of state agricultural experiment stations, defining it as the average of expenditures one and six years prior to the year for which output was recorded, in hopes of testing the hypothesis that resources invested in creating and disseminating knowledge influenced economic growth.

Before presenting the Cobb–Douglas estimates, Griliches tested his assumption of a Cobb–Douglas form for the production function against a CES function, using the now conventional regression of the log of value added per worker on the log of the wage to estimate the elasticity of substitution. Reminding readers that this approach to estimating the CES production function assumed "competitive product and factor markets and equilibrium, correct measurement of all the variables, and an exogenous wage rate," he estimated the regression using various time periods, with and without year dummies, in a distributed lag specification, in first differenced form, and in an instrumental variables specification that used past wage to instrument for current wage. Surveying the array of results, he saw few credible estimates of the elasticity of substitution that were significantly different from unity, and concluded that "there does not seem to be any strong prima facie evidence against the Cobb–Douglas form."

When using the Cobb–Douglas form, Griliches tested, and failed to reject, the hypothesis that the coefficients of the production function were constant over the period of his study, and concluded that these coefficient estimates confirmed the "major findings" of his previous study. The education variable was again statistically significant, and there was again

[51] The data had, for the most part, been assembled by the United States Department of Agriculture (USDA).

evidence of significant economies of scale, with the sum of the relevant coefficients centering on 1.2. Using past input values as instrumental variables for current input values in order to correct for possible simultaneous equations bias did not much change the estimates.

There were some differences, however. The finding of the earlier cross-section study that labor's marginal product was less than, and machinery's more than, their respective costs was not confirmed. Griliches made no effort to square this with the external evidence of changing factor proportions in agriculture that had played a prominent role in his earlier paper. He did, however, again employ the strategy of citing external evidence to bolster the credibility of his results, this time his finding that the implied marginal product of fertilizer was well above its cost:

> Farmers have not remained idle in the face of such a disequilibrium. Between 1949 and 1959 fertilizer consumption grew at the rate of 7.4 per cent per year (more than doubling fertilizer consumption during this period) and continued to grow at the rate of 5.6 percent per year between 1959 and 1962. The estimated equilibrium gap (VMP/Factor price) has declined from about 5 in 1949 to 2.7 in 1959 and 2.4 in 1962
>
> (Griliches 1964, 968).

The coefficient of the novel "research and extension expenditures" variable was positive and statistically significant, surprisingly so, Griliches commented, given the crudeness of the measure. The estimated coefficient was also very stable across specifications estimated using different subsamples. Griliches used the coefficient estimate in some rough calculations of a marginal product of research and extension spending, and concluded that even if agricultural output were valued at half of its market value, the social rate of return to research and extension spending in agriculture was in the neighborhood of 300 percent.

Griliches demurred from using his new production function estimates to conduct a thorough analysis of growth similar to the one presented in Griliches (1963b). He did note, however, that if one simply "used the estimated coefficients ... and data on input and output change over time, it is possible to account for *all* of the observed growth in agricultural output without invoking the unexplained concept of (residual) technical change" (Griliches 1964, 970, emphasis in original), with one third of the growth in agricultural output being attributed to the previously neglected public expenditures on agricultural research.

By 1965, Griliches was at work applying his analytical framework for growth accounting to the manufacturing sector. He presented a "first progress report" on this work in October of that year to an NBER-sponsored conference on production relations. The empirical production function in Griliches's conference paper was estimated using a cross-section data set in which each observation in the sample pertained to an industry in a particular state, and the estimating equation was

$$log\,(V/L)_{ij} = a_0 + a\ log\,(K/L)_{ij} + h\ log\ L_{ij} + \sum_n \beta_n Z_{nij} + d_i + d_j + u_{ij}$$

where i indexed 38 different industries in the sample and j the states. V was value added, L a measure of man-hours, and K a measure of capital services; the Z variables represented various input quality measures, d_i and d_j were coefficients of the dummy variables for industries and states, and u_{ij} was the error term. The equation was derived from the basic unrestricted Cobb–Douglas regression by dividing through by L, so that α was the capital coefficient and *h* measured scale economies.

To create labor quality variables for inclusion in the Z vector, Griliches made use of the 1960 Census of Population, which reported for each of the sample industries in each state the median age of all employees, females as a fraction of all employees, and whites as a fraction of all male employees. The 1960 census did not report state-level information on the distribution of education across employees in each industry, but it did report the distribution of employees across nine occupation categories. Griliches used this information to construct an analog of the education-based labor quality measures used in his previous studies, a weighted average of the mean income for each occupation category, with weights equal to the proportion of the industry's labor force in the state in each occupational category.[52]

Griliches also included in the Z vector a proxy variable for the age of the capital stock, defined as the ratio of the net capital stock to the gross capital stock, the difference between the two being the census respondent's estimate of accumulated capital depreciation. If newer capital was more productive, as posited by the embodiment hypothesis, then this variable would have a positive coefficient. The chief flaw of the variable, Griliches explained, and the one that made this test of the embodiment hypothesis a weak one, was that census respondents had valued capital at its historic cost. This meant that inflation in capital prices would make each dollar's

[52] Griliches used the mean occupational incomes for the south region for observations from southern states, and the mean occupational incomes in the rest of the nation for observations from non-southern states.

worth of old capital appear more productive than a dollar's worth of newer capital, thus masking improvements in capital quality over time due to technical change.

The paper's main estimates were obtained using simple least squares, and were therefore prone to simultaneous equations bias. Griliches experimented rather unsuccessfully with several approaches to avoiding this problem, the least problematic of which appeared to be the inclusion of the dummy variables for industry and state, which would eliminate the portion of simultaneous equations bias due to what Griliches called the "systematic components of the correlation between the disturbance and the independent variables."[53] Still, the use of state and industry dummies also increased any bias due to errors in measurement of the variables. Ultimately, he argued, the collection of longer panels of data was the best strategy for dealing with the simultaneity problem.

Griliches conducted a variety of tests of the Cobb–Douglas assumption of a unitary elasticity of substitution, the results of which led him to conclude that the Cobb–Douglas form was appropriate, "at least for these data" (Griliches 1967, 276).[54] He was more concerned with his assumption that the production function parameters were the same for all industries. In his own defense, he pointed out that a statistical test of the null hypothesis – the slope coefficients were the same in all industries – failed to reject, but admitted that the small number of degrees of freedom for this test made it weak. He also used the graph in Figure 6.3 to argue that allowing a different intercept for each industry's production function (that is, including industry dummy variables in the regression) would ameliorate bias due to an incorrect assumption of common slope coefficients across industry.

[53] In the absence of the state and industry dummies, differences across observations in the unmeasured factors that affected output (which would be reflected by differences in the value of the residual of the production function regression) might also lead to differences across state-industry cells in firms' optimal choices of inputs, giving rise to a correlation between the residual and the measured levels of inputs. However, the inclusion of dummy variables for industry and state would remove from the regression residual all differences in unmeasured factors that were common to a particular industry nationwide, or common to all the industries in a particular state. These shared (across industry or state) differences in unmeasured factors were the "systematic components of the correlation" to which Griliches referred.

[54] This section of the paper included an extensive review of econometric issues raised by attempts to estimate the Constant Elasticity of Substitution (CES) function with either cross-section or time series data, and an explanation of Griliches's own reasons for preferring cross-section to time series versions of the CES regression.

FIGURE 1

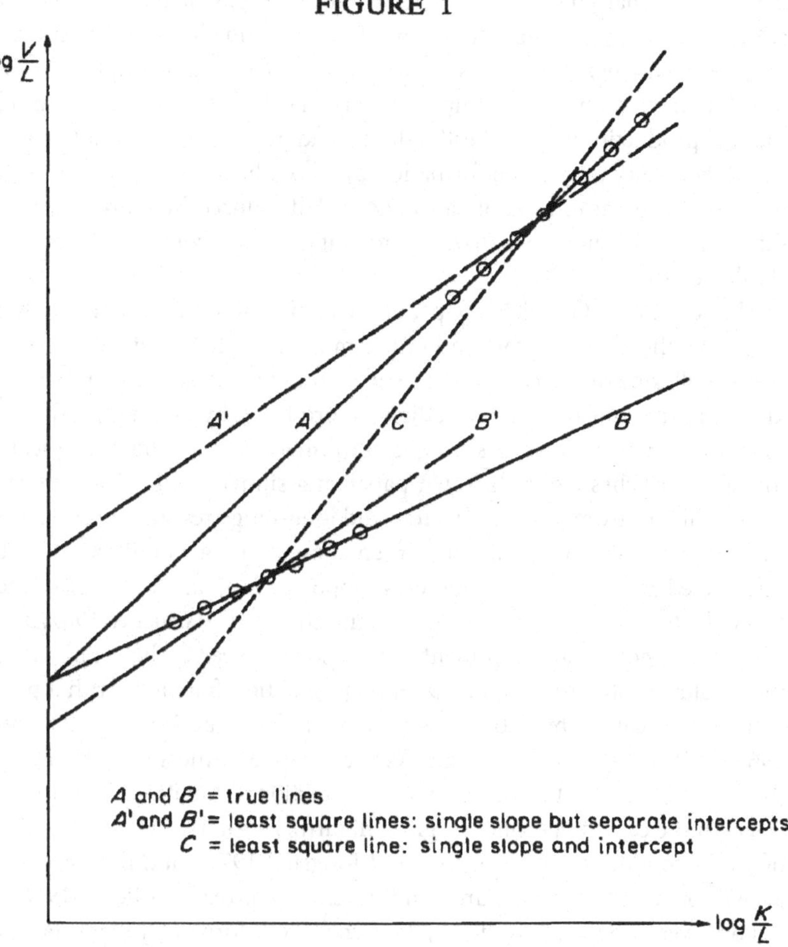

Figure 6.3 Griliches's graphical justification of one of the many econometric tricks he employed to improve the reliability of estimates produced by the cross-section Cobb–Douglas regression

In the paper's introduction, Griliches had used the phrase "fishing expedition" to describe the research he was reporting on, and consistent with that description, he presented estimates from a plethora of Cobb–Douglas specifications: with and without various sets of industry and geographical dummies, with an industry-level capital intensity variable instead of the industry dummies, and so on. His presentation also included the most detailed account to date of his growth accounting framework (that is, a framework that allowed for the possibility of scale economies, deviation of marginal productivities from factor payments, economies of scale, errors in measuring improvements in input quality, and the omission of growth-enhancing variables) as well as the role to be played by production function estimation in implementing that framework.[55] He admitted that the production function estimates he had presented would not provide all the necessary pieces of information to fill out his framework, but he did make use of them in a set of calculations that reduced by more than two-thirds the measured residual in manufacturing from 1947 to 1960 (Griliches 1964, 308–19).

The reaction to Griliches's paper at the conference was a mixture of high praise for the general effort and criticism of the details, but this reflected the overall tone of the conference, which combined deep concern with the known limitations of and contradictions produced by existing production function estimates with a strong commitment to pushing the research forward. Griliches closed his own paper in a similar spirit: "The above is an installment from a relatively large and long-range research program. As such it has no clear beginning or end. Most of the findings must be interpreted as maintained hypotheses supported by data recently examined and to be tested further on data now being collected" (Griliches 1967, 319).

This was not an idle comment. The following year Griliches published the results of estimating Cobb–Douglas production functions with a panel data set created by combining data from the 1954, 1958, and 1963 Censuses of Manufacturing (Griliches 1968). And he continued for the rest of his life to use production function estimation as a tool to research the causes of economic growth, further exploring the contribution of scale economies (e.g., Griliches and Ringstad 1971), and the impact on growth of spending on research and development (e.g., Griliches 1986).

Four years before his death, Griliches and former student Jacques Mairesse wrote an essay analyzing the simultaneity problem as it pertained to production function estimation, and providing a detailed critique of the various econometric procedures that had recently been employed to solve it. All were found wanting. But Griliches and Mairesse concluded, "in spite of all these reservations, the production function framework that we have been analyzing over the last two decades has its uses. It is a major tool for asking questions about rates of technological change, about economies of scale, rates of return to R&D ... and more, whose answer may not be all

55 The conference paper was not published until 1967, however, after the appearance of Griliches and Jorgenson (1966), the definitive formal treatment of Griliches's growth accounting framework.

that sensitive to the biases discussed here. Moreover, we are unlikely to give up this framework just because it is imperfect" (Griliches and Mairesse 1999, 24). I cite this statement for two reasons: First, it shows the persistence of an attitude found in Griliches's first (1957) paper on production function regressions – economists must work with flawed tools, the production function regression is a flawed but useful tool, and it will be more useful if its flaws are well understood. Second, it was an objectively true statement, in that the cross-section production function had become an important general tool for empirical research into economic growth, and would remain so into the twenty-first century.[56]

[56] For example, Griliches (1979), explaining what he called "the production function approach" to the estimation of the contribution of research and development activities to economic growth was cited over 400 times in Web of Science journals between 2001 and 2010. See also Syverson (2001, 332) on the continuing use of the cross-section production function to estimate the weights to be used in constructing outputs over inputs productivity indices.

PART III

CONCLUSION

7

On the Success of the Cobb–Douglas Regression

This book has documented the story of the Cobb–Douglas regression from its early years as an innovative and controversial statistical procedure to the point at which it was coming to be a widely accepted general-purpose tool in empirical economics. In introducing the Cobb–Douglas regression, Douglas was motivated by a broader idea: that stable, quantifiable relationships between the inputs to and outputs of production processes existed and could be discovered through the application of regression analysis to statistical data, and that knowledge of such relationships was relevant to important questions of economic theory and policy. For economists of the early twentieth century, this idea was also innovative and controversial. Douglas used linear regression analysis to measure relationships between inputs and outputs, and embraced the connection seen by other economists between his regression equation and the neoclassical concept of the production function. These initial decisions ultimately helped shape the larger set of techniques developed over the next several decades to explore the research questions embodied in Douglas's broader idea. By the end of the twentieth century, attempts to measure input/output relationships with statistical data had become common, and almost always involved the estimation of the parameters of an assumed production function using a least squares regression procedure.

Why was this procedure, with all its acknowledged flaws, so successful? An identification of the factors that contributed to the success of the Cobb–Douglas regression might suggest more general insights into the factors that determine the success or failure of innovative research techniques in the social and perhaps natural sciences. In the previous chapters, I have occasionally pointed out events and circumstances that I believed help secure the acceptance by a significant number of economists of the Cobb–Douglas regression. In this chapter I synthesize and expand upon those observations, and suggest some more general implications to which they point. My observations and conclusions here are more speculative than those in the rest of the book, and are intended more as prompts for thought and discussion than definitive pronouncements.

Let me reiterate the definition of success with which I began: I call an innovation "successful" when it comes to be used by a large number of researchers, and a significant number of researchers who do not actually use the tool believe that it can produce credible knowledge. This broad consensus on the value of the tool should persist for a while – decades, not years – as evidenced by a steady and substantial stream of peer-reviewed or otherwise professionally approved published research in which the tool is used.

One seemingly obvious candidate for a factor affecting the success of an innovative research technique would be whether that technique produced demonstrably correct answers to the questions that it was designed to address. I do not believe that this had much, if anything, to do with the success of the Cobb–Douglas regression. It is important, however, that over the period covered by this book, applications of the Cobb–Douglas regression produced numbers that were in line with economists' beliefs about the entities its users claimed the regression could measure. In many, though definitely not all, applications, the estimated marginal products of inputs widely believed to be productive were in fact positive, but not outlandishly large, and estimates of the returns to scale of production processes fell within reasonable ranges. Had this seldom or never been the case, I believe that the technique would have been abandoned. The ability to produce (in some instances) such plausible results was a necessary, though not sufficient, condition for the procedure to be widely adopted.

THE LINK TO NEOCLASSICAL ECONOMICS

Another factor that I think was important to the ultimate success of the Cobb–Douglas regression is the fact that the knowledge that it was designed to produce was particularly important to the neoclassical paradigm, which was growing in influence in the decades following the introduction of the technique. The idea of a stable relationship between quantities of inputs employed in production and quantities of output produced was central to the classical economics of the nineteenth century, but it was even more fundamental to neoclassical economics. The marginal productivity theory of distribution posited a much tighter connection between the "laws of production" and the "laws of distribution" than did classical theory, and the idea that those laws of production could be represented by a mathematically expressed "production function" was a key part of the eventually successful movement within neoclassical economics to make mathematics the language of economic theory. By the 1930s, Douglas had linked his regression technique to neoclassical economics in its mathematical mode and its marginal productivity theory of distribution, and had accepted the label "production function" for what the regression was estimating. The neoclassical econometricians reacting to Douglas's research placed more emphasis on this link than did Douglas, making it an important goal of empirical production research to establish more rigorously the relationship between the estimates produced by Douglas's regression and the theoretical production function concept associated with the Walrasian version of marginal productivity theory.

The initial uses of the regression by agricultural economists were not associated with the marginal productivity theory of distribution. Instead, for them, the production function was a tool for prescribing efficiency or diagnosing inefficiency in the allocation of resources. Still, the concept of efficiency that motivated their research was one that emerged from marginalist modes of analysis and neoclassical welfare economics, particularly when the regression was being used to diagnose efficiency in the social allocation of resources by comparing estimated marginal productivities to factor prices. With the successful introduction of the CES production function and the subsequent development of empirical strategies for estimating the parameters of more general production function forms, the relationship between neoclassical theory and the pursuit of Douglas's idea changed. For many of these new procedures, one was required to accept that the equilibrium described by the marginal productivity theory of distribution was approximately true in order to accept the results of the procedure.

Hence, one factor explaining the success of the Cobb–Douglas regression was its link to a paradigm that was growing in strength, a link that was not particularly important to Douglas or Cobb as they initially developed the procedure. Put another way, I would argue that had the neoclassical paradigm declined in importance starting in the mid-1930s, eclipsed perhaps by a more aggregate approach inspired by Keynesianism or the older classical economics, and/or by something closer to what the institutionalist movement hoped for, the Cobb–Douglas regression would have largely disappeared from economic research.[1] The more general

[1] Rutherford (2011, chapter 1) is a good description of the goals of the institutionalist movement in twentieth-century economics.

conceptualizations of Douglas's idea in the 1960s and 1970s based on applications of duality theory would certainly not have occurred.

This is not to say that a strong connection to a flourishing paradigm is necessary to the success of empirical innovations in economics. The development of index numbers as tools for measuring changes in the general level of prices of a diverse set of goods predated the rise of neoclassical economics, and although neoclassical theory provided economists with new tools for evaluating competing approaches to the construction of price indexes and interpreting the evidence they produced, the tool was widely accepted and used by non-neoclassical economists in the twentieth century, and one strongly suspects that it would have continued to be used had the neoclassical approach been abandoned.

In studying the success or failure of research innovations, it can thus be useful to look at the relationship between the innovation and the goals, heuristics, and future trajectories of the paradigm(s) present in the scientific community into which it is introduced, or to various research programs operating within the paradigm(s). Specifically, it is worth examining the extent to which the fundamental assumptions and heuristics of some paradigm must be accepted for the information produced by the technique to be considered valid, and the extent to which the innovation is perceived to be useful in answering the questions that are the subject of high-priority research programs within the paradigm.

FLEXIBILITY OR ADAPTABILITY

Another factor contributing to the success of the Cobb–Douglas regression was its flexibility or adaptability. The statistical procedure first performed by Cobb and Douglas – a linear regression of the log of some output measure on the log of input measures – came to be used by other economists in ways that Douglas had never used it, to answer questions that Douglas had not pursued while using it. But even if they applied the regression to different types of data, or included longer and/or different lists of inputs as independent variables, these subsequent users clearly perceived themselves to be employing the technique that Douglas had introduced – they referred to Douglas's papers, and called the mathematical representation of a production function that underlay their statistical procedure a "Cobb–Douglas production function."

With the Cobb–Douglas regression, a variety of questions on the research agenda of twentieth-century economics could be answered with what was basically the same statistical procedure. The history of the technique shows that this flexibility increased its ability to survive in the face of criticism. The most coherent and thorough critiques of the method were aimed at particular versions of the method, that is, not at the Cobb–Douglas regression in general, but at a particular use of the regression, with a particular type of data, to address a particular set of questions. Many elements of such critiques were moot when the procedure was being applied to a different type of data (e.g., farm-level data rather than industry-level data) or its estimated parameters were being brought to bear on a different question (e.g., what share of economic growth was attributable to growth in labor and capital, rather than whether the marginal productivity theory held at the level of the manufacturing sector).

Historians and sociologists of science have demonstrated that it is common for researchers to come up with ingenious ways to adapt the existing concepts and research techniques of their field such that they can be effectively used to address questions that they were not originally designed to address.[2] It seems apparent, however, that not all newly introduced research tools will prove equally prone to adaptation in this sense, and the general question of what makes a tool a good candidate for adaptation seems one worth considering. In the case of the Cobb–Douglas regression, I believe that certain aspects of the technique itself combined with certain features of mid-twentieth-century economics to increase the likelihood that it would end up being seen as a general-purpose research tool.

To understand why the Cobb–Douglas regression came to be adapted to serve a number of purposes, the first thing to consider is the statistical method of linear regression itself. Although at the time of Cobb and Douglas's article, linear regression was still rarely used in economic research, the procedure is easy to understand and explain graphically or algebraically, and provides an intuitively sensible way of summarizing the relationships between variables. Also, explanations of it were available in the standard textbooks on statistics for economists introduced in the late 1920s. A number of historical studies of the spread of new research methods and devices have emphasized the necessity of face-to-face tutelage of new users by the original innovators and early adapters (e.g., Shapin and Schaffer 1985; Kaiser 2005). However, this potential barrier to dissemination was hardly an issue with the Cobb–Douglas regression. An economist armed with a statistics text could apply the simple least squares

[2] A good recent example is Kaiser's (2005) study of the spread of the Feynman diagram as a research tool in physics.

algorithm to Douglas's original time series data and reproduce his results, or, as with J. M. Clark and Mendershausen, experiment by altering the estimating equation and recalculating the results.

The Cobb–Douglas regression also became a good candidate for adaptation because of the relationship it was designed to measure, that is, the quantitative relationship between factors of production and the amount of output produced. Interest in this relationship had a long history in economics. Important debates between the classical economists hinged on differences over assumptions about the nature of the relationship, and with the emergence and development of marginalist/neoclassical theories, knowledge of the characteristics of the "production function" arguably took on even greater importance. In the marginal productivity theory of distribution, these characteristics helped determine the pattern of income distribution, and neoclassical concepts of efficiency in the allocation of resources were defined in terms of those characteristics. So, empirically derived knowledge of the nature of the production function was relevant to a number of fairly independent sets of questions (What input mixes should farmers employ, and do they seem to be allocating resources efficiently? Is the manufacturing sector competitive? Which industries/sectors of the economy are subject to increasing returns to scale?), which made a method of empirically grounding that knowledge potentially interesting to a wide range of economists.

Also relevant to the adaptability of Douglas's procedure was the fact that by the early decades of the twentieth century, differences in approach among the marginalist pioneers had given rise to several varieties of neoclassical economics. One difference between the varieties was the level of aggregation at which theorizing took place. John Bates Clark was comfortable applying marginal analysis to an assumed aggregate production function, while at the other end of the spectrum Leon Walras and his followers built their theories on the analysis of the choices of individual firms and consumers, assuming a distinct production function for each good. In between, those working in the theoretical tradition established by Alfred Marshall viewed the "industry" – a collection of similar firms making similar products and characterized by a single production function – as a fruitful unit of analysis.

The middle decades of the twentieth century also saw a steady increase in the quantity of data available to economists. These data might pertain to any of a number of levels of aggregation, reporting totals for "industries" or "sectors," or for regional or national economies, or even for individual firms or farms, and they often allowed the creation of defensible measures of "output" or "inputs" tailored to the reported level of aggregation. The heterogeneity within the neoclassical tradition meant that whatever the level of aggregation at which the data were reported, there would be economists whose concept of the production function was such that it seemed plausible to them that Douglas's regression procedure, applied to those data, would produce useful knowledge. The flexibility of the production function concept itself, then, invited variation in the ways that others would alter and apply Douglas's procedure for estimating a production function.

Finally, in the decades following the period covered by this book, another sort of flexibility in the production function concept contributed to further adaptations of the production function regression. By the 1970s, research and pedagogy in economics was dominated by neoclassical modes of analysis, and the production function was a foundational concept in the core economic theories taught to all Ph.D. economists. This makes it unsurprising that economists also developed a tendency to reconceptualize social processes as production processes characterized by production functions, that is, as processes through which some sort of "output" was being created through the transformation of "inputs." The last decades of the twentieth century found economists routinely extending application of the production function metaphor to education, to criminal activity and the prevention of criminal activity, and to technological innovation, just to name a few examples. And where the production function metaphor was applied, the production function regression soon followed as a means of estimating the parameters of the assumed function, along with careful consideration of how one might actually measure the outputs and inputs of the social process to which the concept was being applied. The case of the "education production function" is illustrative: In theory, the output of the educational process is the "human capital" created in students, and the inputs are things like the labor of teachers, the flow of capital services from school facilities and supplies, latent characteristics of the students themselves, and so on. Output is commonly measured using standardized test scores, but sometimes by the post-schooling wages of the students. A variety of approaches to defining and measuring inputs has been employed, with a basic approach being to regress the output measure on per pupil spending on teachers, per pupil spending on physical facilities, and some measure of the family incomes of the students.[3]

[3] Bowles (1970) shows how economists were thinking about and estimating education production functions in the years immediately following the introduction of the concept.

In sum, the case of the Cobb–Douglas regression suggests that one thing to consider in understanding why a research tool becomes a success is its adaptability. This depends not only on characteristics of the innovation itself, like its complexity or cost of use, but also on aspects of the field into which it is introduced at the time it is introduced, including popular conceptual frameworks, theoretical models, and high-priority research questions.

RHETORIC

The surveys in Part I of Douglas's published accounts of his production research reveal two discernably different rhetorical styles: the rhetoric of the objective scientist and the rhetoric of the advocate. In his "objective" mode, Douglas provided long and detailed descriptions of his data-construction procedures, with associated assessments of shortcomings in the resulting samples or series and how those shortcomings might bias estimates produced by the regression. Statistical results that seemed to undermine Douglas's claims for the regression were duly noted along with those that seemed supportive. When in his "advocate" mode, however, Douglas tended to discount or ignore negative evidence, at times even treating evidence he had once identified as negative as if it always had, and should have been, regarded as positive evidence. The rhetoric of the objective scientist is more prevalent in the earlier writings, while the rhetoric of the advocate is more common in the later articles, especially where Douglas is summarizing the past achievements of the research program, but both are often found in the same article. Douglas the advocate is most obvious in passages in which he is defending his procedure against critics, particularly Mendershausen. In such passages Douglas, like a good defense attorney, selects the evidence he wishes to emphasize, and spins that evidence to make it seem as favorable as possible. He concentrates most on what appear to be the weakest arguments of his adversaries, converts others into straw men, and ignores those for which he has no good response.

Whether writing in his objective mode or his advocacy mode, however, Douglas was a skilled communicator. He provided clear explanations of complicated procedures, and was able to describe relatively technical

Harris (2010) reveals the centrality of the concept to modern economic research in education.

matters using nontechnical language, as when, for example, describing how some deficiency in the data would lead his measures to overstate or understate some quantity, which would in turn cause bias in an estimated regression coefficient. He could choose words in a way that made descriptions of dry topics (like which industries were far from the regression line and why) less tedious than they might have been. As an advocate, Douglas was persuasive in the way he constructed arguments. He had an appealing knack for sentence construction, word choice, and metaphor.

In Part I, I also argued that the authors of the articles that contained the most damaging criticisms of Douglas's production research, Mendershausen (1938) and Marschak and Andrews (1944), made rhetorical choices that considerably diminished the immediate impact of their criticisms. Mendershausen used jargon that few economists of the time understood, and a statistical technique that would never be widely taught. To fully understand the criticisms of Marschak and Andrews, readers had to make their way through equations, notation, and mathematical manipulations that most economists of the 1940s, or the 1950s for that matter, were unequipped to decipher without substantial effort, if at all. There were few intuitive verbal explanations of why the key mathematical results were what they were.

Did any of this matter to the success of the Cobb–Douglas regression? I think that perhaps it did. Douglas's desire to "make economics a progressive science," that is, one with a strong empirical component, was widely shared in the economics profession during the interwar period. Further, the subset of those who hoped that the empirical component of economics would be built on what Douglas called the "valuable theoretical scaffolding" of neoclassicism was growing in number. I would propose that this created a significant group of economists who were not directly engaged in production research, or econometrics, or even advanced empirical research, but who were nonetheless excited about the potential of Douglas's research, and hopeful that his empirical methods would prove capable of producing useful knowledge. To use the phrasing of Haidt (2012), these economists, when considering Douglas's research and his claims, took an attitude of "Can I believe this?" rather than the more skeptical attitude of "Must I believe this?" And I think it worth considering the possibility that Douglas won more of these people over than would have someone with less skill in writing, and less willingness to bring the rhetorical style of the courtroom into a scientific debate. Arguably, Douglas's tendency to mix the two rhetorical styles described above increased his persuasive power: When writing in the objective mode, Douglas conveyed the (correct) impression that he was a careful, thorough, and competent empirical researcher with a good command of economics and statistics, which made readers more likely to accept summaries of his research and defenses of his regression procedure that were rendered in the style of an advocate.

It is reasonable to submit that with time, and with the growing sophistication of the mathematical and statistical training received by economics Ph.D. students, enough economists would have had the patience and skill to comprehend, and then communicate in a more accessible way, compelling criticisms like those of Mendershausen and Marschak and Andrews, so that Douglas's claims for his procedure would be assessed on their merits, regardless of how he expressed them. Phelps Brown (1957) did, after all, present many of Menderhausen's criticisms in a more accessible way, and the very damaging criticism of Douglas's cross-section method first made by Tinbergen's (1942) was made by others in subsequent years in more widely read journals. But I think the fact that the most comprehensive and serious critiques of the Cobb–Douglas regression were inaccessible to most economists at the time they first appeared bought valuable time for the technique. By the late 1950s, when the criticisms were being reiterated in a clearer way to an audience more able to understand them, responses to those criticisms had already been developed by the statistically sophisticated agricultural economists who had embraced the Cobb–Douglas regression. They had carefully delineated the circumstances under which the problems identified by Douglas's critics were more or less serious, identified interesting applications of the regression for which those problems appeared to be of little concern, and were developing strategies, for example, the use of panel data or instrumental variables, for mitigating them. By the time that Phelps Brown (1957) attacked the Cobb–Douglas regression as it had been used by Douglas, he was fighting the previous war.

ALLIES

I believe that another important reason for the success of the Cobb–Douglas regression is that, during the fifteen years or so after Douglas published his last original study using the regression, while challenges to Douglas's production research were increasing in number and seriousness, that is, during a time when the Cobb–Douglas regression might have largely disappeared from the economics literature, the new technique attracted a particular type of ally.

As has been documented, responses to Douglas's innovation were many and varied. Some rejected it completely, arguing that nothing of value could be learned from Douglas's results or from further applications of his technique. One subgroup among those responding in this way included those who believed that neoclassical theory was an inappropriate theoretical framework for the analysis of production and distribution, so that an empirical tool embodying neoclassical concepts could only be misleading. Another subgroup accepted neoclassical theory, but believed that the concepts of that theory, by their nature, could not be measured using statistical techniques. A third subgroup accepted both neoclassical theory and the desirability of doing statistical research guided by that theory, but believed Douglas's method to be so flawed as to be irredeemable.

A second type of response came from those I labelled the "friendly critics." They might suggest modifications to the method to correct problems that they had identified, or describe a type of data set (perhaps not yet in existence) from which the method could obtain useful and meaningful results. But these friendly critics never used the method in their own research in any serious or sustained way.

I would argue that the reactions of Earl Heady and Zvi Griliches to the Cobb–Douglas regression represents a third type of response, one that could perhaps also be attributed to Robert Solow. Like many of the "friendly critics," Heady and Griliches both had a sophisticated understanding of the theoretical and statistical issues raised by attempts to estimate production functions with the Cobb–Douglas regression. Unlike those critics, however, Heady and Griliches went beyond simply voicing enthusiasm for the idea of production function estimation, and consistently used the regression in their own research. They defended their own applications of the method, and advocated its use by others. They judiciously discussed the preexisting criticisms of the method, while developing credible arguments as to why these criticisms did not apply to their own applications of the technique, or at least not with enough force to rob their results of usefulness. And accompanying their technical economic and econometric arguments in defense of the method were expressions of what might be called articles of faith: first, that the only way to realize the promising potential of the empirical production function research program was through the repeated application of an as-yet imperfect (but improving) method to as-yet imperfect (but improving) data; and second, that the accumulating results of these repeated applications of the method under less than ideal circumstances would somehow contribute to a better understanding of production relations.[4]

In my own reading and research in the history of economics, I have seen this clear-eyed but optimistic and constructive attitude displayed by some of the early users of other new statistical techniques, new modeling strategies, new conceptual frameworks, and so on. I would hazard the guess that it is associated with a particular personality type, one that is far from universal. I have been sufficiently intrigued by it to offer for consideration the following proposition: When an innovation, that is, a new research tool, technique, or approach, is introduced into economics (or the social sciences, or science) the presence (or absence) of what I will call a "Griliches-type ally" for the innovation will be an important factor in explaining its success (or lack of success).[5]

The Griliches-type ally is not the originator of the innovation, but does actually use the new technique, and displays a solid understanding of how it works as a research tool and of various problems associated with its application to research. S/he has earned the respect of professional colleagues for work or actions aside from those related to his or her use of the new technique. And perhaps most importantly, the Griliches-type ally communicates, by words and example, the attitude that despite its weaknesses, the technique is potentially very valuable, that the best way to realize that potential is to continue using the technique while working to address the weaknesses, and that while this process of improvement is going on, the technique is still able to contribute to knowledge – it is a mistake to put off using the technique until some future time when all of the problems are solved.

4 It is worth noting that Douglas's own work with the Cobb–Douglas regression also displays some of these characteristics, as Douglas was also willing to modify the technique in response to some criticisms, responded to other criticisms with careful and technically sophisticated rebuttals, developed new types of data with which to estimate the regression and encouraged others to do the same, and showed (at times) an open and frank awareness of the limitations of the technique and the results it produced.

5 I decided on "Griliches-type" rather than "Heady-type" because Griliches was more prominent in the profession during his lifetime, and is better known to historians of the discipline.

I believe that the story of the Cobb–Douglas production function provides evidence consistent with my proposition: that as a matter of history, Zvi Griliches and Earl T. Heady played important roles in the diffusion and eventual acceptance by the profession of regression approaches to production function estimation. The positive influence on other empirical economists of their clever uses and well-articulated defenses of the Cobb–Douglas regression were no doubt amplified by their reputations as rising stars in the profession. Beyond that, they taught the method to students. Heady's influence on large numbers of graduate students at Iowa State College is apparent from the essays in Langley, Vocke, and Whiting (1994), and between 1961 and 1974, ten graduate students advised by Griliches went on to publish at least one article in a JSTOR indexed journal in which new estimates of a production function were reported.[6]

Of course, the importance of Griliches-type allies in this single episode (the history of the Cobb–Douglas regression) is also consistent with alternative hypotheses. For example, it could be that almost all innovations attract Griliches-type allies, and then succeed or fail for other reasons. Or it could be that research innovations having the characteristics that lead to success will almost always attract Griliches-type allies fairly quickly, while those without such characteristics will typically lack Griliches-type allies. Distinguishing between the first of these alternative hypotheses and my initial proposition would require a comparative study of successful and unsuccessful innovations, searching for Griliches-types among those engaged in debates over the value of the innovation. The possibility that the second alternative hypothesis is correct raises a thorny "identification problem," in that it is observationally equivalent to my initial proposition. Were this second alternative hypothesis the correct one, it would still be incumbent upon the historian describing the introduction and eventual success or failure of a research innovation to identify and describe the activities of the Griliches-types in the story, as the activities of Griliches-types would probably often be a proximate cause of the innovation's success, that is, an essential part of the process through which those characteristics of the technique that contributed to its success became widely known and understood.

[6] A list of Griliches's graduate students can be found at http://people.bu.edu/cockburn/tree_of_zvi.html.

SOME FINAL THOUGHTS

My discussion of the factors making for the success of Douglas's regression and Douglas's idea includes no mention of broad social trends, ideological and political movements, and so on, as reasons for the success of the Douglas's regression and Douglas's idea. I do not think that these sorts of things played a direct role.[7] As I argued in the introduction, it is ultimately researchers themselves who play the crucial role in deciding whether innovative research techniques are adopted, and they generally do so in their role as scientific researchers, that is, based on criteria developed within the scientific community with which they identify. These criteria tend to be arcane and technical in nature, and their content and evolution relatively unaffected by broader political and social trends.

The four factors that I have highlighted – the link to neoclassicism, the flexibility and adaptability of the technique, Douglas's rhetoric, and the emergence of Griliches-type allies – were mutually reinforcing. That is, along with the prima facie plausibility of the results of Douglas's research with the regression, they were all necessary parts of the process through which the Cobb–Douglas regression became a standard part of the empirical economist's toolbox, and the progenitor of a number of more complex regression procedures for estimating production function parameters. For example, Paul Douglas's rhetorical skills were important in part because they bought time that allowed other researchers to adapt and improve his very flexible procedure. And the presence of a number of able researchers attracted to the task of adapting and improving the procedure owes something to the procedure's perceived potential for answering

[7] It has been argued in various ways that the rise of the neoclassical paradigm was linked to broader social trends, the interests and ideological commitments of powerful social classes, and such. If one grants such an argument, then it is perhaps correct to say that if the perceived links between the neoclassical paradigm and the Cobb–Douglas regression contributed to its success, then whatever social trends or ideological struggles lay behind the triumph of the neoclassical paradigm in the second half of the twentieth century were an ultimate cause of that success. Still, I would argue that research intended to understand the fate of innovative research techniques will do better to focus more narrowly on the relationship between such innovations and the various paradigms, schools of thought, or conceptual frameworks contending for dominance in the scientific community into which it is introduced, leaving aside the important but ultimately tangential matter of how social forces might have influenced the life histories of those paradigms, schools, or frameworks.

important questions associated with the neoclassical paradigm. Likewise, it would be hard to argue that the procedure's link to the neoclassical paradigm would alone have been enough to ensure its success, as several innovative empirical techniques and modeling approaches explicitly designed to advance neoclassically oriented research programs have been introduced since the 1930s and since been largely abandoned.

Finally, it is worth emphasizing that the large number of compelling criticisms of the Cobb–Douglas regression procedure that were articulated during the first 40 years of the regression's life were not enough, even taken all together, to prevent it from succeeding. Many of these criticisms could be classed under the heading "assumptions required for the procedure to produce valid results are not even approximately true." These included, inter alia, assumptions about the match between the statistical measures used to estimate the regression and the theoretical concepts they were intended to represent, about the similarities and differences between the production functions of firms in different industries, and about the sources of variation in the levels of inputs recorded for the different farms, years, or industries in the same sample. The life story of the Cobb–Douglas regression and its descendants in the field of production function estimation involved the emergence of new data, new ways of using Cobb–Douglas, and eventually new regression forms that neutralized some of these criticisms, but also the introduction of new and challengeable assumptions, one of the most noteworthy being the assumption that factor payments in the US economy actually did equal marginal productivities. And still today, one or more of the criticisms of the earliest applications of the Cobb–Douglas regression will be relevant for a modern application of the Cobb–Douglas or other production function regression but seemingly be of little concern to the researcher or those who cite the results of the research.

This last state of affairs, I would suggest, is not peculiar to the case of the Cobb–Douglas regression. Innovative research techniques generally promise something of value to a research community, that is, a means of producing new knowledge and answering questions the community cares about. But it will always be possible to develop logical and coherent criticisms of such innovations. In short, innovations will always have problems. The ultimate success of an innovation depends only partly on the extent to which these problems are actually solved as the innovation develops. It will also depend on the willingness of the community to decide that the unsolved problems and legitimate questions associated with innovation can be ignored without damaging too greatly the validity of the results it produces, and this willingness will, in turn, depend on the community's enthusiasm for the potential of the innovation as a means of advancing knowledge.

References

Abramovitz, Moses. 1956. "Resource and Output Trends in the United States Since 1870." *American Economic Review* 46, no. 2 (May): 5–23.

1962. "Economic Growth in the United States." *The American Economic Review* 52, no. 4 (Sep.): 762–82.

Alford, L. P. 1929. "Technical Change in Manufacturing." In *Recent Economic Changes*, edited by the Committee on Recent Economic Changes of the President's Conference on Unemployment, Vol. 1, 96–166. New York: McGraw Hill.

Allen, R. G. D. 1938. *Mathematical Analysis for Economists*. London: Macmillan and Co.

Arrow, Kenneth J. 1985. *Collected Papers of Kenneth J. Arrow: Production and Capital*, Vol. 5. Cambridge, MA: Harvard University Press.

Arrow, Kenneth J., H. B. Chenery, B. S. Minhas, and R. M. Solow. 1961. "Capital-Labor Substitution and Economic Efficiency." *The Review of Economics and Statistics* 43, no. 3 (Aug.): 225–50.

Aukrust, Odd. 1959. "Investment and Economic Growth." *Productivity Measurement Review* 16 (Feb.): 35–54.

Aukrust, Odd and Juule Bjerke. 1959. "Real Capital and Economic Growth in Norway, 1900–56." *Review of Income and Wealth* 8, no. 1 (Mar.): 80–118.

Ayres, Leonard. 1927. "The Dilemma of the New Statistics." *Journal of the American Statistical Association* 22, no. 157 (Mar.): 1–8.

Backhouse, Roger. 1998. "The Transformation of U.S. Economics, 1920–1960, Viewed through a Survey of Journal Articles." *History of Political Economy* 30 (annual suppl.): 85–107.

Banzhaf, H. Spencer. 2006. "The Other Economics Department: Demand and Value Theory in Early Agricultural Economics." *History of Political Economy* 38 (annual suppl.): 9–30.

Barber, William J. 1985. *From New Era to New Deal: Herbert Hoover, the Economists and American Economic Policy, 1921–1933*. Cambridge, MA: Cambridge University Press.

1994. "The Divergent Fate of Two Strands of Institutionalist Doctrine during the New Deal Years." *History of Political Economy* 26, no. 2 (Summer): 569–88.

Barro, Robert J. 1999. "Notes on Growth Accounting." *Journal of Economic Growth* 4, no. 2 (June): 119–37.

Barton, Glen T. and Martin R. Cooper. 1948. "Relation of Agricultural Production to Inputs." *The Review of Economics and Statistics* 30, no. 2 (May): 117–26.

Bell, Spurgeon. 1939. *Productivity, Wages, and National Income*. Washington, DC: The Brookings Institute.

Benedict, M. R. 1932a. "The Opportunity Cost Basis of the Substitution Method in Farm Management." *Journal of Farm Economics* 14, no. 3 (July): 384–405.

1932b. "The Opportunity Cost Basis of the Substitution Method in Farm Management." *Journal of Farm Economics* 14, no. 4 (Oct.): 541–57.

Beneke, Raymond R. 1994. "On Becoming Distinguished." In *Earl O Heady: His Impact on Agricultural Economics*, edited by James Langley, Gary Vocke, and Larry Whiting, 3–23. Ames: Iowa State University Press.

Berglas, Eitan. 1965. "Investment and Technological Change." *Journal of Political Economy* 73, no. 2 (Apr.): 173–80.

Berman, Edward. 1934. "Review of *The Theory of Wages*." *Annals of the American Academy of Political and Social Science* 174 (July): 182–3.

Biddle, Jeff E. 1996. "H. Gregg Lewis." In *American Economists of the Late 20th Century*, edited by Warren Samuels, 174–93. Cheltenham: Edward Elgar.

1999. "Statistical Economics, 1900–1950." *History of Political Economy* 31 (Winter): 607–51.

2011. "The Introduction of the Cobb-Douglas Regression and Its Adoption by Agricultural Economists." *History of Political Economy* 38 (annual suppl.): 235–57.

2012. "Retrospectives: The Introduction of the Cobb–Douglas Regression." *Journal of Economic Perspectives* 26, no. 2 (Spring): 223–36.

2017. "Statistical Inference in Economics, 1920–1965: Changes in Meaning and Practice." *Journal of the History of Economic Thought* 39, no. 2 (June): 149–73.

Bigge, George E. 1934. "Review of *The Theory of Wages*." *The American Economic Review* 24, no. 4 (Dec.): 688–93.

Bioanovsky, M. and K. D. Hoover. 2009. *Robert Solow and the Development of Growth Economics*. History of Political Economy 41 (suppl.). Durham, NC: Duke University Press.

Black, John (ed.). 1932. *Research in Farm Management: Scope and Method*. New York: Social Science Research Council.

Black, R. D. C., Alfred W. Coats, and Craufurd D. W. Goodwin (eds.). 1973. *The Marginal Revolution in Economics: Interpretation and Evaluation*. Durham, NC: Duke University Press.

Blaug, Mark (ed.) (1999). *Who's Who in Economics* (3rd ed.). Cheltenham: Edward Elgar.

Bloom, David E., David Canning, and Jaypee Sevilla. 2003. "The Effect of Health on Economic Growth: A Production Function Approach." *World Development* 32, no. 1: 1–13.

Bloom, Gordon. 1946. "A Note on Hicks's Theory of Invention." *The American Economic Review* 36, no. 1 (Mar.): 83–96.

Boulding, Kenneth. 1961. "Some Difficulties in the Concept of Economic Input." In *Conference on Research in Income and Wealth, Output, Input, and Productivity Measurement*, 331–46. Princeton, NJ: Princeton University Press.

Boumans, Marcel. 2009. "Dynamizing Stability." In *Robert Solow and the Development of Growth Economics*, edited by M. Bioanovsky and K. D. Hoover, 127–48. History of Political Economy 41 (suppl.). Durham, NC: Duke University Press.

Bowles, Samuel. 1970. "Towards in Education Production Function." In *Education, Income, and Human Capital*, edited by W. Lee Hansen, 11–70. New York: NBER.

Bowley, Arthur L. 1901. *Elements of Statistics*. London: P. S. King & Sons.

Brewer, Anthony. 1991. "Economic Growth and Technical Change: John Rae's Critique of Adam Smith." *History of Political Economy* 23 (Spring): 1–11.

Bronfenbrenner, Martin. 1939. "The Cobb–Douglas Function and Trade-Union Policy." *The American Economic Review* 29, no. 4 (Dec.): 793–6.

1944. "Production Functions: Cobb–Douglas, Interfirm, Intrafirm." *Econometrica* 12, no. 1 (Jan.): 35–44.

Bronfenbrenner, Martin and Paul H. Douglas. 1939. "Cross-Section Studies in the Cobb–Douglas Function." *The Journal of Political Economy* 47, no. 6 (Dec.): 761–85.

Brown, Murray. 1966. *On the Theory and Measurement of Technological Change*. Cambridge, MA: Cambridge University Press.

Brown, Murray and John S. De Cani. 1961. "Technological Change in the United States, 1950–1960." In *American Statistical Association 1961: Proceedings of the Business and Economic Statistics Section*, 74–81. Washington, DC: American Statistical Association.

Burnett, Paul. 2011. "Academic Freedom or Political Maneuvers: Theodore W. Schultz and the Oleomargarine Controversy Revisited." *Agricultural History* 85, no. 3 (Summer): 373–97.

Burns, Arthur F. and W. C. Mitchell. 1946. *Measuring Business Cycles*. New York: NBER.

Cargill, T. F. 1974. "Early Applications of Spectral Methods to Economic Time Series." *History of Political Economy* 6, no. 1: 1–16.

Carson, Carol S. 1975. "The History of the United States National Income and Product Accounts: The Development of an Analytical Tool." *Review of Income and Wealth* 21, no. 2 (June): 153–81.

Chenery, Hollis B. 1960a. "Interindustry Research in Economic Development." *The American Economic Review*, 50, no. 2 (May): 649–53.

1960b. "Patterns of Industrial Growth." *The American Economic Review* 50, no. 4 (Sep.): 624–54.

Chenery, Hollis B. and Tsunehiko Watanabe. 1958. "International Comparisons of the Structure of Production." *Econometrica* 26, no. 4 (Oct.): 487–521.

Christensen, L., D. Jorgenson, and L. Lau. 1973. "Transcendental Logarithmic Production Frontiers." *The Review of Economics and Statistics* 55, no. 1 (Aug.): 28–45.

Clark, J. B. 1908 [1899]. *The Distribution of Wealth: A Theory of Wages, Interest and Profits*. New York: Macmillan.

Clark, J. M. 1928. "Inductive Evidence on Marginal Productivity." *The American Economic Review* 18, no. 3 (Sep.): 450–67.

Cobb, Charles W. 1913. *The Asymptotic Development for a Certain Integral Function of Zero Order*. Norwood, MA: The Norwood Press. https://archive.org/stream/asymptoticdevelo00cobbrich#page/n1/mode/2up

1930. "Production in Massachusetts Manufacturing, 1890–1928." *The Journal of Political Economy* 38, no. 6 (Dec.): 705–7.

Cobb, Charles W. and Paul H. Douglas. 1928. "A Theory of Production." *The American Economic Review* 18, no. 1 (Mar.): 139–65.

Collier, Irwin. 2016. "Amherst. Charles W. Cobb and Paul H. Douglas, 1926." www.irwincollier.com/amherst-charles-w-cobb-and-paul-h-douglas-1926/

Copeland, Morris A. 1929. "The National Income and Its Distribution." In *Recent Economic Changes*, edited by the Committee on Recent Economic Changes of the President's Conference on Unemployment, Vol. 1, 761–844. New York: McGraw Hill.

1937. "Concepts of National Income." In *Studies in Income and Wealth*, Vol. 1, edited by the Conference on Research in National Income and Wealth, 3–63. New York: NBER.

Copeland, Morris A. and E. M. Martin. 1938. "The Correction of Wealth and Income Estimates for Price Changes." In *Studies in Income and Wealth*, Vol. 2, edited by the Conference on Research in National Income and Wealth, 85–135. New York: NBER.

Daly, Patricia and Paul H. Douglas. 1943. "The Production Function for Canadian Manufacturers." *Journal of the American Statistical Association* 38, no. 222 (June): 178–86.

Daly, Patricia, Ernest Olson, and Paul H. Douglas. 1943. "The Production Function for Manufacturing in the United States, 1904." *The Journal of Political Economy* 51, no. 1 (Feb.): 61–5.

Daston, Lorraine J. and Peter Galison. 1992. "The Image of Objectivity." *Special Issue, "Seeing Science," Representations* 40: 81–128.

Day, Edmund E. and W. M. Persons. (1920a). "An Index of the Physical Volume of Production: I. Agriculture 1879–1919." *Review of Economic Statistics* 2, no. 9 (Sep.): 246–59.

(1920b). "An Index of the Physical Volume of Production: II. Mining 1979–1919." *Review of Economic Statistics* 2, no. 10 (Oct.): 287–99.

(1920c). "An Index of the Physical Volume of Production: III. Manufacture 1899–1919." *Review of Economic Statistics* 2, no. 11 (Nov.): 309–37.

(1920d). "An Index of the Physical Volume of Production: III. Manufacture (concluded)." *Review of Economic Statistics* 2, no. 12 (Dec.): 361–7.

(1921). "An Index of the Physical Volume of Production: IV. Agriculture, Mining, and Manufacturing Combined, 1899–1919." *Review of Economic Statistics* 3, no. 1 (Jan.): 19–22.

Debertin, David. 1986. *Agricultural Production Economics*. New York: Macmillan.

Denison, Edward F. 1962. *The Sources of Economic Growth and the Alternatives Before Us*. Committee for Economic Development Supplementary Paper # 13. New York: Committee for Economic Development.

1964. "The Unimportance of the Embodied Question." *The American Economic Review* 54, no. 2, Part 1 (Mar.): 90–4.

Dennison, Henry S. 1930. "Some Economic and Social Accompaniments of the Mechanization of Industry." *American Economic Review* 20, no. 1, Supplement (Mar.): 133–55.

Dickinson, Z. C. 1934. "Recent Literature on Wage Theory." *The Quarterly Journal of Economics* 49, no. 1 (Nov.): 138–46.

Dillon, John L. 1994. "Agricultural Production Function Analysis." In *Earl O Heady: His Impact on Agricultural Economics*, edited by James Langley, Gary Vocke, and Larry Whiting, 52–61. Ames: Iowa State University Press.

Domar, Evsey. 1961. "On the Measurement of Technological Change." *The Economic Journal* 71, no. 284 (Dec.): 709–29.

Douglas, Paul H. 1918. "The Problem of Labor Turnover." *The American Economic Review* 8, no. 2 (June): 306–16.

1919. "Is the New Immigration More Unskilled than the Old?" *Publications of the American Statistical Association* 16, no. 126 (June): 393–403.

1926. "The Movement of Real Wages and Its Economic Significance." *The American Economic Review* 16, no. 1, Supplement (Mar.): 17–53.

1927. "The Modern Technique of Mass Production and Its Relation to Wages." *Proceedings of the Academy of Political Science in the City of New York* 12, no. 3, Stabilizing Business (July): 17–42.

1930. *Real Wages in the United States, 1890–1926.* New York: Houghton Mifflin.

1934. *The Theory of Wages.* New York: Macmillan.

1939. "Henry Schultz as Colleague." *Econometrica* 7, no. 2: 104–6.

1948. "Are There Laws of Production?" *The American Economic Review* 38, no. 1 (Mar.): i–ii+1–41.

1967. "Comments on the Cobb–Douglas Production Function." In *The Theory and Empirical Analysis of Production*, edited by Murray Brown, 15–22. New York: Columbia University Press.

1971. *In the Fullness of Time: The Memoirs of Paul H. Douglas.* New York: Harcourt, Brace, Jovanovich.

1976. "The Cobb–Douglas Production Function Once Again: Its History, Its Testing, and Some New Empirical Values." *The Journal of Political Economy* 84, no. 5 (Oct.): 903–15.

Douglas, Paul H. and Francis Lamberson. 1921. "The Movement of Real Wages, 1890–1918." *The American Economic Review* 11, no. 3 (Sep.): 409–26.

Dupont-Kieffer, Arienne and Alain Pirotte. 2011. "The Early Years of Panel Data Econometrics." *History of Political Economy* 43 (suppl.): 258–82.

Durand, David. 1937. "Some Thoughts on Marginal Productivity, with Special Reference to Professor Douglas' Analysis." *The Journal of Political Economy* 45, no. 6 (Dec.): 740–58.

Easterly, William. 2001. *The Elusive Quest for Growth: Economists' Adventures and Misadventures in the Tropics.* Cambridge, MA: MIT Press.

Ezekiel, Mordecai. 1926. "Studies of the Effectiveness of Individual Farm Enterprises." *Journal of Farm Economics* 8, no. 1 (Jan.): 86–101.

Fabricant, Solomon. 1938. *Capital Consumption and Adjustment.* New York: NBER.

1942. *Employment in Manufacturing, 1899–1939: An Analysis of Its Relation to the Volume of Production.* New York: NBER.

1954. Economic Progress and Economic Change. 34th annual report. New York: NBER. www.nber.org/chapters/c12288.pdf

1959. *The Study of Economic Growth.* New York: NBER. http://papers.nber.org/books/fabr59-2

Ferguson, C. E. 1963. "Cross-Section Production Functions and the Elasticity of Substitution in American Manufacturing Industry." *The Review of Economics and Statistics* 45, no. 3 (Aug.): 305–13.

Fox, Karl A. 1986. "Agricultural Economists as World Leaders in Applied Econometrics, 1917–33." *American Journal of Agricultural Economics* 68, no. 2 (May): 381–6.

1989. "Agricultural Economists in the Econometric Revolution: Institutional Background, Literature and Leading Figures." *Oxford Economic Papers New Series*, 41, no. 1 *History and Methodology of Econometrics* (Jan.): 53–70.

Frankel, Marvin. 1957. "British and American Manufacturing Productivity." University of Illinois Bulletin. Urbana: University of Illinois Press.

Frisch, Ragnar. 1934. *Statistical Confluence Analysis by Means of Complete Regression Systems*. Oslo: Universitetets Økonomiske Instituut.

Fuchs, Victor R. 1963. "Capital Labor Substitution: A Note." *The Review of Economics and Statistics* 45, no. 4 (Nov.): 436–8.

Fuller, Wayne A. 1962. "Estimating the Reliability of Quantities Derived from Empirical Production Functions." *Journal of Farm Economics* 44, no. 1 (Feb.): 82–99.

Gay, Edwin F. and W. C. Mitchell. 1932. "Report of the President and Report of the Directors of Research for the Year 1931." New York: NBER. www.nber.org/chapters/c4299.pdf

1933. "Message of the President, Report of the Directors of Research for the Year 1932." New York: NBER. www.nber.org/chapters/c4151.pdf

George, Henry. 1981 [1979]. *Progress and Poverty*. New York: Schalkenbach Foundation.

Gilfillan, S. C. 1932. "Inventions and Discoveries." *American Journal of Sociology* 37, no. 6 (May): 868–75.

Girshick, M. A. and Trygve Haavelmo. 1947. "Statistical Analysis of the Demand for Food: Examples of Simultaneous Estimation of Structural Equations." *Econometrica* 15, no. 2 (Apr.): 79–110.

Goldsmith, Raymond. 1950. "Measuring National Wealth in a System of Social Accounting." *Studies in Income and Wealth* 12: 21–80.

1951. "A Perpetual Inventory of National Wealth." *Studies in Income and Wealth* 14: 5–74.

1952. "The Growth of Reproducible Wealth of the United States of America from 1805 to 1950." In *Income and Wealth in the United States, Trends and Structure, Income and Wealth Series II*, edited by Simon Kuznets. Cambridge, MA and Baltimore: International Association for Research in Income and Wealth.

Gordon, R. A. 1956. "Population Growth, Housing, and the Capital Coefficient." *The American Economic Review* 46, no. 3 (June): 307–22.

Gordon, Robert J. 1990. *The Measurement of Durable Goods Prices*. Chicago: University of Chicago Press.

Greenwood, Jeremy, Zvi Hercowitz, and Per Krusell. 1997. "Long-Run Implications of Investment-Specific Technological Change." *The American Economic Review* 87, no. 3 (Sep.): 342–62.

Griliches, Zvi. 1957. "Specification Bias in Production Function Estimation." *Journal of Farm Economics* 39, no. 1 (Jan.): 8–20.

1962. "Review of *Agricultural Production Functions* by Earl O. Heady, John L. Dillon." *The American Economic Review* 52, no. 1: 280–3.

1963a. "Estimates of the Aggregate Agricultural Production Function from Cross-Sectional Data." *Journal of Farm Economics* 45, no. 2 (May): 419–28.

1963b. "The Sources of Measured Productivity Growth: United States Agriculture, 1940–60." *The Journal of Political Economy* 71, no. 4 (Aug.): 331–46.

1964. "Research Expenditures, Education, and the Aggregate Agricultural Production Function." *The American Economic Review* 54, no. 6 (Dec.): 961–74.

1967. "Production Functions in Manufacturing: Some Preliminary Results." In *The Theory and Empirical Analysis of Production*, edited by Murray Brown, 275–340. New York: NBER.

1968. "Production Functions in Manufacturing: Some Additional Results." *Southern Economic Journal* 35, no. 2: 151–6.

1979. "Issues in Assessing the Contribution of Research and Development to Productivity Growth." *The Bell Journal of Economics* 10, no. 1 (Spring): 92–116.

1986. "Productivity, R and D, and Basic Research at the Firm Level in the 1970s." *The American Economic Review* 76, no. 1 (Mar.): 141–54.

1996. "The Discovery of the Residual: A Historical Note." *Journal of Economic Literature* 34, no. 3 (Sep.): 1324–30.

Griliches, Zvi and Dale W. Jorgenson. 1966. "Sources of Measured Productivity Change: Capital Input." *The American Economic Review* 56, no. 1/2 (Mar.): 50–61.

Griliches, Zvi and Jacques Mairesse. 1999. "Production Functions: The Search for Identification." National Bureau of Economic Research Working Paper No. 5067, New York: NBER www.nber.org/papers/w5067.pdf

Griliches, Zvi and Vidar Ringstad. 1971. *Economies of Scale and the Form of the Production Function: An Econometric Study of Norwegian Manufacturing Establishment Data.* Contributions to Economic Analysis, Vol. 72. Amsterdam: North Holland.

Grose, Lawrence, Irving Rottenberg, and Robert Wasson. 1966. "New Estimates of Fixed Business Capital in the United States, 1925–65." *Survey of Current Business* 46 (Dec.): 46–52.

Gunn, Grace T. and Paul H. Douglas. 1940. "Further Measurements of Marginal Productivity." *The Quarterly Journal of Economics* 54, no. 3 (May): 399–428.

1941a. "The Production Function for American Manufacturing in 1919." *The American Economic Review* 31, no. 1 (Mar.): 67–80.

1941b. "A Reply to Dr. Mendershausen's Criticism." *The American Economic Review* 31, no. 3 (Sep.): 564–7.

1941c. "The Production Function for Australian Manufacturing." *The Quarterly Journal of Economics* 56, no. 1, pt. 1 (Nov.): 108–29.

1942. "The Production Function for American Manufacturing for 1914." *The Journal of Political Economy* 50, no. 4 (Aug.): 595–602.

Haavelmo, Trygve. 1944. "The Probability Approach in Econometrics." *Econometrica* 12, Supplement (July): iii-115.

1947. "Quantitative Research in Agricultural Economics: The Interdependence between Agriculture and the National Economy." *Journal of Farm Economics* 29, no. 4: 910–24.

Haidt, Jonathan. 2012. *The Righteous Mind: Why Good People Are Divided by Politics and Religion*. New York: Random House.

Hall, R. E. 1968. "Technical Change and Capital from the Point of View of the Dual." *The Review of Economic Studies* 35, no. 1 (Jan.): 35–46.

Hamermesh, Daniel. 2018. "Citations in Economics: Measurement, Uses and Impacts." *Journal of Economic Literature* 56, no. 1 (Mar.): 115–56.

Handsaker, Marjorie L. and Paul H. Douglas. 1937. "The Theory of Marginal Productivity Tested by Data for Manufacturing in Victoria, I." *The Quarterly Journal of Economics* 52, no. 1 (Nov.): 1–36.

1938. "The Theory of Marginal Productivity Tested by Data for Manufacturing in Victoria, II." *The Quarterly Journal of Economics* 52, no. 2 (Feb.): 215–54.

Harries, H. 1947. "The Development and Use of Production Functions for Firms in Agriculture." *Scientific Agriculture* 27, no. 10: 487–93.

Harris, D. N. 2010. "Education Production Function: Concepts." In *International Encyclopedia of Education*, 3rd ed., edited by Penelope Peterson, Eva Baker, and Barry McGaw. Amsterdam: Elsevier.

Heady, Earl O. 1946. "Production Functions from a Random Sample of Farms." *Journal of Farm Economics* 28, no. 4 (Nov.): 989–1004.

1947. "Economics of Farm Leasing Systems." *Journal of Farm Economics* 29, no. 3 (Aug.): 659–78.

1948. "Elementary Models in Farm Production Economics Research." *Journal of Farm Economics* 30, no. 2 (May): 201–25.

1949. "Implications of Particular Economics in Agricultural Economics Methodology." *Journal of Farm Economics* 31, no. 4, Part 2: Proceedings Number (Nov.): 837–50.

1951. "A Production Function and Marginal Rates of Substitution in the Utilization of Feed Resources by Dairy Cows." *Journal of Farm Economics* 33, no. 4, pt. 1 (Nov.): 485–98.

1952. "Use and Estimation of Input-Output Relationships or Productivity Coefficients." *Journal of Farm Economics* 34, no. 5: 775–86.

1955. "Marginal Resource Productivity and Imputation of Shares for a Sample of Rented Farms." *Journal of Political Economy* 63 (Dec.): 500–11.

1957a. "An Econometric Investigation of the Technology of Agricultural Production Functions." *Econometrica* 25, no. 2 (Apr.): 249–68.

1957b. "Organization Activities and Criteria in Obtaining and Fitting Technical Production Functions." *Journal of Farm Economics* 39, no. 2 (May): 360–9.

Heady, Earl O. and John L. Dillon. 1961. *Agricultural Production Functions*. Ames: Iowa State University Press.

Heady, Earl O. and Russell Shaw. 1954. "Resource Returns and Productivity Coefficients in Selected Farming Areas." *Journal of Farm Economics* 36, no. 2: 243–57.

Heady, Earl O. and Schalk du Toit. 1954. "Marginal Resource Productivity for Agriculture in Selected Areas of South Africa and the United States." *Journal of Political Economy* 62, no. 6 (Dec.): 494–505.

Heady, Earl O., Roger C. Woodworth, Damon Catron, and Gordon C. Ashton. 1953. "An Experiment to Derive Productivity and Substitution Coefficients in Pork Output." *Journal of Farm Economics* 35, no. 3: 341–54.

Heath, J. B. 1957. "British-Canadian Industrial Productivity." *The Economic Journal* 67, no. 268 (Dec.): 665–91.

Hendry, David F. and Mary S. Morgan. 1989. "A Re-analysis of Confluence Analysis." *Oxford Economic Papers New Series* 41, no. 1: 35–52.

Hicks, John R. 1932. *The Theory of Wages*. London: Macmillan.

1939. *Value and Capital*. Oxford: Clarendon Press.

Hoch, Irving. 1955. "Estimation of Production Function Parameters and Testing for Efficiency." *Econometrica* 23, no. 1 (Jan.): 325–6.

1958. "Simultaneous Equation Bias in the Context of the Cobb–Douglas Production Function." *Econometrica* 26, no. 4 (Oct.): 566–78.

1962. "Estimation of Production Function Parameters Combining Time-Series and Cross-Section Data." *Econometrica* 30, no. 1 (Jan.): 34–53.

Hogan, Warren P. 1958. "Technical Progress and Production Functions." *The Review of Economics and Statistics* 40, no. 4 (Nov.): 407–11.

Hopkins, J. A., Jr. 1930. "Interpretation of Farm Efficiency Factors." *Journal of Farm Economics* 12, no. 3 (July): 384–402.

Hulten, Charles R. 1992. "Growth Accounting When Technical Change Is Embodied in Capital." *The American Economic Review* 82, no. 4 (Sep.): 964–80.

Intriligator, Michael D. 1965. "Embodied Technical Change and Productivity in the United States 1929–1958." *The Review of Economics and Statistics* 47, no. 1 (Feb.): 65–70.

Jensen, Einar. 1940. "Determining Input-Output Relationships in Milk Production." *Journal of Farm Economics* 22, no. 1 (Feb.): 249–58.

Jerome, Harry.1934. *Mechanization in Industry*. New York: NBER.

Johnson, Glenn L. 1955. "Results from Production Economic Analysis." *Journal of Farm Economics* 37, no. 2 (May): 206–22.

Jones, William O. 1952. "The New Agricultural Economics." *Journal of Farm Economics* 34, no. 4 (Nov.): 441–50.

Jorgenson, Dale W. 1966. "The Embodiment Hypothesis." *Journal of Political Economy* 74, no. 1 (Feb.): 1–17.

1988. "Productivity and Postwar U.S. Economic Growth." *The Journal of Economic Perspectives* 2, no. 4 (Autumn): 23–41.

Kaiser, David. 2005. *Drawing Theories Apart: The Dispersion of Feynman Diagrams in Postwar Physics*. Chicago: University of Chicago Press.

Kanel, Don. 1957. "Discussion: Relative Roles of Survey and Experiment in Farm Management Research." *Journal of Farm Economics* 39, no. 5 (Dec.): 1451–4.

Kendrick, John W. 1956. "Productivity Trends: Capital and Labor." Occasional Paper 53. New York: NBER.

1961a. "Introduction: Productivity and National Income Accounting." In *Output, Input, and Productivity Measurement*, edited by the Conference on Research in Income and Wealth, 1–20. Princeton, NJ: Princeton University Press.

1961b. *Productivity Trends in the United States*. Princeton, NJ: Princeton University Press.

Kjaer, Swen. 1929. *The Productivity of Labor in Newspaper Printing*. Washington, DC: USGPO.

Klein, Lawrence R. 1946. "Remarks on the Theory of Aggregation." *Econometrica* 14, no. 4 (Oct.): 303–12.

1947. "The Use of Econometric Models as a Guide to Economic Policy." *Econometrica* 15, no. 2 (Apr.): 111–51.

1953. *A Textbook of Econometrics*. Evanston, IL: Row, Peterson & Co.

Knight, Frank. 1921. *Risk, Uncertainty, and Profit*. Boston: Houghton-Mifflin.

Knowles, James W. 1960. "The Potential Economic Growth in the United States." Study paper no. 20, prepared for the Joint Economic Committee in connection with the study Employment, Growth, and Price Levels (86th Congress, 2nd session). Washington, DC: USGPO.

Konijn, H. S. 1959. "Estimation of an Average Production Function from Surveys." *Economic Record* 35 (Apr.): 118–25.

Koopmans, Tjalling C. 1937. *Linear Regression Analysis of Economic Time Series*. Haarlem: DeErven F. Bohn.

1945. "Statistical Estimation of Simultaneous Economic Relations." *Journal of the American Statistical Association* 40, no. 232, Part 1 (Dec.): 448–66.

1947. "Measurement without Theory." *The Review of Economics and Statistics* 29, no. 3 (Aug.): 161–72.

Krueger, Alan B. and Timothy Taylor. 2000. "An Interview with Zvi Griliches." *The Journal of Economic Perspectives* 14, no. 2 (Spring): 171–89.

Kuznets, Simon. 1934. "Gross Capital Formation, 1919–1933." National Bureau of Economic Research Bulletin 52. New York: NBER.

1938a. *Commodity Flow and Capital Formation*. New York: NBER.

1938b. "On the Measurement of National Wealth." In *Studies in Income and Wealth*, Vol. 2, 3–61. New York: NBER.

1946. *National Income: A Summary of Findings*. New York: NBER.

1947. "Measurement of Economic Growth." *The Journal of Economic History* 7, Supplement: Economic Growth: A Symposium: 10–34.

1949a. "Suggestion for an Inquiry into the Economic Growth of Nations." In *Problems in the Study of Economic Growth*, edited by Universities-National Bureau Committee on Economic Research, 23–46. New York: NBER. www.nber.org/chapters/c9509.pdf

1949b. "Notes on the Quantitative Approach to Economic Growth." In *Problems in the Study of Economic Growth*, edited by Universities-National Bureau Committee on Economic Research, 117–74. New York: NBER. www.nber.org/chapters/c9509.pdf

1952. "Proportion of Capital Formation to National Product." *The American Economic Review* 42, no. 2 (May): 507–26.

Kuznets, Simon, assisted by Lillian Epstein and Elizabeth Jenks. 1946. *National Product since 1869*. New York: NBER.

Lange, Oscar. 1939. "Is the American Economy Contracting?" *The American Economic Review* 29, no. 3 (Sep.): 503–13.

Langley James, Gary Vocke, and Larry Whiting, editors. 1994. *Earl O Heady: His Impact on Agricultural Economics*. Ames: Iowa State University Press.

Leonard, Thomas. 2016. *Illiberal Reformers: Race, Eugenics, and American Economics in the Progressive Era*. Princeton, NJ: Princeton University Press.

Leontief, Wassily. 1934. "Interest on Capital and Distribution: A Problem in the Theory of Marginal Productivity." *The Quarterly Journal of Economics* 49, no. 1 (Nov.): 147–61.

1951 [1941]. *The Structure of American Economy, 1919–1939*, 2nd ed. New York: Oxford University Press.

Lescohier, Don D. 1935. "The Theory of Wages." *Political Science Quarterly* 50, no. 2 (Jun.): 272–7.

Levinsohn, J. and A. Petrin 2003. "Estimating Production Functions Using Inputs to Control for Unobservables." *Review of Economic Studies* 70, no. 2 (Apr.): 317–41.

Lewis, W. Arthur. 1955. *The Theory of Economic Growth*. Homewood, IL: R. D. Irwin.

Lloyd, P. J. 2001. "The Origins of the von Thünen–Mill–Pareto–Wicksell–Cobb–Douglas Function." *History of Political Economy* 33, no. 1 (Spring): 1–19.

Lomax, K. S. 1949. "An Agricultural Production Function for the United Kingdom, 1924–1947." *Manchester School of Economic and Social Studies* 17: 146–62.

1950. "Coal Production Functions for Great Britain." *Journal of the Royal Statistical Society. Series A (General)* 113, no. 3: 346–51.

Lovell, C. A. Knox. 1973. "CES and VES Production Functions in a Cross-Section Context." *Journal of Political Economy* 81, no. 3 (May–June): 705–20.

MacFarlane, David. 1953. "Review of *Economics of Agricultural Production and Resource Use* by Earl O. Heady." *Journal of Farm Economics* 35, no. 3 (Aug.): 444–5.

Marschak, Jacob. 1936. "An Empirical Analysis of the Laws of Distribution." *Economica New Series* 3, no. 10 (May): 221–6.

Marschak, Jacob and William H. Andrews, Jr. 1944. "Random Simultaneous Equations and the Theory of Production." *Econometrica* 12, no. 3/4 (Jul.–Oct.): 143–205.

Marshall, Alfred. 1948 [1920]. *Principles of Economics*, 8th ed. New York: Macmillan.

Marx, Karl and Friedrich Engels. 1992 [1848]. *The Communist Manifesto*. Oxford: Oxford University Press.

Matthews, Ada M. 1925. "The Physical Volume of Production in the United States for 1924." *The Review of Economics and Statistics* 7, no. 3 (July): 208–16.

McHugh, Richard and Julia Lane. 1983. "The Embodiment Hypothesis: An Interregional Test." *The Review of Economics and Statistics* 65, no. 2 (May): 323–7.

Mendershausen, Horst. 1938. "On the Significance of Professor Douglas' Production Function." *Econometrica* 6, no. 2 (Apr.): 143–53.

1941a. "On the Significance of Another Production Function: A Comment." *The American Economic Review* 31, no. 3 (Sep.): 563–4.

1941b. "A Reply to Dr. Mendershausen's Criticism: A Rejoinder." *The American Economic Review* 31, no. 3 (Sep.): 567–9.

Menze, Robert E. 1942. "An Economic Analysis of Length of Feeding Period in the Production of Hogs." *Journal of Farm Economics* 24, no. 2 (May): 518–23.

Merton, Robert K. 1935. "Fluctuations in the Rate of Industrial Invention." *Quarterly Journal of Economics* 49, no. 3 (May): 454–74.

Mill, John Stuart. 1987 [1848]. *Principles of Political Economy*. Fairfield, NJ: Augustus M. Kelley.

Mills, Frederick C. 1924. *Statistical Methods Applied to Business and Economics*. New York: Henry Holt & Co.

1952. "Productivity and Economic Progress." Occasional Paper No. 38. New York: NBER.

Minhas, Bagicha. 1963. *An International Comparison of Factor Cost and Factor Use*. Amsterdam: North Holland.

Mirowski, Philip. 1991. "The When, the How and the Why of Mathematical Expression in the History of Economics Analysis." *The Journal of Economic Perspectives* 5, no. 1 (Winter): 145–57.

Mitchell, Wesley. 1929. "A Review." In *Recent Economic Changes*, edited by the Committee on Recent Economic Changes of the President's Conference on Unemployment, Vol. 1, 845–914. New York: McGraw Hill.

1936. Retrospect and Prospect 1920–1936. New York: NBER. www.nber.org/chapters/c12282.pdf

1939. *The National Bureau Enters Its Twentieth Year*. New York: NBER.

Mitchell, Wesley, Willford King, Frederick Macauley, and Oswald Knauth. 1921. *Income in the United States: Its Amount and Distribution 1909–1919*, 2 Vols. New York: Harcourt, Brace & Co.

Morgan, Mary S. 1990. *The History of Econometric Ideas*. Cambridge, UK: The Cambridge University Press.

Morgan, Mary S. and Malcom Rutherford. 1998. *From Interwar Pluralism to Postwar Neoclassicism*. Durham, NC: Duke University Press.

Mundlak, Yair. 1961. "Empirical Production Function Free of Management Bias." *Journal of Farm Economics* 43, no. 1 (Feb.): 44–56.

Murray, William G. 1994. "Intellectual Breakthrough." In *Earl O Heady: His Impact on Agricultural Economics*, edited by James Langley, Gary Vocke, and Larry Whiting, 24–8. Ames: Iowa State University Press.

Nelson, Richard N. 1964. "Aggregate Production Functions and Medium-Range Growth Projections." *The American Economic Review* 54, no. 5 (Sep.): 575–606.

Nerlove, Marc. 2001. "Zvi Griliches, 1930–1999: A Critical Appreciation." *The Economic Journal* 111, no. 472: F422–48.

Nicholls, William H. 1948. *Labor Productivity Functions in Meat Packing*. Chicago: University of Chicago Press.

Nittamo, Olivi. 1958. "The Development of Productivity in Finnish Industry." *Productivity Measurement Review* 15 (Nov.): 30–41.

Olson, Ernest. 1948. "Factors Affecting International Differences in Production." *The American Economic Review* 38, no. 2 (May): 502–22.

Page, Eric. 1994. "Obituary: Hollis B. Chenery Dies at 77; Economist for the World Bank." *New York Times*. Sep. 5, 1994.

Parikh, Kirit, T. Srinivasan, and S. Tendulkar. 2005. "To 'Ustad', with Love: A Tribute to Bagicha Singh Minhas." *Economic and Political Weekly* 40, no. 44/45: 4670–3.

Phelps Brown, E. H. 1957. "The Meaning of the Fitted Cobb–Douglas Production Function." *Quarterly Journal of Economics* 71: 546–60.

Phelps, Edmund S. 1962. "The New View of Investment: A Neoclassical Analysis." *Quarterly Journal of Economics* 76, no. 4 (Nov.): 548–67.

Pigou, Arthur C. 1932 [1920]. *The Economics of Welfare*. London: Macmillan and Co. www.econlib.org/library/NPDBooks/Pigou/pgEW57.html

Plaxico, James S. 1955. "Problems of Factor-Product Aggregation in Cobb–Douglas Value Productivity Analysis." *Journal of Farm Economics* 37, no. 4 (Nov.): 664–75.

Porter, Theodore. 1995. *Trust in Numbers: The Pursuit of Objectivity in Science and Public Life*. Princeton, NJ: Princeton University Press.

Reder, Melvin W. 1943. "An Alternative Interpretation of the Cobb–Douglas Function." *Econometrica* 11, no. 3/4 (Jul.–Oct.): 259–64.

1982. "Chicago Economics: Permanence and Change." *Journal of Economic Literature* 20, no. 1 (Mar.): 1–38.

Redman, John C. 1954. "Problems and Possible Solutions in Determining Input-Output Relationships in Agricultural Enterprises." *Journal of Farm Economics* 36, no. 5 (Dec.): 1024–33.

Robinson, Joan. 1933. *The Economics of Imperfect Competition*. London: Macmillan.

Rowe, J. W. F. 1934. "Review of *The Theory of Wages*." *The Economic Journal* 44, no. 176 (Dec.): 684–7.

Rutherford, Malcolm. 2005. "'Who's Afraid of Arthur Burns?': The NBER and the Foundations." *Journal of the History of Economic Thought* 27, no. 2 (June): 109–39.

2011. *The Institutionalist Movement in American Economics, 1918–1947: Science and Social Control*. Cambridge, MA: Cambridge University Press.

Samuelson, Paul A. 1979. "Paul Douglas's Measurement of Production Functions and Marginal Productivities." *The Journal of Political Economy* 87, no. 5, Part 1 (Oct.): 923–39.

Schmookler, Jacob. 1951. Invention and Economic Development. Dissertation, University of Pennsylvania. Ann Arbor, MI: ProQuest/UMI (Publication No. 0007813).

1952. "The Changing Efficiency of the American Economy, 1869–1938." *The Review of Economics and Statistics* 34, no. 3 (Aug.): 214–31.

Schultz, Henry. 1929. "Marginal Productivity and the General Pricing Process." *The Journal of Political Economy* 37, no. 5 (Oct.): 505–51.

Schultz, Theodore W. 1956. "Reflections on Agricultural Production, Output and Supply." *Journal of Farm Economics* 38, no. 3 (Aug.): 748–62.

Schumpeter, Joseph A. 1954. *History of Economic Analysis*. New York: Oxford University Press.

Shapin, Steven and Simon Schaffer. 1985. *Leviathan and the Air Pump*. Princeton, NJ: Princeton University Press.

Shaw, William H. 1941. *Finished Commodities since 1879: Output and Its Composition*. New York: NBER.

Siegel, Irving H. 1951. "Letter to the Editor." *The American Statistician* 5, no. 5 (Dec.): 12–13.

1961. "On the Design of Consistent Output and Input Indexes for Productivity Measurement." In *Conference on Research in Income and Wealth, Output, Input, and Productivity Measurement*, 23–46. Princeton, NJ: Princeton University Press.

Sinclair, Sol. 1947. "Discussion." *Scientific Agriculture* 2, no. 10: 493–4.

Slichter, Sumner. 1928. "Economic and Social Aspects of Increased Productive Efficiency - Discussion." *The American Economic Review* 18, no. 1, Supplement (Mar.): 166–70.

Smith, Victor E. 1945a. "Nonlinearity in the Relation between Input and Output: The Canadian Automobile Industry, 1918–1930." *Econometrica* 13, no. 3 (Jul.): 260–72.

1945b. "The Statistical Production Function." *The Quarterly Journal of Economics* 59, no. 4 (Aug.): 543–62.

Solow, Robert M. 1956. "A Contribution to the Theory of Economic Growth." *The Quarterly Journal of Economics* 70, no. 1 (Feb.): 65–94.

1957. "Technical Change and the Aggregate Production Function." *Review of Economics and Statistics* 39, no. 3 (Aug.): 312–20.

1958a. "A Skeptical Note on the Constancy of Relative Shares." *The American Economic Review* 48, no. 4 (Sep.): 618–31.

1958b. "Technical Progress and Production Functions: Reply." *The Review of Economics and Statistics* 40, no. 4 (Nov.): 411–13.

1960. "Investment and Technical Progress." In *Mathematical Methods in the Social Sciences, 1959*, edited by K. J. Arrow, S. Karlin, and P. Suppes, 89–104. Stanford, CA: Stanford University Press.

1962. "Technical Progress, Capital Formation, and Economic Growth." *The American Economic Review* 52, no. 2 (May): 76–86.

2001. "After Technical Progress and the Aggregate Production Function." In *New Developments in Productivity Analysis*, edited by Charles R. Hulten, Edwin R. Dean, and Michael J. Harper, 173–8. Chicago: University of Chicago Press.

Stern, Boris. 1927. "Productivity of Labor in the Glass Industry." U.S. Bureau of Labor Statistics Bulletin 441. Washington, DC: USGPO.

Stigler, George J. 1941. *Production and Distribution Theories: The Formative Period.* New York: Macmillan.

1947. *Trends in Output and Employment.* New York: NBER.

1961. "Economic Problems in Measuring Changes in Productivity." In *Conference on Research in Income and Wealth, Output, Input, and Productivity Measurement*, 47–78. Princeton, NJ: Princeton University Press.

Stone, Richard. 1939. "Review of *Commodity Flow and Capital Formation*, by Simon Kuznets." *Economic Journal* 49 (June): 308–9.

Syverson, Chad. 2001. "What Determines Productivity?" *Journal of Economic Literature* 49, no. 2 (June): 326–65.

Terborgh, George. 1939. "Estimated Expenditures for New Durable Goods." *Federal Reserve Bulletin* 25 (Sep.): 731–6.

Thomas, Woodlief. 1927a. "The Growth of Production and the Rising Standard of Living." *Proceedings of the Academy of Political Science in the City of New York* 12, no. 3, Stabilizing Business (July): 5–16.

1927b. "Construction of an Index Number of Production." *Journal of the American Statistical Association* 22, no. 159 (Sep.): 315–30.

Tinbergen, J. 1942. "Professor Douglas' Production Function." *Review of the International Statistical Institute* 10, no. 1/2: 37–48.

Tintner, Gerhard. 1944a. "A Note on the Derivation of Production Functions from Farm Records." *Econometrica* 12, no. 1 (Jan.): 26–34.

1944b. "An Application of the Variate Difference Method to Multiple Regression." *Econometrica* 12, no. 2 (Apr.): 97–113.

1952. *Econometrics.* New York: John Wiley.

Tintner, Gerhard and O. H. Brownlee. 1944. "Production Functions Derived from Farm Records." *Journal of Farm Economics* 26, no. 3 (Aug.): 566–71.

Tukey, John W. 1962. "The Future of Data Analysis." *Annals of Mathematical Statistics* 33, no. 1 (March): 1–67.

United States Bureau of Labor Statistics. 1927. "Comparisons of Employment and Productivity in Manufacturing Industries, 1919–1925." *Monthly Labor Review* 24 (May): 16–18.

1928. "Productivity of Labor in Merchant Blast Furnaces." Bureau of Labor Statistics Bulletin 474. Washington, DC: USGPO.

1931. "Technological Changes in the Cigar Industry and Their Effects on Labor." *Monthly Labor Review* 33 (Dec.): 1275–81.

Valavanis-Vail, Stefan. 1955. "An Econometric Model of Growth: U. S. A. 1869–1953." *The American Economic Review* 45, no. 2 (May): 208–21.

Viner, Jacob. 1952 [1931]. "Cost Curves and Supply Curves." In *Readings in Price Theory*, edited by K. Boulding and George Stigler, 198–232. Chicago: Richard D. Irwin.

Vining, Rutledge and T. Koopmans. 1949. "Koopmans on the Choice of Variables to Be Studied and the Methods of Measurement (with Response and Rejoinder)." *The Review of Economics and Statistics* 31, no. 2 (May): 77–94.

Waite, Warren. 1936. "Combination of Factors of Different Efficiency." *Journal of Farm Economics* 18, no. 4 (Oct.): 743–5.

Wall, Burton. 1948. "A Cobb–Douglas Function for the United States Manufacturing and Mining, 1920–1940." In "Report of the Chicago Meeting, December 27–30, 1947." 211–13. *Econometrica* 16, no. 2 (Apr.): 199–215.

Walters, A. A. 1963a. "Production and Cost Functions: An Econometric Survey." *Econometrica* 31, no. 1-2 (Jan.-Apr.): 1–66.

1963b. "A Note on Economies of Scale." *The Review of Economics and Statistics* 45, no. 4 (Nov.): 425–7.

Warren, Stanley W. 1936. "Statistical Analysis in Farm Management Research." *Journal of Farm Economics* 18, no. 1: 169–79.

Wasson, R. C., J. C. Musgrave, and C. Harkins. 1970. "Alternative Estimates of Fixed Business Capital in the United States, 1925–1968." *Survey of Current Business* 50 (Apr.): 18–36.

Wheeler, Richard G. 1950. "New England Dairy Farm Management Project as an Example of the Operating Unit Approach to Farm Management Analysis." *Journal of Farm Economics* 32, no. 2 (May): 201–15.

Woirol, Gregory R. 2006. "New Data, New Issues. The Origins of the Technological Unemployment Debate." *History of Political Economy* 38, no. 3 (Fall): 473–96.

Wooldridge, Jeff. 2009. "On Estimating Firm-Level Production Functions Using Proxy Variables to Control for Unobservables." *Economics Letters* 104, no. 3 (Sep.) 112–14.

Working, E. J. 1927. "What Do Statistical 'Demand Curves' Show?" *The Quarterly Journal of Economics* 41, no. 2: 212–35.

Yarrow, Andrew L. 2010. *Measuring America: How Economic Growth Came to Define American Greatness in the Late Twentieth Century*. Amherst and Boston: University of Massachusetts Press.

Yotopoulos, Panos A. and Jeffrey B. Nugent. 1976. *Economics of Development – Empirical Investigations*. New York: Harper & Row.

You, Jong Keun. 1968. "Embodied and Disembodied Technical Progress in the United States, 1929–1968." *The Review of Economics and Statistics* 58, no. 1 (Feb.): 123–7.

Index

HISTORICAL PERSPECTIVES ON MODERN ECONOMICS

Other Books in the Series (continued from page ii)

Jerry Evensky, *Adam Smith's Moral Philosophy: A Historical and Contemporary Perspective on Markets, Law, Ethics, and Culture* (2005)

Harro Maas, *William Stanley Jevons and the Making of Modern Economics* (2005)

Anthony M. Endres, Grant A. Fleming, *International Organizations and the Analysis of Economic Policy, 1919–1950* (2002)

David Laidler, *Fabricating the Keynesian Revolution: Studies of the Inter-War Literature on Money, the Cycle, and Unemployment* (1999)

Esther-Mirjam Sent, *The Evolving Rationality of Rational Expectations: An Assessment of Thomas Sargent's Achievements* (1998)

Heath Pearson, *Origins of Law and Economics: The Economists' New Science of Law, 1830–1930* (1997)

Odd Langholm, *The Legacy of Scholasticism in Economic Thought: Antecedents of Choice and Power* (1998)

Yuichi Shionoya, *Schumpeter and the Idea of Social Science* (1997)

J. Daniel Hammond, *Theory and Measurement: Causality Issues in Milton Friedman's Monetary Economics* (1996)

William J. Barber, *Designs within Disorder: Franklin D. Roosevelt, the Economists, and the Shaping of American Economic Policy, 1933–1945* (1996)

Juan Gabriel Valdes, *Pinochet's Economists: The Chicago School of Economics in Chile* (1995)

Philip Mirowski (ed.), *Natural Images in Economic Thought: "Markets Read in Tooth and Claw"* (1994)

Malcolm Rutherford, *Institutions in Economics: The Old and the New Institutionalism* (1994)

Karen I. Vaughn, *Austrian Economics in America: The Migration of a Tradition* (1994)

Lars Jonung (ed.), *The Stockholm School of Economics Revisited* (1991)

E. Roy Weintraub, *Stabilizing Dynamics: Constructing Economic Knowledge* (1991)

M. June Flanders, *International Monetary Economics, 1870–*1960: Between the Classical and the New Classical (1990)

Philip Mirowski, *More Heat Than Light: Economics as Social Physics, Physics as Nature's Economics* (1990)

Mary S. Morgan, *The History of Econometric Ideas* (1990)

Gerald M. Koot, *English Historical Economics, 1870–1926: The Rise of Economic History and Mercantilism* (1988)

Kim Kyun, *Equilibrium Business Cycle Theory in Historical Perspective* (1988)

William J. Barber, *From New Era to New Deal: Herbert Hoover, the Economists, and American Economic Policy, 1921–1933* (1985)

Takashi Negishi, *Economic Theories in a Non-Walrasian Tradition* (1985)